BLACK VISIONS

[BLACK VISIONS]

The Roots of Contemporary
African-American Political Ideologies

Michael C. Dawson

THE UNIVERSITY OF CHICAGO PRESS

CHICAGO AND LONDON

Michael C. Dawson is the William R. Kenan, Jr. Professor of Political Science and the College and director of the Center for the Study of Race, Politics, and Culture at the University of Chicago. He is the author of *Behind the Mule: Race, Class, and African-American Politics.*

The University of Chicago Press, Chicago 60637
The University of Chicago Press, Ltd., London
© 2001 by The University of Chicago
Al rights reserved. Published 2001
Printed in the United States of America
10 09 08 07 06 05 04 03 02 01   5 4 3 2 1

ISBN (cloth): 0-226-13860-7

Library of Congress Cataloging-in-Publication Data

Dawson, Michael C., 1951–
    Black visions : the roots of contemporary African-American
political ideologies / Michael C. Dawson
        p.   cm.
    Includes bibliographical references and index.
    ISBN 0-226-13860-7 (alk. paper)
    1. African Americans—Politics and government.   2. African
Americans—Politics and government—Philosophy.   3. African
Americans—Race identity—Political aspects.   4. United States—
Politics and government—1989–.   5. United States—Race
relations—Political aspects.   6. Black nationalism—United States.
7. Feminism—United States.   8. Socialism—United States.
I. Title.
    E185.615 .D394   2001
    320.5′089′97073—dc21

                                                    2001003294

CONTENTS

Figures

Tables

That there are differences between the white and black races is certain, but just what those differences are is known to none with an approach to accuracy.

W. E. B. Du Bois

🔥 This book is motivated by one of the two basic questions that led me to pursue academic research: What motivates individuals to adopt their suite of political preferences? [1] I've addressed this question over the last decade, and *Black Visions* is the latest installment in this stream of research. Let me say a few words about the origins of the project. My first project was concerned with the microfoundations of black political behavior and specifically the relationship between perceived interests and black preferences (Dawson 1994a). Theoretically, I relied on both the bounded rationality and cognitive psychology literature which focused on heuristics. Specifically, if humans are thought to use a satisficing, or "good enough," decision-making calculus that economizes on each individual's political information processing, what were the implications for black public opinion and political behavior? One of the prime theoretical constructs was what I called the black utility heuristic, a terribly clumsy name, I admit, but the basic idea was simple enough. If Bill Wilson and others are correct, and black life chances were overdetermined by race until the 1960s, then during that period it was cognitively efficient, since information is costly, to substitute racial-group interests as a reasonable proxy for self-interest because information on racial-group interests was and is readily available and cheaper than information about one's own, unique situation. One of the questions I addressed empirically was, What was the content of this black utility heuristic? I made a historical argument why perceptions of economic racial-group interests

---

1. The second question is not addressed in this book. Roughly it is, How do changes in the American political economy shape democratic possibilities and group conflict, cooperation, and progress? This is one of the themes central to my next project on black civil society.

are integral to the construction of black identity. Given the social divergence observable in the black population, why don't we see more political heterogeneity? Part of the answer came from understanding the role of institutions and networks within the black community which reinforce racial schema. These networks and institutions, I argue, help to reinforce a sense of group identity and group political consciousness and propagate a racialized view of the world in response to the racialized environment within which African Americans seek to build their lives. Another part of the answer was that there is political heterogeneity among blacks, but it is on the margins, namely the left of the American political spectrum. More important, it is orthogonal to much of American political debate. On issues of taxes, partisanship, the role of government, fiscal policy, and the like, blacks remain on the left and unified—more unified across class than whites, but on issues of the strategy, tactics, and norms of the black quest for social justice, large cleavages can be detected even using the crude instrument of the public opinion survey.

This work was adequate as far as it went, but it did not go far enough. Fifteen years of what one might call ethnographic research or participant observation in black student, trade union, and community organizing made it clear that individuals with similar interests, backgrounds, and experiences could follow radically different paths. It was clear that ideological reasons were cited, usually from the standpoint of interests, for any given political position, but which interests were cited was endogenous or, to phrase it differently, socially constructed. Specifically, which identity or identities were highlighted was often a key feature of one's ideological position. This is still America, so, for the great majority of ideologues, activists, and grassroots blacks, these identities were and are racialized. One sees oneself as a black worker, black feminist, black Marxist, African fighter for diasporic freedom (some of my undergraduates at Michigan had that appellation), and even black conservatives put themselves in the middle of black-centered discourses. The great majority of blacks continue, my previous and current work shows, to see their fate linked to that of the race, but how that linkage gets interpreted is based partly on social position but also partly on ideological orientation.

The current project therefore asks the following questions: Do ideologies play an important political role in the black community? If so, which ones? What are their roots, and what are their effects on black public opinion and on the theory and practice of American democracy?

Black Visions begins to answer these questions. This book takes seriously the ideologies that black activists have historically used in building mass movements and organizations and then analyzes the degree to which they are still present, however transformed, among grassroots African Americans. To the degree that I detect traces of these ideologies in public opinion data, I then ask, What are their roots in African Americans' circumstances, and what effects do these ideologies have on black opinion and practice?

A little foreshadowing is in order. Black ideologies continue to dramatically shape black public opinion. The effects are large enough to warrant a reexamination of our central beliefs about the degree to which ideology does or does not play a role in shaping the preferences of Americans in general. This reexamination would require, I suspect, that we rethink how we conceptualize ideology. Such an attempt would require us to bring into our quantitative models the work that political theorists have done on ideology over the past few decades. I find that there are multiple influential black ideologies. Given the diverse nature of the black ideologies I study, each of the ideological chapters has a slightly different flavor. In the case of black Marxism, an ideology largely unfamiliar to an early-twenty-first-century audience, there is a significant amount of historical work. In the chapter on black feminism, for example, more attention is paid to testing hypotheses found within black feminist thought about the intersection of race and gender. The diversity found within black political thought has led to a series of chapters which hang together but differ from each other in important ways.

I do need to warn the reader what this book is not. It is not a history of black ideologies, although I hope that the analyses suggest a historical grounding. I am a political scientist, not a historian. My comparative advantage, if any, does not lie in historical analysis. Several outstanding historians are working on black ideology within their disciplinary frameworks. Their work informs mine, but mine is not primarily a work of history. Second, I do not present a comprehensive review of all theoretically important black ideologies. Pan-Africanism, for example, is not seriously analyzed, though many serious black theorists have devoted much effort to its development. Part of the reason for not treating it here is that it has not in recent history been as much of a mass force as the other ideologies analyzed in the text. I should also note that many variants of each of the ideologies are not treated in depth. For example, the importance of Trotskyism in black ideologies is not treated. The great theorist C. R. L. James certainly was influenced by that strain of Marxism, and influenced the Detroit activists to some degree. But even in Detroit, where there was a strong black Marxist movement in the late 1960s, the various organizations and cadres by and large ended up in Leninist organizations which rejected Trotsky. Finally, this is not a work on the African Diaspora. Winston James (1998) is one of many scholars who have pointed out the outstanding contributions that West Indian immigrants have made, for example, to black political movements and thought within the United States.

But I am not primarily concerned about origins and foundations in this work. I am more concerned with how ideological currents in the black community shape black opinion, and this is therefore a descriptive work that seeks to detect and outline the relationship between black ideologies and preferences. More theoretically grounded models will come. This work is in a sense both radically incomplete and somewhat unbalanced. It is incomplete in the sense that the analysis of each ideology deserves a book of its own. Both the historical and analytical surfaces are just scratched here. The work is unbalanced in the sense that each chapter highlights different aspects of black ideologies. For example, the black feminism chapter explores more deeply some of the empirical implications of the intersections of ideology and identity than the other chapters. The chapter on black Marxism, on the other hand, provides a fuller historical account, one that may be unfamiliar to many readers. The other central empirical chapters also have flavors of their own. To cover all the ground in each empirical chapter would have taken at least another volume, and much research still needs to be done. Indeed, the work of scholars such as Melissa Harris-Lacewell is already forging new ground in our understanding of how ideology shapes public opinion and is in turn shaped by the context of discourse, or "black talk."

Finally, I provide a tentative answer to a question raised by Don Herzog when I gave a talk outlining the project's preliminary empirical findings at the University of Michigan late in 1997. He cheerfully stipulated that I sounded much like the competent, quantitatively oriented social scientist in my presentation, but he thought that he detected a fairly strong normative strand weaving its way through my discussions of the histories and character of the various black ideologies. He wanted to know what my bottom line was, or, to use King's title from 1967, *Where Do We Go from Here?* That's a fair question, to which I have no comprehensive answer—as I did when I was twenty. The answers seem much more difficult than in 1971, and perhaps the problems are as well. Instead, I'll discuss why I think the entire black ideological project is in crisis, from radical egalitarian to black conservative, and suggest that perhaps this is a problem that should concern us all and not just a small problem of ideological contestation within a small minority community.

[**ACKNOWLEDGMENTS**]

⚜ This project took a long time to complete (multiple administrative re-
sponsibilities can do that to a research schedule). It would not have been
completed at all without the extremely generous aid of a wide range of
individuals and institutions. Ronald Brown was there at the beginning.
He and I were the principal investigators for the National Black Politics
Study that provided data for this and many other projects. Without his
intellectual inspiration and tireless oversight of the data collection, this
work would not have been possible. I will now be able to devote more en-
ergy to our joint efforts. Uday Mehta, Lynn Sanders, Riaz Khan, Carol
Horton, George Sanchez, Robin Kelley, Susan Leibell, Don Herzog,
Nahum Chandler, Don Green, Evalyn Tennant, Dianne Pinderhughes,
Hanes Walton Jr., Jennifer Hochschild, Laura Stoker, Sid Verba, Michelle
Lamont, Bob Shapiro, Theda Skocpol, Ira Katznelson, Manning Marable,
Todd Shaw, Robert Brown, Donald Kinder, Don Herzog, Phil Thompson,
Adolph Reed, Bill Wilson, Michael Hanchard, Barbara Ransby, Bob Starks,
Lisa Wedeen, Frank Sposito, Nancy Burns, Mark Hansen, Ron Suny, and
Cass Sunstein all read parts of the manuscript and provided critical com-
ments that helped improve the work. I apologize to the many more who
were inadvertently left off this list but also provided welcome critical com-
mentary over the years.

Taeku Lee, Zoli Hajnal, Rovana Popoff, Sarita Gregory, Matt Kocher,
and Mark Sawyer all provided outstanding research assistance as well as critical commentary and suggestions as insightful as any I have received. I am
very gratified that many of these colleagues are well along the road of establishing their own careers. Cathy Cohen, Larry Bobo, and Melissa Harris-
Lacewell took the time to give especially close readings of the manuscript,

good-natured critiques, and the encouragement that was desperately needed when I could no longer see the light at the end of the tunnel. To these friends go my deepest thanks.

A number of institutions played an important supportive role. I thank Duke, Princeton, Yale, Harvard, Maryland, Berkeley, UCLA, Michigan, and Columbia for hosting seminars where the work was presented (sometimes more than once). Four institutions played critical roles in providing support for this project. They were the Institute for Social Research at the University of Michigan, the Russell Sage Foundation, the Center for the Study of Advanced Behavioral Sciences, and the University of Chicago. This work was born in the midst of an outstanding Race and Politics Group at ISR. Though most of the participants are no longer at Michigan, without that institutional support this project would never have been attempted. The CSABS is one of the true national treasures available to social scientists. It provided me not only with the support to get most of the writing done, but with a set of tremendous fellows who helped support each other. Victor Nee, Sander Gilman, Jon Krosnick, Hortense Spillars, Roberto Fernandez, and Russell Hardin were particularly energetic in commenting on the work as it unfolded. The Russell Sage Foundation provided generous support for the collection of the survey data that was used for most of the project. The University of Chicago in myriad ways provided an outstanding intellectual environment within which most of the work on the book was completed. In particular, the amazing system of graduate workshops provided critical forums for this work at every stage of development. Two workshops—the Reproduction of Race and Racial Ideologies and American Politics—have earned my special gratitude for repeatedly allowing me to test my ideas.

The University of Chicago Press provided excellent support for this project. I particularly want to thank my editor, John Tryneski, who provided extreme patience, needed prodding, and warm encouragement throughout the life of the project. Nick Murray provided detailed and careful editing of the manuscript. Ira Katznelson and anonymous reviewers provided thoughtful critiques of the manuscript for the press that went beyond what could reasonably be expected from either colleagueship or friendship. I thank each of them. The many warts that remain are my responsibility, not that of the legions of colleagues who attempted to make me see the errors in my ways.

The institution that most nurtured this project was my family. Alice Furumoto has, as always, proved to be the most loving and supportive of partners. My debt to her will never be repaid in full. She is looking forward to my taking up again my neglected duties as household system administrator. This book is dedicated to my parents and our children, with the hope that the quest for racial justice in America does not take too many more generations to complete.

In the area of ideology, despite the impact of the works of a few Negro writers on a limited number of white intellectuals, all too few Negro thinkers have exerted an influence on the main currents of American thought. Nevertheless Negroes have illuminated imperfections in the democratic structure that were formerly only dimly perceived, and have forced a concerned re-examination of the true meaning of American democracy.

Martin Luther King Jr.,
Where Do We Go from Here: Chaos or Community?

CHAPTER 1

Introduction:

The Contours of Black Political Thought

On the eve of the Civil War Frederick Douglass and Shields Green debated whether guerrilla warfare or a lightning raid was the best armed strategy to free their enslaved race. This debate represented a monumental ideological shift for Douglass, who had led the successful opposition to Henry Highland Garnett's call for an armed insurrection of slaves at the 1843 National Negro Convention.[1] As Garnett and Douglass had disagreed fifteen years earlier at the Buffalo convention, these two former slaves would part ways. Green accompanied John Brown on the fateful road to the attack on Harper's Ferry. Then as now, radically different visions of

1. I am indebted to Michael Hanchard for bringing to my attention this vignette, which he uses to open his article, "Racial Consciousness and Afro-Diasporic Experiences: Antonio Gramsci Reconsidered."

1

the road to freedom would shape and divide the black community as it searched for freedom in America.

Competing visions of freedom and the means to gain that freedom had confronted one another within black communities decades before the debate between Frederick Douglass and Shields Green on armed strategies to free their still-enslaved cousins. Taking to arms versus using "legitimate" politics, protesting versus voting, and looking towards socialism versus capitalism have all been seriously considered as viable options by many blacks throughout the centuries-long quest for black freedom, justice, and self-determination. Competing visions of freedom led Frederick Douglass to consider both armed struggle and the Republican Party as vehicles to freedom. Competing visions of freedom led Booker T. Washington to worry about law and order while Ida B. Wells fiercely led anti-lynching crusades in the early years of the twentieth century. Competing visions of freedom during the 1920s and 1930s led many Harlemites into both the Communist Party and the largest black nationalist organization in American history— Garvey's Universal Negro Improvement Association. Converging and increasingly dark visions of a racist America led Malcolm X and Martin Luther King Jr. to share increasingly similar visions of freedom toward the ends of their respective lives during the 1960s. Competing visions of freedom at the end of the century have led Jesse Jackson and Clarence Thomas to hold nearly opposite views of the role the American state should play in advancing the welfare of African Americans. Over the centuries black activists, elites, and intellectuals have forged these and other visions of freedom into black political ideologies which offer both a more or less consistent vision of freedom and a roadmap for the journey to freedom. These visions of freedom are ideological visions. Ideologues craft ideologies which contain portraits of the good society, of state/civil-society relations, and of political morality. In turn, grassroots African Americans have reinterpreted and applied these ideologies in ways not always anticipated, or approved of by activist and elite ideologues. Throughout black history these different visions of freedom have been influential in shaping black political attitudes and practice. At other times, these ideologies have been quiescent, having a barely noticeable effect on either political practice or debate within black communities.

These ideologies, and the discourses around them, form the core of black political thought, which historically has not only captured the range of political debate within the black community, but has also produced one of the most trenchant critiques of the theory and practice of American "democracy." This book examines these ideologies and their origins, which have influenced African Americans to seriously consider the political program of the Black Panther Party in the 1960s, overwhelmingly endorse Jesse Jackson in the 1988 presidential campaign, and favorably view Louis Farrakhan of the Nation of Islam in the 1990s. The study of black political thought is important not only to the study of the political dynamics of the black community, but also to an understanding of how, during critical historical periods, black political thought has played a vital role in shaping political debate and action in America.

In this book, I ask several questions about black ideologies. Which historically important black ideologies still have a presence within contemporary black public opinion? When present, how do the "mass" versions differ from the conceptions of their elite and activist codifiers? What structural and psychological factors make individuals more or less likely to adopt any particular black political ideology? How do these ideologies shape black public opinion? Finally, what are the likely consequences of racial political ideologies for the theory and practice of American democracy?

ORIGINS AND APPROACH

Situating black political ideologies and discourses within the larger polity's discourse necessitates answering the following question: Do blacks and whites share common beliefs, speak the same political language, have common understandings of the same events, and share conceptual categories of politics? Further, when blacks and whites debate politics, do they mean the same thing even when they use the *same* language? Or in Habermas's terms, is there a lack of shared understanding and common interpretation of "our lifeworld" (Habermas 1984)? Without a shared understanding of commonly experienced political events, blacks and others could reach very different conclusions and trigger different political responses. Strengthening our comprehension of the contours of African-American ideologies is a prerequisite for answering these questions and for understanding both the politics of the black community and interracial politics.

This book is based on the first national survey that focused on the ideological and political beliefs of African Americans. That this was the first survey of its type is symptomatic of how far short social scientists in this century have fallen of the goal set forth by W. E. B. Du Bois in 1897:

> The American Negro deserves study for the great end of advancing the cause of science in general. . . . If they miss the opportunity—if they do

the work in a slip-shod, unsystematic manner—if they dally with the truth to humor the whims of the day, they do far more than hurt the good name of the American people; they hurt the cause of scientific truth the world over, they voluntarily decrease human knowledge of a universe of which we are ignorant enough, and they degrade the high end of truth-seeking in a day when they need more and more to dwell upon its sanctity. . . . That there are differences between the white and black races is certain, but just what those differences are is known to none with an approach to accuracy. (Du Bois 1986, 597–98)

While the essentialist phrasing of the early Du Bois may cause some nervous shudders, the fact that race is socially constructed does not negate the fact that systematically different patterns of outcomes are produced within a racially stratified society. These different outcomes shape individual life chances as well as the perceptions of society, thereby providing the basis for the huge racial gulf in public opinion—a gulf that persists but about which we know little a century after Du Bois issued his call. But Du Bois also issued a call to study the dynamics within the black community with the best research tools available, and (not surprisingly) we know much less about difference within the black community, whether gendered, based on class, or on different degrees of integration into the black community, than we do about racial differences in public opinion.

In the realm of African-American ideologies, we do not know enough about how increasing divisions among African Americans have affected black understanding of and support for core concepts within American and black political thought, such as citizenship, equality, black power, self-determination, separation, integration, and justice. Each of these concepts has a long history within black politics, and each has been the object of struggle among African Americans (Pinderhughes 1987). Constellations of concepts come together to form political ideologies within black political movements. For example, the concepts of separation, self-reliance, and self-determination are all associated with various forms of black nationalism.

Ideology is defined here to mean a world view readily found in the population, including sets of ideas and values that cohere, that are used publicly to justify political stances, and that shape and are shaped by society. Further, political ideology helps to define who are one's friends and enemies, with whom one would form political coalitions, and, furthermore, contains a causal narrative of society and the state. Cognitively, ideology serves as a filter of what one "sees" and responds to in the social world.[2]

In order to better understand black ideologies, it is important for the theory and research communities to understand how political discourse developed in the black community, the degree to which it differed from discourse in the American polity at large, and equally how it influenced and was influenced by discourses in American society. There is a pragmatic as well as theoretical need for a better understanding of African-American ideologies, since ideologies shape, or at lest inform, political action (Skinner 1988).

However, the ways in which ideologies shape political action is as determined by historical context as are the meanings of the concepts and principles themselves, which are shaped within a history. Even if we superficially examine a strain of ideological discourse such as black nationalism, we find that its proponents are in important ways engaged in political debate with American society even as they try to convince blacks of the need to distance themselves either spiritually, economically, politically, or socially from white America. On the other hand, even such a European-originated descendent of the Enlightenment as Marxism is to some degree transformed (as Cedric Robinson, Robin Kelley, and others have argued) as it becomes reinterpreted to better fit the realities of black life by each generation of activists and intellectuals in the black community (Kelley 1994; Robinson 1983).

Increasing our understanding of African-American political discourse requires us to understand how concepts that reappear in black political debate change over time or are interpreted differently within a given time period. Let's take the concept of "black nation," a fairly common concept in what has been called black political thought. The term has a long and

2. This working definition of ideology is drawn substantially from conversations with Lynn Sanders and the work she has done on ideology, race, and public opinion. For an extended discussion of her approach see Sanders, 1995a. It is also consistent with how historians such as Bailyn (1967), Foner (1980), and Oakes (1990) have used the concept. For a similar treatment of the cognitive mechanisms that underlie ideology and belief systems see Allen et al. (1989) and Dawson (1994a). This view of ideology is considerably different from how some recent public opinion specialists have treated the concept. Zaller (1992) in his important book treats ideology as "a mechanism by which ordinary citizens make contact with specialists who are knowledgeable on controversial issues and share the citizens' predispositions." Stimson (1991) uses the concept of "policy mood" as a substitute for ideology. Smith and Seltzer (1992) provide a good review of the tendency in public opinion work to treat ideology as a mechanism that provides constraint among political attitudes. While, the approach used here shares some of the same attributes as these approaches, they are too reductionist and ahistorical for our current purposes. The approach used here is similar to the definition of ideology used by Smith in his discussion of black ideological diversity (Smith 1993). See Chapter 2 for a more extensive discussion of how public opinion research has treated the question of ideology.

honored history in black political discourse. The concept of a "black nation" has shifted both over time and across discourse communities during the same period. As Higginbotham explains, the concept of a black nation is part of an old tradition among black nationalists (and a newer one among black radicals). Martin Delaney described African Americans as a "nation within a nation" as early as the 1850s (Higginbotham 1993). It was used by black Civil War veterans when they petitioned the victorious Union government in the name of the "poor colored nation." In the 1920s the term was used both within the Garvey movement and by black cadres within the Communist Party of the United States who, with significant aid from the leadership of the Communist International, forced the concept on white American communists. It appeared once again among black nationalists and black Marxists in the context of the black liberation movement of the late 1960s and early 1970s. There is evidence of the concept's continued use among grassroots African Americans into the late 1970s, as one elderly urban resident argued that "we are our own nation" (Gwaltney 1980). It is difficult to believe that a black Union veteran from the 1860s, a 1920s communist, or a member of the Nation of Islam in 1970 shared a similar understanding of the term "black nation."

Concepts such as "black nation" and "freedom" mean different things to different people and different groups in different places at different times. Wittgenstein argues that the meanings of concepts such as "black nation" are constructed within given historical contexts (Wittgenstein 1958). Interpreting these concepts' meanings is not impossible; we can use "characteristic experiences" and notions of each concept's essential elements to be able to say that various versions of "the black nation" have the same meaning (Wittgenstein 1958). There was significant agreement, for example, among the newly freed slaves after the Civil War that freedom meant autonomy in (re)forming families, the ability to work small plots of land, and power to refuse to work large plantations if they so chose (Dawson 1994a; Foner 1988; Jaynes 1986; Ransom and Sutch 1977). During the same period, blacks had profound disagreement with southern *and* northern whites about all of these components of freedom. The meaning of freedom had shifted for blacks by the time of the turmoil of the Civil Rights era to encompass full citizenship rights and active participation in the economy. Again, there was profound disagreement with whites (as well as some disagreement within the black community) over the meaning of freedom.

Ideologies serve to anchor meanings. Ideological activists often use ideologies as mechanisms that can "fix" the meanings of key concepts such as *nation, self-determination,* and *freedom* across time and context. Black feminists and black nationalists of our era explicitly attempt to define and fix the meaning of *woman*. Attempts to establish definitive definitions can be the cause of intense political conflict. Since the late nineteenth century, for example, one social definition of the term *woman* has attempted to regulate the status of women as public leaders of black movements, ranging from the extremely effective anti-lynching leader, Ida B. Wells, to leaders in the Civil Rights and Black Power movements like Ella Baker and Angela Davis. Many male leaders argued that these women's place was back in the private sphere of the home. Both nationalist and Pauline Christian narratives have been interpreted to mean that black women should not desire social and political equality but should treasure and preserve their roles as the guardians of hearth, home, and the morals of the community.

We must guard against the belief, however, that ideologies such as black nationalism, the black variants of liberalism or feminism, or any other ideology are themselves fixed throughout time or space. Black nationalism's attitude toward Africa during the middle and late nineteenth century was very different from that of the nationalist activists of the 1960s and 1970s. The nineteenth-century nationalists believed it was their responsibility to "civilize" the "dark" continent (Moses 1978). Nationalists during the second half of the twentieth century were studying the writings of the late leader of the liberation movement of Guinea-Bissau (Amilcar Cabral) to learn what African lessons could be applied to black struggles in the United States. The writings of Nkrumah of Ghana, Fanon of Algeria, and Walter Rodney of Guyana, as well as those of other diasporic activists and theorists were highly influential among black activists during the period of African independence and national liberation that coincided with the period of the Cold War. The slogan of some of these activists that the "East was red, and the West was ready" suggested a reversal of the assumed direction of liberating influences across the Atlantic. What does remain constant across evolving notions of nationalism is the belief that race represents both the fundamental reality and the fundamental analytical category for understanding the plight of blacks in the Americas—that race remains the fundamental axis around which blacks need to be mobilized for liberation.

Again, we must remember that ideologies are socially constructed and reconstructed within particular social, economic, and political contexts. Viewing ideologies as constellations of political concepts constructed out of politically laden language helps us realize that while ideologies are so fluid that they are extremely difficult to pin down, the relationships of political concepts within ideologies allow us to compare them if we are careful about context and do not insist on any absolute or final definition for any ideology (Wittgenstein 1958). A central concern of this book is to consider *how similar* are the members of the "family" of ideologies that African Americans have forged over the centuries, not only to each other, but also to the dominant ideologies found within the United States.

The best way to study changes in black ideologies is not to focus on only a few canonical texts or authors, but to try also to understand how various concepts were used within various black activist and grassroots communities. One reason for this approach is that once an ideological discourse enters the public realm, control is lost, no matter how tightly an ideology is scripted by ideologues and activists (Dolan 1994). Once such a discourse enters the public sphere(s), it becomes shaped and reshaped. This is not just a feature of ideology, as Arendt would argue. Dolan argues that Arendt wants to label as ideology that which

> replaces the real world constituted in a genuine public sphere. Such a fiction departs from the world in that it presents events as inevitable, ordered, and necessary; it tells a story with a beginning, a middle, and an end implicit in the beginning; it seems to consist of particular experiences that follow from some general principles; and above all, it conceals the radical contingency of political life, in which purposes are transmuted into unanticipated projects and acts take on meanings their agents could not have intended or predicted. (Dolan 1994, 169)

Ideologies do have this property to a significant degree; however, these fictions can tell us quite a bit about how the world is perceived, and in the case of oppositional ideologies, they have generative (as well as totalitarian) possibilities. Black feminists and nationalists, as well as black liberals and Marxists, all envision futures which differ from the dominant understanding of the American Dream (Dolan 1994; Thompson 1984). All ideologies, including the American mythos, seek to define and control debates by providing a "script" of scenarios with which to think about the political world (Sanders 1995a).[3] Some discourses—liberal ones, for example, or many variants of feminism—have as part of their ethos open public discourse. All ideologies, however, claim at least local, if not universal, sovereignty over the future at least of civil society and often of the polity as well. Ideologues

---

3. See Schank and Abelson (1977) for an early, influential explanation from artificial intelligence research about how the concept of scripts can be used to model belief systems. In addition to Sanders's outstanding discussion of race and the ideology of the American creed, see Horton (1995) for a discussion of ideological alternatives to American liberalism. According to Horton, many of these ideologies were defeated at least partly because of the exercise of racism.

and activists attempt to use ideologies in order to define the limits of the permissible within both private and public realms. Many feminists, for example, have argued for restrictions on speech that they find promotes harm to women as well as on actual practices, such as genital mutilation.

Theorists such as Arendt and Habermas worry that ideologies seek to establish bonds that prevent the "rational" deliberation deemed necessary for democratic processes and institutions. Indeed, American liberalism has some of the characteristics that worry these theorists. First, American liberalism is constructed with its own set of fictions. The version of American ethnic and race relations celebrated by theorists who work within this tradition bears little resemblance to historical reality, but does represent well the standard American liberal myth: "The United States is a political nation of cultural nationalists. Citizenship is separated from every sort of particularism: The state is nationally, ethnically, racially, and religiously neutral. At least, this is true in principle, and whenever neutrality is violated, there is likely to be a principled fight against the violation. The expression of difference is confined to civil society" (Walzer 1992, 9).

This depiction of historical support for this version of "neutrality" is patently at odds with the historical record. Smith (1997), for one, demonstrates how both grassroots and elite Americans have at times enthusiastically embraced such violations. Almost all African-American theorists, on the other hand, have severely challenged the idea that the United States has followed the principled path described by Walzer, or, indeed, that America can even be generally considered a "just" country. A few decades earlier, conservative theorists such as Storing attacked King for his refusal to acknowledge America as a "just country" (Storing 1995). Indeed Storing's ideological vision for America refuses to find a place for the activist, nonviolent protest which is central to the black liberal vision out of which King emerged. Conflicts over these ideological visions have often entered public debate within the United States. Former Senator Dole, for example, challenged historical standards which took "too critical" a view of the polity by emphasizing such factors as the long history of slavery and racial oppression.

While it is naive to obsess about the deformities introduced into democracies by ideologies (they are with us all the time), it is also problematic to believe that the egalitarian goals of democracy are advanced by a blind preference for "rational" deliberation. As Sanders demonstrates, deliberative debates are fundamentally shaped by societal inequalities of power and thus often promote the inequalities that democratic debate is supposed to alleviate (Sanders 1997). When sorting out the effects of black political ideologies on African-American as well as American politics, one should focus both on discourse communities within the black community and within other U.S. speech communities. A key aspect of this analysis is an assessment of the relative levels of power between discourse communities. For that matter, one should also focus internationally, when we consider the importance of non-U.S.-based theorists and activists of African descent on black debates and movements within the United States.

It is also critical to focus on the dynamic properties in the development of black political thought. For example, it is a mistake to try to understand the work of activists such as Du Bois and King as temporally coherent; we cannot assume that their early work easily fits into the same philosophical framework as their later work. Just as it is difficult to reconcile the "young Marx" with later versions, it is hard to believe that the political thought of Malcolm X in 1961 and his beliefs in early 1965 can be easily reconciled within a single theoretical framework. Consequently, historical specificity and nuance are important factors to account for when modeling contemporary black ideologies. Public opinion data on black ideologies must be understood in the context of a multivocal set of discourses that have occurred both within the black community and between the black community and other communities for more than two centuries.

HISTORICAL TENDENCIES IN BLACK POLITICAL THOUGHT

The discourses that encompass black political debate are centered around six distinct political ideologies. These have evolved as a result of the continued ideological conflict which has been a constant feature of black politics since at least the early nineteenth century. While the antebellum Negro Convention movement of the first half of that century can be viewed as the first major forum for black ideological debate, it was the Reconstruction era that provided the first opportunity for African Americans to combine ideological debate with high levels of political activity and mobilization (Brown 1989; Foner 1988; Saville 1994b). Brown's description of black politics at the 1867 Virginia state constitutional convention illustrates the significant degree to which ideological debate and political mobilization were combined in black politics. At this juncture ideological debate was a mass activity for the black community. She reports that during points of heated controversy, black delegates turned to blacks in the gallery as they made their addresses on the convention floor. The purpose was to gain support for their position and to gauge the wishes and sentiments of the community at large. Furthermore, outside the convention, mass meetings were held where children, women, and men debated and voted on major issues. These were not merely mock assemblies; the most radical black Republicans argued that major convention issues should actually be settled at these mass meetings and that delegates would attend the convention to cast the community's vote.

The political ideology and behavior of the Virginia delegates is said to be a product of an African-American world view in which the moral, spiritual, and material development of the community is at least as important as the development of the individual (Dawson 1994a; Foner 1988). Brown argues that African Americans held a communal world view during the Reconstruction period. Lewis describes the importance for African Americans of perceptions of collective racial interests in the political and economic spheres of black life several decades later during the Depression era (Lewis 1991). To a great extent, Brown's description of a communal world view during Reconstruction and Lewis's discussion of a similar world view among blacks in the midst of the Great Depression are similar to Jencks's (1990) definition of "communitarian unselfishness." That is, individuals develop a politicized sense of racial identification which influences both their ideological view of the social world as well as their political behavior (Allen, Dawson, and Brown 1989; Dawson 1994a).

A communal approach to politics continues to influence African-American political life. This point is made clear in a number of empirical voting studies which indicate that racial concerns shape not only political perceptions and attitudes but candidate choice and participation (see Campbell et al. 1960; Dawson 1994a; Tate 1993). Group-based racial politics have developed historically to such a degree that many African Americans' political preferences are shaped by the belief that their individual life chances are linked to the fate of the race (Dawson 1994a). This sense of linked fate is a product of the individual's interaction within both informal and formal African-American sociopolitical networks. These networks include the black media, the black family, and religious and community-based organizations. These networks and institutions have been largely responsible for crystallizing the shared historical experiences of African Americans into a sense of collective identity, and they have also played a key role in shaping the development of black political ideologies. Neither the communal nature of black politics nor the strong sense of the majority of blacks that their fate is linked to that of the race prevent political conflict from raging within black communities. The fact that two African Americans can believe that their fate is linked to that of the race does *not* mean that they agree on how best to advance their own and racial interests. Black ideological conflict occurs precisely over what constitutes the best political path for the race.

Core Concepts of Black Political Ideologies

Several ideologies have developed within black political thought, and the adherents of each have contested for dominance within the black community throughout black history. The continued importance of political conflict over black ideologies and the legacies of the political leaders who popularized them can be seen in conservative Clarence Thomas, nationalist Kwame Toure (Stokely Carmichael), and Marxist Amiri Baraka (LeRoi Jones), all claiming to be followers of Malcolm X. Ideological confusion can be limited by specifying the key components of black political thought.

Black ideologies contain positions on classic questions from political theory such as the role of the state, the perfectibility of human nature, how to view the law, and the moral and strategic standing of the use of violence. But more important, *black* political ideologies must also answer several questions about African Americans' relationship to the state and other racial and ethnic groups within U.S. society. Black ideologies answer the following questions:

- How is blacks' position in society explained? What specific roles are race, class, and gender assigned?
- Who or what is the enemy?
- Who are friends; with whom is one willing to form coalitions?
- What attributions are made about the nature of American society and the state?
- What is the nature of whites? Are they by nature hostile to blacks; are they too tied to the "benefits" of racism to abandon racism; or are they basically good and able to become willing partners in the quest for racial justice? (This list, of course, is not exhaustive of the possibilities found historically in black political thought.)
- What degree, if any, of either tactical or strategic separation (social, political, economic, cultural) from whites is desirable or necessary?
- What stance should African Americans take toward what has been labeled the "American Creed," "American Liberalism," and the "American Liberal Ideology"?

The relationship between black political ideologies and "American" liberalism is critical for framing the book. Many, mainly white, commentators on black ideology have forcefully argued that black political thought falls comfortably within the realm of liberal democratic thought and practice. Just as many, mainly black, scholars have argued that black political thought and practice can be read as a rejection of American liberalism. I marshal a significant amount of textual, historical, and quantitative evidence to support the following propositions. First, as can be expected from a discourse that exists partially within the framework of a larger discourse, black political thought contains ideological currents that are firmly within the boundaries of American liberalism, broadly construed. Black variants of liberalism, with one moderate exception, have been transformed by the historical experience of African Americans in ways which not only stretch the traditional boundaries of mainstream American liberalism, but also contain elements which are decidedly antiliberal. Finally, black political thought contains ideological trends, such as black nationalism, which not only cannot be made to march under the liberal banner, but have enjoyed significant mass support during several historical epochs, including the present period.

The great majority of black theorists challenge liberalism as it has been practiced within the United States, not some abstract ideal version of the ideology.[4] It is a form of liberalism that celebrates the boundaries between the public and private. Most (white) Americans have had more faith in markets, the voluntary associations of civil society, and local governments than in a strong central state. The American Creed, the form of liberalism that has dominated American society in practice, also eagerly promotes a rugged (and gendered) individualism while remaining skeptical about establishing a strong central state. It is a form of liberalism of which the great majority of black theorists and activists, including black liberals, have been skeptical. Let me be clear—as Holmes, Waldron, Shklar, and others demonstrate in their analyses of the history of the liberal tradition—that there is no necessary contradiction between the liberal tradition in *theory* and black liberalism. The contradiction exists between black liberalism and how liberalism has come to be understood in practice within the American context.

Black ideologies directly challenge the idea of what Dolan characterizes as a single "national mythology" (Dolan 1994, 5). The universal acceptance of liberalism is one of America's national mythologies. From Hartz to modern theorists, the claim that "nothing is waiting; American[s] . . . have to recognize that there is no one out there but separated, rights-bearing, voluntarily associating, freely speaking, liberal selves" (Hartz 1955; Walzer 1990, 15). One example of the American national myth of a universal consensus around liberalism is provided by some of the writing of Michael Walzer. He has argued, for example, that Martin Luther King's speeches represented the best of a "palpable [American] tradition"—one which,

---

4. I go into much more detail on how I view liberalism and black political thought in chapter 6.

when invoked, we as a nation would disagree with only in regard to the timing and method of implementation (Walzer 1990, 14). We will see in chapter 6 not only that King harbored deep doubts about whether white Americans in fact supported that tradition, but also that he began to harbor deep doubts about the goodness of the tradition itself. Perhaps even more fundamentally, I will argue that certain aspects of King's thought were well outside of the American Creed. Indeed, with the exception of black conservatism, all black ideologies contest the view that democracy in America, while flawed, is fundamentally good. Theorists such as Michael Walzer are able to argue that "America has been, with severe but episodic exceptions, remarkably tolerant of ethnic pluralism (far less so of racial pluralism).[5] I don't want to underestimate the human difficulties of adapting even to a hyphenated Americanism, nor to deny the bigotry and discrimination that particular groups have encountered. But tolerance has been the cultural norm" (Walzer 1992, 44). A central theme within black political thought has been not only to challenge such characterizations of the nation's propensity for tolerance, but also to insist that the question of *racial* injustice is a central problematic in *American* political thought and practice, not a minor problem that can be dismissed in parentheses or footnotes.

Some black ideologies challenge the single American mythos from within liberal political thought. These are radical egalitarianism, disillusioned liberalism, and conservatism. However, some black challenges represent the interaction of race with other constitutive hierarchies of power. Black feminism challenges American liberalism on an ideological foundation based primarily on analyses of the intersection of race and gender, although some forms of black feminism account for intersections with sexuality and class as well. Black Marxism challenges American liberalism on the basis of analyses of the intersection of race and class. As mentioned above, black nationalism critiques American liberalism and builds an alternative vision based on taking race as the fundamental analytical category of concern to African Americans. All of these black ideologies are similar to other oppositional ideologies to the degree that self-definition and rejection of external definitions of the political, social, and economic self are central to their visions.

Six historically important black political ideologies were identified for study. They were the radical egalitarian, disillusioned liberal, black

---

5. Walzer, of course, has not been identified as primarily a liberal theorist, but even he has argued that the best polities are proving to be liberal polities, which only need occasional communitarian correcting (Walzer 1990).

Marxist, black nationalist, black feminist, and black conservative ideologies. The following sections provide suggestive sketches of each of these ideological tendencies. Full descriptions of each ideology's development and current status within black political thought are provided in chapters 3–6.[6] The six ideologies are the key ones that were identified from reading black political history and thought. There is nothing sacred about the number six. Many other commentators have identified two or three separate ideologies. My examination of the historical record identified three that could be clearly viewed as liberal ideologies. Other scholars' categorizations will surely differ from mine. Black liberal ideologies have been present within black political thought since before the founding of the nation. The language of the founding was adapted to black political needs. As will soon be detailed, I have identified three important liberal ideological strands. Just as important as liberal ideologies are the ideological challenges to liberalism that have emerged from black politics. The oldest challenge to black liberalism comes from black nationalism. To a people subjugated on the basis of their race, an ideology based on racial liberation that tended to cast the enemy also in racial terms provided a certain persistent attraction. Other challenges to liberalism were based on ideologies which had their roots in the intersections of race and gender, on one hand, and race and class on the other. This categorization of black ideologies loses much of the richness that they have had historically. This reduction in richness is a necessary feature of the process of abstraction, which allows us to better analyze broad historical patterns and the effect of black ideologies on contemporary public opinion. Some of the richness of these ideologies is hinted at in the following chapters. Short preliminary descriptions are provided now to give readers an overview of the ideological landscape.

Radical Egalitarianism

The radical egalitarian ideology typifies the optimistic phase of such important African-American intellectuals and activists as Frederick Douglass, Ida B. Wells, the pre-1930 Du Bois, and the pre-1967 Martin Luther King Jr. This ideology is typified by the coupling of a severe critique of racism in American society, an impassioned appeal for America

---

6. Independently derived, these six ideologies bear a family resemblance to the six ideological families, or "traditions," that Robert Goodin identifies. One should note the absence of "anarchism" from my list as perhaps the most significant difference. Anarchism has found little support of any kind among African Americans.

to live up to the best of its values, and support for a radical egalitarian view of a multiracial democratic society (Howard-Pitney 1990). On the Fourth of July, 1852, Frederick Douglass bluntly stated,

> The Fourth of July is yours, not mine. You may rejoice, I must mourn. To drag a man in fetters into the grand illuminated temple of liberty, and call upon him to join you in joyous anthems were inhuman mockery and sacrilegious irony. Do you mean, citizens, to mock me, by asking me to speak today? . . . There is not a nation on earth guilty of practices more shocking and bloody than are the people of the United States at this hour. (Douglass 1969b, 441, 445)

Douglass exhorts the crowd to make America live up to its principles by taking up the abolitionist cause. Over a century later King makes a similar but more hopeful plea. King's "I Have a Dream" speech provides perhaps the classic modern expression of this ideological viewpoint.

> When the architects of our republic wrote the magnificent words of the Constitution and the Declaration of Independence, they were signing a promissory note to which every American was to fall heir. . . . It is obvious today that America has defaulted on this promissory note in so far as her citizens of color are concerned. Instead of honoring this sacred obligation, America has given the Negro people a bad check; a check which has come back marked "insufficient funds." (King 1986i, 217)

This characterization of America provoked attacks by theorists who had a more benign view of American history. As Herbert Storing argued in an article attacking King shortly after his assassination, "Many whites and blacks today have forgotten [that America is] a fundamentally decent and just civil society, in which men are protected and encouraged in the pursuit of happiness, [and this] is a rare and precious thing" (Storing 1995, 258). Storing argued that even black moderates such as King were doing real harm to the polity by calling for civil disobedience, given both the subversive nature of civil disobedience and the fundamentally just nature of American democracy.

However, this ideological tradition strongly emphasizes that actively pressuring American society and the state is critical for achieving black justice. Douglass argued that "power concedes nothing without a demand," while Ida B. Wells argued that black activism was largely responsible for the decrease in lynching during the early decades of the twentieth century

(Wells 1970). King himself summarizes this view by stating that "the Negro will only be free when he reaches down to the inner depths of his own being and signs with the pen and ink of assertive manhood his own emancipation proclamation" (King 1986e, 246).

Other components of this ideological tendency include support for a strong central state which promotes equality combined with respect for individual liberty and self-reliance. Capitalism is criticized but considered reformable. Racism is seen as a vile ideology that will disappear after vigorous debate and social action demonstrate the untruthfulness and moral bankruptcy of its basic principles and assumptions. Alliances with all other people of good will, including white Americans, are considered vital to the quest for racial justice and achievable through a variety of mechanisms, including scientific explanation and moral suasion. The use of violence, except in self-defense, is rejected.[7]

Disillusioned Liberalism

The disillusioned liberal is typified by the post-1930 Du Bois and Dr. King in his last years. America is viewed by adherents of this ideological vision as fundamentally racist; segregation is seen not as a goal, but as a stage which must be tactically planned for in the very long struggle for racial equality. The capitalist system is seen as a fundamental part of the problem, but liberal, egalitarian, democratic American values are still embraced to a significant degree (Cone 1991). However, white racism is considered to be fundamentally entrenched among whites. By 1967 the optimism of King's 1963 speech, "I Have a Dream," has disappeared: "Let me say that we have failed to say something to America enough. . . . However difficult it is to hear, we've got to face the fact that racism still occupies the throne of our nation" (King 1986h, 676).

Du Bois had become thoroughly pessimistic by the late 1930s. He argues in *Dusk of Dawn*,

> I began to realize that the heights and fastnesses which we black folk were assailing could not in America be gained by sheer force of assault,

7. While most activists and intellectuals rejected most uses of violence as exceedingly self-defeating, the majority, including major figures such as Du Bois, Ida B. Wells, and Douglass, supported African Americans' right to engage in self-defense. King was exceptional for his suspicion even of violence in defense of oneself, one's family, or the community.

because of our relatively small numbers. They could only be gained as
the majority of Americans were persuaded of the rightness of our cause
and joined with us in demanding our recognition as full citizens. This
process must deal not only with conscious rational action, but with irrational and conscious habit, long buried in folkways and custom. Slowly
but surely I came to see that for many years, perhaps many generations,
we could not count on any such majority; that the whole set of the white
world in America, in Europe, and in the world was too determinedly
against racial equality to give power and persuasiveness to our agitation.
(Du Bois 1986, 776)

Scientific evidence about the true conditions and nature of African
Americans and their communities (in Du Bois's case) or moral suasion (for
King) are considered woefully inadequate for mobilizing the majority of
whites as part of a struggle for black racial justice. Whites are considered
either too wedded to the material gains derived from a racist system or
too indifferent to make reliable allies. There is more of an emphasis on
building the political and economic power of the black community as part
of the strategy for gaining equality and admission into American society.
This is often an unstable ideological position; those who become disillusioned, particularly if they remain committed to activism, move on to other
ideological positions such as nationalism, Marxism, feminism, and occasionally conservatism (Dawson 1994a).

Black Marxism

Black Marxism is an ideology which adapts the tenets of Marxism to
the situation of African Americans. Leading figures have included Cyrill
Briggs, Du Bois, Richard Wright, and Angela Davis. In addition to emphasizing the central role of the capitalist system, *black* Marxism also emphasizes *race* as a fundamental category and *spirituality* to a degree not
found in traditional Euro-American Marxism (Dawson and Wilson 1991;
Robinson 1983). Black Marxists have often emphasized the political principle of self-determination and the material question of land as fundamental for understanding revolutionary dynamics within the United States—
often to the consternation of their white comrades. Black communist
theoretician Harry Haywood argued from a position within the Communist International that the black struggle in its own right had a revolutionary character—a position that was at odds with the views of most of the

predominantly white American party leadership: "The black freedom struggle is a revolutionary movement in its own right, directed against the very foundations of U.S. imperialism, with its own dynamic pace and momentum" (quoted in Franklin, 1995, 163)

Further, black Marxists throughout the twentieth century, such as Du Bois, Richard Wright, and others, were skeptical about claims which characterized white workers as a revolutionary group. They were more likely to search for allies among those waging anticolonial struggles outside of the United States and among the black petite bourgeoisie. This was at least in part due to the constant infusion of talent from other parts of the Americas into indigenous black political movements and debates. The contributions of those such as Cyril Briggs, C. R. L. James, Claudia Jones, and George Padmore helped to broaden African Americans' understanding of their place in what many saw as a global struggle (or struggles) for black freedom. Euro-American imperialism was the enemy, Du Bois argued: "Empire; the domination of Europe over black Africa and yellow Asia, through political power built on the economic control of labor, income, and ideas. The echo of this industrial imperialism in America was the expulsion of black men from American democracy, their subjection to caste control and wage slavery. This ideology was triumphant in 1910" (Du Bois 1986, 623–24).

In conclusion, this ideology proposed "united front" tactics which would ally progressive classes and individuals within the black community while linking with other progressive movements and forces outside the black community.

Black Conservatism

The most marginal tendency during most historical periods has been black conservatism. However, during the late nineteenth and early twentieth centuries, Booker T. Washington was the dominant figure in black politics and set the terms of ideological debate for much of the first half of the century long after his death in 1915.[8] Since the election of Ronald Reagan, black conservatism has come back into prominence. Key ideological

---

8. Washington's ideas had little force in persuading the black grassroots; see Rosengarten (1974) for the view of Washington by a fellow black, rural resident of Alabama. Washington, however, had enormous power due to the degree of resources that were invested in him by white corporate and governmental elites.

traits include reliance on self-help, an attack on the state as a set of institutions that retard societal progress in general and black progress in particular, and belief in the antidiscriminatory aspects of markets, all in the name of service to the black community. Political strategies are considered inferior to strategies based on economic development for bringing about black progress. Further, any strategy or policy which diminishes the "honor" of African Americans by allowing one to hold the perception that blacks are receiving an undeserved benefit is considered both immoral and counterproductive. Finally, claims that blacks have suffered special oppression and deserve special consideration are rejected for a number of reasons, including the view that blacks are one of several groups that have suffered disadvantage and therefore should receive no special consideration.

Black Feminism

African-American women have played a continual role in the struggle for black freedom and justice. By the last half of the nineteenth century, black women were collectively asserting their rights as women and as African Americans (Carby 1987; Wells 1970). The women of the Combahee River Collective argued in 1977, "It was our experience and disillusionment with these liberation movements [the feminist and black movements], as well as experience on the periphery of the white male left, that led to the need to develop a politics that is antiracist, unlike those of white women, and antisexist, unlike those of Black and white men." (Combahee River Collective 1981, 211). Modern proponents of this ideological perspective include Barbara Smith, Audre Lorde, Patricia Hill Collins, and bell hooks. Some of the distinguishing characteristics of black feminism, or "womanist philosophy," include a tendency to see the struggle of African-American women as being more holistic and universalist than that of most white feminists, a greater emphasis on and concern for the entire community, and a tendency to see race, gender, and sometimes class as the fundamental analytical categories (Brown 1990b; Higginbotham 1992; Walker 1993). Black feminists argue that it is the *intersection* of gender with race and class which requires African-American women to battle against multiple forms of oppression (Collins 1991; Crenshaw 1990; Locke 1987). As Brown argued, "Because they have been created outside the experiences of black women, the definitions used in women's history and women's studies assume the separability of women's struggle and race struggle. They allow, belatedly, black women to make history as women or as Negroes but not as

'Negro women.' What they fail to consider is that women's issues may be race issues and race issues women's issues" (Brown 1990, 174).

One implication of this analysis is that black feminists are usually sympathetic toward forming alliances outside of the black community; they see themselves as struggling against both patriarchy and white supremacy. Supporters of this ideological perspective are especially critical of ideologies which include as core elements claims about the "natural" leadership role of black men and contain essentialized views of gender roles.

Black Nationalism

Black nationalism is the second oldest (after radical egalitarianism) ideological tendency found within black political thought. Core concepts include support for African-American autonomy and various degrees of cultural, social, economic, and political separation from white America. Race is seen as *the* fundamental category for analyzing society, and America is seen as fundamentally racist. As Garvey has argued,

> Some Negro leaders have advanced the belief that in another few years the white people will make up their minds to assimilate their black populations, thereby sinking all racial prejudice in the welcoming of the black race into the social companionship of the white. Such leaders further believe that by the amalgamation of black and white, a new type will spring up, and that type will become the American and West Indian of the future. This belief is preposterous. I believe that white men should be white, yellow men should be yellow, and black men should be black in the great panorama of races, until each and every race by its own initiative lifts itself up to the common standard of humanity, as to compel the respect and appreciation of all, and so make it possible for each one to stretch out the hand of welcome without being able to be prejudiced against the other because of any inferior and unfortunate condition. (Garvey 1986, 26)

Leading personages espousing this ideology include Martin Delaney, Marcus Garvey, and Malcolm X (Moses 1978; Stuckey 1987). Black nationalists are suspicious of alliances with those outside of the black community and argue that minimally strong unity must be built within the black community before alliances with others can even be considered (Carmichael and Hamilton 1967; X 1965). The fact that Africa holds a special place as the "motherland" for most black nationalists leads many (not all) to see all people of African descent as at least the spiritual allies of African Americans. Some versions of black nationalism are in theory open to alliances with other nonwhite social movements; others reject all such alliances. One consequence of this racialized world view is that virtually all other ideological perspectives are considered to be the tools of white oppressors. Historically, this has led to fierce clashes between black nationalists and black socialists, while in the contemporary period similar clashes have occurred between black nationalists and black feminists.

What distinguishes all of these ideologies from their counterparts in white society is that they all claim to have been developed out of the historical experiences of African Americans. While ideologies such as Marxism and conservatism can be found in Western culture, they (and the other ideologies such as liberalism and feminism) have been to some degree modified by their incorporation within the black experience.[9] Many analysts of these ideologies claim that they are distinct because they have the following components which characterize African-American political thought. (1) They explicitly take as their point of view African Americans, or some segment of the African-American community (Collins 1991; Robinson 1983; Stuckey 1987). (2) They embrace more firmly communalism or holistic approaches, even in individualistically oriented ideologies such as the radical egalitarian version of liberalism (Brown 1990b; Dawson 1994b). Hord argues that in black philosophy the "self" is only actualized and achieves fulfillment through the community—"I am because we are" (Hord and Lee 1995). (3) There is more likely to be a spiritual component built in, even in ideologies such as black Marxism (Robinson 1983; Stuckey 1987). Finally, (4) the link between theory and practice is considered to be organic; the epistemic basis for knowledge is as likely to be derived, according to some theorists, from practical activity as from abstract reasoning (Brown 1990b; Collins 1991; Dawson and Wilson 1991; Robinson 1983).

I do not argue that each of these ideologies forms a neat, separate set of ideas and values. One would expect that, given the common context in

---

9. Indeed, it is the recognition of the set of dual influences on black ideologies that leads me to come up with more categories than many analysts of black ideologies. For example, I agree with Smith's (1993) argument that ideological diversity marks black political discourse and practice. However, if one does believe that Euro-American political thought has had a consistent influence on black political thought, one must deconstruct ideological categories such as "integrationism" into their liberal philosophical components. At the same time, if one also wishes to argue, as I do, that the historical experience of African Americans has had a transformative effect on European systems of political thought, one must specify how the new, transformed ideologies differ from those found in mainstream, Western political thought.

which each ideology has developed, these ideologies would share ideas and concepts. These ideologies grew out of the ideas that were available to African Americans. Thus they were not only informed by the indigenous political ideas of the black community, but also powerfully shaped by the set of political concepts and values available in the general American society. For example, the concept of self-determination is found both in the black nationalist and black Marxist ideologies, just as a strong individualist strain is found in the various black liberal traditions.

The core concepts of African-American political thought have developed out of the experiences of slavery and the forced separation of the races during the period of retrenchment that followed the post–Civil War Reconstruction period. Concepts such as equality, freedom, self-determination, integration, and nationalism have all developed as part of attempts by various segments of the African-American community to propose strategies for the advancement of black racial interests. The core concepts of black political thought have, as noted, been the object of fierce debate and conflict within the black community. For example, the extremely large following of Marcus Garvey at the beginning of the century promoted black nationalism and waged war with those such as Du Bois and A. Philip Randolph and the organizations they represented (the early NAACP for Du Bois). Du Bois and Randolph in turn militantly promoted social equality as both a goal and a strategy for African Americans. However, although proponents of these concepts have been in conflict with each other, they all framed their proposals as critical to the advancement of the race. Modern black conservatives, for example, are just as likely to frame their analyses as being critical to the advancement of the African-American cause as are black nationalists. In the next section we consider both the institutional bases and the character of the sites within which black political thought has developed. We also examine the importance of the black counterpublic for the development of black political thought.

BLACK POLITICAL THOUGHT
AND THE BLACK COUNTERPUBLIC

Black political thought evolves and develops through the clash of ideologies which typifies political debate among African Americans. The discursive site for these debates has historically been the black public sphere, or more precisely, the black counterpublic. The concept of a black counterpublic sphere that interacts with other spheres within American society is useful for understanding how the ideologies contained within black political thought both develop semi-autonomously and interact with the political debates coursing throughout the polity.

The idea of a black counterpublic is needed because for most of American political history, blacks were excluded from the "American" bourgeois public sphere. Just as feminist critics have pointed out that Habermas's concept of the bourgeois public sphere is both exclusionary and hegemonic, there are several aspects of Habermas's formulation which render it inappropriate as a model for black politics (Fraser 1989; Ryan 1989). First, Habermas consistently presented a romanticized version of Western European history (Eley 1989; Fraser 1989). A number of scholars have demonstrated that historically existing bourgeois public spheres were always exclusionary. Gender was a prime basis for exclusion, and spheres were formed in some circumstances as a patriarchal alternative to already existing spheres in which women's voices were prominent (Fraser 1989; Ryan 1989).[10] What emerged in these and other Western polities were a variety of alternatives to the bourgeois and post-bourgeois public spheres that facilitated women's and other excluded groups' access to public life. Several scholars explicitly connect the stratification of a society and the creation of alternative subaltern counterpublics (Fraser 1989; Ryan 1989). We can restate the thesis of Fraser and others as follows: Alternative public spheres have developed in Western democracies, at least in keeping with the fundamental constitutive stratification lines of a given society.

By fundamental constitutive stratification lines I mean that, historically, societies of which we have records have been organized systematically to provide favorable outcomes for privileged groups. Favorable outcomes include material goods, life chances (including the ability to capture resources), status, individual autonomy (consider the role of women in many societies, or of slaves), and ideological privileging/degradation of a *group's* place in the social order. Most, perhaps all, societies on record which reach a certain stage of development have at least two such organizing principles. These are gender and how economic activity (including the distribution of

---

10. According to Fraser, Habermas makes four incorrect assumptions in his discussion of the European bourgeois public sphere. First, she argues that it was not (is not) possible to "bracket" differences within the sphere in such a way that citizens can "deliberate as if they were social equals." Second, she argues that Habermas is wrong to the degree that he suggests that the creation of multiple spheres represents a move "away from . . . greater democracy." Third, she argues that an emphasis on the common good tends to privilege the goals of the most advantaged sectors of a society. Fourth, she argues that it is not necessary for a functioning democratic public to have a "sharp" demarcation between the borders of civil society and the state.

resources) is organized.[11] These systems of stratification produce social groups which are systematically excluded from the *bourgeois* public sphere. However, I agree with Fraser (1989) that the claim that these groups are excluded from *the* public sphere is an *ideological* claim, since it privileges the bourgeois sphere as being *the only sphere* of consequence for discourse that is capable of critiquing the state and its policies.

With the capital accumulation generated by European colonialism and the slave trade, the potential for "race" to become an organizing principle was created. Race, gender, and class, are, of course, socially constructed and historically contingent. In the case of race, there is nothing deterministic about race becoming a constitutive organizing principle. There is no automatic mechanism which required race (and racism) to become a constitutive organizing principle. However, I argue that it does become such a principle for the United States. Race became a key, some argue *the* key, constitutive line of stratification within the United States.

Historically, the racial stratification that has shaped the United States coalesced into a *racial order*. The American racial order assigned racial groups various degrees of citizenship rights, legal status, relationships to the security apparatus, places in the economy, and the amount of status to be conferred on members of each racial group. What has generally not been understood about the American racial order was the extremely high degree of connection between African-American (and white) citizenship status during a given era, and the place of racial groups in the economic hierarchy. A few scholars have argued that the American racial order closely tied (and still ties) economic, political, and social status together (Arnesen 1994; Shklar 1995).

For example, during the period between 1890 and 1906, when blacks were being disenfranchised in one southern state after another, white members of the railway brotherhoods connected their demand for the end of black seniority rights to political disenfranchisement by arguing that further economic subordination should accompany political disenfranchisement (Arnesen 1994). They argued that "to admit Negroes, the Southern members declared, would be tantamount to admitting that the Negro is the 'social equal' of the white man," (Arnesen 1994, 1628). The ideological

---

11. I'm agnostic about "which came first," or if they came at the same time, as many (e.g., de Beauvoir) argue. However, the anthropological research of Christine Ward Gailey supports the view that "gender hierarchy emerges in association with class relations and state structures" (Gailey 1987, xv).

rationale at the beginning of this century for removing blacks from jobs at the same time that they were being removed from the polity was that "[we are] unalterably determined that America shall be and remain a white man's country," according to an editorial in the *Jackson (Tennessee) Daily Sun* (Arnesen 1994, 1625). It took a general order by the national government before the railroads would pay equal pay to blacks for equal work.[12] From the end of the Civil War to the advent of the Civil Rights movement of the mid-twentieth century, economic coercion, official and "unofficial" violence, and the power of local state authorities were used to appropriate black property and drive blacks from employment markets. During this period, neither black property rights, employment rights, constitutional rights, nor human rights were protected by the state or respected within civil society.[13]

As some argue today, the racial order also contained a script about the moral unworthiness of African Americans as justification for the denial of citizenship rights and exclusion from broad sectors of civil society (Dawson 1995). African Americans were considered both mentally inferior ("cognitively disabled" to use the current jargon) and morally bankrupt and therefore undeserving not only of citizenship, but also of a "valued place" within the economic hierarchy. This view of blacks as incapable of joining either civil society or the polity appears in the writings of the founders (e.g., Jefferson). State-supported white supremacy and the propagation of the view that blacks were inferior persisted well into (if not throughout) the twentieth century. During World War I the leaders of the American expeditionary force sent the French high command a pamphlet titled *Secret Information Concerning Negro Troops*. Within the pamphlet they starkly outlined the status of blacks in the United States: "Although a

---

12. This is yet another example of the need for central state intervention in civil society for the achievement of racial justice (Arnesen 1994). The hundreds of examples throughout black history of appeals being made to the central state (and sometimes being answered) helps to explain the centrality of the state as a vehicle for social change in central black political ideologies. Black support for a strong central government can be significantly explained by the federal government's relative support in protecting black claims for property rights and human rights against public and private expropriators in the states and local communities (Dawson 1994a).

13. For multiple examples of this process and how these incidents often became crucial in fostering the activism of key black leaders and shaping their ideological orientations, see Giddings (1984), who describes the lynching of successful store owners in Memphis as a critical event in the career of Ida B. Wells; Du Bois's description of the lynching of Sam Hose in *Dusk of Dawn* (1986); and Harry Haywood's description of his father being beaten and forced to flee his job and city (Franklin 1995). Richard Wright describes similar incidents, as does Frederick Douglass (Douglass 1969a; Wright 1966). Twentieth-century examples can be found in the narrative of Alabama sharecropper Nate Shaw (Rosengarten 1974).

citizen of the United Sates, the black man is regarded by the white American as an inferior being with whom relations of business or service are only possible. . . . The vices of the Negro are a constant menace to the American who has to repress them sternly" (Franklin 1995, 150). As late as the 1940s, a minor league manager could ask Branch Rickey (the owner of the Brooklyn Dodgers, who was about to integrate major league baseball with Jackie Robinson) in amazement, "Do you really think they're human?"

This racial order and its ideological components not only served to formally exclude African Americans from participation in the American bourgeois public sphere; it also encouraged the exclusion of blacks from subaltern counterpublics such as those associated with the labor, populist, and women's movements of the late nineteenth century. However, the black counterpublic sphere is the product of *both* the historically imposed separation of blacks from whites throughout most of American history (which was associated with exclusion from the "official" public sphere) and the embracing of the concept of black autonomy as both an institutional principle and an ideological orientation. Since Reconstruction, African Americans' notions of autonomy have included not only personal autonomy and liberty (which often led to clashes with white managers on how work was organized), but a community-based concept of autonomy which "embraced familial and community relationships as well" (Holt 1982a, 299; Brown 1989; Saville 1994a). Black discourse since the Civil War has emphasized both the building of autonomous political, economic, and social institutions within the black community and the demand for full citizenship rights, including the right to participate fully in debates critical to shaping the future of the nation.

Thus, the formal expulsion of African Americans at the end of the nineteenth century from official spheres of public discourse and decision making and the informal exclusion of African Americans from the mainstream of most of the oppositional movements at the time led to a dual strategy that was followed by African Americans for the first two-thirds of the twentieth century. On one hand, through the political agitation of those such as anti-lynching leader Ida B. Wells and the protests of organizations such as the NAACP, African Americans, using a variety of tactics and approaches, struggled to reinsert themselves into the channels of public discourse. Simultaneously, an active counterpublic persisted through organizations such as the active Negro Women's Club movement, the journals, meetings, and activities of the fledgling civil rights organizations, the small but active literary circles among black women and men, the activities and debates of black academics, and the black church. The blossoming of black organizational forms in the political, economic, and social arenas, when combined with the outburst of the Harlem renaissance, led to a strengthening of the black counterpublic and increased the pressure for African-American inclusion, both in official discourses as well as oppositional publics. These twin processes should be seen as part of a single, dialectical process. The activities of most of the major black leaders and many of the black organizations in the first half of the twentieth century, with the notable exception of Marcus Garvey, were important in both arenas. Ida B. Wells, who helped to shape debate about lynching not only nationally but internationally, was also a key figure in the debates within the early Negro Women's Club movement (Giddings 1984; Wells 1970). Similar dual roles were played by activists ranging from Du Bois and Randolph to the early black cadre in the U.S. Communist Party (Naison 1983).

Tensions grew within the black counterpublic as what Fraser called bourgeois masculinist norms were argued to be appropriate for black discourse and participation by some black (mainly male) leaders. One consequence of the adoption of the rules of the game from the dominant society was a shift in black politics from the type of inclusionary participatory debate described by Brown during the early stages of Reconstruction to the consistent attempts described by Wells and others to limit the participation of women in black public discourse (Brown 1989; Wells 1970). However, at the same time that powerful forces within the black counterpublic were attempting to impose (non–racially based) dominant norms, there were currents in the debates within the black counterpublic that provided the basis for both a devastating critique of American political institutions and values as well as some suggestions about possible theoretical and institutional alternatives. Historically, it was during this period of the late nineteenth and early twentieth centuries that we see the development of many features of the role that the black counterpublic would come to serve. Through the work of the Negro Women's Club movement, black women's activism became a crucial link between the by then somewhat separated women's suffrage and black rights movements—a role that African-American feminist groups continue to play to a significant degree. We also see radical critiques of American society flourish within the black community and also become disseminated to some degree through the writings of those such as Du Bois. Throughout this period, which also witnessed the emergence (and suppression) of a radical trade union movement, we see African-American activists both within and outside of the trade union movement argue that an understanding of racial subordination, of white supremacy, had to be a central feature of any non-reductionist critique of

American society. All of these trends would play a part in the interaction of racialized counterpublics throughout most of the twentieth century.

THE AFRICAN-AMERICAN COUNTERPUBLIC AND AMERICAN LIBERALISM

This view of the black counterpublic serving as a site not only for the criticism of existing American democratic institutions and practices but also for a severe interrogation of American liberalism runs counter to the claims of some recent theorists. Several scholars have argued recently that African Americans have embraced and made good use of American liberalism as a powerful source of opposition to slavery and white supremacy. Foner argues that nineteenth-century black political thought and, indeed, modern black political thought and activism are grounded in "the republican traditions of the eighteenth century, particularly as expressed in the Declaration of Independence and the Constitution" (Foner 1984, 60). Greenstone (1993) places Frederick Douglass in the same liberal reform tradition as John Adams and Daniel Webster. Oakes makes the connection between black political thought and liberalism explicit:

> If any group of Americans might have been expected to repudiate liberalism for its complicity in the defense of slavery, racism and economic inequality—African-Americans are that group. The fact that black political leaders consistently claimed the liberal tradition as their own therefore constitutes a major problem in the history of American political culture. [He goes on to say] . . . black political thought . . . has never been divorced from the liberal tradition. From the late eighteenth century to the late twentieth, blacks have successfully harnessed the themes of liberalism to the struggles against various forms of inequality. (Oakes 1992, 24, 27)

There are several fundamental problems with the uncomplicated, if comforting, celebration of the location of black political thought solidly within the mainstream of American liberalism. First, there is a tendency not to fully appreciate the range of discourse during any given period within the black counterpublic. Instead there is an overreliance on a few prominent historical figures.[14] In particular, the importance of black nationalism,

---

14. This is less true of Foner, who, in a variety of short papers and in his massive work on Reconstruction, does consider a wide range of discourse within post-emancipation black society. How-

the main challenger to the dominant trend of radical liberalism throughout most of the history of black political thought, is systematically underrepresented. Except during the period of Reconstruction, black nationalist intellectuals and activists have played an active role in the black counterpublic. It should not be surprising that in a society stratified by race, where African Americans have been systematically excluded from the bourgeois public sphere as well as many counterpublics, where even in the twentieth century the idea that African Americans could freely choose their roles and associations in good liberal fashion seems ludicrously naive, nonliberal theoretical perspectives which emphasize the primacy of community are prominent in the black counterpublic. Both a lack of appreciation for the autonomy of the black counterpublic and the ideological blinders of many scholars, which lead them to miss the significance of major nationalist movements (such as that of Marcus Garvey, of organizations such as the Nation of Islam, and of intellectuals such as Martin Delaney), contribute to the lack of theorizing about the relationship between black nationalist thought in the black counterpublic and American liberalism.

The dynamics of interracial discourse are also partly responsible for the widespread lack of familiarity with the nonliberal components of black political thought. For most of black history, the discourses of the black counterpublic have been partly hidden from view. To a significant degree, debates such as those between Shields Green and Frederick Douglass constitute part of the hidden transcript of a subaltern people (Scott 1990).[15] As Sanders has conclusively demonstrated, interracial dialogue within the United States is marked by both blacks and whites adopting more moderate and conventional political standpoints than when they talk among themselves (Sanders 1995a, 1995b). Thus, the antiliberal tendencies of black political discourse are to some degree masked, *especially when blacks and whites are directly debating politics.*

Second, even during periods when the political rhetoric of African-American activists was consistent with the liberal tradition, the actual political practice within black communities has had decidedly nonliberal

---

ever, Foner's ability to make sweeping generalizations about black political thought is hindered by the fact that the period he knows best is the one period in American history when African Americans were both most optimistic and most prone to accept, albeit critically, American liberalism. His judgments on liberalism and black political thought for other historical periods do not show the same appreciation for the nuances of black political discourse as those of his work on Reconstruction.

15. The presence of John Brown at this conversation can hardly be considered typical of white access to black strategic discussions.

elements. Perhaps the most obvious example of a nonliberal (some would say antiliberal) political tradition within black politics has been the consistent demand that *individual* African Americans take political stands that are perceived by the *community* as not harming the black community.[16] This norm is often systematically backed by community sanctioning and censoring of those perceived as transgressors. The work of Brown, Saville, and Foner details how during Reconstruction black Democrats were considered traitors, stripped of community-derived benefits, and publicly condemned and humiliated (Brown 1989; Dawson 1994b; Foner 1988; Saville 1994b). This tradition remains strong even today, when growing social and economic divisions within the black community have led to considerably less consensus on the "black" tradition than has existed in even the recent past. Black supporters of the Republican Party are disdained by most African Americans with the same high level of frigidity as the Republican Party itself (Dawson 1994a). Black conservatives such as Glenn Loury have complained throughout the recent period that they are ostracized and treated as traitors by other African Americans because of their conservatism. In the academy, liberals are periodically appalled as the most recent darling of the conservative establishment becomes pilloried by a chorus of black academics. Many African-American academics see the situation in radically different terms. Perceived attacks on the black community are not seen as the result of a courageous and creative talent, but as rank opportunism that imperils a community already under siege. More recently, black feminists, radicals, and liberals have challenged many of the supporters of the Million Man March who argued that any criticism of the march was a betrayal of the black community. While we can assess the empirical validity of either view in any given case, the tradition of a public community censoring and sanctioning of those seen as attacking the community represents a decidedly antiliberal tendency within black political practice.

Third, virtually all of the major ideological tendencies within black political thought (except the historically weak trend of black conservatism) have strongly deemphasized the privileged nature of private property. Former slaves such as Douglass would have found foul the idea of compensating former slave owners for their former "property." By the 1930s, Du Bois, who foreshadowed many of the transitions that African-American intellectuals would make in the 1960s, had abandoned much of the liberal

---

16. Implicit in this passage is a view of liberalism, one not shared by all liberals, that privileges individualism as a central concern. In chapter 6 I more fully discuss the construction of liberalism(s) that are central to my task and discuss more specifically the antiliberal elements within black liberalism(s).

tradition in which he had earlier put so much faith. Fairly typical is this passage from *Dusk of Dawn:*

> It was clear to me that agitation against race prejudice and a planned economy for bettering the economic condition of the American Negro were not antagonistic ideals but part of one ideal; that did not increase segregation; the segregation that was there and would remain for many years. But now I proposed that in economic lines, just as in lines of literature and religion, segregation should be planned and organized and carefully thought through. This plan did not establish a new segregation; it did not advocate segregation as the final solution of the race problem; exactly the contrary; but it did face the facts and faced them with thoughtfully mapped effort. (Du Bois 1986, 777)

Du Bois's work in his later years provides an example of the need to better understand the autonomy of the black counterpublic and the reasons why black discourse cannot be confined within the boundaries of American liberalism. Du Bois is but one of many black intellectuals and activists who became members of an active black left. The black left had strong ties with white leftists, particularly during the heyday of the Communist Party USA, but it still represented an autonomous force within the black community that was fully engaged with other intellectuals, activists, and members of the black counterpublic (Kelley 1990, 1994; Naison 1983; Robinson 1983; Stuckey 1987).

While the black left had its doctrinaire wing(s) as well as a more social-democratic element, even the beliefs of those who composed the latter ran seriously counter to the tenets of mainstream (i.e., "white") American liberalism. As the following passage from King's last presidential speech to the Southern Christian Leadership Conference (SCLC) demonstrates, even relatively moderate black leaders have tended to place demands on the state and limits on property that stretched the boundaries of liberalism:

> We [must] honestly face the fact that the movement must address itself to the question of restructuring the whole of American society. There are forty million poor people here. And one day we must ask the question, "Why are there forty million poor people in America?" And when you begin to ask that question, you are raising questions about the economic system, about a broader distribution of wealth. When you ask that question, you begin to question the capitalistic economy. And I'm simply saying that more and more, we've got to begin to ask questions

about the whole society. We are called upon to help the discouraged beggars in life's marketplace. But one day we must come to see that an edifice which produces beggars needs restructuring. . . . What I'm saying to you this morning is that communism forgets that life is individual. Capitalism forgets that life is social, and the kingdom of brotherhood is found neither in the thesis of communism nor the antithesis of capitalism but in a higher synthesis. It is found in a higher synthesis that combines the truths of both. Now, when I say question the whole society, it means ultimately coming to see that the problem of racism, the problem of economic exploitation, and the problem of war are all tied together. These are the triple evils that are interrelated. (King 1986a, 260)

These criticisms are not meant to deny that there is a strong liberal theme within black political thought. The last statement by King, made at the height of his radicalism, still contains strong liberal elements. However, American liberalism is usually defined in such as way as to privilege the autonomy and liberty of the individual, skepticism of central state power, and the sanctity of private property (Greenstone 1993; Oakes 1992; Waldron 1993). In summary, any sustained examination of the history of discourse within the black counterpublic quickly reveals two important features. First, strong historical traditions exist within black political thought and practice that diverge from the major tenets of American liberalism in important ways. Second, even the very strong liberal elements within black political thought include explicit critiques of the "consensual" version of American liberalism as foundational components.

One implication of these two features of the discourse within the black counterpublic is that we cannot view black political thought as fully situated within American liberalism.[17] What stance to take toward discourse within the black counterpublic has been problematic for politicians, political activists, and scholars who work within the liberal tradition, due to the nonliberal and radically transformed liberal currents found within the historical black counterpublic. Two strategies predominate. One is to ignore the discourse entirely. Forests of work on American political thought

17. An additional consequence of not fully recognizing the diversity and autonomy of discourse within the black counterpublic has been the tendency to view black political discourse through the lenses of binary oppositions such as "black nationalism vs. assimilation" (Oakes 1992). As Pinderhughes (1987) and Reed (1992b) both argue, such an approach to black political thought provides inadequate analytical power and impoverishes the task of attempting to understand the dialectic between a relatively autonomous, indigenous discourse within the black counterpublic and the discourse between those within the subaltern counterpublic and the dominant public about the nature and future course of the American polity.

totally ignore political discourse among African Americans—Reed (1992b) provides a good review of works in this genre. The second strategy has recently become more popular, and that is to assert that black political thought is within the mainstream and therefore to ignore or dismiss the tendencies within black political thought that diverge from the liberal tradition.[18]

The formal and "informal" exclusion of African Americans from the polity provided a political basis for the official public sphere to ignore (except for purposes of surveillance) the black counterpublic well into the middle decades of the twentieth century. Interest in the black counterpublic rapidly increased in the 1960s, however, due to the combined pressures of the collapse of the legalistic mechanisms for excluding blacks from formal participation within the polity, the exponential growth of a black social movement which was responsible not only for the collapse of Jim Crow but also for a general increase in militancy in U.S. society, and the widening of the base and an increase of activity within the black counterpublic. Throughout American history there continued to be an exchange between the black counterpublic and other publics. The careers of Douglass, Wells, Du Bois, and King, among others, were marked by the range of contacts and debates they had with whites, both as individuals and as representatives of major black organizations (in the cases of Wells, Du Bois, and King). No period since the Reconstruction era was as marked by the intensity of political debate and practice in the black community and by meaningful political exchanges and pragmatic cooperation between blacks and whites as was the 1960s.[19] However, during the 1970s a set of transformations within the black community, the American economy, and the American political system not only served to reduce once again the level of

---

18. This strategy is seldom used by American conservatives, who are often quick to recognize (if not exaggerate) the radical and antiliberal elements of black political thought and practice. The conservative critiques of King during the Civil Rights era, of Jesse Jackson's campaigns during the 1980s, and (more recently) of the failed nomination of Lani Guinier as assistant attorney general for civil rights provide three modern examples of this phenomenon.

19. It is no coincidence that both academics and private pollsters began to pay more attention to black public opinion during this period. The increased activity had an inherent regulatory function, as the study of black public opinion was seen within the framework of "race relations." Pollsters were less concerned about the historical development of black thought and discourse than with how blacks viewed American society and groups within American society; trends within black public opinion (Were blacks becoming more radical and dangerous?); and which sectors of the black community were most disruptive. It is not surprising that the spurt of attention given to black public opinion by organizations such as the University of Michigan's American National Election Studies (1972) and the Harris organization (several major studies in the late 1960s and early 1970s) died down once African Americans were once again no longer viewed as a threat to domestic "tranquillity."

interracial exchange and cooperation, but also seriously undermined the black counterpublic. These developments would also have serious consequences for ideological competition within black political thought.

THE TRANSFORMATION AND UNDERMINING OF THE BLACK COUNTERPUBLIC

One often overlooked but critical feature of Habermas's formulation of the nature of the public sphere is the importance of the institutional bases for the bourgeois public sphere. Nancy Fraser's description of the feminist counterpublic also has at its base a wide variety of institutional forms, including media and artistic outlets, bookstores, academic centers, and community service and other organizational sites (Fraser 1989). Similarly, throughout black history numerous black institutions have formed the material basis for a subaltern counterpublic. An independent black press, the production and circulation of socially and politically acute popular black music, and the social and political activities of the black church have provided consistent institutional bases for the black counterpublic since the Civil War. The most important organization during each historical epoch, always intimately tied to the black counterpublic, has been the black church (Higginbotham 1993). In addition, each period's subaltern counterpublic has had a variety of secular organizational bases. Examples include the Negro Convention movement of the antebellum period, the Union Leagues of Reconstruction, the Negro Women's Club movement of the late nineteenth century, the multitude of organizations and debate that surrounded the Garvey movement, and the civil rights organizations of the early 1960s. Indeed, one mark of the 1960s and the early 1970s was the proliferation of both sacred and secular organizations within the black community that were engaged in both intense political debate and practice. Church-based organizations such as the SCLC (Southern Christian Leadership Conference), student organizations such as the black student unions, black workers' caucuses that spread like wildfire in settings as diverse as universities and auto plants, and community-based Civil Rights and Black Power organizations all provided bases for a vibrant black counterpublic. They were centers of debate over the direction of the black liberation movement as well as over the relation that black political action would have to the massive political mobilization that was occurring outside of the black community. They also provided an environment which closely linked political debate to political action. Figure 1.1 provides a rough diagram of the overlapping sets of discourse communities that provided the foundation for

Figure 1.1   Intersections between black and white discourse and activist communities, 1966–1972

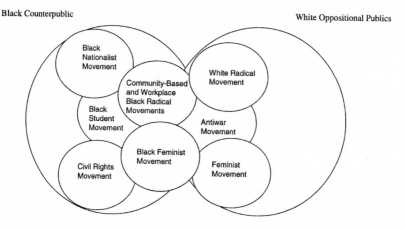

many of the social movements of blacks and whites during the height of the activism of a generation ago.

Unfortunately, a number of developments both within American society and the black community severely undermined the institutional foundation for the black counterpublic as well as black access to white-dominated publics. The combination of state repression and internal dissension destroyed or severely harmed many Civil Rights and Black Power organizations. The state, mainly but not exclusively through the FBI's Counterintelligence Program (COINTELPRO), systematically targeted civil rights, black student, and black militant organizations. State activities included the harassment of Dr. King; the instigation of intragroup violence; the filing of numerous charges against black activists, often tying them and their organizational resources up in court for years; and, in the case of Chicago Black Panther leader Fred Hampton, assassination (Carson 1981, 1991; Garrow 1981; McAdam 1982).

The disintegration of the progressive and nationalist organizational bases of the black counterpublic was aided in the middle 1970s by the near fanatical attention that both leftist forces dominated by people of color and black nationalist forces devoted to the twin themes of "theory building" and, even more specifically, "party building." The cadrification of groups as diverse as the New York–based, predominantly Puerto Rican Young Lords organization, the groups that came out of the radical black labor organizing of Detroit's DRUM (Dodge Revolutionary Union Movement) movement, the Chicano-based August Twenty-Ninth movement, and the originally nationalist Congress of Afrikan Peoples meant that experienced blacks (and other organizers of color) were pulled out of the student movement, labor movement, cultural activities, and community organizations to form small study groups and fight (all too often violently) with each other, all in the name of building a myriad of "vanguard" political parties. Organizations such as the African Liberation Support Committee of the early and middle 1970s, which were able to mobilize tens of thousands of African Americans across the United States in the name of both African and black liberation while facilitating theoretical debate about the future of black liberation, were destroyed through this process as group after group degenerated into small sects.[20]

A structural shift in the U.S. economy away from manufacturing and toward low-wage service industries also contributed to the erosion of the institutional base of the black counterpublic, especially its points of contact with other oppositional forces. One of the critical aspects of the shift in the American economy, a shift that much of the industrialized world would experience throughout the 1970s and 1980s, was the shift from Fordist economic arrangements to a capitalist regime that emphasized flexible accumulation (Harvey 1989). In the United States, increased competition from Western Europe, Japan, and the newly industrial countries accelerated this process, as did the increasing attempts by producer countries (e.g., oil producers) to control the flow and price of raw materials, which had devastating effects on income and wages, as evidenced by the decline of the real standard of living in the United States after the oil shocks of the early 1970s.

What is not as well understood—indeed, it is usually totally missed—is that the Fordist regime in the United States integrated the racial and economic orders. For blacks, the Fordist regime meant that black economic gains were concentrated in the state and manufacturing sectors (see Dawson 1994a for a review). These two sectors constituted the economic bases for the black middle and working classes, the heart of most twentieth-century black protest movements. This was a racialized economic order, because blacks were incorporated into the industrial order on a racially subordinate basis. One trenchant example is provided by Whatley and Wright (1994), who describe how foundry-work wages went from high to

---

20. Reed (1999b) provides an excellent analysis of this dismal history. Reed's analysis is somewhat too attentive to East Coast developments at the expense of the development of the radical wings of the black movement in other parts of the country, and he underestimates the role of the state in aiding the disruption and disintegration of black radical movements.

low as the workforce shifted from white to black. The system of white supremacy shaped labor markets and wages, as well as the human capital endowments that black workers could bring into increasingly competitive and high-skill labor markets. However, the shift to a system of flexible accumulation, which led to smaller workplaces, more homogenous workforces, and the weakening of labor unions, eviscerated the moderate-wage bases of the black working and middle classes; in addition, under the new regime, blacks were more likely to suffer from racial discrimination in the labor markets (Kirschenman and Neckerman 1991; Johnson and Oliver 1990). Further, the spatial aspects of this transformation left inner cities economically devastated as their economic base was removed and large sectors of urban minority residents lived in increasingly poor neighborhoods.

The transformation in the political economy had several major consequences. The impoverishment of the black working class as its base in both manufacturing and public employment disappeared sharpened class divisions; much of the stable black working class now found its financial existence seriously imperiled (Dawson 1994a). From the fourth quarter of 1974 through the fourth quarter of 1992, there were only *five* quarters in which black unemployment was below 10 percent (data compiled by author from Citibase electronic database). In all five of those quarters the black unemployment rate was more than 9 percent. States that had previously high levels of black industrial workers, such as Illinois and Michigan, were very hard hit. The state of nearly permanent economic depression in many black communities harmed their organizational base. Black organizations shrank and disappeared when their financial status worsened and their programs were seen as less relevant to solving the problems of a devastated economy. During this period, as during the great majority of the period since 1955, the black unemployment rate was, on average, twice that of whites. The devastation of the economic base was accompanied by a significant decline in the political and economic strength of American trade unions. Although the trade union movement from the 1930s to the 1960s never provided a panacea or the basis for multiracial mass organizing for which many on the left hoped, it did provide one of the few settings within which non-elite blacks and whites interacted and (occasionally) cooperated politically. It also provided a training ground for many of the black activist forces of the 1960s and for many future black elected officials such as Detroit's previous long-term mayor, Coleman Young. After the 1970s, the trade union movement's ability to serve either as a site for interracial political discourse or as a valuable training ground for a wide range of black activists was severely attenuated.

As many have documented, the transformation of the American political economy combined with the dismantling of the formal mechanisms of segregation fostered the growth of various segments of the black middle class (see Dawson 1994a for a critical review). Formal segregation and the entire white supremacist system of Jim Crow provided a monumental common target not only for African Americans, but also for many liberal and progressive whites. As King (1967) and others argued, white support declined due to the shifting of the Civil Rights movement to the North, where it was increasingly perceived as focusing on economic demands. Black and white interracial cooperation plummeted, and, more often than not, in political arenas ranging from local contests for mayor to national presidential politics, blacks and whites found themselves on opposite sides. The political gap between blacks and whites continued to grow through the early 1990s as different events such as the subway shootings by Bernard Goetz, the election and reign of Ronald Reagan, and the presidential campaigns of Jesse Jackson were assigned radically different meanings by blacks and whites (Dawson 1994a). By the early 1990s, points of intersection between white and black discourse communities had largely disappeared, with the partial exception of the continued discourse between feminist women of color and white feminists. Labor unions, the military, and even college campuses no longer provided the arenas for interracial debate that they once did. Differences that emerged out of traumatic national racial conflict further eroded the desire to engage in interracial discourse. The complicated reactions of many blacks and whites to the O. J. Simpson verdict were not portrayed in the American media; the media's portrayal of these reactions as a simple example of interracial division fed the tension between racial communities.

The dismantling of the formal barriers of segregation combined with the sharpening of economic divisions within the black community also problematized black political discourse. The lack of a single, agreed-upon goal served to unmask the political relevance of already existing social cleavages. The sharpening economic divisions led to a divergence in black mass opinion on questions such as whether policies of economic redistribution were desirable (Dawson 1994a). Just as important—perhaps even more so when considering the various purposes of subaltern publics as described by Fraser (1989)—is that economic divisions are strongly associated in African-American mass opinion with division over the degree to which race is seen as the driving force in creating black disadvantage. Class cleavages also underlie differences over what strategies African Americans should adopt at this time. Specifically, economic disadvantage—of both the individual and the community—is strongly associated with a racialized view of the world and a greater probability of support for black nationalist policies and organizational forms (Cohen and Dawson 1994, 1993; Dawson 1994a, 1995).

The new economic regime further intensified divisions within the black community and disintegration of the black counterpublic as a new wave of black elected officials provided a buffer class that helped to delegitimate protest and circumscribe "acceptable" political discourse within the black community. Three parallel processes were at work as many black elected officials cooperated in the narrowing of the black agenda through the 1970s and the 1980s. First, black elected officials at the local level inherited cities that were devastated by the economic earthquake described above. They were severely limited in their ability to meet the demands of their disadvantaged constituents. Second, as black elected officials began to have aspirations that required attracting votes outside of the black community, they (with the moderate exceptions of those such as Jesse Jackson and Harold Washington) deemphasized both their explicit racial appeals and political agendas that included economic redistribution—historically a fundamental political demand of the black community (Dawson 1994a; Persons 1993). Finally, many black elected officials became incorporated into the new ruling regime of race relations management, which functioned as a regulatory buffer dedicated to incremental changes in race relations and even smaller improvements in the economic plight of the poor (Hill 1994; Reed 1999b).

While the economic divisions within the black community are politically important, Morrison's (1992a) and Henry's (1990) analyses of the death of black political unity were triggered not by a conflict generated by class cleavages, but by the turmoil that erupted among African Americans after the nomination of Clarence Thomas and the subsequent charges of sexual abuse leveled by law professor Anita Hill. Throughout African-American history, black women have played a leading role in the struggle against white supremacy and struggled as well with the patriarchal attitudes of many black men and some black women, who believe that black women should play a subordinate role—if any active role at all—in the struggle against oppression. They have also struggled to get the issues of particular concern to black women included as part of the black "agenda" (Cohen 1994; Davis 1981; Giddings 1984; Wells 1970). The increasing dissatisfaction with (1) the lack of political attention devoted to issues of special significance for black women (e.g., patriarchal ideologies being used to justify the subordination of women not only in black nationalist and church-based formations, but also in some black "left" organizations), and (2) the vulgar and brutal misogyny of black leaders such as Eldridge Cleaver and Stokely Carmichael helped fuel the explosion of black feminist and womanist organizations, literatures, presses, and debates. The increasingly vocal belief advanced by some African Americans that the surest way to understand the black condition was by understanding the intersection of race, gender, and class and the white supremacist, patriarchal, and classist systems of stratification that mapped the terrain of American society (Crenshaw 1990) clashed with openly patriarchal analyses of the black condition of many black activists and intellectuals. Many supporters of Justice Thomas, for example, claimed that no black men who are in a position to achieve power should ever be publicly criticized, even if their politics differed immensely from the politics of 85 percent of blacks, and even if they had previously used power to abuse less powerful members of the black community. The demand for uncritical support of blacks in positions of power and the relegation of the specific concerns of black women to secondary status was seen as increasingly intolerable. As Morrison states, "In matters of race and gender, it is now possible and necessary, as it seemed never to have been before, to speak about these matters without the barriers, the silences, the embarrassing gaps in discourse" (Morrison 1992a, xxx).

Taken together, the disintegration of the institutional bases of the black counterpublic since the early 1970s and increasing black skepticism regarding the existence of a bundle of issues and strategies that define a "black agenda" should lead us to question whether we can assert that a subaltern counterpublic exists—and if it does, how "healthy" is it now? The racial system of stratification which helped provide the material basis for the historic counterpublic still exists. American society is nowhere near the idea described by Charles Taylor when he asserted,

> From the democratic point of view, a person's ethnic identity is not his or her primary identity, and, important as respect for diversity is in multicultural democratic societies, ethnic identity is not the foundation of recognition of equal values and the related idea of equal rights. . . . In other words, from the liberal democratic point of view, a person has a right to claim equal recognition first and foremost on the basis of his or her universal human identity and potential, not primarily on the basis of an ethnic identity. (Taylor 1992, 88)

And I argue that Baker (1993) exaggerates when he claims, "Any of us might encounter simply in our daily travels a black, Vietnamese-American, potential MBA, Ivy-League, basketball-playing woman who is fully at ease with the transnational, material, and indisputably hybrid spaces in which she dwells" (Baker 1993, 70). He misses the point. Certainly, it is past time to reject essentialist definitions of race, gender, and other socially constructed categories. As Reed states, "Of course race is real, but it is real only in the way that all social constructs are real. Its reality is always contingent on historically circumscribed contexts of meaning and patterns of social stratification. The success of civil rights activism in defeating the regime of official racial segregation, for example, . . . has helped to give rise to recent efforts to nail down a new, historically appropriate summary construction of black identity" (Reed 1992b, 138–39).

Some identities still are more salient than others in the political, economic, and social realms. A new wave of empirical research conclusively demonstrates that where one can live, for whom one is likely to vote, whether one is likely to encounter discrimination based on stereotypes when entering the labor market, and whether one's culture and intelligence are considered inferior were still structured by race in the 1990s (Dawson 1994a; Jencks 1992). Wealth, a prime determinant of life chances, is structured by racial inequalities (Oliver and Shapiro 1995). The dismantling of the formal structures of segregation, however, combined with the increasing importance of identities based on other structures of stratification require that a black subaltern counterpublic would have to be reconstituted based on a new understanding of the nature of the issues, including those addressing patriarchy and economic oppression, that will move to the fore. Without such a broadening of what is understood to be on the "black agenda," a unifying set of discourses and political agenda will not come to be.

CONCLUSION

How have black political thought and, more specifically, black political ideologies developed, given the disintegration of the institutional base of the black counterpublic and increased ideological conflict within the black community? The rest of this book is devoted to answering this question. The turmoil that accompanied the Anita Hill–Clarence Thomas hearings strongly suggests that some black ideologies are alive and well not only among intellectuals and activists, but also among the black grassroots. However, black discourse in the mid-1990s is also filled with complaints about leadership vacuums, the lack of a common agenda, and other commentary, which suggests that contemporary black political ideologies may be inadequate to provide guidance in the difficult times that face black communities. The rest of this book concentrates on answering the following questions:

- Which political ideologies are supported by blacks?
- Which sectors of the black community are more likely to support which ideological constellation?
- How do structural factors such as individual social location, embeddedness in black information networks, and the spatial location of individuals in various types of neighborhoods shape individual ideological orientations?
- How do black ideologies shape black public opinion?

Chapter 2 sketches my theoretical approach to the study of black public opinion and black ideologies. I differentiate between how ideology differs for political theorists and public opinion researchers. The empirical and theoretical relationships among some forms of black popular culture, the black counterpublic, and black ideologies are also introduced. Chapter 2 concludes by introducing the reader to the 1993–94 National Black Politics Study, which provides the data for much of the analysis. The level of support for each ideology is presented in this chapter. Chapters 3–6 each sketch the historical development of each African-American ideological challenge to American liberalism. Each of these chapters also analyzes the relationship between black political ideologies and contemporary black popular culture. The chapters also consider the effect of black ideologies on various forms of civil and political participation. Chapter 3 analyzes the support for and consequences of black nationalism. The interaction of gender and black feminism is the central theme of chapter 4. The elusive quest for understanding the intersection of race and class and the equally elusive quest for building a black socialist movement are examined in chapter 5. The many transformations by blacks of the liberal creed, including conservative transformations, form the subject of chapter 6. Each chapter also presents evidence about the presence of each ideology within contemporary black public opinion and the ideology's influence on black public opinion. Chapter 7 concludes the book with speculation about the future development of several black political visions and their importance for understanding the theory and practice of American democracy.

The American Negro deserves study for the great end of advancing the cause of science in general.

W. E. B. Du Bois

CHAPTER 2

Black Ideologies and Black Public Opinion

🏔 The relative homogeneity of black public opinion has been generally considered one of the few certainties of modern American politics. While some scholars have challenged the claim of homogeneity in black public opinion, the popular wisdom has been that African Americans constitute one of the few remaining solid American voting blocs, and that the ideology of the African-American mass public is narrowly bound.[1] While most commentators place African Americans on the liberal side of the traditional liberal-conservative ideological divide, more sophisticated observers suggest that a separatist-assimilationist ideological divide exists as well.

---

1. For a sampling of work that discusses cleavages in the black mass public, see Cohen 1994; Dawson 1994a, 1994b; Pinderhughes 1987; and Reed 1999b.

Dramatically divisive conflicts within the black community have become public over the past several years. These conflicts have been centered around events such as the Anita Hill–Clarence Thomas hearings, debates over the views of leaders of the Nation of Islam, as well as the relatively brief tenure of Ben Chavis as leader of the NAACP. More recently, the ideological struggles around the Million Man, Million Woman, and Million Youth marches have commanded attention within and outside of the black community. These events have demonstrated to the nation ideological fractures which do not neatly fall along the liberal-conservative or assimilationist-separatist fault lines. These conflicts have been driven in part by long-standing ideological cleavages which have historically shaped black politics but have until recently been hidden from many observers outside of the black community. These conflicts reflect the many ideological divisions that transcend both the usual liberal-conservative and even the assimilationist-separatist categorization schemes.

This chapter begins to describe the contours of African-American ideologies in the 1990s. Black ideologies such as black nationalism have long intellectual traditions, and substantial social bases, and they are the focus of contemporary debate within the black community (Brown 1990b; Bracey, Meir, and Rudwick 1970; Cohen and Dawson 1994; Higginbotham 1993). Research has shown that black ideologies are important determinants of African-American preferences and behavior (Dawson 1994a; Dawson 1994b; Smith 1993; Tate 1993). Theoretical and empirical research into ideology, however, has been limited for several reasons. Many social and political theorists view ideology as a phenomenon that undermines the democratic system itself as well as the ability of citizens to be critical participants in shaping a just and good society.[2] Some social theorists worry that charismatic leaders can use ideology to manipulate mass publics for undemocratic ends (Eagleton 1991). Public opinion researchers take a more agnostic view about whether ideology plays a positive or negative role within democratic polities. They do, however—at least since Converse's seminal work in 1964—doubt the efficacy of ideologies for shaping American public opinion and political action. The lack of academic attention directed toward ideology is ironic, Eagleton comments, given the undeniable force that ideologically driven movements have in our modern world. Marxist, free market, religious, and a multitude of nationalist ideologies

2. For a good introduction to the multiple meanings and uses of the concept of ideology, see Eagleton 1991.

quite literally battle, often bloodily, for supremacy in both civil and external wars. I agree with Eagleton that we must view ideology "as an organizing social force which actively constitutes human subjects at the roots of their lived experience," though I don't agree that ideology necessarily aids in "the general reproduction of the social order" (1991, 222). I argue that without detailed examination of ideologies within specific historical contexts, we cannot predict whether any specific ideology serves a positive or negative role, or whether it has any effect on public opinion. I find the content of some ideologies highly objectionable, but that is a normative judgment on my part. Whether ideologies have an effect on political behavior is, however, an empirical question. The foundations for the empirical investigation of black ideologies are laid in this chapter.

The degree to which structural and ideological forces shape public opinion has been consistently debated within both social and public opinion theory.[3] Public opinion researchers, however, have rarely had the opportunity to determine the degree to which social structure(s) other than individual social location shape both black ideologies and political preferences.[4] This chapter also extends our understanding of the impact of the interaction between social structure and black ideologies as well as, more generally, black public opinion. Social structures such as those of class also play an important role in shaping of black politics. Indeed, another central argument of this book is that social structures shape African-American ideologies. The structures of urban residential segregation and neighborhood poverty, for example, affect not only black opinion but African Americans' entire view of the political and social world (Cohen and Dawson 1993; Massey and Denton 1993; Wilson 1987).

First, I continue the discussion begun in chapter 1 of the way ideology is viewed within this book. I discuss ideology from the standpoint of some trends within political and social theory and then try to "reconcile" that view of ideology with that found among public opinion researchers and historians. Then I discuss the role of social structures in shaping black ide-

---

3. See Sanders 1995a for an excellent discussion of this issue, which is also addressed in a variety of other works (Dawson 1994b; Sanders 1995b; Zaller 1992). Habermas's (1989) work on the public sphere has influenced one recent strand of thinking regarding the relationship among social structures, institutions, and public opinion.

4. Exceptions to this claim include Cohen and Dawson (1993), who were able to show that the level of neighborhood poverty shaped black public opinion, and Bobo and Gilliam (1990), who demonstrated that the degree of black incorporation into local political structures was also critical for understanding black public opinion.

ologies. I next lay the groundwork for analyzing the institutional bases of black ideologies. Finally, I describe the contours of the distribution of the six black ideologies identified in chapter 1 among African Americans and establish the bases for analyzing the effects of these ideologies on black preferences.

IDEOLOGY, HISTORY, AND PUBLIC OPINION

Political and social theorists of both the left and the right have attacked the phenomenon of "ideology" for corrupting virtuous political processes. Both views agree that ideology is "false," that ideology deceives the masses, and that the deception serves the ruling regime, whether that regime is a bourgeois, capitalistic, liberal regime, a totalitarian regime of the left, or an authoritarian regime of the right.[5]

Ideology and Critical Theory

Marxist social theorists, including those associated with the Frankfurt school, view ideology as the capitalist tool aimed at consensually deflecting the masses from their true class interests (Rorty 1994; Thompson 1984; Žižek 1994). The media are seen as accomplices in the process of homogenizing the opinions of citizens in society, with dire consequences for democratic debate, critiques, and participation (Habermas 1989; Žižek 1994). Scholars on the left agree with Arendt that ideology masks the divisions among grassroots citizens and also provides the important function of masking the ills of the society (Dolan 1994; Thompson 1984; Žižek 1994). They agree as well that ideological thinking does not allow for the self-reflection that is necessary for critical political theorizing and action (Horkheimer 1972).

Habermas in particular is concerned that the consumerist ideology associated with the economic gains achieved after World War II in much of the West has led to a degradation of the bourgeois public sphere. The

---

5. Reading my notes for this chapter, the only conclusion I could come to on the status of ideology in political and social theory was that it was bad, bad, bad. Less facetious, and perhaps on the extreme end of negative evaluations of ideology, is the opinion of Kenneth Minogue, who sees all ideology as "oppositional" (Eagleton 1991). More to the point is his view that ideologies are typified by their "hostility to modernity: to liberalism in politics, individualism in moral practice, and the market in economics" (quoted in Eagleton 1991, 6). Many theorists may disagree with the specifics of his critique, but the tone is not unusual.

middle and upper working classes traded the ability to critique and, to some degree, to regulate the state for the pabulum produced by the consumerist society of *Father Knows Best*. The perception that markets are just and the ability to achieve autonomous liberty have combined, argues Habermas, to gut the very desire of citizens to participate in politics. Elaborate spectacles, hero worship, and rituals replace and suppress the critical debate that marks the public spheres of healthy democracies (Dolan 1994; Lane 1962; Žižek 1994). These processes corroded the once-dense network of civil associations, political parties, political clubs, and social movements which provided an organizational infrastructure for critical public spheres and democratic societies. Black theorists such as Adolph Reed argue that this same consumerist ideology and its associated cultural and artistic products are blinding African Americans, thus aiding the deterioration of black critical analyses of American politics and society.

The critics of ideology do recognize that which ideology is *dominant* at any given time, which is *politically important* in a given society, is historically contingent (Arendt 1966; Horkheimer 1972). Ideologies form, are articulated, and take root among the grassroots as a result of specific social processes (Horkheimer 1972). The process of white racial backlash, for example, often helps provide an atmosphere within which black nationalism flourishes. Specific ideologies are also more likely to flourish among specific social groups and associated sets of interests (Habermas 1989). Historically, various forms of liberalism have generally flourished among an upwardly mobile and successful black middle class; cultural nationalism has flourished among a sector of the middle class that is often on the verge of impoverishment; while in our period black nationalism has taken strongest root among the desperately poor. These patterns do *not* have the status of historical *law*. Eagleton reminds us that "what is represented is never some 'brute' reality" (Eagleton 1991, 208). It is easy to find examples of middle-class nationalists, bourgeois Marxists, and proletarian liberals throughout the twentieth century. As Horkheimer argues, it is easy for members of any class stratum to be "corrupted" by ideology (Horkheimer 1972).

Ideologies not only rise and fall in response to historical changes in their social base and social forces such as technological change, but each ideology is itself transformed by these historical forces (Arendt 1966; Horkheimer 1972). Confusion can result if the analyses of ideologies are taken out of historical context. As suggested in chapter 1, the concept of a "black nation" does not mean the same thing to a black Civil War veteran, a supporter of Marcus Garvey, a black communist sharecropper during the 1930s, a member of the Nation of Islam during the 1950s, a 1960s Black

Panther Party member, or 1970s black Leninist. Because ideologies are "implicated" in social life, are grasped and transformed by the members of society, they have creative potential in both the social and political realms (Thompson 1984). In the end, however, even critical theorists who argue that ideology has a creative potential agree with their peers that ideology fundamentally warps the democratic process, regardless of historical context, through its promotion of a dangerously false, fictional portrayal of the world.

Nietzschean-inspired but left-oriented political philosophers also find ideology more stultifying than illuminating and equally the tool of the dominant classes. As often happens in times such as these, when the left is immersed in its own defeat, the writings of political philosophers such as Hannah Arendt, who are not normally identified with the modern left, are used to inspire the creation of a leftist political movement that is not based on ideology. Arendt and her supporters argue that ideology is representative of an immanence that submerges identity and ultimately the individual in a faceless sea of beings whose identity and lives are inextricably tied to the state (Arendt 1958, 1966; Dolan 1994; Dumm 1994). Indeed, even ideologies which claim to oppose the established order, such as black nationalism, are criticized (justly) because they are seen as seeking to define a single identity, a single mode of being, which is defined as virtuous (in this case "virtuous" = "authentically" black). In many versions of black nationalism, for example, it is not possible, adherents claim, to have a feminist identity and simultaneously hold a black, let alone a nationalist, identity.[6]

To the degree that ideologies are associated with naturalized, essentialist, identities, they "paralyze" the ability to engage in the performative, creative politics that allow for the greatest individual freedom and collective democracy. Like the critical theorists, Arendt views ideologies as the promoters of dangerous fictions (Arendt 1958). Even more important than their fictional nature is that modern ideologies swallow identity and produce conformity, that they have the sinister character of robbing individuals of the possibility of acquiring *virtù*, of being politically virtuous. If we are all the same, how can we recognize virtue or excellence of any kind? Black ideologies, however, generally do not celebrate individual virtue. Even black "conservatives" (who are really a form of "liberals"), insist that virtue cannot be achieved unless one is willing to fight to bring along one's cousins as either individuals or classes advance. Contrary to Arendt's view of modern society (she is extremely hostile to society and the social), all

6. See chapter 3 for some examples of such claims.

black ideologies affirm that individual advancement and excellence are not only possible within society, but they cannot be achieved without society (Arendt 1958; Dolan 1994).

Arendt's view of ideology is consistent, in at least one respect, with that of public opinion researchers. She does believe that elites are the true ideologues, at least in being able to understand and grasp the complete, "consistent" worldview of any given ideology. The "masses" are only capable of a vague, inconsistent, appreciation of ideologies, an understanding that must be continually reinforced by the spouting of ideological clichés and the performance of rituals (Arendt 1966). Ideologies are not only closed systems of thought, which use (fake) scientificism to explain everything that needs to be explained, but—and this is their most dangerous aspect— ideologies of the totalitarian type use an "inescapable" historical logic to arrive at conclusions that result in terror. This "tyranny" of logic leads people to view everything as either black or white, to view any historical event as "inevitable," and always drives those who use this methodology to the "worst conclusion" (Arendt 1966). Indeed, this type of logic is very apparent within many black and other ideologies. The extreme Christian Right, the logic of white supremacist ideology, and extreme forms of some black nationalisms (see chapter 3 for details) all exhibit the characteristics that lead Arendt to condemn ideological thinking. But the "fictive" nature of ideologies does not always lead their adherents to interpret political and social life according to the "worst conclusion." While black ideologies vary in the extent to which they use the logic that Arendt finds poisonous, or in their general levels of pessimism, blacks in all historical periods, including the present, find much evidence to support interpretations of American life that are consistent with the "worst conclusions." Indeed, most blacks, even middle-class blacks (to the bafflement of many whites), believe that "worst conclusion" analyses arise not from too much indulgence in ideological thinking, but from sober analyses of the realities of race in America. Nevertheless, Arendt and her followers reject ideologies, not only because they impede the development of independent citizens who participate in open political spaces, but also because they are viewed as deeply corrupting of both citizens and politics (Honig 1993).

A common feature of all these critiques of ideology is their assertion that a single, universal ideology dominates society. Many scholars critique Habermas's treatment of the public sphere on the grounds that he assumes a single bourgeois sphere, and it is equally incorrect to assume that a single ideology operates within societies that have heterogeneous populations and multiple public spheres. The multiple publics and counterpublics which are a part of civil society in a complex, multiracial polity like the United States—a society which historically has featured societal inclusions and exclusions based on multiple social cleavages and hierarchies such as race—are the bases of the multiple ideologies that flourish across and within America's diverse public spheres. The diverse social movements and communities which produce these public spheres and counterpublics include a wide range of political, social, and religious institutions which provide the infrastructure for critical debate and social change. Just as ideology can sustain oppressive regimes, ideology can sustain the resistance that is developed out of counterpublics such as the black public spheres of the nineteenth and twentieth centuries.

The forcible separation of blacks from whites in the late nineteenth century led to the formation of a separate black counterpublic (Brown 1989, 1995; Dawson 1994a, 1994b; Higginbotham 1993). The separate counterpublic had as its institutional foundation the set of autonomous organizations that the black community had built since the Civil War. The black church was particularly critical for providing an independent secular as well as sacred organizational basis for the black community. Even before the Civil War, the Negro Convention movement provided an autonomous forum for northern black political and ideological debate. Independent information sources such as black newspapers also became common during this period in the North. Frederick Douglass's *North Star* provided a forum for ideological debate in a black newspaper. During the antebellum period David Walker's *Appeal* offered one ideological vision of what blacks needed to end their oppression, and Delany's *The Condition, Elevation, Emigration, and Destiny of the Colored People of the United States* offered another. After the smashing of what Du Bois called "Black Reconstruction" in the 1870s, autonomous black information sources proliferated. Newspapers and journals under the leadership of those like Ida B. Wells, T. Thomas Fortune, and Du Bois himself not only agitated for the particular ideological perspective of the editor, but also provided forums for ideological debates during the dark three quarters of a century that followed the smashing of democracy and budding black political power in the South. The violent transition from the era of Reconstruction to the triumph of white supremacy which marked the era of Redemption forced blacks to turn inward in their debates, although never exclusively inward. Political discussions and organizing within black churches combined with the development of secular organizations such as the Niagara Movement and the NAACP in the early twentieth century to encourage the expansion of a black counterpublic. Black women played a central role in this expansion through activities ranging from church-based organizing to the production and discussion of a variety of literary works (Carby 1987; Higginbotham 1993). Many black women and their organizations had to fight to avoid being excluded from the black counterpublic, just as those active in the black counterpublic had to fight for a hearing in the publics and counterpublics of the larger society, which were universally dominated by white supremacy (Giddings 1984; Guy-Sheftall 1995; Higginbotham 1993; Wells 1970).

The result of a flourishing counterpublic was the accelerated development of autonomous black ideologies, which began to differ markedly from their white counterparts. Historically, there had always been differences even between the version of liberalism embraced within the black community and the version that would become dominant in the second half of the nineteenth century. The progressive, republican version of American liberalism, with its small-producer, communitarian overtones, was defeated by the end of the nineteenth century (Foner 1980, 1988; Horton 1995). Black and white ideological convergence on forms of liberalism with economic equality at their core ended with the defeat of American republicanism. But black nationalism had a sufficient social base throughout the nineteenth century, except during Reconstruction, to insure that substantial sectors of the black community were always at odds with all of America's versions of "the" liberal tradition. But by the late nineteenth century, we see stark differences not only between black nationalism and "mainstream white" ideologies, but between black liberalism, black socialism, and even black conservatism and their white counterparts. The pattern would be repeated in the mid-to-late twentieth century as significant differences grew between the black and white versions of feminism. What constitutes the differences between the "black" and "white" versions of these ideologies is one of the central themes of the following chapters.

The development of these black ideologies throughout the nineteenth and twentieth centuries illuminates several problems with the skeptics' theoretical view of ideology. First, and most obviously, societies which are marked by racial apartheid are not only likely to develop separate public spheres, but those spheres themselves become the bases for the articulation of divergent, often conflicting, group interests. The subordinate group, in particular, is likely in bourgeois democratic societies to perceive ideology through the lens of whatever social cleavage is the basis of its historical oppression, whether its members believe their oppression to be based on religion, class, or (in the American case) race. These separate public spheres are the venues through which multiple ideologies flourish. Between dominant and subordinate group spheres, we historically see differences in *which* ideologies are influential in a given period, and divergence in *how* the putatively same ideologies are understood and practiced.

The second problem is that black ideologies decisively demonstrate that ideologies can be produced by the opposition, loyal or not, and not just by a ruling race, clique, or class. As we shall see, black ideologies are almost always highly critical of both the hegemonic American liberal world view of any given period and the actual functioning of the American state and the place of blacks in civil society.

Third, black political thought and its associated ideologies are forged, to use Arendt's phrase, by men (and women) of action (Arendt 1958). Within black political thought, the distinction between the "contemplative" and the "active" life has been neither a luxury most black intellectuals could historically afford nor one that made pragmatic or philosophical sense to the activists and intellectuals who were developing, debating, codifying, and implementing the ideologies which are at the core of black political thought. Black public spaces, the black *polis*, has been historically constituted by those engaged in *both* the creation of speech and action. Indeed, the worthiness of black political speech has often been judged by the claims of the speaker to have engaged in political action. The black public sphere has had much in common, ironically, with Arendt's views of a properly constituted *polis*, despite the flourishing of ideological activity within the black counterpublic. Pragmatic work and the close connection between theory and practice have marked black feminism, nationalism, and liberalism every bit as much as they have marked black Marxism. Even intellectually oriented black liberals like Du Bois in his "early" years, let alone dedicated activists like Ida B. Wells and Martin Luther King, Jr., were more organically engaged with the pragmatic and theoretical connection between theory and practice than many, particularly academic, Marxists.

Black political actions, however, would not have garnered Kant's approval. Kant argues that human sociability and morality are founded on decency, on "good manners." For Kant, this decency is the mark of rational, adult behavior (Honig 1993). Blacks, like women of all races, are often accused of being politically "childlike" and irrational. Storing's critique of King shortly after King's assassination is in part based on outrage over King's and other African Americans' having had the bad manners to protest what blacks believed to be an unjust society (Storing 1995). But when people are barred because of their group membership from participation in public spheres, or even in counterpublics, then political rudeness is not only appropriate but often necessary. Black political ideologies, whether liberal, Marxist, feminist, nationalist, or even conservative, are very noisy and often impolite. Sadly, this is often the only way one can be heard. And the propensity of black political thought and black politics to politicize the "social" would have equally offended Arendt's sensibilities. Arendt's public spaces, according to Honig, are marked by the banning of the social to the private sphere. But issues such as slavery and the inability to protect private property and *one's own person* from white expropriation and violence, even after slavery was ended, led to repeated calls by blacks in the nineteenth and twentieth centuries for national state intervention in the "private" sphere. Part of being oppressed is the reality of thinner barriers between public and private. Indeed, the politicization of "private" concerns such as labor, family practices, and status must be seen as inevitable under these conditions, and we should not be surprised when the oppressed turn to ideologies that explain both politics and society as being intimately connected. We should not be surprised when people in this position turn to ideology not only to explain their lot, but also to provide a vision of the road out of oppression. Ideologies, as the critics claim, can sustain relations of domination, but oppositional ideologies provide their own sustaining narratives of resistance and eventual triumph. All black ideologies provide visions of triumph, but each has a substantially different vision of a triumphant future. Which black ideology becomes dominant, if any, will greatly shape the future of both black and American politics.

Another View of Ideology

My use of the concept of ideology has more in common with how historians have used the concept than with how it has been used by the theorists that I have discussed. This approach also draws on Lane's classic public opinion study on ideology (Lane 1962). Ideologies provide the member of a polity with a worldview, with constellations of ideas with which to organize their understanding of the political world (Bailyn 1967; Foner 1980, 1988; Kerber 1990).[7] Foner argues that ideologies remain coherent even though they contain "internal ambiguities" and that they embody sets of

---

7. Kerber (1992) independently uses the same phrase, "constellation of ideas," that I had begun to use when I first started working on this project.

"values, hopes, and fears" in addition to a commitment to a "particular so-cial order" (Foner 1980). Fields agrees and argues that ideologies are "re-fractions of objective reality in human consciousness" and are real (Fields 1982, 150–51). She also agrees with both Bailyn and Foner when she ar-gues as follows:

> Ideologies offer a ready-made interpretation of the world, a sort of
> hand-me down vocabulary with which to name the elements of every
> new experience. But their prime function is to make coherent—if never
> scientifically accurate—sense of the social world. Therefore, new expe-
> rience constantly impinges on them changing them in ways that are dia-
> bolically difficult for the detached observer, let alone the engaged par-
> ticipant, to detect. . . . But far the more common situation in the history
> of ideologies is that instead of dying, the same vocabulary attaches itself,
> unnoticed, to new things. (Fields 1982, 155)

Ideologies change over time according to Fields and Horkheimer, and each era uses ideology to interpret political texts, events, and move-ments in those eras during which ideologies are politically influential (Horkheimer 1972; Fields 1982). From this perspective, we can think of ideologies as representing everyday, commonsense knowledge of the polit-ical world—as lenses through which political information is focused. The ideological lenses of opposing groups often lead them to understand the same political event from two (or more) stunningly different perspectives. When black slaves read and preached about the Bible, they focused on the story of Moses and the overthrowing of the unjust Pharaoh, the slave owner. Black activists have tended to focus on the Declaration of Indepen-dence and its emphases on equality and individual rights. Racial conserva-tives have focused more on the Constitution and its emphasis on states rights. The American revolutionaries found inspiration in Cato's letters and viewed every action of the British Crown as another part of a Royal scheme to enslave the colonies (Bailyn 1967). The ideology of the slave owners encouraged them to interpret Lincoln's election in the "worst pos-sible light"—to use Arendt's phrase (Foner 1980, 1988). Again the Ameri-can revolution provides examples which resonate with our current situa-tion. Perhaps even more than blacks and whites in the late twentieth century, British and American radicals shared a common political heritage, common vocabulary, and common sets of texts. Yet, because of their dif-ferent ideological lenses, the corruption of the British government had a much greater effect on this side of the Atlantic as the Americans connected this corruption to their ideological belief that the Crown and its ministers were dedicated to the destruction of American liberty (Bailyn 1967).

Ideological belief in the corruptness of an oppressive regime can lead to the type of worst-case reasoning that Arendt finds so worrisome. The American revolutionaries were well aware of this phenomenon. Bailyn has one conservative American revolutionary making the following argument:

> Acts that might *by themselves* have been upon many considerations excused or extenuated derived a contagious malignancy and odium from other acts with which they were connected. They were not regarded according to the simple force of each but as parts of a system of oppression. Every one, therefore, however small in itself, became alarming as an additional evidence of tyrannical designs. It was in vain for prudent and moderate men to insist that there was no necessity to abolish royalty. Nothing less than the utter destruction of the monarchy could satisfy those who *had* suffered and thought they had reason to believe they always *should* suffer. (Bailyn 1967, 144)

The conspiracy theories (often rooted in bitter experience) associated with ideological thinking are ultimately tied to sets of interests that are perceived as "diametrically opposed" (Foner 1980). Ideologies, like interests, have concrete social bases; to be effective, they must be consistent with the fears, anxieties, and hopes of their holders, as well as with existing discourse patterns (Bailyn 1967; Lane 1962). Ideologies may have diverse sources (Garvey's nationalism drew on Plato and Marxism, among other sources), but they must be consistent with the political and social understanding of a substantial segment of the target population. Ideologies are not rigidly fixed in stone, however; they change with political events, with changes in a political economy, with changes in other major social processes, or as a result of momentous events.

How do ideologies evolve yet hold together? First, we need to consider that ideologies are language games that have neither totally precise boundaries nor fully internally consistent sets of rules. Ideologies exhibit both a fluidity and openness which prevent the development of rigid boundaries or "complete" descriptions. The contingent nature of rules is critical in language games. As Wittgenstein argues, the rules of language games are "made up as we go along" (Wittgenstein 1958, 39). This is especially true for theorists and ideologues who are also activists, who are trying to solve the specific political problems that confront them during a given era. Eras marked by powerfully salient ideologies are also often marked by turbulent political movements and serious political upheavals. So the Abbé Sieyès had to be creative in adapting his ideology while creating a revolutionary document that matched the rapidly changing conditions. In the end *What Is the Third Estate?* would prove enormously influential in the French Revolution (Sewell 1994). Black activists during the turbulent 1960s were in the process of creating, revising, and implementing several ideologies during a period of rapid political and social change. It is because ideologies are constituted out of language and ideas that they are instruments for creative, imaginary action as well as being able to inspire and guide creative political movements (Sewell 1994; Thompson 1984). While ideologies, particularly oppositional ideologies, are designed to spark the imagination, they still must be consonant with the key social forces and discourses of the times. When they are, as Sieyès's document was, they can be powerful instruments for shaping political action (Sewell 1994). Because ideas are important, and specifically because ideologies can provide powerful guides to action, we see fierce social and political battles over which ideology should be adopted as well as over the proper interpretation of any given ideology.

Ideological battles, Thompson argues, are over words and meanings. While Lincoln's, Douglass's, and Webster's definitions of "liberty" shared many similarities, they also exhibited important differences reflected in the significant political cleavages that divided the nation on the eve of the Civil War (Greenstone 1993). In modern black political debate, how should we interpret the meaning of "self-determination?" Does it mean that blacks should separate from the United States? Or "only" that blacks should be able to choose their political affiliations? What does "the right to self-defense" mean? Does it mean that when attacked because of their race, blacks have the right defend themselves by any means necessary? A majority of blacks would support this interpretation. Or does it mean that if some group has a history of attacking blacks unjustly, blacks have the right to eliminate them first? The latter interpretation did not enjoy substantial support among blacks and led to several violent deaths on both sides during the 1960s and the 1970s.

Ideological conflicts can expose what seems to be "spheres" of consensus as potential sites for conflict (Thompson 1984, 132). Once ideological concepts are part of public debate and contestation, they are out of the "control" of the original speaker (Norton 1993). Thus the result of ideological conflict is unknowable precisely, because originating activists cannot predict with which meanings their tomes and pronouncements will be invested. Ideological conflicts will always be with us, but, as Reed reminds us, the results of these conflicts are directly tied to how they're embedded in the social practice, movements, and institutions of the day (Reed 1992a).

These battles over meanings are not "winnable" in any definitive sense; it is not possible, as Wittgenstein reminds us, to draw a boundary around black nationalism (or black Marxism for that matter) which would enable us to say whether the Black Panther Party were "in" or "out" of some set of ideological walls. There is "not *one genuine* proper case of description," whether we are trying to describe objects we see or language constructs that share a certain "resemblance" but around which precise boundaries are impossible to draw (Wittgenstein 1958, 200). Black nationalism shares features and distinctions which are common across eras, but even within a particular era it is impossible to identify an "ideal type" of any given ideology. Because the interpretation of language is a subjective process, differences will arise in the interpretation of the "meaning" of language games such as ideologies. But for such conflict to be critical in shaping the politics of a community, there must be a "shared matrix of meaning," a "discursive formation" within which the terms of debate are understood (Eagleton 1991, 195). Part of the task of this book is to sketch which "distinctions/sets of rules" (to use Wittgenstein's phrases) are associated within given ideological patterns both over time and within our own era, and then determine which ideological constellations are associated with which segments of the black community.

But before I can describe, even partially, the dimensions of black political ideologies, I must emphasize that, arbitrary or not, grammatical rules are embedded within each black political ideology. These rules define not only limits of the permissible ("blacks should put the interests of their race first"), but also the limits of the understandable (Wittgenstein 1958). Ideologies cannot be debated without a common understanding of the language over which the debate is occurring and in which the debate is embedded.

Part of the "grammatical" rules which define any given language game—in our case political ideologies—are the norms, values, and "central practices" common within a given political community (Greenstone 1993). To be more precise, before one can decide on the truth or falsity of a given event, one must be speaking the same language, playing by the same rules of interpretation. One of the basic problems of black/white discourse in the United States is that blacks and whites often bring radically different understandings of the social world, with radically different sets of political vocabularies and radically different understandings of central political institutions and events to political conflicts and debates. The grammatical limits of all but one black ideology allow massive state intervention in the private economy, while this option has become increasingly impossible even to speak about in the white liberal tradition during the late twentieth century. To a significant degree, a political community is defined by these shared grammatical rules and semantic understandings. When some groups, such as black nationalists, disagree on both the rules and who is in the community, significant political conflict is often unavoidable. Blacks in general, not just the nationalists, have historically had very problematic relationships vis-à-vis who is defined as being a "good" American as well as what is considered the acceptable grammar of American politics. To the degree that language and practice are "inseparable," blacks have had a very tortured relationship to the American polity (Hess 1993).

Different language rules lead to differences in perceptions of institutional rules. Markets are distrusted by blacks, and are certainly held in lower esteem than the national state. Whites, with a very different social experience in the United States, tend to reverse this ordering (Dawson 1997). The different experiences of blacks and whites with institutions such as markets and the state are a concrete demonstration that two different sets of rules have existed for blacks and whites with respect to these and other major political, economic, and social institutions in this country. These different histories reflect the different experiences of each race (and often of subgroups within races) with the economy and different struggles for liberal rights. The rules by which each race has had to interact with these institutions have led to different ideological visions about what constitutes the good society (Dawson 1994a, 1997).

Part of the task in describing black ideologies, then, is to detail which are the key bindings and the key concepts about which followers of an ideology must agree. More globally, members of a political community would at least share agreement about the key issues and differences around which ideological debate occurs. Consensus does not imply unanimity, but it does suggest that a substantial body of opinion exists which sets the terms of debate on a given set of issues. Used in this sense, one assertion that is carried through this book is that blacks and whites imperfectly form a common political community.

There are three key bindings that exist (1) between a community and the relevant rules of inclusion, (2) between rules and institutions, and (3) between rules and ideology. First, within a political community in which meaningful ideological debate flourishes, agreement must exist about whom, more or less, that community comprises and about the rules by which that community is governed. In this case the rules include the common understandings, norms, values, key historical events, and common language which govern the political life of the community. Within the black community, such understandings, among others, exist around the importance of emancipation, the high value of equality as both a political goal and normative principle, the language of reparations (even though disagreements exist on the priority/value of reparations), and the historic importance of black nationalism. There must also be consensus about the bindings between rules and institutions. Such a consensus exists around beliefs about the rules with which the police and similar agencies interact with the black community, the frequency with which blacks experience discrimination in a variety of markets, and the likelihood of systematic discrimination in the implementation of state policies. Bindings between rules and ideologies include shared terms of debate about the prevalence of white racism, the desirability of independent black organizations, and the importance of Malcolm X as a black leader (one white professor during the 1980s at the University of Michigan, for example, could not understand why middle-class blacks were up in arms when he attacked Malcolm X, just as white Trotskyites in the 1970s could not understand why a very large and angry crowd of working-class black students at a California junior college ran them off campus for verbally attacking Malcolm X during a rally commemorating the anniversary of his assassination).

But an understanding of the rules of the game only solves part of the of the problem. There still must be shared meanings which ground ideological debate. When blacks talk about equality, they are generally talking equality of outcomes.[8] Now black conservatives may attack Martin Luther King, Jr.'s view that true equality will necessitate the implementation of quotas, but there is a shared frame of reference that grounds the debate (King 1967). Similarly, while during the late 1960s there was great debate in the black community about the merits of the slogan "Black Power!" there were stunning differences between blacks and whites about *what* the slogan actually meant. Blacks understood "black power" to mean black pride or that blacks should get their fair share. Whites believed it to mean that blacks wanted to place themselves above whites (Aberbach and Walker

---

8. When I speak of "equality of outcome," I am not speaking of a view which demands that we all end up with absolutely equal distribution of goods. I am speaking of the common assumption within black opinion and thought that commitment to equality should be demonstrated not only by equality of opportunity but also by a more equal distribution of goods. *How* equal is a source of contention within black political thought, as it has been within Western thought more generally.

1970). The conflict among blacks over the phrase centered on the contention of those such as King, who argued in 1967 that while the concept had some merit, and blacks needed power, the phrase and the concept did more harm than good. The grounds for debate about the phrase were very different in the black and white communities. Without shared understandings, ideological debates can take a surreal but deadly turn as opponents (or "friends") find it impossible to understand each other because they lack a common vocabulary with which to communicate. This can be especially serious if, as in the American case, the participants in political conflicts believe that they are indeed using the same language. These ideological conflicts are unimportant, of course, if, as the seminal public opinion researchers of our era believe, ideologies do not affect political behavior or opinion, or if the grassroots are incapable of ideological thinking.

NOT SO INNOCENT: RACE, IDEOLOGY, AND PUBLIC OPINION

Americans are ideologically innocent, according to the leading public opinion researchers within the United States. Kinder argues in an excellent review essay, "One conclusion is perfectly obvious, however: the field of public opinion has been far too occupied with the ideological possibility . . . the vast majority of Americans were thoroughly innocent of ideology" (Kinder 1983, 390–91).

Public opinion researchers in the United States have argued for three decades that ideology plays virtually no role in shaping American public opinion. Converse even argued against the term, if not the concept, because "A term like *ideology* has been thoroughly muddled by diverse uses. We shall depend instead upon the term *belief system*, although there is an obvious overlap between the two" (Converse 1964, 207). The concept of ideology is here reduced to that of a belief system, which is itself reduced to "a configuration of ideas and attitudes in which the elements are bound together by some form of constraint or functional interdependence" (Converse 1964, 207). The reason for employing such a strategy in the empirical study of the effects of ideologies on public opinion is that, among the grassroots, ideologies are messy. This Converse finds unacceptable from the standpoint of research design: "An adequate mapping of society . . . would provide a jumbled cluster of pyramids or a mountain range, with sharper delineation and differentiation in beliefs from elite apex to elite apex but with the mass bases of the pyramids overlapping in such profusion that it would be impossible to decide where one pyramid ended and another began" (Converse 1964, 256).

For Converse and his followers, ideological belief systems are composed of abstract, deductive systems of thought which are highly constrained and organized. Each component of a belief system evokes all the others. This abstract system of deductive thought is removed both from considerations of social groups and from other aspects of everyday life. Only a small sector of the highly educated and activist public is capable of ideological thinking of this type, according to Converse and Kinder (Converse 1964; Kinder 1983). As education declines, access to the type of information necessary for ideological reasoning declines, and abstract reasoning also declines as people use "lower" forms of considerations, such as group attachments and everyday life experiences, to structure their political "reasoning." Converse describes his understanding of the process in his seminal article:

> These objects shift from the remote, generic, and abstract, to the increasingly simple, concrete, or "close to home." Where potential objects are concerned, this progression tends to be from abstract, "ideological" principles to the more obviously recognizable social groupings or charismatic leaders and finally to such objects of immediate experience as family, job, and immediate associates. . . . Most of the stuff of politics—particularly that played on a national or international stage—is, in the nature of things, remote and abstract. (Converse 1964, 213)

This is an extraordinarily elitist and misguided view of the connection between ideology and politics. We should not be surprised that when using this definition of ideology, Converse finds only about 2.5 percent of the population engaged in "true" ideological reasoning and only another 9 percent or so capable of even remotely ideological thinking.[9] Converse and Kinder's vision of ideology is so abstract that it is removed from the field of politics.

One aspect of the deductive abstractions that are defined as ideologies is the importance of labels. It is not enough that packages of ideas cohere and influence political opinion and behavior; true ideologues are also able

---

9. Interestingly, Converse's and Kinder's description of the status of informed opinion among grassroots Americans is most consistent with a belief that false consciousness is rampant among the "masses." As Eagleton (1991) points out, to believe in strong versions of false consciousness, one must believe that ordinary citizens are so ill-informed and cognitively ill-equipped that they can believe in institutions and social orders that are completely at odds with their own interests.

to correctly name ideologies such as black nationalism, liberalism or feminism (Converse 1964). So if you found a Black Student Union on a college campus, circa 1969, and three-quarters of the membership could recite the Black Panther Party's ten-point program verbatim, believed in the rights of self-determination and self-defense, organized around starting black studies programs, practiced democratic centralism, and followed the political platform of the Panthers, even though 99 percent of the students were not party members, would we be comfortable with saying that dozens of black student unions were dominated by ideological thinking, even though most of these same students would not know that the ideology was a form of revolutionary nationalism? This description fits the students on many campuses in California, ranging from the working-class students at community colleges like Laney College in Oakland to upwardly mobile working- and middle-class students at schools like San Francisco State and the more privileged students at the University of California and Stanford.

Ideology becomes even more abstract in the more recent work of prominent public opinion researchers. Converse was extremely well versed in the theoretical literature on ideology and crafted his research in direct response to that literature. With Zaller's sophisticated study of modern public opinion, the rupture between social and political theory on ideology on one hand and empirical research on the other is complete. Zaller explicitly rejects the previous notions of ideology which were based in social theory. For him ideology has a more functional role: "Ideology, in this view, is a mechanism by which ordinary citizens make contact with specialists who are knowledgeable on controversial issues and who share the citizens' predispositions. As such, ideology can make a valuable contribution to democratic politics in a society in which people are expected not only to have opinions about a range of impossibly difficult issues, but to use those opinions as the bases for choosing leaders and holding them accountable" (Zaller 1992, 327). How do we know what type of ideology is at work? Ideology is the work of specialists "sharing a common predispositional bent" (Zaller 1992, 328). Conservative economic policy is what conservative economists say it is, and (to continue with Zaller's example) conservative foreign policy becomes what conservative foreign policy experts say it is.

The immense difference posited by modern public opinion researchers between the masses and the elites in the ability to reason ideologically in a cogent way does ironically remind us of the images of the manipulable and politically unsophisticated grassroots of Arendt and Habermas. But where in the political and social theory of Arendt and the Frankfurt school ideology was the evil tool of dominant classes to sway the masses, for public opinion researchers the *only* group *capable* of ideological thinking are the educated and dominant elites. Politics, or at least political reasoning is for the elites. Uninformed and uninterested "citizens" get their cues through the media and other sources, follow the leader(s), and remain cheerfully uninformed (Kinder 1983; Zaller 1992). In addition, unlike Arendt and other social and political theorists, public opinion researchers believe that the "fact" that dominant, well-informed elites guide the grassroots is actually healthy for democracy. Let those who have the resources and the stakes be the ones that pay attention to politics and help guide the vast majority of the rest, who remain uninformed. Everyday life absorbs people, according to Kinder, not "affairs of state" (Kinder 1983). But if society is organized around race, and racial conflict is part of everyday life, and if our stories of the world are also organized around race, race is profoundly political and profoundly ideological, at least for blacks, and—one would suspect—for whites and others as well.

One consequence of this transformation in the way public opinion researchers view ideology is that ideologies and ideological reasoning have become separated from social groups. While most clearly apparent in Zaller, the seeds of this transformation can be found in Converse. Like Lane, Converse argues that the constraints on, and the roots of, ideologies can often be found in social groups (Lane 1962). Indeed, Lane sees the close connection between group ideology and community as problematic for democratic societies. Democracy requires individualist detachment and what Arendt would call loneliness to function properly (Arendt 1958; Lane 1962). But for Converse the large fraction of the public that uses group thinking in their political reasoning processes is in fact far removed from ideological thinking. Converse is well aware that traditionally specific ideologies such as Marxism or nationalism have been tied to specific groups and sets of interests, such as those of classes and nations. But he argues that in modern democratic societies, group identities are not that salient, and even when they are salient, they only span a narrow range of issues; thus, the public fragments into several narrow-issue publics, none of which are overarching. Of course public opinion researchers in the 1980s and 1990s have shown how the politics of race indeed structures the entirety of American public opinion (Carmines and Stimson 1989; Kinder and Sanders 1996). Converse's crystalline view of ideologies as highly abstract, deductive belief systems led him to argue at the height of the Civil Rights movement that the fact that several policy questions in a national survey on blacks were highly correlated with each other, and not with items about the size of government, states rights, and other more abstract principles, was an example of non-ideological group thinking.

My understanding of ideology leads me to believe that in a society structured by racial cleavages, the type of high correlation observed by Converse is actually an excellent example of ideological thinking, a type of ideological ordering of the world that we now know became more widespread and persists today. For a few hundred years, blacks have been made quite aware of "their" identity, and substantial research has shown that racial identity remains central to African Americans (Dawson 1994a; Tate 1993). To use Converse's language, there are a number of linking mechanisms between blacks' social locations, their racial identities, and various (generally unsatisfactory) aspects of their social, economic, cultural and political worlds. Indeed, as Katznelson (among many others) argues, racial oppression has led blacks to view the political world "holistically," and indeed blacks are quite prone to connect a series of demands across issues not usually connected in American politics (Katznelson 1982). It is empirically and theoretically plausible that blacks do engage in racially based ideological thinking. Whether they do so at higher levels than other Americans, while an interesting question, is beyond the scope of this study.

This study asks the following questions from the standpoint of both intellectual inquiry and what activists on the ground might expect. First, what is the relationship between how ideologues and elites formulate an ideology and how it is transformed by grassroots blacks seeking to understand and change their social world? This view of ideology looks at grassroots blacks neither as passive receivers of ideology nor as incapable of adapting ideologies to their own pragmatic needs, even over the objections of any given ideology's originators. I will also consider three different standards for measuring the presence of an ideology among grassroots African Americans. One standard is that of traditional public opinion researchers: Do the concepts within an ideology cohere with each other? Most activists and "ideological intellectuals" would be delighted if people adopted their package of ideas as a whole. Thus, support for black self-determination, for example, also evokes the idea that blacks constitute a nation, which also evokes the idea that blacks should have a separate nation. But that is too high a standard. To continue with this example, both black Marxism and black nationalism would claim the first two elements, while most black Marxists would have rejected the third (of course many would have rejected the second as well). There is sufficient overlap between ideologies to make it simply unreasonable to believe that these elements automatically evoke each other. This brings us to a second standard. How disappointed would most black leaders be if they had two million followers, all of whom believed all five points of their five-point program, even if each element did not automatically evoke the other for most members of their following? The second question is to what degree is there broad support within the black population for different ideological packages? Finally, in either case of looking at the packages of ideological components or of looking at coherent belief systems, how well do they predict other elements of black public opinion? Do some ideologies influence only narrow ranges of issues, while others have more general impact? The answers to these questions, while of intellectual importance, also have important consequences for the theory and practice of American democracy.

STRUCTURE

We start by introducing the data and taking a preliminary look at the role of social structure in shaping contemporary African-American political ideologies. The sections that follow describe the foundations of the analyses presented here.

The Data

The following analyses use survey responses from the 1993–94 National Black Politics Study (NBPS). The data for the NBPS was obtained from a probability sample of all black households. A total of 1,206 telephone interviews were completed. Each interview was approximately forty-five minutes in length. To be eligible, respondents had to be both black and at least eighteen years old. The survey was conducted between November 20, 1993, and February 20, 1994. The response rate was 65 percent.[10] The two main substantive foci of the study were to provide instrumentation for (1) the analysis of relationships between black ideologies and their determinants and consequences and (2) the relationship of black worship to black public opinion. Before we begin to model black ideologies, however, we need to take a closer look at the measures of structure available in the NBPS. While ideological position does not follow *automatically* from social location, I do predict that social location does structure ideological position (Eagleton 1991).

---

10. The principal investigators were Ronald Brown of Wayne State University and Michael Dawson of the University of Chicago. The study was administered through the University of Chicago. The Russell Sage Foundation provided a generous grant for the collection of the data.

Table 2.1   Distributions of selected social location variables

Gender

	Frequency	Percent
Men	425	35.2
Women	781	64.8
Total	1,206	100.0

Valid cases 1,206   Missing cases 0

Family Income	Percent
Less than $10,000	14%
$11,000–$20,000	24%
$21,000–$30,000	22%
$31,000–$50,000	24%
More than $50,000	16%

Valid cases 1,113   Missing cases 93

Social Structure

Social structures involve two components. First, they are associated with a distribution of resources. For example, labor markets structure the availability of jobs, their location, and the level of wages. Second, social structures are associated with schemas (sets of rules). For example, schemas associated with labor markets include rules for entering and leaving the market, normative behaviors for those intending to be ongoing participants, and sets of identities tied to different locations within the market.[11]

A significant amount of work has theorized and tested the influence of various forms of social structures on black ideologies and black public opinion. Structure has been theorized to have multiple roles in shaping black ideologies and black public opinion. In keeping with the multiple manifestations of structure as seen by Sewell and others, I focus on three particular kinds of structure which I consider as plausible determinants of black public opinion: (1) social location, (2) spatial situation, and (3) access to black information networks.

Social location dramatically affects an individual's resources and life chances. It also provides a set of "normative" social roles that shape an individual's identity. Social locations that are posited to play key roles in

11. The definition of structure that I use in this essay is borrowed from William Sewell's essay, "A Theory of Structure" (1992).

shaping black public opinion are socioeconomic status, gender, and level of concentrated poverty. Tables 2.1 and 2.2 display the distribution of these locations within this sample. For example, many social theories, including pluralism, Marxism, and rational choice theory, conceive of public opinion and individual preferences as being strongly shaped by self-interest, which in turn is believed to be shaped by class or social position. Thus, as far back as the early 1960s, social theorists such as Robert Dahl were predicting that the growth of the black middle class would lead to a decline in black political homogeneity (see Dawson and Wilson 1991 for a review). Although numerous scholars have speculated about the importance of self-interest in building support for black conservatism, research has yet to find evidence that black conservatism is based on significant class differences (Dawson 1994a; Hamilton 1982). Similarly, black feminists and others have argued that the intersection of several different social locations (those determined by race, gender, and class) has facilitated a unique ideological standpoint for black women (Collins 1991; Crenshaw 1990; Locke 1987). There has also been both theorizing and empirical work on the degree to which class makes one more or less receptive to black feminism. Research has also shown that ideologies such as black nationalism, and related ideologies such as black autonomy, are associated with class cleavages within the black community (Dawson 1994a; Tate 1993).

A second critical structure that is posited to influence black public opinion is the spatial location of the respondent. The degree of concentrated poverty and degree of racial segregation have been extensively discussed as factors in the availability of material resources, the construction of social roles and identities, and the societal judgments regarding those who occupy given spatial locations (Massey and Denton 1993; Wilson 1987). Concentrated poverty among blacks has been shown to lead to social isolation, which in turn leads to greater suspicion of other groups within American society (Cohen and Dawson 1993). Further, the economic devastation found within some inner cities has been theorized to cause not only an increase in black nihilism but also an attenuation of black political consciousness (Marable 1983; West 1993). Concentrated segregation is supposed to contribute to an oppositional and racialized orientation on the part of African Americans (Massey and Denton 1993).

The effect of concentrated poverty on black ideologies and public opinion was measured using a set of dummy variables for three different levels of concentrated poverty: 10–20 percent, 21–30 percent, and 31 percent and over. These categories were determined by measuring the level of poverty within each respondent's census tract. This was the same set of

Table 2.2   Distribution of concentrated poverty

Percentage of Homes in Poverty in Respondent's Census Tract	
Less than 10%	19%
11–20%	29%
21–30%	23%
More than 30%	29%
Valid cases 1,183 Missing cases 23	

categories used by Cohen and Dawson (1993) in their study of the effects of neighborhood poverty on black public opinion in Detroit. The dummy variables are used in accordance with the argument of Wilson (1987) and others that qualitative social differences exist between poor neighborhoods and those with the most concentrated levels of poverty.[12] Just as the NBPS allows one to determine the level of poverty at the census tract, one can also measure the level of racial concentration. Since there are much higher levels of racial concentration (remember that affluent blacks are also likely to live in racially segregated neighborhoods), there is less theoretical and empirical work which would suggest a conceptual design for determining the level at which one would expect effects from "hypersegregation." Therefore, a continuous measure of the percentage of black respondents in a census tract was used to test hypotheses about the effects of structural segregation on black public opinion. The distribution of concentrated poverty is displayed in table 2.2.

Black information networks compose the third structure studied for its effect on black public opinion. Information networks are associated with resources (such as information and the goods and institutions through which information is conveyed) and with schemas (such as the rule that news from the "grapevine" is more reliable than information from outside the black community). These networks constitute a factor of black social life which complicates the analysis of black public opinion. Sophisticated public opinion researchers are once again providing strong evidence that much of American public opinion is elite-driven (Page and Shapiro 1992;

---

12. Further justification of the use of these particular measures of concentrated poverty appears in Cohen and Dawson (1993). In many of the later analyses, a composite ordinal-level variable that combines all four levels of poverty is used to preserve degrees of freedom. Analyses of the national sample reveal very little difference between the dummy-variable and the ordinal-variable versions of measures of concentrated poverty. This was not true when using the denser spatial data available to Cohen and Dawson in their study of black attitudes in Detroit.

Stimson 1991; Zaller 1992). Black discourse, however, is often cast in the form of being oppositional to mainstream American politics and is the product of activists or *counter-elites* (Dawson 1994b; Lee 1997b). Consequently, non-elite sources (particularly "nonwhite" or "nonmainstream" sources) of information, must be considered as critical in shaping black ideologies ranging from black nationalism to radical liberalism. In the domain of black public opinion, Zaller's two-message model of opinion formation is inadequate because black citizens hear not only both sides of the "official" debate, but also multiple views emanating from the black community.

We must carefully consider the specific historical development of black political discourse. African-American elites have generally had relatively modest class backgrounds. Ida B. Wells was from a middle-class family; Malcolm X had a more disadvantaged background. Even today most black activists do *not* come from an upper-class background, though many do come from backgrounds that are privileged by black standards. Further, historically, the institutions of the popular white press, as well as cultural and artistic resources, have generally been unavailable for transmitting information and messages to most African Americans, and they still perform a limited role in transmitting information within the black community (Dawson 1994a). Therefore, analyzing black public opinion is complicated by the multivocal nature of discourse within the black community and by the influence on black public opinion of a stream of information from "white America" that is often at odds with the information transmitted within the black community.[13] While two-message models are a step in the right direction (Zaller 1992), black public opinion needs to be conceptualized and eventually modeled as a process of diffusion and contestation, with polarizing streams (crudely "white" and "black") often competing for attention.[14] Simultaneously, significant diversity and contestation is found within "black" information streams, part of which concerns the definition of the origins of various ideological tendencies. For example, at the heart of the claim made by nationalist elites that black feminism and black feminists should be dismissed is the argument that black feminism should be

13. See Dawson (1994a) for a discussion of racial polarization in black and white interpretations of political and social events ranging from the evaluations of the Black Panther Party, the Bernard Goetz incident, American military interventions, the Reagan presidency, and Jesse Jackson's candidacy for president in 1984 and 1988.

14. Historically, external black attention has been focused on whites. Whether this is changing or has changed in cities such as Miami or Los Angeles is an interesting empirical question which is unfortunately not testable with the data available from this study.

viewed as part of a "white" information stream "designed" to subvert black progress.

While exposure to "white" information is hard to model directly using NBPS data (although class should give us a proxy), measures of exposure to various black information sources are provided.[15] Table 2.3 provides data on the degree to which African Americans are exposed to various sources of "black" information.

Use of the more limited measures of integration into black information networks available in the 1984 and 1988 National Black Election studies was shown to reinforce blacks' racial identity (Dawson 1994a). The National Black Politics Study used a more inclusive set of indicators: the black information networks scale, designed to measure respondents' exposure to black information sources, including various forms of black culture, was constructed of the eight variables listed in table 2.3. Exposure to rap music was included in this scale because claims have often been made that rap music serves an information function within the black community. The black information scale has reasonable properties.[16]

There is evidence that integration into black social networks does reinforce black identity and lead to a more racialized world view (Dawson 1994a), just as social location and spatial situation are expected to shape black ideology. The degree to which one is integrated into black information networks is likely to be constrained by other structures; more precisely, it may be shaped by the social isolation which derives from concentrated poverty.

Spatial-situation variables have mixed effects on the likelihood of exposure to black information. Those in extremely poor neighborhoods are less likely to read the standard metropolitan (white) newspaper. On the other hand, the more segregated the neighborhood, the *more likely* one is to read a black newspaper. These results are robust and stand up even when the social location variables which measure one's access to resources are included in the equations.[17] Thus, concentrated poverty tends to increase one's *informational isolation* from "white" news sources. On the other hand, increased segregation tends to slightly increase one's exposure to some specific forms of black news outlets.

15. The pervasiveness of television viewing in America makes it reasonable to believe that most sectors of the black community are exposed to the "official" news that matters.

16. The Cronbach alpha score for this scale was .62.

17. These analyses are not reported here but can be obtained from the author.

Table 2.3   Indicators of exposure to black information networks

Have you read a novel by a black author like Toni Morrison in the past *year*?
Yes   44%
No   56%
Valid cases 1,200   Missing cases 6

Gone to a Movie like *Boyz N the Hood* or *Malcolm X*?
Yes   72%
No   28%
Valid cases 1,206   Missing cases 0

Have you in the past *week* read a black newspaper?
Yes   55%
No   45%
Valid cases 1,206   Missing cases 0

Read a black magazine like *Ebony* . . . or *Jet*?
Yes   81%
No   19%
Valid cases 1,206   Missing cases 0

Listen to rap music?
Yes   48%
No   52%
Valid cases 1,206   Missing cases 0

Listen to a black news program on the radio?
Yes   78%
No   22%
Valid cases 1,204   Missing cases 2

Watched a black TV program on cable?
Yes   72%
No   28%
Valid cases 1,202   Missing cases 4

Watched a black TV program on a non-cable station?
Yes   80%
No   20%
Valid cases 1,199   Missing cases 7

Table 2.4   The determinants of exposure to black information sources

Variable	Dependent Variable Exposure to Black Information Sources Coefficient (SE)
Gender (1 = woman, 0 = man)	—[a]
Family income	.13 (0.02)
Age	−.34 (.03)
Education	—
Percentage of blacks in census tract	—
Census tract poverty 11–20%	—
Census tract poverty more than 31%	−.03 (.02)
Belong to black organization? (0 = yes, 1 = no)	−.10 (.015)
Is interviewer perceived as white? (1 = yes, 0 = no)	−.02 (.017)
Constant	.81 (.04)

Source: 1993–1994 National Black Politics Survey
Notes: These are OLS estimates. All variables coded 0–1.
[a]A dash denotes that the result is not statistically significant.
$n = 1008$
adjusted R^2 = .20
Standard error of estimate = .21

Table 2.4 presents evidence on the determinants of one's total exposure to black information sources. When one analyzes the predictors of one's total exposure to black information (as measured by the scale described above), it becomes clear that the three critical predictors of being tied to black information networks are whether one belongs to a black organization, age, and the degree to which one's family has financial resources.

Younger, organizationally connected, and more affluent blacks are exposed more to black information networks. Organizational connections can compensate somewhat for the lack of resources. So for our purposes, one's placement in the structure of black information networks is shaped by the nature of one's spatial and social location structures. The 1993–94 National Black Politics Study is the first national survey that allows researchers to explore the effects of all three types of structures on black public opinion.

As I have noted however, one key concern of black social, political, and cultural theorists has been the degree to which disruptions in the black social structure and major shifts in the American political economy have undermined the black counterpublic. One avenue of speculation that this manuscript explores is that new forms of black information networks—indeed, entirely new black counterpublics—have emerged which form new bases for black critical discourses.

DIS BEAT DISRUPTS:
BLACK COUNTERPUBLICS, IDEOLOGY, AND RAP

This beat obstructs the justice of the peace
And the quiet in your neighborhood tonight.

—George Clinton

Tremendous changes have occurred within the black public sphere in which activists such as Ida B. Wells, W. E. B. Du Bois, Marcus Garvey, Martin Luther King, Jr., Malcolm X, Angela Davis, Amiri Baraka, and Barbara Smith debated, polemicized, and organized.[18] While a few of those leaders are still active, the black public sphere of the turn of the twentieth century is vastly different than even that of the 1960s and 1970s. Movies, cable television, rap music, and cyberspace, some cultural critics argue, have become integral elements of that sphere and perhaps even replaced the traditional speakers' corners, union halls, ballrooms, and activist newspapers and magazines as the main sites of the black counterpublic.

Such vehicles as speaker's ballrooms (the sad and important role of the Audubon Ballroom where Malcolm X was assassinated comes to mind) and activist-oriented magazines played important roles in the past. Tables 2.5

18. Parts of this chapter appeared in Dawson 1999: "Dis Beat Disrupts: Rap, Ideology, and Black Political Opinion," in *The Cultural Territories of Race: White and Black Boundaries*, ed. Michèle Lamont (Chicago: University of Chicago Press, 1999), 318–42.

Table 2.5   *Negro Digest/Black World* frequencies: Black ideology by five-year intervals, 1942–1976

Year	Marxism	Nationalism	Conservatism	Liberalism	Feminism
1942–1946	11	0	50	125	12
1947–1951	—	—	25	57	7
1952–1956	—	—	—	—	—
1957–1961	—	—	—	—	—
1962–1966	4	21	6	14	2
1967–1971	4	16	0	1	1
1972–1976	10	28	1	12	2

Source: *Negro Digest* and *Black World*, 1942–1976. *Negro Digest* did not publish or circulate from 1951 to 1961.

and 2.6 show that both the *Negro Digest/Black World* (same magazine, changed name), and the still active *Black Scholar* have been active sites for black ideological contention. Indeed, a quick perusal of the tables shows how the Marxist/nationalist debate comes to a head in the early and middle 1970s and declines from there. The emergence of black feminism is also clearly seen. Table 2.6 suggests that in recent years there has been a shift away from the more radical ideologies.

There has been also been a shift in the sites where preferences are shaped and ideological contestation occurs. Cathy Cohen, for examples, calls our attention to the harm done by some rap music and by television programs such as *Living Color* in promoting dangerously negative stereotypes of black gays and lesbians (Cohen 1994). Vigorous debate and organizing is occurring in black cyberspheres. The well-attended Black Radical Congress of 1998 fostered a spirited, on-line debate between prominent black nationalists, radicals, and other ideologues both before and after the conference. Similarly, the organizers of the Million Youth and Million Woman Marches were active in cyberspace. Voting registration drives and

Table 2.6   *Black Scholar* frequencies: Black ideology by five-year intervals, 1969–194

Year	Marxism	Nationalism	Conservatism	Liberalism	Feminism
1969–1973	6	32	4	7	10
1974–1978	34	25	5	15	10
1979–1983	15	10	0	9	23
1984–1988	12	10	0	20	14
1989–1994	3	4	2	11	4

Source: Data compiled from *The Black Scholar: Journal of Black Studies and Research*, 1969–1994.

national conferences are being announced on e-mail lists. There are critical questions about which African Americans are likely to be involved in the more interactive forms of the new counterpublics: Internet access is still relatively limited among African Americans and their organizations. Of perhaps greater concern is the passive nature of many of the new media. Interaction, some argue, is not a component of watching movies, listening to the radio, or watching television. Others argue that there is an active underground poetry/hip-hop scene, book clubs are flourishing among blacks, and that intense political debate can be generated by either music or movies. In the chapters that follow I comment on the most analyzed and most controversial of these new vehicles for ideological politics—rap music.

Can new black discourses, new black counterpublics, and new black centers for debate over the future of the race be rebuilt on a new black popular culture? Or is placing any political faith in this new culture at best ridiculously naive and perhaps even dangerous, as the many critics of contemporary black popular culture argue. Certainly not all elements of black popular culture are argued to be either potential sites for political resistance or the most backward or banal of black artistic endeavors. Black classical music, or jazz, is popular among political activists of most persuasions, even if it doesn't now have the same political status that it had during the Civil Rights and Black Power eras. During the 1960s, however, writers such as Amiri Baraka (then known as the Pulitzer Prize–winning author LeRoi Jones) claimed when talking about the new generation of jazz artists that "there was a kind of race pride or consciousness that animated the musicians and their music," and Frank Kofsky could equally plausibly argue that "bebop can therefore be viewed in its social aspect as a manifesto for rebellious black musicians unwilling to submit to further exploitation." (Jones 1967, 209; Kofsky 1970, 57). Cultural critics such as Tricia Rose believe that rap is this generation's answer to bebop. She argues that rap continues "the long history of black cultural subversion and social critique in music and performance" (Rose 1994, 99). For Rose, not only does "dis beat disrupt," but rap represents "the central cultural vehicle for open social reflection on poverty, fear of adulthood, the desire for absent fathers, frustrations about black male sexism, female sexual desires, daily rituals of life as an unemployed teen hustler, safe sex, raw anger, violence, and childhood memories." (Rose 1994, 18). Rap provides a political outlet for the disenfranchised of the black inner-city, and provides "alternative interpretations of key social events such as the Gulf War, the Los Angeles uprising, police brutality, censorship efforts, and community-based education" (Rose 1994, 18).

But great controversy surrounds the music, and detractors of the new black music abound. Adolph Reed starkly represents the point of view of the detractors when he bleakly argues that even representatives of the so-called political wing of hip-hop culture "spew garbled compounds of half-truth, distortion, Afrocentric drivel, and crackerbarrel wisdom, as often as not shot through with reactionary prejudices" (Reed 1992a, 228). While Reed is generally suspicious of any claim that artistic production created for capitalist markets can play a progressive role, he says that the "black power consumerism" of the 1960s, while "parasitic" on black power ideology and the Black Power movement, was at least continually critiqued by both. The current black artistic consumerist fad, according to Reed, is neither critiqued nor influenced by a dynamic mass movement.

This view is not exactly compatible with that of Michael Dyson and other defenders of the more specifically political veins of rap. When discussing Public Enemy, the most famous/popular political rap group, Dyson proclaims that "PE has maintained its integrity and vision. . . . *It Takes a Nation of Millions to Hold Us Back* lunges far beyond anything in rap's past to help secure its future. . . . *It Takes a Nation* gave the genre ideological vitality" (Dyson 1996, 166). Houston Baker waxes equally poetic when he declares: "Rappers had been prophetic with respect to tensions between black urban youth and metropolitan police authorities" (Baker 1993, 33–34). For these scholars, the new black culture represents the cutting edge of a rejuvenated, critical, black public sphere—a space that would encourage in black Americans the ability to critique the racist ills of American society, as well as provide a social space which facilitates the process of consciousness-raising necessary for rebuilding the black movement. For Baker, this is particularly true for black youth. He sees it as potentially the last "outpost of teenage redemption" (Baker 1993). Our youth may yet be saved by rap.[19]

A middle ground is taken by Ransby and Matthews in their essay "Black Popular Culture and the Transcendence of Patriarchal Illusions" (1993). They also caution us that even political rappers popularize backwards points of view when they argue, "Even lyrical brews concocted with a distinctly militant flavor are frequently laced with enough counterproductive and counterrevolutionary messages, especially with regard to gender and the status of women, to dull their potentially radical edge." (Ransby and Matthews 1993). While they make the common and correct point that

---

19. This belief that rap is a possible salvation for black youth leads him to attack critics of rap in print (see Baker 1993 for one of many examples).

popular culture, whether in the form of wearing the X symbolizing Malcolm X or listening to the "undirected rage" of political rap, is no substitute for political action, they also point out that the vicious attacks on women have their roots not only in previous black cultural forms such as the blues and the toasts, but in American popular culture more generally. Such sentiments, they point out, including the less violent ones that attempt to relegate black women to a secondary role, potentially rob black mobilizations of half their potential force and leadership.

These visions of the relationship between rap and the black community are radically different from each other. Certainly the Dyson/Baker vision of rap as a site for contestation and black renewal clashes with Reed's view, which sees as fraudulent any assertion that rap can provide an impetus to political knowledge, let alone a guide to action. In each of the following chapters I outline and test several sets of assertions about the relationship of rap music to black political ideology (specifically to black nationalism and feminism) and to African-American political beliefs. The analyses demonstrate that both exposure to rap music and the belief that it constitutes an important resource of the black community play substantial roles in shaping black political opinion, both directly and indirectly. The normative and practical consequences of such a relationship are considered in the conclusion.

Why Rap?

Why focus on rap? Rap is certainly the most visible and debated black art form in contemporary America. Youth of all races have embraced rap and rap artists. It is easily accessible on radio and television. Movie soundtracks routinely and prominently feature rap artists. Sports superstars cut rap records, as have some Superbowl winning teams. Rap artists have become television and movie stars in their own right. Sadly, rap music garnered even more attention in late 1996 and early 1997 due to the murders of two of the most popular gangsta rappers, Tupac Shakur and the Notorious B.I.G.

On the other hand, it is not just right wing forces and Tipper Gore that attack rap as being detrimental to the black community. Black religious leaders such as Calvin Butts have led protests against rap as a damaging force in the black community. Rappers themselves argue that they are both serious providers of needed knowledge for the black community and a source of inspiration for at least the young. Controversial and popular rapper Ice Cube describes the role of rappers as follows: "We call ourselves underground street reporters. We just tell it how we see it, nothing more, nothing less" (Kelley 1994, 190).

In concentrating on rap, I evaluate four sets of claims which add specificity to the disputes that we observed between a number of scholars of rap. Each set of claims is discussed before the results of the analyses are evaluated. The four set of claims follow:[20]

1. Rappers represent the new "griots" of contemporary Africa America.[21] As the "CNN" of the black community, rap music plays a vital role in rebuilding a dynamic black public sphere. One function of a critical public sphere is to provide the timely and accurate information necessary to make informed political decisions. From this perspective, rappers as modern griots provide a "pro-black" source of information which in turn provides a necessary, but not sufficient, basis for forging a vibrant, black civil society within which ideological debate would flourish and political mobilization proceed.

2. Rap music provides a contested, critical space that contributes to the political education of the black community. Further, rappers themselves are *ideological partisans* who attempt to persuade their audience, the black community (or at least the "righteous" sectors of the black community) to a "correct" ideological orientation. If the first point at least implies neutrality (we're just "telling it like it is"), this perspective requires a critical political viewpoint.

3. The economics of the production and marketing of rap constricts the ability of rap artists to make a positive contribution to the black community. Others argue that rap music provides the most "authentic" source of commentary on the economic devastation of the black community and its most disadvantaged residents.

4. The gender politics of rap, despite the presence of strong women rappers such as Queen Latifah, is overwhelmingly reactionary and contributes to the high level of misogyny, homophobia, and anti-black-feminist sentiment within the black community. Some have

20. For a fuller discussion of these four claims, see Dawson 1999.

21. The term *griot* comes from the West African oral history tradition. Traditionally griots served the rulers of African empires, such as that of historical Mali. They provided a record of the history of the kingdom and the ruling family, acted as advisors to the court, and were often accomplished musicians as well.

argued that gangsta rap in particular contributes to both sexually oriented violence and generalized violence within the black community. Intercommunity violence as well as misogyny and homophobia are argued to do grave harm to the ability to build a black public sphere capable of including the viewpoints of the entire black community

A Preliminary Analysis of the Determinants of the Consequences of Rap

If Reed and like-minded critics are right, exposure to rap should have one of two effects on black political opinion and preferences. First, rap should have very little effect in politicizing blacks when it comes to mobilizations against the structures of power that progressive critics find oppressing. So, for example, a positive cultural force would influence African Americans to take a critical stance toward America's large multinational corporations. Second, and even more important, the critics argue, rap music encourages the rampant degradation of women, homophobia, and what we saw Reed characterize as "backward prejudices." Even Dyson agrees that some of the lyrics of the most political of groups, such as Public Enemy's anti-Semitism, "marred their revolutionary agenda" (Dyson 1996). The basic predictions are that exposure to and emphasis on rap leads to "negative" attitudes, but not to positive consciousness raising.

Those who see rap as playing a positive role would argue that the good outweighs the bad, that rap music provides a potential basis for political mobilization, political education, and progressive discourse. This set of predictions, particularly from radical and liberal defenders of rap, focuses on a positive correlation between rap and a variety of political views consistent with a radical agenda. Nationalist defenders of rap, particularly the rappers themselves, would also argue that rap should be positively connected to building nationalist ideology among African Americans. They also may argue, especially if they are strongly allied with the Nation of Islam, that promoting hostility toward gays, lesbians, and whites is healthy for the black community. The following sections examine preliminary evidence about the degree to which contemporary black public opinion data supports these hypotheses. More detailed, multivariate models of both the determinants of rap and its effect on black ideologies are considered in each of the ideology chapters.

Table 2.7 displays simple bivariate relationships between several attitudes and beliefs and both exposure to and support for rap music. Males,

Table 2.7 Distribution of exposure to and support for rap music according to selected structural factors

Variable	Percentage Exposed to Rap	Percentage Supporting Rap as a Positive Force
Gender		
Male	54.35	40.74
Female	44.05	38.20
(χ^2 df, p-value)	(11.72, 1df, Pr = .001)	(.6054, 1df, Pr = .437)
Age		
18–29	78.39	70.48
30 and older	38.10	28.55
(χ^2, df, p-value)	(134.02, 1df, Pr = .000)	(125.08, 1df, Pr = .000)
Education		
Less than high-school	31.25	30.08
High school degree	46.01	35.12
Some college	58.49	49.58
College degree or greater	47.11	39.36
(χ^2, df, p-value)	(32.66, 3df, Pr = .000)	(15.873, 3df, Pr = .001)
Urbanicity		
Rural/County area	47.92	34.15
Small town	41.57	35.21
Small city	55.09	39.85
Suburb	54.80	44.37
Large City	45.02	38.56
(χ^2, df, p-value)	(10.199, 3df, Pr = .017)	(3.04, 4df, Pr = .551)
Degree of linked fate		
None	40.23	34.78
Little	46.43	37.36
Some	51.65	44.76
High	51.57	40.12
(χ^2, df, p-value)	(10.199, 3df, Pr = .017)	(5.3015, 3df, Pr = .151)
Interviewer perceived as white		
Yes	39.84	29.56
No	49.57	41.82
(χ^2, df, p-value)	(7.625, 1df, Pr = .006)	(10.074, 1df, Pr = .002

Source: 1993–1994 National Black Politics Study

the young, the more educated, the urban, and those who believed their fate to be linked to that of other African Americans are more likely to have consistent exposure to rap music. Given the controversy over rap music in the mainstream media, it is not surprising that those who perceive the survey interviewer to be white are less likely to report consistent exposure to rap. Gender, on the other hand, makes no difference in whether blacks evaluate rap as a positive force. Age most decidedly does—a gap of 40 percentage points separates approval for rap voiced by young blacks from approval by older blacks. The only other significant and substantial relationship reported in table 2.7 is that blacks who believe they are being interviewed by an African American are more than 10 percentage points more likely to voice their approval of rap.

We will see in what follows that exposure to rap music does indeed shape black ideologies and black public opinion. Whether new media and artistic forms can provide a basis for a reconfiguration of black counterpublics remains to be seen. But it is certainly apparent that these new forms can affect black politics and public opinion. In the concluding section of this chapter I introduce the black ideologies which are at the heart of many black political discourses and which influence the content of the new black media and the new black arts.

THE BLACK IDEOLOGICAL CLUSTERS

Chapter 1 briefly introduced the core components of each of the six main ideologies embedded in black political thought. While more nuanced definitions and analyses are presented in the following chapters, table 2.8 provides the first glimpse of their degree of support within contemporary black public opinion.

The categories "true believer" and "true hater" need explanation. The "true believers" are the African Americans who agree with *all* of the component questions used to construct each ideological scale. Similarly the "true haters" are blacks who reject *all* elements of an ideology.[22] As can be seen, all of the ideologies, except one have modest to moderate levels of key supporters. Only one is rejected in its entirety by large numbers of blacks. Firm supporters outnumber core opponents in ratios which range from approximately 9:1 to 20:1. Two caveats must be immediately made. First, there is more than a little racial and economic discontent among African

---

22. The list of questions used in constructing all six ideological scales appears in appendix table A1.1

Table 2.8 Black ideological true believers and true haters

Ideology	True Believers	True Haters
Black Nationalism	37%	4%
Black Feminism	19	2
Black Marxism	34	2
Disillusioned Liberalism	40	2
Black Conservatism[1]	1	20

Source: Compiled by Prof. M. Dawson from 1993–94 National Black Politics Survey.
[1]The constructions of the Black conservatism and the Radical Egalitarianism ideological scales share the same component questions (see Table A1.1). As a result, their percentage distributions of "true believers" and "true haters" are transposed. Instead of presenting the distributions of both ideologies, this table presents only those of the Black conservatism scale.

Americans. Seventy percent of all African Americans believe that the society *and* legal system are unfair to blacks *and* that the economic system is unfair to poor people (data compiled from NBPS by the author). Blacks may be liberals, but they are by no means even vaguely satisfied with the status quo, as we shall see in chapter 6. Even more stunning is the low level of support for black conservatism, both absolutely and relative to the other ideologies. Only black conservatives have more entrenched opposition than support. Their support is minuscule, and the solid opposition is formidable. Subsequent chapters present much more detail about the supporters and opponents of each ideology.

CONCLUSION: A LOOK AHEAD

Black ideologies enjoy substantial support within the black community. Each of them must confront the American liberal tradition, distinguish itself as a "black" ideology, and present a vision of how to achieve black justice, equality, and collective development. The chapters that follow discuss in detail how the activists of each ideological tradition attempt to distinguish their programs from each other as well as challenge the hegemonic status quo.

As we analyze each ideology, we must also pay attention to how each is presented both within the black counterpublic as well as in the dominant public spheres and counterpublics of the American republic. Where the greatest overlap has existed between black and white public spheres, we have witnessed increases in both state building projects and the progressive politics that attend state building projects within the United States. On the other hand, as Spillers brilliantly details in her analysis of the Moynihan

Report, often the price of admission into American civil society is black abandonment of core ideological principles such as equality for women in the workplace and the home (Spillers 1987). How each ideology fares in negotiating the tortuous terrain of race in American politics is the subject of the remainder of this book.

I believe in a pure black race.

Marcus Garvey

CHAPTER 3

Visions of a Black Nation: Black Nationalism
and African-American Political Thought

▟▟▟ "Black nationalism" is the second oldest ideological tendency found within black political thought. More important, black nationalism has provided the most enduring challenge to both the black and white liberal traditions. Black nationalism provides an ideological challenge to the *legitimacy* of American liberalism. Even so, Harold Cruse's sympathetic treatment of black nationalism in his seminal book, *The Crisis of the Negro Intellectual*, describes this ideological trend as the "rejected strain" (Cruse 1967, 4). Cruse goes on to argue that just as black liberalism (which he conflates with other "integrationist ideologies") can trace its historical roots to the mid-nineteenth century and leaders such as Fredrick Douglass, black nationalism can trace its roots back to the same period and "Douglass's barely remembered contemporaries" such as "Martin Delaney, Edward Blyden, Alexander Crummell, Henry M. Turner, and George Washington

85

Williams." (Cruse 1967, 5). Barely remembered or not, popular support for black nationalism continues to be based on the time-tested skepticism in black communities that, when it comes to race, America will live up to its liberal values. As is generally true with nationalist movements, and specifically true in American history, black nationalist movements are often reactive in nature, a political and ideological response to what is seen as an oppressive racial order (Cruse 1967; Kiss 1996). Cruse concludes that black political history can be seen as being fundamentally shaped by the conflict between nationalism and what he sees as its "integrationist" rivals: "American Negro history is basically a history of the conflict between integrationist and nationalist forces in politics, economics, and culture, no matter which leaders are involved and what slogans are used." (Cruse 1967, 564). The nature of this conflict shifts because the nationalist vision itself evolves as it adapts to different historical epochs. At its core, however, black nationalism represents the most racialized of African-American ideologies.

Black nationalists' theoretical vision of black liberation continues to be based on the contention that understanding the plight of blacks and achieving black salvation must be based on taking *race and racial oppression* as the central feature of modern world history. American versions of liberalism—indeed, all versions of European descent—are seen as philosophical and political systems which are at best promising in theory, but which in practice systematically exclude blacks. Black nationalists, like many nationalists throughout the world (as well as sympathetic analysts with a more liberal, universalist orientation), reject the belief espoused by John Stuart Mill that the institutions of a liberal democracy would guarantee full inclusion, leaving no segment of a population permanently marginalized (Kiss 1996). This viewpoint sees American liberalism as a hypocritical failure to the degree that it denies the benefits of liberal citizenship to blacks in the United States. Malcolm X in the last year of his life demanded in the name of nationalism that liberal democratic practices and citizenship rights be extended to African Americans. His rhetorical appeals on this point were more similar than dissimilar to those of Martin Luther King, Jr. Within two years of each other, each was arguing that America had not lived up to its contract with African Americans. During his "I Have a Dream" speech in 1963, Martin Luther King, Jr. accused the United States of bouncing a check to blacks, while Malcolm X argued in 1965,

> Man, how could you think you're an American when you haven't ever had any kind of an American treat over here? You have never, never.

Ten men can be sitting at a table eating, you know, dining, and I can come and sit down where they're dining. They're dining; I've got a plate in front of me, but nothing is on it. Because all of us are sitting at the same table, are all of us diners? I'm not a diner until you let me dine. . . . Just because you're in this country doesn't make you an American. No, you've got to go farther than that before you can become an American. You've got to enjoy the fruits of Americanism. You haven't enjoyed the fruits. You've enjoyed the thorns. You've enjoyed the thistles. But you have not enjoyed the fruits, no sir. (X 1965, 172)

At worst, liberalism is seen as an active component of a rapacious system that is founded on the oppression of blacks. Liberalism is described as a dangerous language game designed to lure blacks and others to not only accede to their own oppression, but to kill and die in the service of its maintenance (Madhubuti 1994; Yeshitela 1988). From such an ideological perspective, liberalism is viewed as antithetical to the interests of blacks, and white liberals (either philosophical or political) are viewed at the least with great suspicion. Many nationalists view liberals as no different in essence from white-robed Klan members. Many nationalists argue that by *nature* white and black interests are opposed to each other. Even nationalist organizations such as the Black Panther Party, which was often berated by other nationalists for its advocacy of alliances with whites, argued that the special status of African Americans and the disparities of power between blacks and whites made racially separate organizations and strategies necessary. Consequently, core concepts of black nationalism include not only support for African American autonomy and self-determination, but various degrees of cultural, social, economic, and political separation from white America.

Not only is race is seen as *the* fundamental category for analyzing society, but America is seen as fundamentally racist. Garvey, the founder of modern black nationalist movements, argued,

Some Negro leaders have advanced the belief that in another few years the white people will make up their minds to assimilate their black populations, thereby sinking all racial prejudice in the welcoming of the black race into the social companionship of the white. Such leaders further believe that by the amalgamation of black and white, a new type will spring up, and that type will become the American and West Indian of the future. This belief is preposterous. I believe that white men should be white, yellow men should be yellow, and black men should be black in the great panorama of races, until each and every race by its own initiative lifts itself up to the common standard of humanity, so as to compel the respect and appreciation of all, and so make it possible for each one to stretch out the hand of welcome without being able to be prejudiced against the other because of any inferior and unfortunate condition. (Garvey 1986, 26)

Because most black nationalists are suspicious of alliances with those outside of the black community, they argue that firm unity must be built within the black community before alliances with others can even be considered (Carmichael and Hamilton 1967; X 1965). Alliances, nationalists argue, must be built between groups that have roughly commensurate levels of power. They cannot usefully be entered if blacks are operating from a position of relative or absolute powerlessness. The fact that Africa holds a special place as the "motherland" for most black nationalists leads many (not all) black nationalists to see people of African descent as at least the spiritual allies of African Americans. Some versions of black nationalism are in theory open to alliances with other, nonwhite social movements; others reject all such alliances.

One consequence of this racialized world view is that virtually all other ideological perspectives are considered to be the tools of white oppressors. Historically, this view has led to fierce clashes between black nationalists and black socialists. By and large, in the current period, the clashes between black socialists and nationalists have been replaced by battles between black nationalists and black feminists.[1] Historically, these clashes have been centered around the perceived need of black liberals, feminists, and socialists to forge alliances outside of the black community. Further, black socialists have viewed class-based conflict within the black community not only as inevitable but often as desirable.

More recently, challenges to what black feminists have characterized as nationalists' blatantly patriarchal and often misogynist views of women have also fueled conflict between activists in the black feminist and nationalist camps. Patriarchal perspectives on the nature of society and the role

---

1. During the 1920s, Garvey's nationalists were in fierce conflict with the cadre of the African Blood Brotherhood, who became the core of black presence within the CPUSA during that period. Similar conflicts marked the Black Power era and continued well into the period of the African Liberation Support Committee.

of men and women in struggles for black liberation are one of the ideological commonalties between black nationalism and other ideological orientations. I address this argument in more detail in subsequent chapters. The propensity of many black Marxists (and of American Marxists in general) to see work as male and the proletariat as a male preserve, and the influence of black ministers in liberal-led movements such as the Civil Rights movement have helped to reinforce patriarchal norms and moral authority throughout black discourse and in activist circles (Kelley 1994; Ransby 1995). Black nationalists have argued since the 1960s that concentration on an "alien" philosophy such as feminism detracts from the black struggle for freedom and justice. Nation of Islam leader Minister Farrakhan is just one of many black leaders who have made this point. Rap groups such as Public Enemy have often voiced the same sentiments in their music, which has a large following among many segments of the black community. Nationalists often challenge the very idea of gender equality, focusing instead on gender difference and different gender roles for black women and black men. At the time nationalist theorist Ron Karenga argued, "Equality is false; it's the devil's concept. Our concept is complementarity. Complementarity means you complete or make perfect that which is imperfect, the man has the right not to destroy the collective needs of his family; the woman has the two rights of consultation and separation if she isn't getting what she should be getting" (quoted in White 1990, 73).

There are exceptions: Haki Madhubuti has passionately argued for women's equality, against America's rape culture, and against many forms of attacks against and degradation of black women (Madhubuti 1994). However, most nationalists remain extremely skeptical of ideological orientations that are felt to originate outside of the black community.

Despite the call by many nationalists for ideological purity, others have attempted to combine black nationalism with a variety of the other ideologies. Some branches of the Black Panther Party adopted a version of black nationalism which was a hybrid blend of Marxism and nationalism (this was the "official" position of the Panthers). Other branches were much more nationalist in orientation. Feminist scholars such as Patricia Hill Collins have also attempted to provide a synthesis between nationalism and other ideologies (Collins 1991). These combinations fuse challenges to liberalism based on race with challenges based on class or gender.

Nationalism in all of if its various forms has developed over the decades among African Americans partly as a response to blacks' strict exclusion from the benefits of American liberalism, and partly as a way for blacks to distance themselves politically, socially, and culturally from what were seen as the hegemonic, racist narratives and practices of a corrupt system of white supremacy. This persistent perspective of black nationalists resembles that of the anticolonial nationalists in India and elsewhere (Chatterjee 1993). A common characteristic of anticolonial and antiracist nationalism is the tendency to substitute a new hegemonic narrative that assigns precise roles to members of their nations and denies that differences exist between members of the nation (Chatterjee 1993; Dyson 1993). Indeed, according to Chatterjee, most nationalisms and the systems of belief and practice they oppose share the Hegelian view of family, and by extension, community and nation, which suggests that one's natural, predetermined, prepolitical affiliations are set at birth (1993).

By the late twentieth century, black nationalism had once again become a nationally prominent ideology, challenging white supremacy and "moderate" black ideologies alike. Relatively unchallenged by its traditional radical rival (black radicalism has been much weakened by the forces described in chapter 1), only black feminism has consistently presented a progressive critical alternative to nationalism. Greeted with unease by much of the black middle class, and with horror by many whites, nationalism was increasingly embraced by the poor, in particular by young men.

In the remainder of this chapter we first consider black nationalism as a form of nationalism. This discussion is followed by a review of modern black nationalism. The key components of black nationalism are then identified. I conclude with a discussion of who are the black nationalists in contemporary black public opinion and how black nationalism is shaped by and in turn shapes black public opinion.

BLACK NATIONALISM AS A FORM OF NATIONALISM

I'm tired of that one-nation-under-God boogie-joogie. We are ourselves. We are our own nation, or country, whatever you want to call it. We are not one tenth of some white something! That man has got his country, and we are our country. . . . We don't need them to do what we do. They need us more than we need them.

John Oliver, black worker, early 1970s

We are a nation. The best of us have said it, and everybody feels it. I think it was Frederick Douglass who said we were a nation within a nation. . . . We don't really agree with white people about anything important. If we were in power, we would do almost everything differently

than they have. We are a nation primarily because we think we are a
nation.

Hannah Nelson, piano teacher, early 1970s

A fundamental problem for all nationalists, but a particularly acute problem for black nationalists, is the central concept of a separate black nation.
Nationalism is fundamentally centered around the concept of "nation,"
whether it is defined in terms of the nation constituted as a state, as a primordial people, or as a historical cultural community (combinations are of
course possible). Boundaries are another critical aspect of the definition of
nations. Boundaries are of course in part spatial, defining (usually) the ter-
ritorial expanse of the nation. Just as important, however, are the boundaries constructed to define which people belong to the nation; as one leading, Chicago-based nationalist remarked in 1996, "There's some black
people I wouldn't want to be part of a black nation." What, according to
Calhoun, can be "problematic" about such a sentiment is "the nationalist
claim . . . [that] national identity is categorical and fixed, and that somehow
it trumps all other sorts of identities, from gender to region, class to political preferences, occupation to artistic taste" (Calhoun 1994, 311). As both
my nationalist friend and Calhoun suggest, the nationalist project entails
determining the membership of the community and, consequently, determining who is allowed to speak.

Black nationalists have grappled with three overlapping definitions of
"the" black nation. The first is built on state power and land. The second
defines African Americans as more than "just another American ethnic
group" but as a separate, oppressed people, a nation-within-a-nation, with
the right to self-determination. A third, usually less political, conception of
"the" black nation defines it as a community with a defined and unique
spiritual and cultural identity. All three definitions of the black nation presume that people of African descent within the borders of the United States
have at least some common interests based on their race or their common
history of racial subjugation.[2]

Another common theme among activists of all three traditions of
black nationalism is an emphasis on self-determination. Blacks should be

---

2. This definition is not, of course, unproblematic. For example, much literature assumes that
when one speaks of the black population in the United States, one is speaking of the descendants of
slaves. This view leaves untheorized how to think about Caribbean and African immigrants, not all
of whom were the descendants of slaves. Even in the case of immigrants descended from slaves, it is
likely that the slave experience was not in the American South.

able to define their own destiny, whether their orientation toward black nationalism is spiritual, cultural, economic, or political. The concept of self-determination is not limited to nationalist discourses. Communists, and even some liberals (particularly black liberals, or white American liberals talking about populations of certain countries outside the borders of the United States) have also made the term their own. Whether self-determination is defined as primarily a cultural goal or a political one is a major dividing line between black activists (Franklin 1984). Relatively few activists—Malcolm X was the most notable exception—embrace both the political and cultural aspects of self-determination. Nevertheless, a defining characteristic of all black nationalism is the absolute acceptance of the principle that blacks within the United States should define their own destiny.

Finally, another critical component of nationalism is its emphasis on self-reliance. Self-reliance is closely connected to self-determination, as Garvey makes clear in the following argument: "Chance has never yet satisfied the hope of a suffering people. Action, self-reliance, the vision of self and the future have been the only means by which the oppressed have seen and realized the light of their own freedom" (Garvey 1986, 1). This is a common sentiment among black nationalists—one can only rely on one's own efforts to gain freedom and justice.

Self-reliance becomes connected in twentieth-century black nationalism to a variety of concepts such as community control, independent black political parties, and the need to build autonomous cultural and spiritual institutions. But a central aspect of almost all black nationalist thinking and practice is the linking of the need for self-reliance to a program of economic nationalism. Harold Cruse argued, for example, that economic nationalism has played a largely unacknowledged role in building communities such as Harlem into important black enclaves. He assigns an important role, for example, to Philip A. Payton, who "was a disciple of Booker T. Washington." He argues that blacks' movement into Harlem was "engineered" by Payton (Cruse 1967, 21). In the mid-twentieth century the Nation of Islam pioneered efforts to build black small businesses, and other nationalists developed cooperative farms in the South (the latter efforts were met with intense hostility by white private citizens and local and state governments in the South during the 1960s and 1970s). Efforts to build food cooperatives, restaurants, bookstores, independent black presses, and other small businesses were part of the economic agenda of the Nation of Islam and many other black nationalists. Parallel efforts, mostly unsuccessful, were also launched by entertainers in the twentieth century to gain control of black artistic products, particularly black music. These efforts at establishing an independent black economic base continued to be important part of the nationalist agenda at the dawn of the twenty-first century.

While black definitions of nationalism overlap in many organizational and historical contexts, they have sometimes led to deadly differences. Some members of the Black Panther cadre, who upheld a position roughly equivalent to the nation-within-a-nation position, were shot in the late 1960s by cultural nationalists. These same conceptualizations of the black nation can be found in contemporary black discourse, and they find varying degrees of mass support. I begin with the conception of a black nation based on land. The central project of these nationalists is to build a black state.

Toward a Black State: Land and the Black Nation

At the core, this nationalist tradition defines the nation as a group of people with primordial, even if historically constituted, ties. A nation is a group of people who are defined by community and some sense of "naturalness" in the ties that bind—a set of ties and bonds that are based on gendered concepts of the family. The term *family* is used and defined both in its immediate sense of a unit which has at its heart the physical reproduction of the nation, and in the metaphysical sense of the nation as one large, united family. Families are said to have "heads," and so must nations. Not all belong to the family, and the family must be protected from internal and external threats. Thus nations are about power: The power to define who belongs and who does not is critical to nationalist projects. Ultimately, some group—and often individuals—claim the leadership of the nation as the father claims to be head of the family. This claim has been interpreted by some nationalists as meaning that to be head of the "black" family, to be "head of the nation," must mean to be head of state. Garvey made this point explicitly: "I asked 'Where is the black man's Government?' 'Where is his King and kingdom?' 'Where is his President, his country, and his ambassador, his army, his navy, his men of big affairs?' I could not find them, and then I declared, 'I will help make them'" (Garvey 1986, 126).[3]

3. Compare the following quotation from *The Prince*. There are striking similarities between Garvey's thought about a nationalist project and Machiavelli's republican project: "And if, as I have said, one wished to see the virtue of Moses, it was necessary for the people of Israel to be enslaved in Egypt; and to know the greatness of the mind of Cyrus, that the Persians be oppressed by the Medes; and [to know] the excellence of Theseus, that the Athenians be dispersed—so, at present, if one

Many black nationalists of the modern era continue to promote Garvey's view that black liberation could only come with the reclaiming of the land and the creation of the revolutionary "Afrikan" state. One militant, Pan-Afrikan organization argued in the early 1980s at a national meeting of black activists that "an independent, revolutionary, Afrikan national state will be the basis for the liberation of our people from racism and capitalism" (Document A 1980).[4] From the late 1960s on, influential nationalist organizations such as the Republic of New Africa argued for the liberation of five southern states (a common demand of both black nationalists and the Leninist left from the mid-twentieth century through the mid-1980s). This demand can be traced among both black nationalists and the black left to early-twentieth-century nationalists associated with the Garvey movement. Many of the cadres from the Garvey movement would take their concern about building a black homeland and black nation into organizations ranging from the Nation of Islam to the Communist Party of the United States.

This is the version of the "black nation" that is most closely tied to the common conception of the nation as the fundamental basis for the modern nation-state. But black nationalists have recognized since the time of Delany in the mid-nineteenth century that *the location of the land of the black nation is highly problematic, as is the establishment of a state when the territory for the black nation has been identified.*[5] For some nationalists, such as Garvey in the early twentieth century, the quest for a black state was part of the natural order of the world. Each people was to have its own government.

For others, such as Delany, the reason to seek a separate black state for African Americans was America's demonstrated dedication to the perpetual subjugation of Africans throughout the world. After arguing (1) that there exist throughout the world enslaved nations-within-nations, (2) that we all believe in equality, and (3) that America is the true home of "colored people" in the United States, Delany shifts his rhetorical focus to the

---

wishes to know the virtue of an Italian spirit, it was necessary that Italy be reduced to her present terms, and that she be more enslaved than the Hebrews, more servile than the Persians, more dispersed than the Athenians, without head, without order, beaten, despoiled, torn asunder, overrun, and having borne every sort of ruin" (Machiavelli 1980, 151). See Hill 1987 for Garvey's intentional modeling of some of his essays on Plato's dialogues. See Dawson (n.d.) for a systematic comparison of Garvey and Machiavelli.

4. Please see the appendix for information about Documents A and B. Since I have removed the identifying information from them, they are not entered in the references, although I cite them as sources in the text.

5. Delany in 1852 proposed various sites in the Western Hemisphere, such as Nicaragua. By 1861, however, he was proposing the Niger Valley in Africa (Delany 1993).

critical plight facing African Americans in the decade before the Civil War, after the passage of the heinous Fugitive Slave Act:

> We must abandon all vague theory and look at the *facts* as they really are; viewing ourselves in our true political position in the body politic. To imagine ourselves to be included in the body politic, except by express legislation, is at war with common sense, and contrary to fact. We are politically, not of them, but aliens to the laws and political privileges of the country. . . . What then shall we do?—What is the remedy?—is the important question to be answered. (Delany 1993, 157–59; emphasis in the original)

He goes on to argue for the creation of a free black state in the Western Hemisphere. Delany's argument is similar to that of nationalists of many stripes as well as many disillusioned black liberals. In different historical periods, both Du Bois and Malcolm X argued that blacks within the United States were fooling themselves if they believed that the United States was going to live up to its democratic, liberal commitments and become racially just anytime in the foreseeable future. However, what weds Delany's nationalism to Garvey's is that both embrace the idea of a separate state as a solution to the problem of continuing black oppression.

While some nationalists have suggested parts of the Western hemisphere outside of the boundaries of the United States, the common choices of black nationalists for over a century have centered around a territory and state either within the United States (usually located in the "black belt" of the South) or in Africa.[6] The call to build an autonomous black nation on land in North America has reverberated among black activists throughout the twentieth century. An early call for a black homeland (outside of Africa) was advanced by Cyril Briggs in 1917 as editor of the *Amsterdam News* (Haywood 1978; Kelley 1994). He demanded a "colored autonomous state" within the United States (Kelley 1994, 106).

Briggs is a key figure for understanding black nationalism in the twentieth century. Briggs, founder of the short-lived but extremely influential African Blood Brotherhood, promoted the idea of an independent black nation within the United States in both the nationalist *and* communist movements of the United States. Briggs and his comrades, such as Otto Hall, were members of the Garvey movement and would later join the Communist

---

6. The phrase *black belt* does not refer to the concentration of black people (except by "chance") but to the rich soil of the plantation belt.

Party. Indeed, the African Blood Brotherhood countered Garvey's emphasis on a return to Africa with the proposition that the black nation be built in North America (Haywood 1978). Ironically, from 1920 through 1980 the main proponents of a black nation in the United States (usually identified with the black belt South) were revolutionary nationalists, such as the Republic of New Africa, African People's Party, and The Nation of Islam (during some periods) on one hand, and Leninist communist organizations that were either predominantly black or had significant black membership, such as the Communist Party of the United States (CPUSA) and the multitude of black Leninist organizations that were one of the legacies of the black power movement of the 1960s and 1970s. The differences between land-oriented nationalists and communists were large and often bitter. But black communists (and their allies) focus on land, and fundamental insistence on the right of self-determination would lead to frequent racially based splits in American communist movements, and the more than occasional emergence of black united fronts that included both communists and nationalists (which often ended in ugly "divorces").

Cultural nationalist Karenga argues that the land question "is still a burning one [that] is not solved by non-believers dismissing it as utopian." (1993, 178). African Americans have craved land as a material base for independence, autonomy, and power. Blacks have tried to gain land, or control over the institutions associated with it in territories where they have resided, since the era of slavery. Black attempts to form free communities of escaped slaves, redistribute the land of Confederate leaders, form free communities of farmers in the West, set up an independent state in Mississippi the 1960s, and fight for community control have historically been attacked by governments at all levels and by "independently" organized whites. During the Civil War, for example, it was usually *Union* troops who protected Confederate plantations that were being redistributed by freed slaves. Black essayists ranging from the great black anti-lynching leader Ida B. Wells to novelist Richard Wright have repeatedly demonstrated how black property and land was violently seized by whites. Black folklore, often with more than a little historical accuracy, tells how both state and federal governments cooperated to seize the black-owned sea islands of South Carolina and Georgia and turn them into the corporate resorts they are today. The bitterness of African Americans over their inability to protect their land, property, and families and to determine the course of their lives has led each generation of blacks up to the 1970s to consider the possibility of forging a collective existence independent of the United States. In most eras, however, levels of support for actually establishing a separate state have been very low. Still, the enduring strength of black nationalism speaks to the deep resonance that the idea of safe, autonomous, free, black communities has had with African Americans.

A Nation within a Nation:
A Landless Quest for Self-Determination

We're nationalists because we see ourselves as a nation within a nation. But we're revolutionary nationalists. We don't see ourselves as a national unit for racist reasons but as a necessity for us to progress as human beings and live on the face of this earth. We don't fight racism with racism. We fight racism with solidarity. We don't fight exploitative capitalism with black capitalism. We fight capitalism with revolutionary socialism.

> Bobby Seale, Chairman of the Black
> Panther Party for Self-Defense, 1993

(1) We want freedom. We want power to determine the destiny of our Black Community. We believe that our people will not be free until we are free to determine our own destiny.

> First point of the Ten-Point Program
> of the Black Panther Party for Self-Defense

For at least a century and a half, many blacks have argued that they belonged to a separate nation confined within the borders of the United States. A major distinction between these nationalists and the state-oriented ones is that a contiguous territory is not defined. Their similarity derives from the view of both traditions that blacks are an oppressed nation with the right to self-determination.

The status of land and statehood is ambiguous among the theorists who embrace the nation-within-a-nation thesis. "Revolution is always based on land!" Malcolm X argued in his speech entitled "The Black Revolution" (X 1995, 277). Yet the land over which the black revolution is to be fought was never specified. Most of the speech concentrates on the hypocrisy of American liberals and democracy, the possibility of the first nonviolent revolution, and the need for blacks to control the critical social, political, and economic institutions of their community.

Community control and the characterization of blacks' plight as that of an internal colony are two of Malcolm X's central themes in that and many of his other speeches. This framing of black oppression has some significant consequences. One is that it identifies other oppressed and colonized peoples of the United States and the international community as the "natural" allies of African Americans. A corollary is that it becomes relatively straightforward to envision the quest for black justice and freedom as a liberation struggle. This is especially true of the period after World War II when the vocabulary of national liberation struggles had become readily available. It is no coincidence that from the middle 1960s through most of the 1970s black activists in their rhetoric, and in some cases in their practice, drew connections between what was called during the Black Power era the black liberation movement and the national liberation struggles of the Third World.

Delany made this connection over a century earlier when he connected the condition of blacks in the United States to that of the oppressed peoples of Europe (specifically the Poles, Jews, gypsies, etc.). By the 1960s, not only is the connection of similar condition constantly made, but the rhetoric, tactics, and strategies of the Chinese communists, Vietnamese guerrillas, North Koreans (the Panthers found their philosophy of *Juche*, translated as "self-determination," particularly attractive), Palestinians, Algerians (through Fanon's great classic *The Wretched of the Earth*), Mozambiqueans, and the revolutionaries of Guinea-Bissau under the leadership of the PAIGC and Amilcar Cabral, were embraced as models for black liberation. Many, but not all, nationalists of this generation followed Malcolm X's lead:

> Now the black revolution has been taking place in Africa and Asia and in Latin America. Now when I say black, I mean nonwhite. Black, brown, red, or yellow. Our brothers and sisters in Asia, who were colonized by the Europeans, our brothers and sisters in Africa, who were colonized by the Europeans, and in Latin America, the peasants, who were colonized by the Europeans, have been involved in a struggle since 1945 to get the colonists, or the colonizing powers, the Europeans, off their land, out of their country. (X 1995, 276–77)

Malcolm X goes on to declare that these peoples were involved in "real" revolution, revolution centered around the just liberation of land. The lack of an easily identifiable land base within the United States, however, leads to an ambiguity in goals that the national liberation struggles of the Third World escape at least partially. While the united fronts that typified these liberation struggles often included a mix of elements (nationalists, socialists, and communists among others), they could at least agree on a minimum program of national independence. In 1926, T. Thomas Fortune characterized the plight of the African American as follows: "There is no more miserable person than the one who can be said to be a man without a country" (Fortune 1973, 159). Forging political programs is tricky when people are convinced of the utter corruption of the society within which they are confined, but they do not believe that the establishment of an independent state is either desirable or pragmatic. Further, unlike the black socialists, feminists, or liberals whom we discuss later, nationalists in this category believe that blacks are severely constrained when looking for allies, particularly white allies. Not only is the proletariat considered backward and white liberals (regardless of class) hypocritical, but whites are considered to be by nature the enemies of blacks. Thus, even white feminists are considered agents of a corrupt and evil people. "Good white people," in this paradigm, are those who support the autonomous black liberation struggle. This point was made not only by Malcolm X, when he ironically argued that "good" white people were those who followed the difficult road of John Brown, or Kwame Toure (then Stokely Carmichael) when he called for good white folks to organize poor whites and leave organizing blacks to blacks, but also by Eldridge Cleaver, seen as the main proponent of alliances with whites within the Black Panthers—an organization which was itself viewed as suspiciously friendly toward whites by other nationalists.[7]

One natural extension of the position that blacks constitute a nation within a nation is the view that blacks must control the government and economic institutions of the black community. Malcolm X and other nationalists have translated the struggle for land within the context of the United States to a struggle "to gain control of the land and the *institutions that flow from that land*" (X 1995, 284; emphasis added). James Jennings advocates this position for the current period:

> Black empowerment activism, however, focuses on control of land. Indeed, the question of land control is major under a politics of empowerment. It surpasses affirmative action, job discrimination, or school integration as priorities; many Black activists I interviewed felt that control over land or urban space was much more important than other issues. Under the political umbrella of empowerment the issues that are supported focus on institutionally strengthening the Black community. . . . A third position regarding the politics of land [the other two being the African and Black Belt alternatives] and race emerged in the

7. Indeed, even at this late date, Karenga dismisses the Panthers from 1968 on as nothing more than stooges for the white left (Karenga 1993, 177).

last two decades; this position posits that Blacks should control economically and politically the land occupied in the American city. (Jennings
1992, 77–78)

Thus land becomes actualized programmatically within the nation-within-
a-nation tradition through seeing the land as spatially located within urban
black communities, as the basis for community control of black institutions,
and through the calls for reparation, which often include the Reconstruction era claim of forty acres and a mule (or their modern equivalent) and
claims to the acres of land appropriated by whites (often at gunpoint or
through government chicanery) over the past several decades. The land
that one would control in this case is literally the land under one's feet;
ownership was to be determined by use and occupation, according to one
revolutionary nationalist during the early 1970s (Baraka 1997, 154). The
process through which the black nation was to become strong enough to
enforce its claims of self-determination and land was described by Amiri
Baraka, the leader of the Congress of Afrikan Peoples in the early 1970s, as
"a cultural nation striving . . . to seize the power to become a political nation" (Van Deburg 1997, 136–37).

In addition to supporting the call for self-determination and land,
black activists in this tradition seek to take the plight of African Americans
before international bodies—typically, in the mid–twentieth century—
the United Nations. Since the founding of the United Nations, black activists have charged that blacks have been the victims of genocide and argued
that the massive human rights violations against blacks should be heard by
the United Nations under the rules that allowed colonies, territories, and
similarly oppressed peoples to bring their cases forward. Du Bois, Paul
Robeson, Malcolm X, and the Black Panther Party are just some the activists who have led such campaigns. Nationhood, sometimes implicitly, often quite explicitly, is fundamental to efforts to bring the plight of the
African American people before international bodies.

Community Nationalism?
Disillusioned Liberals and the Reality of Racism

Not all black nationalist movements, however, have been centered
around immediate concerns with liberating a territory and building a new
nation. The Reverend Eugene Rivers III, argued for a "new nationalism"
in the October/November 1995 issue of the *Boston Review:*

For more than forty years the integrationist conception of racial equality has dominated the nationalist alternative. But skin color still determines life chances; millions of blacks continue to be excluded from
American life: segregated residentially, educationally, and politically.
Moreover, racial barriers show no signs of falling, and affirmative action
is all but dead. Committed to racial equality, but faced with a segregated
existence, we need to rethink our identification of racial equality with
integration, and reopen debate about a sensible nationalist conception
for racial equality. . . . Blacks constitute a "nation-within-a-nation."
(Rivers 1995)

Rivers's nationalism, he claims, is consistent with the liberal tradition
and the project of the black quest for equality—a stance that places him
significantly outside of the tradition of Garvey. His concern is with "advancing community," and he rejects "a separatist repudiation of the American nationality." This form of nationalism can be thought to fall in the
category of ethnic nationalism, which Kiss argues embraces "a politics of
identification with and allegiance to a nation, a collectivity defined by what
its members regard as a shared descent, history, and culture." (Kiss 1996,
290). Kiss goes on to stress that this type of identity and nationalism is
highly subjective and constructive, that nationalism is given meaning by
politics and structured by politics. Nationalism, a strong historical force, is
nevertheless generally reactive to particular historical forces, particularly a
social and political order perceived as oppressive. This form of ethnic nationalism is not, however, tied to a conception of nation that has at its center a definable homeland.

The community nationalist variant of black "nationalism" enjoys
strong mass support (as we shall see). It incorporates the concept I have
called black autonomy and includes the concepts of self-determination,
black control of political and economic institutions in the black community, and the building of autonomous black organizations; it rejects separatism and withdrawal from the state, and sees itself as consistent with
black liberalism (Dawson 1994a). That this ideological constellation is associated with nationalism is clear from the data we will examine. Whether
it is truly a form of nationalism, even though it does not contain a central
concept of a black nation, is a theoretical question which will be discussed
throughout the chapter.

Rivers wants to focus black attention inward, to build strong autonomous institutions, reconstruct the indigenous black counterpublic, and

forge an independent economic, social, cultural, and political agenda. Rivers is right to say that his agenda is consistent with a broad black historical tradition that embraces equality, is not attached to integrationism, and rejects assimilation. But is it nationalism? The remainder of this chapter explores the contours of modern black nationalism as synthesized by activists, ideologues, and intellectual elites and as interpreted, embraced, and ultimately transformed by the African-American grassroots.

MODERN BLACK NATIONALISM

Black nationalism is once again a vibrant force in African-American popular culture. At the center of the popular resurgence of black nationalism in the 1980s was an iconized portrait of Malcolm X—most commonly seen in the ubiquitous display of the letter X in this nation's cities during the late 1980s. However, Malcolm X provides both an inspiration and a problem for adherents of black nationalism. Malcolm X was at the cutting edge of those attempting to construct a *political* program within a black nationalist framework, and his work inspired an entire generation of militant activists during the late 1960s and early 1970s. However, by the end of his life Malcolm X was consciously and visibly moving *away* from black nationalism as a guiding ideology. It is no accident that Malcolm inspired African-American activists with a *socialist* orientation, such as the Black Panthers and the Marxist incarnation of the Congress of Afrikan Peoples, as much as he inspired nationalists in organizations such as SNCC (Student Nonviolent Coordinating Committee) or US (Karenga's United Slaves). During the last year of his life, he even refused to allow the term "black nationalism" to be used to describe his politics (Breitman 1967). To a significant degree, Malcolm was adopting aspects of a "Third World" socialist agenda. The nature of Malcolm X's ideology during the last year of his life remains a matter of great controversy among African-American activists and intellectuals. For example, Asante (1988) attacks the idea that Malcolm ever moved away from nationalism. On the other hand black communists such as Baraka have claimed equally strenuously that Malcolm X represented a revolutionary, working-class perspective within the Black Liberation movement of the 1960s (Baraka 1991b). Perhaps his own words best summarize his position; Malcolm made the following statement in January of 1965:

> I believe that there will ultimately be a clash between those who want
> freedom, justice, and equality for everyone and those who want to con-

tinue the systems of exploitation. I believe that there will be that kind of clash, but I don't think it will be based upon the color of the skin, as Elijah Muhammad had taught it. . . . However, I do think that the European powers, which are the former colonial powers, if they're not able to readjust their thinking of superiority toward the darker-skinned people, whom they have made to think are inferior, then the lines can easily be drawn—they can easily be lumped into racial groups, and it will be a racial war. (X 1965, 216)

This move away from nationalism conflicts to a significant degree with the nationalist message found in rap songs by groups and artists such as Public Enemy, Sister Souljah, and X-Clan, and contradicts the political programs promoted by nationalist organizations such as the Nation of Islam. By the end of his life, Malcolm no longer viewed the struggle of African Americans in America as primarily a racial struggle but as part of a worldwide struggle of the "oppressed vs. the oppressor" (Breitman 1967). Consequently, we must find a model other than that provided by Malcolm X if we are to understand the political foundation of the black nationalist resurgence in popular, urban, black political thought.

Marcus Garvey provides a better model for understanding twentieth-century black nationalism, for he is the pivotal figure in its growth. As with Malcolm X, there are many competing images and interpretations of Garvey's political thought and practice. Molefi Asante in *Afrocentricity* categorically states, "Garveyism, ... was the most perfect, consistent, and brilliant ideology of liberation in the first half of the twentieth century. In no nation in the world was there a philosophical treatment of oppressed people any more creative than Garveyism." (Asante 1988). Howard-Pitney describes Garveyism as "a potent, black, civil religion promulgating the idea that there was no promising future for blacks in America." (Howard-Pitney 1990). Wilson Moses, on the other hand, depicts Garvey as a fairly orthodox descendant of nineteenth-century conservative black nationalists who "appealed to the emotions more than reason, so that for many it [Garveyism] was more of a religious than a political experience" (Moses 1978). Garvey presents an analytical problem for both his followers and detractors. Garvey led the largest secular organization in African-American history. This fact is either ignored or dismissed by his detractors due to the alleged "backwardness" of African Americans in the early twentieth century. But as Asante persuasively argues, "Garvey made sense, common sense to the people; they went for [Garvey's] position because it rang true" (Asante

1988). Critics of Garveyism need to understand what it is about his political thought that made such stringent black nationalism popular to many African Americans not only at the beginning of the twentieth century, *but also at its end.* However, supporters of Garveyism would be well advised to study his political thought from several angles in order to understand why his political program lost support and fell so quickly into organizational oblivion.

Garvey was the quintessential black nationalist: ranging in his thought from issues such as self-determination, "the highest human calling," to miscegenation (1986, 17–18), Garvey encompassed all aspects of nationalism. Africans throughout the world should have only one purpose, argued Garvey—building the African nation. And they should only look to other Africans for personal and political companionship. At one extreme (see the preceding citation regarding miscegenation) Garvey could be read as justifying lynching, and in practice did ally himself with the Ku Klux Klan on a temporary basis. This tendency for the most extreme forms of black nationalism to tactically ally themselves with the most extreme elements of white racism has always caused nationalists problems, whether it was Cuffe and his colleagues allying themselves with pro-slavery elements or Garvey speaking favorably of the Klan's views on racial separation.

One difference between Garvey and many later nationalists was his overwhelming emphasis on Africa. U.S.-based nationalists today, while often concerned with a homeland (the Republic of New Africa, for example), are often less wedded to Africa as the potential site. Malcolm X, for example, considered Africa "our Motherland" and was a champion of solidarity with African liberation movements, but still focused most of his theoretical and practical work on a program of liberation for blacks in the United States (X 1997, 110). We now turn to an analysis of the major political trends within modern black nationalism. We start with the most prominent black nationalist of the late twentieth century, Minister Louis Farrakhan of the Nation of Islam.

SPIRITUAL ROOTS: AFRICAN-AMERICAN CULTURAL NATIONALISM

Cultural nationalists emphasize the need for a return to black spiritual renewal, a return to the source, the need for metaphysical liberation as the foundation for black liberation. Knowledge of self is based on knowledge of the roots and traditions of one's own people, without which there is no spiritual, social, political, or moral advancement. Nation of Islam founder Elijah Muhammad argued this point:

> First, my people must be taught the knowledge of self. Then and only then will they be able to understand others and that which surrounds them. Anyone who does not have a knowledge of self is considered a victim of amnesia or unconsciousness and is not very competent. The lack of knowledge of self is a prevailing condition among my people here in America. Gaining the knowledge of self, makes us unite in a great unity. (Farrakhan 1989, 1)

The Cultural Nationalism of Minister Farrakhan

The denial of difference and the emphasis on racial unity present difficulties to nationalists in general and cultural nationalists in particular. Nationalists must either cite ignorance or traitorous behavior when confronted with blacks who do not subscribe to the nationalist viewpoint. That all *groups* of blacks have the same interests is fundamental to this variant of the ideology. Class divisions and gender divisions cannot produce fundamental differences because race is the category by which one's lot is determined. Blacks who act against the interests of other blacks are, therefore, traitors. And traitors are dealt with harshly according to Minister Farrakhan. A harsh nationalism is found in the minister's speech celebrating Garvey's centennial: "There's a new student coming up. He's in Howard today, he's in M.I.T. and Harvard today, he's in high school today. He looks like a bopper, but he's mean, and he's watching his counterpart in Azania preparing neckties, necklaces for the collaborators, and he's getting ideas" (Farrakhan 1989, 217).

Such discipline is the basis for the self-knowledge which leads to righteousness, and since blacks are chosen by God, they must live up to God's commands as interpreted by his prophets, and God has chosen blacks for a special mission: "Blacks are going to rule whether you like it or not. If you don't want to live under black power, then you have to get off the planet, and move quickly! But we will not rule because we are black; we will rule because God says he wants to try you now, and see how you act" (Farrakhan 1989, 230).

Here Minister Farrakhan was following the teachings of his teacher, the Honorable Elijah Muhammad, who taught an earlier generation of members of the Nation of Islam, "Allah (God) has decided to place us on top with a through knowledge of self and his guidance" (Muhammad 1997, 99). Being the chosen people demands and is linked to profound levels of self-reliance. Muhammad demands that blacks "get up and go to work for self" (Muhammad 1997, 103). Blacks must "build [their] own homes, schools, hospitals, and factories" (Muhammad 1997, 104). Such a spiritual task demands the severest discipline. Thus, one must rule through fear as God rules, and as a father rules his children. Not surprisingly, Farrakhan supports Islamic law and supports the death penalty for a wide range of sexual acts such as adultery and homosexuality. Blacks must rule and be ruled with an iron hand because of the corruptness of whites. Whites, according to Minister Farrakhan are objects of contempt: "[The] Caucasian was a vessel made for dishonor. He's like a vile olive branch grafted in. He ain't natural, he's not a natural branch, he's grafted among the peaceful people" (Farrakhan 1989, 247). Blacks can become honorable themselves only by renouncing whites and all the dishonorable aspects of white society—which is everything, since the source is polluted—and by embracing blacks. The corruptness of whites was a common theme for cultural nationalists.

Cultural nationalists' interpretation of the principle of self-determination in the great majority of cases also ruled out alliances with whites. Garvey argued that there are not any good whites: "Fundamentally, what racial difference is there between a white Communist, Republican, or Democrat?" (Ofari 1970). His answer is of course, none, although white capitalists can be used to better serve blacks, according to Garvey. But the bottom line is that one does not ally oneself with the wicked. And one only allies oneself with anyone outside of the race when it is in the interests of the race and when blacks are themselves already strongly organized. As one leading nationalist argued at a meeting of black faculty who were debating whether to support the American Indian movement during the siege at Wounded Knee in the early 1970s, "What have Indians done for us lately?"

And for nationalists, as for many other black activists, the personal is the political. Sister Souljah railed against blacks who had white friends or engaged in political work with whites: "What is the definition of a 'good white'?" I said, "There is no such thing!" (Souljah 1994, 85). She went on to say that one of the problems with interracial dating is that "the white girl represents the people who, throughout history, have caused the destruction of African culture, the African family and the African values system" (Souljah 1994, 86). For Souljah, and many similar nationalists, black authenticity is founded on both the love of black people and the complete rejection of whites.

Self-knowledge necessitates not only a rejection of whites, but also the love of self and a return to one's roots. Authentic return to a black spiritual source also means a spiritual return to Africa for many cultural nationalists, though for the Nation of Islam it means a "return" to Islam.[8] For both, Islamic and non-Islamic cultural nationalists, however, "traditional" (white) Christianity is viewed with deep suspicion. The institution of the church is often seen as dominated by hostile white institutions and their "Negro" representatives. From the beginning, the white Christian church's role is seen as facilitating the enslavement of Africans:

> The slaveholders' reasons for Christianizing the enslaved Africans
> began with their perception of Christianity as a way to reinforce and
> maintain dominance. Thus, in 1743, a white minister prepared a book of
> dialogue for slaveholders to teach enslaved Africans which stressed con-
> tentment and thanks for being enslaved and ended by saying, "I can't
> help knowing my duty. I am to serve God in that state in which he has
> placed me. I am to do what my master orders me." (Karenga 1993, 231)

Karenga, Farrakhan, and other nationalists have more ambivalent views toward the black church. They realize that historically it has played the role of the strongest independent black institution. It also provided a space for the development of a black spiritual community with some ritualistic roots in African ceremonies (Stuckey 1987). Finally, black theology also has a tradition of liberation theology, which has provided a spark and leadership for black rebellions (Cone 1991; Lincoln and Mamiya 1990; West 1982). Cultural nationalists in general, and the Nation of Islam in particular, however, are at best ambivalent about the current black church. Not only is the pacifist orientation of the church-led Civil Rights movement suspect, but black preachers are often argued to be dominated by white secular and sacred authority:

> Today, [America], as the Revelation of John prophesied, the head of the
> church (the Pope of Rome) helping her deceive Negroes and keep them

---

8. The status of Islam for blacks caused some controversy among nationalists of earlier generations; some nationalist students of African history claimed that Islam was a great destructive force of African civilizations. Williams makes this claim in his influential *The Destruction of Black Civilizations*. The strength of the Nation of Islam and the conversion of other nationalists such as Malcolm X, the former Rap Brown, and many former Panthers to the Sunni tradition has made Islam a more accepted religion not only in the black community in general, but among black nationalists as well.

in the church so that they may be destroyed with her. The only thing
that will hold the Negro is his belief in whites as a people of divinity.
They hold to his religion (Christianity), which they use to deceive
everyone they possibly can. It was through Christianity that they
got their authority over the black, brown, yellow, and red races. . . . It
is laughable and saddening to see the so-called Negro preachers reading and preaching from the Bible while they do not understand it.
(Farrakhan 1989, 27)

Karenga viewed the black church, particularly its nationalist wing, led
by ministers such as Albert Cleage of Detroit's shrine of the Black Ma-
donna, as making a particularly important contribution through the promotion of black liberation theology (Karenga 1993). These institutions
provided the foundation for rebuilding the African-American cultural and
spiritual values, which cultural nationalists see as critical.

Indeed, building uniquely black spiritual rituals, festivals, and organizations has been central to cultural and other nationalists at least since
the Garvey movement. Karenga originated the Kwanza holiday to be "very
relevant to building family, community and culture." (Karenga 1988, 31).
While it is a self-conscious synthesis, Kwanza is to provide a "cultural anchor" for "any claims of cultural authenticity." Authentic African (American) culture becomes one of the critical standards by which all acts completed by blacks, most specifically including political acts, are to be judged.
The acts of black men must be righteous because, according to Farrakhan,
blacks are the chosen people: "Whether you know it or not, Black man,
God has chosen you. . . . You are pure gold, Black man. Chosen by god,
now, to do a mighty work" (Farrakhan 1996, 65).

This understanding of disciplined self knowledge and self-determination which forms the Nation of Islam's view of the role of black men also
generated a view of politics as an extension of righteous behavior, a tool
with which to achieve the race's destiny. Politics is governed, as it is for
all nationalists and for many of the followers of the other black ideologies,
by the principle of self-determination. For nationalists, and many non-
nationalist blacks as well, political action cannot achieve the goal of self-
determination and independence unless closely linked to economic empowerment. In this realm the cultural nationalists fully agreed with other
nationalists. Farrakhan echoed Malcolm X's famous passage when he argued in his speech "Politics without Economics" that "politics without economics is symbol without substance" (Farrakhan 1989, 201). One cannot
be politically autonomous without also being economically independent.

Not surprisingly, the quest for political and economic autonomy was closely connected to the task of building strong black institutions, as it was for the majority of African Americans. Farrakhan continued in the same essay as follows: "There is both a duty and need to build autonomous black institutions, [and if] we forget that we have a duty and a responsibility to build institutions for ourselves, then we put ourselves more at the mercy of our oppressors than we were prior to 1954 and 1966" (Farrakhan 1989, 202).

Again echoing Malcolm X, Farrakhan argued that black power was necessary since African Americans shared in none of the fruits of America: "They don't treat you like a tax-paying citizen. They treat you like a piece of property, and that is all that Black people have been in America, something to be used. And now that you have no more utility, you and I are facing death in America, because the Black man and woman have become obsolete" (Farrakhan 1989, 203). Farrakhan's argument closely tracked that of Malcolm X twenty years earlier. Malcolm X, of course spoke directly to this point, as we saw in the statement quoted earlier about blacks not being diners at the table.

Black power was seen as an antiracist strategy. The emphasis on race was seen as a necessary, if not sufficient, condition for ensuring that the leaders, organizations, and strategies offered to blacks would be in the race's interest. Farrakhan's explanation was reasonably typical of that offered by many nationalists. Color comes first, but justice is more important:

> We are not racist at all, for it's better to elect a white man that is just,
> than to elect a Black man simply because he's Black if he refuses to apply
> the principles of justice and equity. So at some point we will grow to
> look beyond color [but we aren't at that point yet]. We must look at
> color first, because we have been deprived because of our color, so it is
> natural that we should want a man who is in there because of our color.
> (Farrakhan 1989, 229)

As we will see later, most blacks believe that blacks better represent blacks than whites *and* that no candidate deserves support just because they are black. While nationalists such as those from the Nation of Islam and Sister Souljah are suspicious of democracy, and those involved in fighting a war cannot afford democracy (Souljah 1994, ixv), some involvement in the electoral politics and the state are necessary both for survival and to advance the race's political agenda. Cultural nationalists, including the Nation of Islam nationally and many local forces, are increasingly entering the electoral arena (Jennings 1992). Some of these forces involved themselves in voter registration drives during the 1996 presidential election. Other nationalist forces in cities such as Chicago attempted to organize the youth, including those in gangs, to enter the electoral process in order to increase the flow of economic resources into the black community as a result of both public and private initiatives such as empowerment zones.

Political strategies are less important to cultural nationalists than to other nationalists. The political system is corrupt, and alliances are generally unwise propositions for African Americans. Politics are important to the degree that they can leverage economic and other resources for the black community. Regardless of how important politics may be to these forces, however, politics remains overwhelmingly the business of men.

The role of women for the Nation of Islam and many cultural nationalists is that of producer of the fruit of the nation and protector of its mores. The Honorable Elijah Muhammad, for example, made the following pronouncement in his foundational work, *Message to the Blackman in America:* "The Woman is man's field to produce his nation. If he does not keep the enemy out of his field, he won't produce a good nation. If we love our vegetable crops, we will go out and turn up the leaves on that vegetable stalk and look carefully for worms that are eating and destroying the vegetables. We will kill that worm—right?" (Farrakhan 1989, 37).

This view of black women demands that black men protect and embrace black women as the complement to their own existence—but not necessarily on the basis of equality. Karenga rejected the idea of gender equality. Even when equality between men and women is recognized, it is based on the understanding that men and women have different roles to play in African society. The organizers of the Million Man March emphasized the need for the men of the community to come together and take their place at the head of the family and community.

The "natural" roles of men and women in the African community mean that it is a crime, quite literally, to have relationships outside of the race or with those of the same gender. Garvey sets the tone early in the century: "But not all white men are willing to commit race suicide and to abhor their race for the companionship of another. The men of the highest morals, highest character, and noblest pride are to be found among the masses of the Negro race who love their women with as much devotion as white men love theirs" (Garvey 1986, 17–18).

Those who sleep with their own gender are equally "deviant" according to the Nation of Islam and many other nationalists. While a "nation can rise no higher than its women," according to the Honorable Elijah Muhammad, the perceived narrowness of the role of women in nationalist philosophy has been a great source of conflict between black nationalists, black feminists, and many others. Nationalists argue in return that they are rejecting white, Western, culturally imperialist notions of gender equality in order to seek a more "natural" balance between men and women in society.

While cultural nationalists reject the West and its products, other nationalists embrace some Western traditions as having producing useful tools for liberation. Many revolutionary nationalists have adopted the critique of capitalism and imperialism found in the philosophy of their sometime comrades, the black socialists.

Revolutionary Nationalism

All Power to the People! Black Power to Black People!

We repudiate the capitalist economic system. We recognize the class nature of the capitalist economic system and we recognize the dynamics involved in the capitalist system. At the same time we recognize the national character of our struggle. We recognize the fact that we have been oppressed because we are black people even though know this oppression was for the purpose of exploitation.

Eldridge Cleaver, Minister of Information
of the Black Panther Party for Self-Defense

Revolutionary nationalists were the heirs of the legacy left by Malcolm X during his last years, just as cultural nationalists are the progeny of Marcus Garvey. Revolutionary nationalists viewed the project of national liberation as one which demands relentless struggle against the structures of white supremacy within the United states, the worldwide forces of European imperialism, and the black exploiters of African Americans. While they are the heirs of a tradition solidified and reenergized by Malcolm X, the tradition itself goes back at least to Cyril Briggs and the African Blood Brotherhood. The ABB (discussed both earlier in this chapter and in more historical detail in chapter 5) would eventually become the first major source of black communists in the early twentieth century. But they, like a myriad of black leftist organizations during the following decades, started with a revolutionary nationalist ideology. Briggs stated in 1920 that the goal of the organization was to "Adopt the policy of race first, without, however, ignoring useful alliances with other groups." (Briggs 1997, 36). This policy would be adopted by other revolutionary nationalist groups later in the century, such as the Revolutionary Action Movement (RAM) of the 1960s. The ABB was perhaps the first black *organization* to advocate a "state of their own" on behalf of African Americans (Van Deburg 1997, 97).[9] While many of the original cadre came from the West Indies, the ABB also attracted native black activists such as Harry Haywood to its ranks.

The leadership of the ABB would eventually turn toward the newly established Soviet Union for theoretical guidance. During the 1960s, however, many revolutionary nationalists attempted to forge a nationalist ideology that substantially borrowed from versions of Marxism found in the Third World. Under the name of either "scientific socialism" (The Congress of Afrikan Peoples in the 1970s) or African Socialism (The African People's Revolutionary Party), they have looked historically to the Third World, particularly Africa, for revolutionary inspiration and guidance. Amilcar Cabral of Guinea-Bissau, Frantz Fannon, and Kwame Nkrumah were all African revolutionary leaders and theorists who found favor with revolutionary nationalists in the United States during the second half of the twentieth century. These leaders, as well as Asian and Latin American communists, were usually favored over European and white American leftists because the latter were alleged to have a severe lack of understanding of the place of race in shaping American society and oppressing blacks.

Self-determination and the liberation of blacks were seen as the primary goal, not proletarian revolution. Malcolm X emphasized the importance of self-determination on all fronts in virtually all of his writings: "We assert that we Afro-Americans have the right to direct and control our lives, our history, and our future rather than have our destinies determined by American racists" (X 1997, 109). The need for self-determination was linked to the need to build *black* organizations, even though support would be accepted from any honest quarter. Typical was the following passage from the "Basic Black Unity Program" of the Organization of Afro-American Unity, the organization Malcolm X was attempting to build in the last year of his life:

> We must face the facts. A 'racial' society does exist in stark reality, and not with equality for black people; so we who are non-white must meet the problems inherited from centuries of inequalities and deal with the present situations as rationally as we are able. The exclusive ethnic quality of our unity is necessary for self-preservation. We say this because:

9. Pan-Africanism is a variant of revolutionary nationalism. It has had less popular support than either cultural or revolutionary nationalism over the years. Support for Pan-Africanism among the black grassroots is directly tested in the analyses that follow.

Our experiences backed up by history show that African culture and
Afro-American culture will not be accurately recognized and reported
and cannot be respectably expressed nor be secure in its survival if we
remain the divided, and therefore the helpless, victims of an oppressive
society. (X 1997, 113–14)

He went on to state that they welcomed the support of all people of goodwill as part of the struggle, but that black organizations must be organized
along racial lines. There is a racial order within the United States (my term
again; Malcolm X's phrase is "racial society") which required, at least during that period for Malcolm, that blacks control their own organizations.

Earl Ofari, writing five years later in 1970, also argued that revolutionary nationalists had to emphasize the *national* aspects of the black struggle
because black oppression had a special character that blacks alone faced in
the United States. David Hilliard also linked the nature of the organizational form to the need for black self-determination while he was chief of
staff for the Black Panther Party: "We stand for self-determination; we
fight to let individuals and people decide their own fates. . . . We're a colony, a people with a distinct culture who are used for cheap labor. The only
difference between us and, say, Algeria, is that we are inside the mother
country" (Hilliard and Cole 1993, 140).

The Panther slogan, "Nationalist in form, socialist in action," captured well the sentiment of one significant wing of the revolutionary nationalist movements of the Black Power era. While the media and some of
the leaders of these organizations focused on the commitment of these
organizations to armed struggle, the great majority of the day-to-day work
of organizations such as the Black Panthers (before they were enmeshed
in monumental court cases) was dedicated to the type of service-oriented
community organizing with which many European socialist organizations would have felt comfortable. Some organizations, such as the African
People's Revolutionary Party, concentrated most intensely on student organizing. Others were part of broad-based united fronts oriented toward
electing the first wave of black mayors. Two central demands of revolutionary nationalists which predate Malcolm X (although he championed
both) were the demand for reparations and for bringing the subject of black
oppression before an international tribunal such as the United Nations.
Both demands were also frequently adopted by black Marxists as well as by
many black liberals and feminists.

The core of this political program, which guided many revolutionary
nationalists of this period, including many outside of the Panther Party, is

Table 3.1   Program of the Black Panther Party for self-defense

The Shadow of the Panther: The Ten-Point Program, What We Want, What We Believe

1. We want freedom. We want power to determine the destiny of our Black Community.
2. We want full employment for our people.
3. We want an end to the robbery by the capitalists of our black community.
4. We want decent housing fit for shelter of human beings.
5. We want education for our people that exposes the true nature of this decadent American society. We want education that teaches us our true history and our role in the present-day society.
6. We want all black men to be exempt from military service.
7. We want an immediate end to POLICE BRUTALITY and MURDER of black people.
8. We want freedom for all black men held in federal, state, county, and city prisons and jails.
9. We want all black people when brought to court to be tried by a jury of their peer group from their black communities, as defined by the Constitution of the United States.
10. We want land, bread, housing, education, clothing, justice, and peace. And as our major political objective, a United Nations–supervised plebiscite to be held throughout the black colony in which only black colonial subjects will be allowed to participate, for the purpose of determining the will of black people as to their national destiny.

[Followed by the Declaration of Independence]

---

expressed in their now famous Ten-Point Program. This program (see table 3.1) served as an ideological guide for political practice for dozens of organizations and was widely reprinted by groups outside of the Panthers (see Ofari 1970 for one of many examples).

After the downfall of the Black Panther Party in the early 1970s, virtually the entire revolutionary nationalist movement worked on African liberation support activities, mainly through the African Liberation Support Committee (ALSC).[10] The Panthers concentrated less on African

---

10. A long history of locally successful black activist movements extends beyond the demise of the Panthers and the Civil Rights movement well into the 1970s. This history is largely unwritten and, indeed, unknown or unrecognized by most historians of the period. The African Liberation Support Committee would be centrally featured in any such history. ALSC organizers were able to organize massive marches in support of African liberation on the continent and black liberation within the United States. Many local chapters also had impressive histories of local work. A strength of this organization was that it included a wide array of black activists and community people. Particularly active in the ALSC were black nationalists and black Marxists. Although conceived of as a broad united

liberation and more on community service programs, which included free breakfast for children, medical care, and legal service programs. At their height, the Panthers had more than thirty chapters sponsoring these programs and a newspaper with a claimed circulation of 100,000 that promoted these programs in every region of the country (Hilliard and Cole 1993). The rationale for these programs was described by Hilliard:

> We made the programs our priority. The military was second. All of it was based on an effort at socialism. We were going to show the community how to survive by using socialist ways and thinking and economics. At the same time we went and talked to the merchants and tried to talk them into supporting these programs. We were trying to create a new reality based on independence, self-reliance, self-struggle, and autonomy. (Hilliard and Cole 1993, 239)

The characterization of the black liberation struggle as one of national liberation also had important consequences for the alliance strategy pursued by revolutionary nationalists. Both the ideological orientation and pragmatic concerns demanded seeking allies outside of the black community. The most natural allies of the most disadvantaged segments of the black community were the black middle class, other people of color at home and around the world, and—perhaps potentially, but definitely last on the list—revolutionary and progressive whites. These groups often forged close alliances with radical organizations from other communities of color. The Black Panthers in the East and Midwest had strong ties to Puerto Rican radical groups, particularly the Young Lords, and also had some contact with radical groups centered in Chinatown, such as the Red Guards (Hilliard and Cole 1993; Shakur 1987). Across the country, Panthers worked with both groups of white supporters and white radical organizations such as Rising Up Angry and the Peace and Freedom Party.

While most nationalist organizations of all descriptions thought that the Panthers worked too closely with whites, there were some common themes that all revolutionary nationalists from Malcolm X on shared. First, all revolutionary nationalists followed the dictate of Malcolm X that "we must control the politics and the politicians of our community. They must

---

front, ALSC finally fell apart in most regions of the country as various organizations of all persuasions became embroiled in bitter and occasionally violent conflicts with each other and experienced severe internal disagreements as well.

no longer take orders from outside forces" (X 1965, 21). This was closely connected to the belief expressed in Malcolm X's "Declaration of Independence," that whites had to prove themselves. Further, all revolutionary nationalists strongly believed that progressive and revolutionary whites should attempt to organize in the white community—a sentiment which would earn a hearty amen not only from nationalists but from many black socialists, liberals, and feminists. One consequence of this orientation toward alliances, is that, unlike the black socialists, who often tried to build multiracial revolutionary organizations, revolutionary nationalists ranging from the Black Panther Party to the African People's Socialist Party worked with organizations of whites organized into separate support groups. Some nationalist organizations, such as the Congress of Afrikan Peoples and the Revolutionary Action Movement, were willing to ally with other revolutionary people of color, but they insisted that whites were the enemy. Some extreme versions of this strand of nationalism argued that it was better to ally with blacks who opposed black power, such as Roy Wilkins, than with even white radical lawyers who were trying to defend black nationalists from severe repression (Van Deburg 1997).

The alliance policy of the Panthers and others caused tensions among the ranks and leadership. Shakur was not alone when she described her reluctance to work with whites. Not only were there individuals in these organizations who were uncomfortable working with whites, but some chapters of the Panthers were more nationalist than others. This experience was repeated in many nationalist organizations as they adopted an increasingly socialist orientation. The experience of an exodus from the Panthers of more the more nationalist members after Cleaver's rapid expansion of coalitional activities was repeated in many nationalist organizations, such as the Congress of African Peoples, as they turned more toward Marxism.

Alliance policy was hardly the only source of tension to be found within these organizations. Several theoretical tensions contributed to inconsistencies within revolutionary nationalist organizations. There were divisions within both the movement and individual organizations over how to understand and address divisions within the black community. While they were less prone than cultural nationalists to assert an identity of interests among African Americans, they were still hesitant to identify *class* as a fundamental division within the black community. Characterizing the black liberation struggle as a national liberation struggle meant that all blacks were victims of racist hierarchy and potentially members of a united front. Thus, Malcolm X and his followers tended to characterize middle-class antagonists as racial traitors, not necessarily as class enemies of the black masses. Malcolm X's famous dictum about trusting the field Negro instead of the house Negro had more to do with the racial loyalties of each class than the class interests of either.

The type of Marxism which appealed to these organizations often varied as well with the various brands of Marxism or Leninism to be found in the Third World, all of which had proponents in the black community, sometimes within the same organization. These inconsistencies were readily apparent in practice. Shakur is just one of many former members of the Panthers and other organizations who describes fierce struggles with deadly implications about the role of violence in the black movement and the presence of tendencies which can only be characterized as gangsterism (Brown 1992; Hilliard and Cole 1993; Shakur 1987). This ideological confusion arose partly because revolutionary nationalism was often a transitional phase on the road to black socialism for organizations such as the Panthers and SNCC, which were oriented neither around Pan-African liberation (as was the African People's Revolutionary Party) nor the creation of a separate black state (as was the Republic of New Africa).

An additional source of some ideological and rampant practical tension was argument over the role that women should play within these organizations specifically, and with regard to black liberation more generally. Many of these organizations asserted the formal equality of women, as do many Marxist organizations. Malcolm X partially recanted his view on the secondary role of women when he said, in praise of Fannie Lou Hamer of the Mississippi Freedom Democratic Party, "One does not have to be a man a to fight for freedom; all you have to be is an intelligent human being" (X 1965, 135). A deep distrust of women, however, can be still found in *The Autobiography of Malcolm X*. Consistent emphasis on masculine styles of leadership, the encouraging of a "warrior" culture, the public and pronounced misogyny of prominent leaders (ranging from the physical abuse of women to pronouncements by SNCC and Panther leaders that the role of women was best exercised in bed) led to the frequent demoralization of women in these organizations, the continual exodus of many the most talented women, and a consistent gap in theory and practice (Brown 1992; Giddings 1984; Shakur 1987). While many talented women remained to work with and lead, the tensions due to sexist theory and practice within these organizations was never resolved and contributed to the downfall of most of them.

A final source of tension was to be found outside of the revolutionary nationalist movement. The revolutionary and cultural nationalists engaged in what could fairly be termed a war which led to the death of several cadres and which still simmers a generation later. Revolutionary nationalists argued, as did Black Panther leader Huey Newton, that "culture itself will not liberate us. We're going to need some stronger stuff" (Ofari 1970). Ofari made one of the more class-based critiques of cultural nationalists, arguing that they represented the interests of a backward black business class which acted as the agent of an exploitative white corporate power structure (Ofari 1970). Cultural nationalists continued to argue just as fiercely that revolutionary nationalists were the dupes of white leftists out to subvert the black liberation movement. These divisions, which were actively encouraged by the COINTELPRO program of the FBI, contributed to the lack of a united nationalist movement after the death of Malcolm X in 1965. J. Edgar Hoover, director of the FBI, took a personal interest and targeted militant nationalist organizations for disruptive, often violent, activities. His definition of dangerous black nationalist organizations is stunning in its expansiveness. For example, he lumped together by name SNCC, King's SCLC, RAM, the moderate liberal organization CORE, and the Nation of Islam (Van Deburg 1997).

During the early 1970s, as the revolutionary nationalist movement came under fierce attack, nationalists were shifting in different directions. The shift that many individuals and organizations made toward black Marxism is described in fuller detail in chapter 5; the foundations for what would become by the 1990s community nationalism were established during this period. One component of this new, pragmatic nationalism was a deepening involvement with electoral institutions. Community control demanded control over not only the economic institutions of the black community but the politicians and political institutions as well. Black Power advocates during this era saw transforming the American state as a central task for African-American politics, and reformist electoral politics would not be sufficient. A critical meeting of activists and politicians came together in Gary, Indiana, in 1972, and the declaration from this convention proclaimed, "A major part of the challenge we must accept is that of redefining the functions and operations of all levels of American government, for the existing governing structures . . . are obsolescent" (National Black Political Convention 1997, 141). To lead such an assault on the "racist" state, one needed an independent black political party. Such a party would enjoy substantial support today, as we shall see. In 1970, nationalists defined such a party, which was to be the organizational formation for building the black nation: "What we are talking about is a national, international, nationalist, Pan-Africanist political party which will be the model for the nation becoming." (Baraka 1997, 145). Again the electoral connection was to be in the service of community control of resources, not careerist politicians: "You must control everything in the community that needs to be controlled. Anything of value: any kind of antipoverty program, politicians, celebrities, anything that brings money, resources into your community, you should control it. You understand that? Anything of value in your community, you have to control it, because if you don't control it, the white boy controls it" (Baraka 1997, 149).

While militant in tone, the electoral push by many nationalists was connected to a defensive shift toward a more pragmatic and more conservative nationalism. By the late 1960s, blacks in liberal civil rights organizations such as CORE and SNCC had become disillusioned and shifted toward nationalism. While SNCC cadres such as Kwame Toure embraced a revolutionary Pan-Africanism, CORE activists embraced a more conservative separatism that emphasized economic development. Roy Innis, the CORE leader, called in 1969 for a new social contract that would give blacks peaceful control of their own communities, "Separation," he argued, "is a more equitable way of organizing society" (Innis 1997, 178). This was economic nationalism with teeth; Innis, for example, explicitly discussed the need to control the public budgets in black communities, a significant set of resources.

A more direct form of economic revitalization was closely linked to the form that the reparations movement took during this period. The demand for reparations for blacks has been prominent during several periods of American history; today, for example, several cities—including the District of Columbia, Chicago, Detroit, and Cleveland—have passed resolutions supporting reparations as a result of black popular pressure (Van Deburg 1997). Reparation has been a central theme in black political life. James Forman led a major drive for reparations during the late 1960s which enjoyed some limited success. The scope of the program included an African development component, support for African national liberation movements, a Black Anti-Defamation League, support for black universities, the establishment of jobs, community communication centers, and support for National Welfare Rights Organization, and the establishment of a black strike fund of $20,000,000 in 1970 dollars. The entire demand was for half a billion dollars. Reparation has been the quintessential black demand for arousing broad and deep support among blacks and hostility among whites. While the movement soon died out as Foreman and others moved in other directions, the demand for reparations has survived as a component of black public discourse and community nationalist ideology to the end of the twentieth century.

The revolutionary nationalist movement as well as the black Marxist movement all but collapsed during the 1970s. Both revolutionary wings of the black liberation movement received significant attention from the police agencies of the state. The combination of internal dissension, repression, and the lack of support in the black communities for strategies tied to violent revolution all contributed to the decline of this movement. While some revolutionary nationalist organizations, such as the African People's Socialist Party, continued their work in this period, the revolutionary nationalist movement ceased to be a national, organized force in black politics by the end of the 1970s. What dominated the non-Islamic nationalist movement of the 1990s was a synthesis of some of the elements of revolutionary nationalism, Pan-Africanism, and cultural nationalism.

Community Nationalism in the 1990s

An affirmation of self-determination and unified commitment to self-sufficiency through economic and human development; political empowerment; and international policy and development by African Americans in the interest of people of African descent throughout the African world community, our youth, and future generations.

Preamble of "The Manifesto of the Million Man March"

What I label community nationalism, which Jennings ably describes but labels "black empowerment politics," combines elements of both revolutionary and cultural nationalism (Jennings 1992). The class divisions are gone; indeed, black business entrepreneurs have pride of place, as they do in the ideology of the Nation of Islam. Business is seen as the key to black economic development, and political development without economic development is considered nonsense. Politics, however, has not totally disappeared. Electoral campaigns are waged to gain political as well as economic control of the institutions and resources of the black community. The concept of self-determination is strongly supported even if, as alluded to earlier, the concept of nation has a very ambiguous status. Ties to Africa are once again featured as a central part of the nationalist program. Black liberation at home cannot be separated on any level from the liberation of Africans throughout the world. There are strong antiliberal elements in this program. Women are decidedly not equal in theory or practice.

One organization in Chicago that followed these tenets targeted for ouster every black incumbent woman in the city council. The "Manifesto of the Million Man March" in each section of its program has a section outlining the duties of black men. No such section exists anywhere in the document which outlines the duties of black women. Those who disagree with the program of community nationalists, either locally or, as we saw with the critics of the Million Man March, nationally, are labeled as traitors to the race.

The document which outlines the programmatic aims of this ideology is the "Manifesto of the Million Man March" (Starks 1995). A central theme of the document is economic self-sufficiency. Business is the key element emphasized in the economic plan. Curiously, a job program is not mentioned, let alone developed anywhere within the manifesto, even though the central policy demand of the black community for nearly two decades has been for increased employment opportunities (Dawson 1994a, 1995). The only mention of a "trade union" policy concerns diasporic *trading* unions designed to promote trade and business among people of African descent. The long history of black critical engagement in trade unions is not reflected anywhere in the document.

The leading role that black men are to play in the process of building the black community is considered critical. "We mandate that all black men through the entire African World Community in cooperation with Black women take immediate control of our communities as First Priority" is typical of the emphasis on the leading role envisioned for black men. Community control and self-determination demand loyalty. Just as Pan-African nationalists attempted to ban black Marxists from their African liberation activities a generation earlier, blacks with loyalties outside of the black community are to be shunned. The statement that "[black] loyalty must stand above any party, organization, institution, individual, or group outside of the African World Community," from the Million Man March manifesto is very similar to the position taken by one nationalist organization in organizing the efforts for a National Black United Front in 1980: "It would probably be wise to allow for a period of consolidation of Pan-Afrikan forces before the front is exposed to other tendencies" (Starks 1995; Document A 1980). Another nationalist organization argued in 1980 that only organizations that were 60 percent black should be allowed to join a Black United Front (Document B 1980). Cultural authenticity is critical as well. The manifesto argues that "throughout the entire African World Community, . . . we are pledged to the establishment of African cultural dominance within individual communities. We are willing to reaffirm the uniqueness of our culture and take the best of its traditions" (Starks 1995).

Most of the policy positions in the manifesto are widely supported within the black community. It outlines a program of community control of the black community, electoral actions designed to maximize black empowerment, support for black businesses, and the defense of both affirmative action and antidiscrimination programs. The strong thrust to build autonomous black institutions within the black community is also strongly supported within the black community, as we shall see. This version of community nationalism has more of a separatist aspect than the one proposed by Rivers (discussed earlier in this chapter), but it has more in common with historical nationalist antecedents than does Rivers' version. This version also has the support of more organizational forces actively attempting to implement it. Community nationalism is likely to continue enjoy very strong support and provide a challenge and alternative to black liberalism for the foreseeable future.

But who supported community nationalism in the 1990s? The next section begins the empirical analysis by probing more deeply the question, Who are the black nationalists?

WHO ARE THE BLACK NATIONALISTS?

We return now to the question we began to explore in Chapter 2, considering it from a variety of viewpoints. We will address the question of which African Americans fit the profile of the committed black nationalist. Historically, we have seen two ways that African Americans have conceptualized a black nation. First, there is the relatively well supported notion that blacks constitute a nation within a nation. As we saw, half of the modern black community agrees with the statement that blacks constitute an internal black nation and not "just another ethnic group." When combined with the other principles of black nationalism, we find that 20 percent of African Americans agree with this version of nationalism, which combines the perspective of a separate people and the need to control and build autonomous black institutions.[11] This form of nationalism is not particularly gendered. Approximately 20 percent of both men and women support the "people" oriented definition of nationhood.

Not surprisingly, there is much less support among African Americans for the separatist version of black nationalism. Only 10 percent of blacks support all elements of this version of the ideology. Further, this

---

11. See appendix table A3.1 for question wording, the items which compose the scale, and the statistical properties of the scale.

Figure 3.1 Smoothed Black Nationalism distribution using normal and Epanechinikov estimators

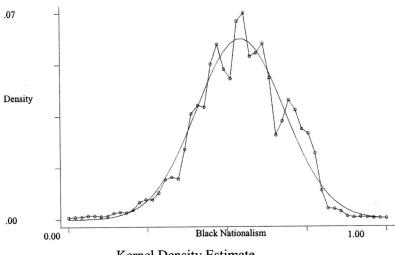

Kernel Density Estimate

	Observations	Mean	Std. Deviation	Minimum	Maximum
Black Nationalism	1,072	0.54	0.15	0	1

Source: 1993–1994 National Black Politics Survey

version is gendered with a small but statistically significant gap between men and women. Black men support the separatist version of black nationalism slightly more than black women.

The distribution of black autonomy shown in Figure 3.1 indicates that there is very little hard opposition to, and only modest hard support for, black autonomy. However, the position of the mean (.54) indicates that there is broad support for a moderate position in favor of controlling, building, and supporting institutions in the black community. As a reminder, what we found in Chapter 2 was that black nationalism was strongly present in black public opinion, but that it took the form labeled here as community nationalism. Neither the nation-within-a-nation nor separate nation items are found to cohere successfully with the other items of "community nationalism," which I have labeled the black autonomy orientation in the appendix material (table A3.1).

THE ANTECEDENTS AND CONSEQUENCES OF CONTEMPORARY BLACK NATIONALISM

The purpose of this section and its counterparts in the following chapters is not to develop a "true" model of support for black nationalism or the ideologies analyzed in later chapters, but to initiate an assessment of the effects of black ideologies such as black autonomy and structural factors such as concentrated poverty on some components of black public opinion (see King 1989 for a discussion of the problems involved in trying to model "truth"). Consequently, a set of basic controls described in the appendix is used to model the effects of black nationalism (and in later chapters, the other ideologies) on components of black public opinion. All of variables as well tables of results appear in the appendix (tables A3.1 and A3.2). The controls are included to provide greater confidence that we can first isolate the effects of social structure on the likelihood of support for a nationalist (or other) ideology, and then isolate the effects of espousing such an ideology on black public opinion and political preferences.

First, we probe the effect of one's location in various social structures on ideological belief. Next, given that the political effects of rap are germane in the arena of black nationalism, we explore the effects of exposure to rap music on the likelihood of supporting black nationalism. Then we analyze the effects of black nationalist beliefs on black public opinion. Finally, we consider the implications for American politics of large shifts in the percentage of African Americans that support nationalism.

Social Structure and Black Political Ideologies

In this section we asses the role of social structure in fostering support for black autonomy. The sets of variables described in Chapter 2 measuring the structural factors of social location, spatial position, and ties to black information networks are included. To review, social location is measured through indicators of gender, family income, education, and age. Spatial situation is represented through indicators of concentrated poverty and degree of neighborhood segregation. Ties to black information networks are measured through an index of exposure to black news and artistic products. Also included are measures which tap the degree to which blacks believe that their fate is linked to that of other African Americans and the degree to which whites are perceived to be faring economically better than blacks. I showed in detail elsewhere that blacks' belief that their fate is tied to that of other blacks serves as a powerful component of racial identity (Dawson 1994a). I also argued that the historic economic subordination of African Americans has helped to forge blacks' relative assessment of black/white economic status into another powerful influence on black public opinion. The perceptions that one's fate was linked to the race and that whites were faring better than blacks both had a radicalizing effect across a variety of domains. They are included here as general factors likely to shape black ideological orientations. Finally, Sanders (1995b) has decisively shown that perceptions of the race of the interviewer shapes how respondents filter and understand the political terrain of the interview process. The coding for these variables is provided in appendix table A1.1.

The beliefs that one's fate is linked to that of other blacks and that blacks are worse off economically than whites, integration into black information networks, and youthfulness all increased the likelihood of supporting black autonomy (regression results can be found in table A2.1). One surprising result is that, in contrast to the findings of earlier research (Dawson 1994a), income was not a strong predictor of this orientation.[12] On the other hand, the importance of the perception of the belief that one's fate is linked to that of the race replicates results achieved using earlier studies and further confirms the theoretical importance of this variable for modeling black public opinion. Believing that one's fate is linked to that of the race is a powerful predictor of support for all of the black ideologies except black conservatism. Political ideology, for blacks, is tied strongly to black racial identity. If one views race as a factor in determining one's chances in life, then one is more likely to view the political world through oppositional political lenses.

More specifically, a *nationalist* view of the political world is also tied to how embedded one is within black information networks. The importance of exposure to black information networks is consistent with the claim made earlier that those who had a nationalist-like orientation had reasonable access to black information conduits. Black discourse encourages both nationalism and its surprisingly close ideological cousin, disillusioned liberalism. Black nationalism is particularly embedded within black discourses and communities, and it is the only ideology for which membership in a black organization is a significant predictor.

---

12. Comparison of the indicators of black autonomy and black nationalism in the NBPS and the 1984–1988 National Black Election Panel Study suggests that the increase in support comes primarily from a shift among affluent blacks.

If *embeddedness* within black society encourages nationalist perspectives, then there is at least suggestive evidence that *alienation* from mainstream (i.e., white) American society also encourages nationalist ideology. That the young are most likely to lean toward autonomy is consistent with the perceptions of observers of black culture who claim that black youth are disaffected with American society and provide a fertile ground for nationalist appeals. Indeed, the change in the importance of class as a predictor of nationalist sentiments can be explained with the same logic. The shift of affluent black Americans into the camp of the racially disillusioned explains why class is no longer a significant predictor of black nationalism. In the early 1990s after a number of traumatic national events, the black middle class became politically similar to their less affluent cousins. (Bobo et al. 1995; Dawson 1996). As racial discontent spreads across groups within the black community, so does support for black community nationalism.

Community Nationalism, Rap Music, and Black Public Opinion

This section addresses the effect that exposure to and support for rap music have on support for community nationalism. It is necessary to jointly model exposure to rap and support for community nationalism since those who are nationalists may prefer rap music, and rap music may simultaneously encourage black nationalism. We start with the determinants of increased exposure to rap. The results are displayed in table A2.18. Age is by far the strongest predictor of exposure to rap. Rap is the music of the young. At the extremes of the adult age range, an eighteen-year-old is 76 percent more likely to have listened to rap than someone in her nineties.[13] Even a thirty-year-old is at least 20 percent more likely than a fifty-five-year-old African American to have recently listened to rap. A few other indicators have modest effects on exposure to rap music. Women are 7 percent less likely than men to have listened to rap. The number of years of education is also negatively associated with likelihood of listening to rap. Those who believe their fate is linked to that of other blacks are slightly more likely to have listened to rap, although in this case the direction of causation is more difficult to pin down.

---

13. The percentages discussed in the text were obtained by converting logit coefficients to probabilities.

The next set of results illuminates the effects that both the exposure to and approval of rap have on the formation of black public opinion. One central question is whether rap promotes black nationalism. As discussed earlier, political rap in particular is often identified with black nationalism. First, we must answer the following question: Do people who are black nationalists seek out rap, or does approval of rap make one more likely to adopt black nationalism, or do rap and black nationalism simultaneously constitute each other? The simultaneous equation analyses described in table A2.20 show convincingly that those who approve of rap are more likely to adopt community nationalism; however, those who uphold a nationalist ideology are no more likely to approve of rap than their non-nationalist cousins. This should not be a surprising result. While rap musicians such as Sister Souljah, Paris, X-Clan, PE, and Brand Nubian all consciously promoted nationalism as an ideology, and artists such as Ice Cube implicitly advanced nationalist sentiments, many nationalist activists and leaders have voiced strong criticism of rap music, particularly gangsta rap. Nationalist leaders and writers such as Minister Farrakhan of the Nation of Islam and Haki Madhubuti consistently argue that black men should show greater "respect" for black women (Farrakhan 1989, 1996; Madhubuti 1994). Indeed, Madhubuti makes a number of impassioned pleas which argue that men must be an integral part of building an antirape culture and combat the pervasive misogyny in the black community. Similarly, Bakari Kitwana worries that gangsta rap in particular not only promotes violence against and disrespect for black women, but can also contribute to the genocidal levels of violence suffered by black men at each others' hands (Kitwana 1994). On the other hand, the relatively constant, if not consistent, message from numbers of rap songs promoting the attitude that "we should control our thang" does seem to correspond with a modest increase in the probability of supporting community nationalism. Thus, when we try to assess the effect of rap on black public opinion, we can be confident that it is not an indirect proxy for support for community nationalism. As many supporters confidently predicted and rap's detractors feared, appreciation for rap encourages support for black nationalism.

The strongest predictor of belief that rap represents an important information source for the black community is, not surprisingly, exposure to rap. Those who have listened to the music are nearly 40 percent more likely to support the positive view of rap. The young are also, not surprisingly, more likely to reject the belief that rap represents a destructive force in the black community. Exposure and age are the only two significant predictors of approval of rap music. Rap is not particularly the music of an alienated middle class, nor the province of the most disadvantaged segments of the black community.

Appreciation of rap increases support for a number of items that are correlated with support of black nationalism. Rap artists such as Paris and Public Enemy sprinkle their cuts with praise for Louis Farrakhan. Farrakhan's speeches are often sampled for use in many groups' materials. Both exposure to and appreciation for rap increase the likelihood of supporting Farrakhan by 16 percent. Supporters of rap are also slightly more likely to support teaching black children African languages.

The great majority of the politically oriented rap groups have very violent antipolice songs, but this theme is not confined to political rap. Groups on the border of political and gangsta rap such as Ice T, Ice Cube, Geto Boys, and the NWA all have had songs that show the most extreme contempt for the police. This theme transcends subgenres and is prevalent in the rap of artists such as LL Cool J who are not closely identified with gangsta rap (Rose 1994). Thus it is predictable that greater exposure to rap increases the probability by 10 percent that African Americans believe police to be part of the problem of violence in the black community and not part of the solution. This is a result likely to reinforce the beliefs of those who see rap as the authentic voice of the most disadvantaged and those alienated members of the black community who "tell it like it is," the CNN of the inner city, to use Chuck D's phrase, as well as the beliefs of critics from the *right*, such as police organizations and other government officials who worry that rap incites the black community to commit acts of violence against the police.

Those who believe that rap music provides an information source for the black community are also nearly 10 percent more likely to think it is necessary for blacks to form an independent political party than those who do not.[14] On the other hand (in analyses not displayed in table A2.6), neither approval of nor exposure to rap has an impact on the probability that blacks believe in a separate nation. Support for a separate black nation is confined to a sufficiently small proportion of the black community as to remain unaffected by rap, unlike other indicators that are correlated with support for black nationalism. Be that as it may, exposure to rap leads to a

14. In all cases exposure to rap had similar effects to beliefs that rap played an important role as a communication medium in the black community. While the sizes of the effects were similar, we should remember that these are direct effects and do not take into account the indirect contribution that exposure to rap has, since it is also a predictor of the approval of rap.

view of society where the problems of Americans are not only defined by race, but the solutions to these problems are to be found within the ideology of black nationalism.

Finally, the results displayed in the appendix show that rap does not affect how blacks feel toward whites. Equally surprising, given the notoriety of lyrics such as Ice Cube's and Geto Boys' anti-Asian rhymes, rap does not affect black attitudes toward immigrants except indirectly to the degree that it increases support for community nationalism (which does directly predict anti-immigrant attitudes). Similarly, exposure to rap music does not directly affect whether one believes that other people of color and poor people generally make suitable allies for African Americans. There is a mixed message in much of rap concerning other people of color. Blacks and Latinos are often linked in descriptions of the unfairness and harshness of ghetto life, while Asians are routinely demonized as oppressors of blacks only one step above the level of whites. While rap plays a limited role in shaping African-American acceptance of various political ideologies and black political attitudes, a more powerful role in shaping black political attitudes can be attributed to the ideology of community nationalism.

Community Nationalism and Black Separatism

Not surprisingly, black autonomy is the best predictor of support for the components of more separatist forms of black nationalism. Community nationalism provides a base for these more separatist-grounded variants. Black autonomy has strong links to black nationalism. For example, moving from the low to high end of the black autonomy scale increases the probability of supporting the formation of a black political party by 88 percent. Moving from one end of the scale to the other raised one's warmth toward Minister Farrakhan of the Nation of Islam 34 degrees, while reducing one's warmth toward whites by 16 degrees. Black community nationalism leads directly and strongly to support for many of the more separatist policies that black nationalists have historically espoused.

Table A2.2 in the appendix shows that support for both the nation-within-a-nation and separate-nation perspectives is closely predicted by support for black autonomy. When included in the estimation, the ideological construct of black autonomy overwhelms all the other predictors except for being tied to black information networks in the case of support for the nation-within-a-nation thesis. Similarly, table A2.6 shows that those with the autonomy orientation are much more likely to believe that

Africa is African Americans' "special homeland." While not equivalent to black nationalism, black autonomy strongly predicts support for many of the core components of traditional black nationalism.

Another central component of black nationalism is the belief that blacks should control and build the economic institutions of the black community. A two-item scale comprising support for shopping at black stores and control over the economic institutions of the black community was constructed (this scale has a relatively strong alpha reliability of .62, (see table A3.2 for details). By far the strongest predictors of support for economic nationalism are the perception that whites are better off financially than blacks and being embedded in black information networks (see table A2.3). Believing that one's fate is linked to that of the race and belonging to an organization working on behalf of blacks are also strong predictors of support for economic nationalism. Again the combination of racial consciousness with being embedded in black networks and organizations provides the best predictor of support for various forms of black autonomy and nationalism (Dawson 1994a). All of the progressive ideologies—black Marxism, black feminism, and radical egalitarianism—correspond to a greater likelihood of support for economic nationalism, but by far the strongest ideology predicting economic nationalism was disillusioned liberalism (see table A2.4). As we shall see, disillusioned liberals are extremely similar in their preferences to community nationalists.

The effects of support for black autonomy on black nationalism are extremely consistent, robust, and powerful. Remember, these effects are reported after controls for age, income, education, race of interviewer, racial identity, and the other structural measures have been added to each equation.

With one exception, black feminism has a weak effect on indicators of black nationalism. In contrast to supporters of black autonomy, those with black feminist orientations are more likely to reject the view that the status of African Americans should be characterized as that of a nation within a nation. Black conservative orientations, on the other hand, have a consistent but moderate effect on indicators of black nationalism. Black conservatives are significantly more likely to reject nationalism than other blacks, and more likely to feel warmth toward whites than other blacks. In political conflicts around black nationalism, conservatives and those who support independent black institutions often find themselves on opposite sides of the conflict.

Community Nationalism and Black Public Opinion

In turn, community nationalism has a wide range of effects on other ideologies and black public opinion, as well as on the core components of the nation-oriented components of black nationalism (see tables A2.5–A2.8). For example, adherents of community nationalism clashed with the adherents of black feminism over the question of whether the disease AIDS is the result of an antiblack conspiracy. Those oriented toward nationalism believed this was true, while those with feminist positions were more likely to see AIDS as resulting from tragic natural causes. An increase in community nationalism would lead to even greater belief in the existence of antiblack conspiracies. Bear in mind that the consistent revelations about government misdeeds in the black community, ranging from the medical crimes of the Tuskegee experiments to the FBI's COINTELPRO operations during the Civil Rights and Black Power era, and the wide coverage of possible CIA involvement in crack distribution in the black community periodically serve to reinforce the belief in such conspiracies across a wide range of African Americans who hold a variety of ideological orientations.

Black nationalism has scattered effects on black public opinion (see the appendix for the full set of analyses). The effects of the ideologies in general are more scattered when looking broadly at black opinion, although orientations toward black autonomy again play an impressively consistent role in shaping black opinion. Those with black autonomy orientations tend to reject the view that whites can represent black districts as well as blacks. For most African Americans, descriptive representation is still a necessary if not sufficient requirement for substantive representation.[15] As expected, those with autonomy orientations were more likely to believe American society is unfair (as do the great majority of African Americans). Black feminists were more likely to reach out to other groups in order to form coalitions, while those with orientations toward autonomy were more likely to reject the idea that immigrants should have an equal chance at jobs. Those who supported black autonomy were also more likely to see America's large corporations as unfair to blacks.

Black ideological orientations had powerful effects in shaping black public opinion. The effect of views toward black autonomy were particularly consistent in broadly shaping black opinion, while orientations toward

---

15. The raw marginals indicate that 65 percent of respondents believed that blacks best represent majority black districts, and 35 percent believed that whites could potentially do as well.

the other ideologies had greater and more consistent effects, as we shall see, within specific domains.

Political Implications of Ideological Shifts

The importance of black political ideologies can be further demonstrated by considering how far key items of black opinion shift as a result of shifts in the underlying ideological structures. Large shifts in support of forming an independent black political party have been observed in the early 1990s. Between 1988 and the end of 1993, support for an independent black political party doubled to 50 percent after declining during the preceding decade (this represented a shift of approximately two-thirds of a standard deviation). Even more radical shifts of black public opinion have been observed. Bobo and his colleagues observed shifts of a standard deviation among upper-income blacks between the period immediately preceding and immediately following the Simi Valley verdict. The verdict was seen by many blacks as absolving the police officers involved in beating Rodney King. The shifts across the black community were in the direction of becoming more alienated, more convinced that America was a racially unjust society, and more convinced that remaining racial inequalities were due to racial discrimination (Bobo et al. 1995).

Shifts in black public opinion can be induced either by "shocking" events such as the Simi Valley verdict or as a result of somewhat more gradual shifts in the structure of black ideologies. The political implications of the second type of shift can be seen by showing the effects of shifts in black ideology on selected components of black public opinion.[16]

The results suggest that shifts in black autonomy can have large effects on black public opinion, even when we control for a large number of other factors. Shifting by one standard deviation causes support for formation of a black political party to increase by 15 percent (see table A2.9). Even a shift of half of a standard deviation (not displayed here) causes shifts of 7–8 percentage points in mean support for a black political party. Shifts in black autonomy cause substantial if not as spectacular shifts in a number of other variables of political significance. A black community that is solidly in favor of an independent black political party, becomes even more

16. These proportions were obtained by first estimating probit equations using the variables that produced the estimates in appendix. Then the estimates (using the original probit coefficients) were recalculated after inducing a shift in black autonomy ranging from −1 to +1 standard deviations. The probabilities were then obtained using the cumulative distribution function; see table A2.9.

anti-immigrant, more solidly antipolice, and more solidly conceives of itself as a separate nation with a shift of one standard deviation in black autonomy. Although sizable, such shifts can be found in contemporary black opinion. Shifts in support of black autonomy would cause both the broadest and deepest effects on black public opinion.

CONCLUSION

Black nationalism's likely future and its impact on black and American politics are examined in the conclusion of this book, but some things need to be said even at this early point. Black nationalism not only has a long and prominent history in black political thought and practice, but remains, particularly in its "community nationalism" variant, a strong force in black politics and public opinion. Black nationalism grows in force when the nation is perceived to have turned its back on blacks. This period clearly falls in that category. Black nationalism has become a pervasive influence in black life. Black nationalism is embedded in the music, journals, magazines, and cyberspace networks of the black community.

Many aspects of black nationalism fall outside of the liberal tradition, a factor that mainstream scholars of race tend to ignore. Some of the antiliberal aspects of some forms of black nationalism present dangers to the black community. One of dangers is that those "motivated by ethnic nationalism can come to believe that only members of their own groups should have any moral claim, or be entitled to political voice" (Kiss 1996, 293). This is a problem that was found for example in some of the teachings of Elijah Muhammad. For the Honorable Elijah Muhammad, not "all human beings have the same basic moral status"; the white race and its works were evil (Kiss 1996, 296; Muhammad 1997). More subtly, it is important to avoid what Calhoun calls the "pseudo-democracy of sameness" (Calhoun 1994, 327). As black feminists and others have argued, the nationalist impulse has produced both the reality and the illusion of shared interests and unity, but it has also served to mask severe disagreements over strategy, tactics, and goals within the black community. Truly democratic discourse must acknowledge these differences and allow for a politics of difference as well as one of unity.

Nevertheless, some aspects of black nationalism, including that of community nationalism, continue to garner enduring support. While it may be possible, as Calhoun (1994) would have us believe, to build a diverse society without needing either communism or nationalism to bind the society, both black nationalism and its black leftist and feminist cousins have the potential for a strong political base as long as an oppressive racial order assigns blacks to the bottom of multiple hierarchies. Just as nationalism has inspired peoples throughout the world in the modern era, black nationalist rhetoric continues to be able to mobilize African Americans. Black nationalist themes still find resonance in black communities within the United States, as they have periodically throughout the twentieth century. This is true, though support for the more separatist strands has dissolved. It is no coincidence that some aspects of the manifesto of the Million Man March were very similar to the set of recommendations that Harold Cruse had outlined for the black community a generation earlier. But we should not forget that Cruse was not only calling for the economic revitalization of the black community through a program of economic nationalism where blacks became "owners" and not merely producers; he also encouraged what today we would call a revitalization of black civil society and a more energetic set of black public discourses (Cruse 1967, 84). Indeed, the type of "liberal" nationalism that Rivers (1995) calls for would require both a vigorous civil society and a democratic black counterpublic. It would be akin, perhaps, to some of the allegedly liberal nationalisms that can be found in other parts of the world. Sadly lacking, however, in some other, more popular, modern black nationalisms is Cruse's commitment to a vigorous, democratic, black public sphere. Nevertheless, the continuing strength of black nationalism as an ideology as well as a political force should vividly remind us of the complicated contours of black political thought.

While our men seem thoroughly of the times on almost every other
subject, when they strike the woman question they drop back into
sixteenth century logic.

Anna J. Cooper

I came to the conclusion before our relations ended that our white
women friends were not willing to treat us on a plane of equality
with themselves.

Ida B. Wells

CHAPTER 4

A Vision of Their Own:
Identity and Black Feminist Ideology

Celia, a black girl of fourteen, was purchased by Robert Newsome in
the state of Missouri. As Higginbotham reports, Celia was "repeatedly
raped" and by the time she was nineteen she was ill, had one child, and was
pregnant (Higginbotham 1992). When Newsome tried to once again rape
her in June of 1855, she protested and stated she would defend herself.
When he ignored her and continued his attempt, she defended herself and
killed Newsome. By Missouri law at the time, *any* woman had the right to
defend herself. Other Missouri statutes explicitly specified racial differences
using terms such as "white female" or "Negro" women, but Missouri's rape
statute referred only to "women" without specifying race. In order to find
her guilty and uphold her death sentence, Higginbotham argues, the state
court had to find that as a slave woman, she did not fall into the category

of "woman." She was hung in December of 1855 after the still birth of her child. Not just Celia's race, nor just Celia's gender, but the combination of her status as woman and slave put Celia in a special hell especially produced for black women by the evil legacy of American slavery.

Black feminists and others argue that this legacy continues with us today. Precisely such abhorrent crimes led many antebellum black women, such as Harriet Tubman, Maria Stewart, and Sojourner Truth, to use every means at their disposal to combat slavery at least as fiercely as their better known male brethren such as Frederick Douglass and Henry Highland Garnet. Indeed, Tubman's contributions as a military leader during the Civil War and as leader of the underground railroad surpassed in ferocity the contributions of her abolitionist brethren. Her leadership of the campaign near the Combahee River in South Carolina freed 750 slaves and inspired the naming of a critically important black feminist collective of the early 1970s.

Half a century later Ida B. Wells was following in the footsteps of her foremothers—fighters such as Harriet Tubman and Sojourner Truth. Wells was one of the most articulate, innovative, militant, and *effective* black activists in American history. T. Thomas Fortune, prominent newspaper editor and black activist from the turn of the century, described Wells in glowing terms. But Fortune was cautious and worried that she would not receive proper recognition.

For Wells, whose political theory was several decades ahead of most of her contemporaries, who led an international lynching campaign that decisively contributed to the ending of lynching in three states, who started settlement house work among African Americans in Chicago, and was a pioneering newspaper editor in Memphis, is hardly known today, even in the city that became her home. As far as most Chicagoans know, including black Chicagoans, the only legacy that Wells has left us is a very run down public housing project. Why isn't Wells enshrined in both the pantheon and canon of black leaders and theorists?

The puzzle goes deeper. In his great work *Dusk of Dawn*, W. E. B. Du Bois explained that Wells was one of only two activists from the Niagara Movement who were not invited to be founding members of the NAACP. He stated: "All save Trotter and Ida Wells Barnett came to form the backbone of the new organization." We know that Trotter was too nationalistic to join the interracial NAACP, but we are not told why Wells was not invited. She had extensive experience working with whites on both sides of the Atlantic. Holt, however, finds a more telling quotation from Du Bois concerning Wells and the NAACP. Du Bois chillingly stated, "Nothing more than membership was expected of her in the NAACP" (Holt 1982b, 52). She faced opposition from other quarters as well. When she was elected financial secretary of the Afro-American Council in 1904, the *Colored American* newspaper stated: "We are compelled to regard her election . . . as an extremely unfortunate incident. She is a woman of unusual mental powers, but the proprieties would have been observed by giving her an assignment more in keeping with the popular idea of women's work and which would not interfere so disastrously with her domestic duties. The financial secretary of the Afro-American Council should be a man." (Giddings 1984, 110–11). Giddings goes on to report that the paper suggested she be made head of the women's auxiliary.

Wells also faced opposition from white women activists of the period. Mary Ovington, who concurred with Du Bois's action in blocking Wells, stated, "[Black women are] ambitious for power, often jealous, very sensitive, (but) they get things done." Wells's response was, "She has basked in the sunlight of the adoration of the few college-bred Negroes who have surrounded her, but has made little effort to know the soul of the black woman; and to that extent she has fallen far short of helping a race which has suffered as no white woman has ever been called upon to suffer or understand" (Wells 1970, 327–28).

She had an even fiercer disagreement with Frances Willard of the Women's Christian Temperance Union, a large and important women's organization. Willard was known in England as the "unknown queen of American democracy." Wells, however, accused Willard of a silence that aided and abetted lynching. Indeed, Willard is quoted in Giddings as saying, "The colored race multiplies like the locusts of Egypt, and the grogshop (liquor store) is its center of power. . . . The safety of women, of childhood, of the home is menaced in a thousand localities." The myth of the drunken black male rapist is used here by Willard to advance women's "rights." (Giddings 1984, 90–91). When Wells pointed out these statements and the segregated nature of the Temperance Union, Willard's allies tried to get her banned in England, and vilified her in the American press. The *Times* stated that black men were indeed prone to rape more than other men, then went on to attack Ida B. Wells as a "slanderous and nasty mulatress that was looking more for income than outcome" (Giddings 1984, 92).

Wells's life is emblematic of a central theme within black feminist thought—that a black woman, no matter how talented, can face stiff opposition from within both the black movement and the women's movement. While never successfully silenced during her lifetime, she has been effectively written out of black, women's, and American history for a number of decades. Nor is this an isolated instance; the active black women writers' movement of the turn of the century was ignored until many black, female literary critics documented their importance, and so were most of Wells's political contemporaries. This is true as well for more recent activists, such as Ella Baker, who were central to organizing and leading the Civil Rights movement (Baker, for example, was a field secretary for the SCLC and was instrumental in founding the Student Nonviolent Coordinating Committee). All were ignored by contemporary historians until rescued by scholars who have been predominantly black women.

The examples of the horrors faced by Celia and the travails undergone by Wells represent the core of many problems that are the central theoretical concerns of black feminism. Black feminists have argued for generations that the intersection of race, class, and gender, which has defined the social position of black women at the bottom of an often brutal American hierarchy of power, has shaped the political agendas and ideological projects of black feminists. Thus, for example, many black feminists have argued that they do not have the luxury of fighting on just one front, be it just for women, just for blacks, or just for the poor, or just for lesbians, but must, due to their intersecting social locations, fight on all or some combination of these fronts. Further, black feminists during both the nineteenth and twentieth centuries have been united in the belief that black activists such as Wells, Nannie Burroughs, and Anna Julia Cooper were correct in fighting for the rights of women within the context of the ongoing struggles of the black community. Therefore, the great majority of black feminists have followed these predecessors in rejecting both the separatism of some of their white feminist sisters and the patriarchal insistence of some of their black brothers on maintaining the distinction between a male public domain and a female private domain. The historical example provided by the life of Ida B. Wells, however, illustrates another central theme of black feminist thought. As often as not, black feminists must face sexism from within the black movement as well as racism from the women's movement at the same time they are struggling to combat what they perceive as the cumulative effects of multiple disadvantages.

These themes have been prominent in the writings of black women such as Sojourner Truth and Maria Stewart since before the Civil War. Another consistent theme in black feminism is that the quest to eliminate patriarchy and white supremacy must be connected to the liberation of the entire black community (Brown 1989; Roberts 1997). This holistic approach has led some within this tradition to reject the term *black feminism* in favor of a term with roots inside the black community These black women prefer the term *womanism*. Both those who adopt the term *black feminists* and those who prefer *womanist* believe that this concern with eliminating all oppressions and the emphasis on community necessitate a more communal approach that rejects the liberal individualism of the dominant society. Liberalism, with its strong emphases on public and private spheres, and on the autonomous individual, is consistently rejected, particularly in black feminist writings from the 1970s and 1980s, as being inadequate for the liberation of black women or the black community. In slightly different fashion, black feminist traditions have been as skeptical of the American liberal tradition as have black nationalist traditions.

These three central premises have historically composed the core of black feminist ideology. These premises have also often put black feminists in conflict (often not of their own choosing) with a variety of other ideological forces ranging from black nationalists to white feminists, black conservatives, black Marxists, and many black liberals. Black feminists have been criticized by some white feminists and many black nationalists for their insistence on the need to build ties across multiple racial categories as well as with black movements that often embrace either implicitly or explicitly patriarchal norms. Black feminists see the process of education and struggle as necessary in order to build progressive coalitions capable of confronting the variety of structural, social, and economic disadvantages that confound generations of African-American women.

One consequence of their standpoint, especially in this period (although these themes can be found in any historical era during which black women are active; i.e., all periods) is that black nationalists in particular have often accused black feminists of traitorous behavior. Black feminists and their allies have fiercely replied that any program which does not incorporate the agenda of black women cannot, by definition, be considered as a serious strategy for black liberation. The 1990s have seen extremely fierce struggles over these issues. The Clarence Thomas–Anita Hill hearings and the Million Man March provide two examples (the former example will shortly be considered in more depth). Given the increasingly severe level of ideological debates that blacks are being drawn into in the American polity, and the high stakes of issues such as affirmative action, inner-city social problems, and welfare, these debates are likely to become more frequent and perhaps fiercer in the future.

In this chapter I consider how black feminists, or womanists, have transformed feminist ideology based on their historical experiences, social position, and indigenous efforts to build multiple movements within the black community and between the black community and many other communities. First, the contours of modern black feminism are traced. The analysis section then discusses the antecedents and consequences of black feminism, and analyzes the results from the intersection of gender and racial identity for black respondents. I then take a more detailed look at these issues for black women and conclude by discussing the role of black feminism in contemporary ideological debate.

MODERN BLACK FEMINISM

The adherents of black feminism exhibit more agreement on what constitutes the political core of their ideology than the adherents of any other black ideology. While codified relatively late—the modern form was forged during the early 1970s—black women have adopted and agitated for political agendas remarkably similar to those found in modern black feminism for over a century. Maria Stewart, for example, was writing about the problems that black women faced due to the intersection of race and class as early as 1832 (Sheftall 1995).[1] Before the war, Sojourner Truth had to assert her right to speak for women to both white and black abolitionists, and then assert her right to be heard, as did white women abolitionists. Immediately following the war, Truth demanded that black women be extended the vote at the same time as black men, arguing that black men and black women worked equally hard, and that black women should have equal rights with black men. She also voiced suspicion about what would happen to black women's rights if they were not taken care of at the same time as those of black men (Truth 1995a).

The enormously talented Anna Julia Cooper wrote the first black feminist book in 1892 in a career that is actually longer than that of W. E. B. Du Bois (indeed she is his contemporary). She argued that black men were underdeveloped within the black community and that black women should play a key role in maintaining the community's political discipline in the face of vicious hostility and racism (Cooper 1995). Indeed, during many periods of the nineteenth century, black women would play a key role in maintaining a political discipline so strict that it violates liberal norms of the autonomous individual citizen (Brown 1989; Higginbotham 1993; Saville 1994b). Historians such as Elsa Barkley Brown use this evidence to point out that the political practice of Cooper and her sisters across the

---

1. Unless otherwise noted, the historical material for this section was drawn from Beverly Guy-Sheftall's introduction to her excellent collection of black women's writings (Sheftall 1995).

nineteenth century can help us to understand that the black community functions by a communitarian ethic, rather than a liberal ethic which prizes individual autonomy.

Nannie Burroughs, a critical and energetic leader, worked to build a women's movement inside the National Baptist Convention from a feminist perspective from 1900 through 1960. Her political approach also combined her concern with race and gender with concerns about class (Higginbotham 1993; Sheftall 1995). One of the earliest adaptations of the term *feminist* by a black activist can be found in the work of Elsie McDougald in 1925. During the same period, Amy Jacques Garvey, Marcus Garvey's second wife, was promoting a feminist perspective within the largest urban black nationalist organization in history, the two-million-strong Universal Negro Improvement Association (UNIA). It is ironic, given the importance of the organization and, more important, the iconic centrality her husband has had as the patriarchal originator of modern black nationalism (see chapter 3), that *this* Garvey promoted several political positions from *within* a powerful nationalist movement which modern black nationalists would consider anathema. Garvey not only argued that if the black nation was to be liberated, black women should be active in all spheres of public and private life, but also argued for the ability of women to control their own bodies through birth control. Most prominent black nationalists today argue that a women's place is in the home, and many see birth control and the support of other reproductive rights as part of a white genocidal attack on the black community.

At the same time their colleagues were fighting for a black feminist perspective within the nationalist UNIA, black communist women were having an even more difficult time in the substantial black wings of the American Communist movement. Some cadres, such as Claudia Jones, were able to get the special problems of black working women (e.g., domestics) on the communist organizing agenda. Jones also criticized white women for their racism toward black women—reminding them that their own liberation was tied to black women's liberation. In general, however, American Marxists of all races remained hostile toward both the larger women's movement in general and the agenda of black women activists for several decades to come.

During the Civil Rights movement, black women such as Ella Baker played critical roles as key national organizers for organizations such as the Southern Christian Leadership Conference and in the formation of the Student Nonviolent Coordinating Committee and other important movement organizations. Baker and numerous other women (e.g., Frances Beale), however, bitterly complained about the patriarchal attitudes they encountered at every turn. Ministers, who dominated the leadership of the Civil Rights movement, actively opposed any public recognition of the leadership role played by black women (Ransby 1996). Some black nationalists (see Giddings 1984) had only the most vile pronouncements to make about the role of women being (to be semipolite) to produce the next generation of warriors, while organizations that followed Leninist principles, such as the Black Panthers—whose party program upheld equality for women— were as vulgar as the nationalists and perhaps even more violent in their quotidian sexism (Brown 1992; Hilliard and Cole 1993; Shakur 1987).

Perhaps the ultimate insult, according to many contemporary black feminists, was that when they began to participate in the predominantly white wing of the women's movement, seeking support and alliances, they were met by the same patronizing and racist gestures that confronted Wells at the beginning of the twentieth century in every domain, from theorizing about gender to the group and personal dynamics of the movement itself. Faced by what these activists and theoreticians saw as extremely high levels of sexism within the black movement, and equally high levels of racism within the women's movement, black and other women of color began their own organizations. The National Black Feminist Organization was formed in 1973. By 1977, the Combahee River Collective had published a major statement on black feminism. This document is often cited as a central founding document of modern black feminism. The rest of this section examines the key theoretical components and claims of modern black feminism. I start with the central claim that the condition of black women can only be understood by recognizing how the intersection of race and gender shapes the social location of black women in the United States.

The Intersection of Gender and Race

"A Black Feminist Statement," published by the Combahee River Collective, foreshadows the main theoretical themes that would develop in black feminist thought over the next two decades. The writers of "A Black Feminist Statement" came together partly as a result of the many disappointments that they had experienced in movements that concentrated predominantly on either race or gender: "It was our experience and disillusionment within these liberation movements, as well as experience on the periphery of the white male left, that led to the need to develop a politics that was antiracist, unlike those of white women, and antisexist, unlike those of black and white men" (Combahee River Collective 1981, 211).

Their disillusionment with the two movements, however, was not confined to disgust with the virulent racism and sexism which they faced. The failure to understand that one could not just focus on one or the other as the primary oppression in society meant that neither movement could adequately address the forms of disadvantage faced by black women and often led both movements to dismiss, willfully or otherwise, the claims of black women as peripheral to the main show (Brown 1989; Brown 1992; Combahee River Collective 1981; Crenshaw 1990; Higginbotham 1992, 1993). Recognizing that black women faced double jeopardy, however, was not theoretically sufficient either. One had to realize that the social position of black women (and others) is structured in the interactions of these power hierarchies, not just experienced as additive, parallel oppression. For example, black women who had to work to help support their families could not ride in the "Ladies" car during the Jim Crow era. Similarly, bathrooms in the South were labeled during this period as being for "black women" or "white ladies" (Higginbotham 1992). Higginbotham argues, for example,

> Feminist scholars, especially those of African-American women's history, must accept the challenge to bring race more prominently into theories of analyses of power. The explication of race entails three interrelated strategies, separated here merely for the sake of analysis. First of all, we must define the construction and "technologies" of race as well as those of gender and sexuality. Second, we must expose the role of race as a metalanguage by calling attention to its powerful, all-encompassing effect on the construction and representation of other social and power relations, namely, gender, class, and sexuality. Third, we must recognize race as providing a site of dialogic exchange and contestation, since race has constituted a discursive tool for both oppression and liberation. (Higginbotham 1992, 252)

The view that these intersecting social locations are mutually constitutive has several political implications. First, in order to be truly free, black women—indeed, *all* those interested in a progressive political agenda—cannot simply take on one form of disadvantage but must fight on multiple fronts. Anna Julia Cooper made this argument in 1893 when she argued, "We take our stand on the solidarity of humanity, the oneness of life, and the unnaturalness and injustice of all special favoritism, whether of sex, race, country or condition. If one link of the chain be broken, the chain is broken" (Brown 1992, 177). Barbara Smith echoed this theme nearly a century later when she argued for the following position:

> The reason racism is a feminist issue is easily explained by the inherent definition of feminism. Feminism is the political theory and practice to free all women: women of color, working-class women, poor women, physically challenged women, lesbians, old women, as well as white economically privileged heterosexual women. Anything less than this is not feminism, but merely female self-aggrandizement. (Smith and Smith 1981, 61)

Another political implication of this viewpoint is that no group of women, especially not a group of largely privileged, middle-class women, can presume to universalize its experience and claim to speak for all women in general and black women in particular. Barbara and Beverly Smith argue, "Women of color are very aware that racism is not gender-specific, and it affects all people of color. We have experiences that have nothing to do with being female, but are nonetheless experiences of deep oppression . . . and even violence" (Smith and Smith 1981, 121). There are two implications of this standpoint. One is that black feminists argue that they cannot support separatism, be it the racial separatism of black nationalists or lesbian separatism. The Smiths and Audre Lorde, for example, argue that as black lesbians, they have no privilege to fall back on and must therefore ally themselves with progressives wherever they can be found. A further implication is that black feminists are critical of both feminist scholarship and black scholarship that ignores the experiences of black women. Brown criticizes some white feminist historians for not taking into account the experiences of black women such as Maggie Lena Walker or Ida B. Wells because they are considered "race women" (Brown 1992). Brown argues that because they do not understand how race and gender intersect, they miss a vital component of feminist history. Brown and other feminists also claim that the political costs of this mistake are very large since, consciously or unconsciously, many white feminists and their organizations find themselves unable to grasp the key issues facing women of color while at the same time claiming to speak for all women. These political problems can explode into firestorms when black feminists get called traitors or worse by those within the black community who see them as tools of the devil.

Racism, Sexism, and the Search for Allies

One trope that is found in much of the historical work of black feminists is that black men have often asserted their "rights to be men" by restricting the rights of black women (Brown 1995; Higginbotham 1993).

This theme is prominent in the black feminist historiography of the second half of the nineteenth century, which saw a severe diminution in the public roles available to the masses of black women.

Sexism in the Black Movement

Contemporary black feminists also face resistance from multiple sources. First, the expectation on the part of many African Americans that political unity is both necessary and demanded has served, in the opinion of many black feminists, to silence women within the black community. Audre Lorde made precisely this point in her collection of essays, *Sister/ Outsider*:

> The threat of difference has been no less blinding to people of Color. Those of us who are Black must see that the reality of our lives and our struggle does not make us immune to the errors of ignoring and misnaming difference. Within Black communities where racism is a living reality, difference among us often seem dangerous and suspect. The need for unity is often misnamed as a need for homogeneity, and a Black Feminist vision mistaken for betrayal of our common interests as a people. (Lorde 1984, 119)

Higginbotham agrees when she argues,

> Afro-American history has accentuated race by calling explicit attention to the cultural as well as socioeconomic implications of American racism but has failed to examine class and gender positions that men and women occupy in black communities—thus uncritically rendering a monolithic "black community," "black experience," and "voice of the Negro." Notwithstanding that this discursive monolith most often resonates with a male voice and as the experience of men. (Higginbotham 1992, 256)

The emphases on unity and the suppression of difference led black women to be called traitors when they criticized Clarence Thomas's nomination to the U.S. Supreme Court or even when they protested their exclusion from the Million Man March. In both cases black feminists were told that (1) they were not black and (2) they were the tools of the oppressors of black people. Even a milder version of this criticism has black feminists following too closely the lead of white women. Nationalist leader

Ron Karenga still argued in the 1990s, "Moreover, . . . much of the [black feminist] literature follows too closely white feminism without recognizing and taking into consideration vital differences. In fact, even when black women use the category "womanist," there is little theoretical development of its distinctness as a defining characteristic of black feminist thought" (Karenga 1993, 42).

Another common criticism of black feminists throughout African-American history has been that it is inappropriate for black women to play a leading role in fighting for black freedom and justice. Just as Wells at the height of her critical public successes against lynching was asked by some men to step down because "a man should have got the job" as secretary to the Afro-American Council, so successful black women organizers in the National Baptist Convention in the early twentieth century, Shirley Chisolm during the 1960s, and dozens of women cadres in SNCC and the Black Panther Party were told that their talents were not needed or were better utilized at home. This attitude on the part of some black nationalists and others was a large part of what motivated the women of the Combahee River Collective to leave the black organizations they belonged to and form a black women's collective: "Feminism," they argue, "is nevertheless very threatening to the majority of Black people because it calls into question some of the most basic assumptions about our existence, i.e., that sex should be a determinant of power relationships." (Combahee River Collective 1981, 215). They go on to criticize the following passage as an example of the devastating patriarchal beliefs that were common in the nationalist and, indeed, the broader movement:

> We understand that it is and has been traditional that man is the head of the house. He is the leader of the house/nation because his knowledge of the world is broader, his awareness is greater, his understanding is fuller, and his application of this information is wiser. . . . After all, it is only reasonable that the man be the head of the house because he is able to defend and protect the development of his home. . . . Women cannot do the same things as men—they are made by nature to function differently. Equality of men and women is something that cannot happen even in the abstract world. (Combahee River Collective, 1981, 215.

Throughout the decades black women activists such as Maggie Lena Walker and Amy Jacques Garvey have argued that African Americans cannot afford to have half of the population staying at home out of the trenches. Generally, black feminists have argued that the arguments against the participation and leadership of black women in political and civil action have at their base a patriarchal and often homophobic set of beliefs that consigns black women to the private sphere tightly enclosed within the space of the traditional bourgeois family (hooks 1984; Lorde 1984; Smith and Smith 1981). But black feminists also argue that while patriarchy and homophobia within the black community are largely responsible for the resistance to black feminism within the black community, some of the responsibility for this resistance can be traced to the character of the predominantly white branches of the feminist movement.

Racism in the Women's Movement

Black feminists have argued that mainstream feminism in the United States has been plagued since its modern founding with a universalist perspective that is both classist and racist. In her 1984 work, *Feminist Theory: From Margin to Center*, bell hooks angrily attacks Friedan's standpoint in the *Feminine Mystique*. She sarcastically comments on the irony of believing that the standpoint of middle-class, white women is the most "advisable" for speaking for all women. She continues,

> White women who dominate feminist discourse, who for the most part make and articulate feminist theory, have little or no understanding of white supremacy as a racial politic, of the psychological impact of class, of their political status within a racist, sexist, capitalistic state. [Theorizing of this kind] is another example of wishful thinking, as well as the conscious mystification of social division between women, that has characterized much feminist expression. While it is evident that many women suffer from sexist tyranny, there is little indication that this forges "a common bond among all women." There is much evidence substantiating the reality that race and class identity [have] created differences in quality of life, social status, and lifestyle that take precedence over the common experience women share—differences which are rarely transcended. (hooks 1984, 4)[2]

2. There certainly has been work by white feminists that have wrestled with the intersections of race, class and gender as well as those with sexuality (see Young 1990 and 1997, and Haraway 1992 for just two examples). Other feminists still strongly argue that gender trumps race and class Okin (1991) argues for example "The very early formative influence on children of female parenting, especially, seems to suggest that sex different [*sic*] in a gendered society is more likely to affect one's

Lorde was also troubled by what she saw as the conscious exclusion of women of color—both as subjects with agency and as equal partners in the theoretical project of feminism—by white feminists. In an often-anthologized open letter, Lorde harshly attacks Mary Daly's *Gyn/Ecology:* "To imply, however, that all women suffer the same oppression simply because we are women is to lose sight of the many varied tools of patriarchy. It is to ignore how those tools are used by women without awareness against each other" (Lorde 1984, 67). She goes on to say that it is not "acceptable" to believe that "assimilation into a western european herstory" provides the necessary route for feminists of color to be accepted (Lorde 1984, 69). Papering over difference can only help patriarchal forces and provide a false and weak unity among women.

Racial blindness, however, is only one of the major complaints that black feminists have regarding many feminists in the mainstream. Black feminists like hooks in 1984 considered mainstream American feminism to be bourgeois. This criticism was made with two different connotations, usually simultaneously. On one hand, from the Combahee River Collective statement on, the great majority of black feminists argued that issues of class had to be directly confronted. Black women were often poor women, and the realities of working and poor women were being totally ignored by the women's movement. But a second connotation can be found in the work of black feminists such as hooks (1984) and Brown (1989). Becoming equal partners in a liberal republic is (1) antithetical to the communitarian tradition of African Americans, particularly the tradition of black women, and (2) since this society is structured along lines other than those of gender, just which men were women supposed to become equal to? According to hooks,

> This broad definition . . . raises problematic questions. Since men are
> not equals in white supremacist, capitalist, patriarchal class structure,
> which men do women want to be equal to? Implicit in this simplistic
> definition of women's liberation is a dismissal of race and class as factors
> that, in conjunction with sexism, determine the extent to which an indi-
> vidual will be discriminated against, exploited, or oppressed. Bourgeois
> white women interested in women's rights issues have been satisfied
> with simple definitions for obvious reasons. Rhetorically placing them-

---

thinking about justice, than for example, racial difference in a society in which race has social significance, or class difference in a class society" (p. 194).

selves in the same social category as oppressed women, they were not anxious to call attention to race and class privilege. (hooks 1984, 18)

Crenshaw argued that both the patriarchal attitudes of the antiracist black movement and the racial blindness of the antisexist women's movement severely limit the ability of black women to have their claims addressed. This disadvantage is clearly seen in American judicial decisions. Courts, for example, have ruled that black women's claims are too particularistic to entitle them to represent either black men or white women; however, any claims made on behalf of their intersecting status as blacks and women are rejected because the category "black woman" is not recognized by the courts. This is an especially bitter finding, argued Crenshaw, because white men are allowed to make reverse discrimination claims in the courts precisely because of their status as both white and male. The tendency for institutions and movements to unsuccessfully attempt to force black women into a category based on either race or gender, but not both, would prove to be particularly explosive in the Thomas–Hill hearings.

The Thomas–Hill Hearings

Black feminists have spent considerable time analyzing traumatic episodes that highlight the interaction between race and gender in the United States. One of the most analyzed sets of events were those surrounding the testimony of Anita Hill. Reading black writers in a variety of venues quickly makes it clear that while black women took the lead in defending Anita Hill from racist and sexist attacks that came from multiple sources, as Nellie McKay and others point out, a complicated set of interactions between gender and race made the affair even more traumatic for black feminists and their supporters than was apparent at the beginning of the process. Some black women, such as nationalist Julia Hare and colleagues of hers around the country, accused Anita Hill of being a traitor, of betraying both Clarence Thomas and the black community. Nathan and Julia Hare went so far as to state that blacks who opposed Thomas were "white-oriented, assimilationist 'coconut' [brown outside, white inside] feminists and their hangdog male cohorts" (Hare and Hare 1992, 37). Obviously these women and their less than fully male flunkies were the tools of whites (Hare and Hare 1992). While some black men agreed, a very small minority organized to support African-American women in Defense of Ourselves, the group of black women that initiated a campaign to defend Hill much as black women came together a century earlier to defend anti-lynching leader Ida B. Wells when she was attacked by the white press and some black male leaders for not knowing her place.

As Sheftall and others have argued, a significant reason that this case exploded into the public consciousness is that African-American women were increasingly less willing to silence themselves in the name of some mythic unity which could only be built if black women submerged their claims (Sheftall 1995). Nellie McKay developed this point further:

> Exposing a situation that called into question the sexual conduct of a black man, to those minds, Anita Hill committed treason against the race. This was the most serious infraction she could make against the understood inviolability of race loyalty. This loyalty espouses that the oppression that black men have suffered and continue to suffer at the hands of the white world entitles them to the unqualified support of black women, even to their self-denial. Interestingly, there are no circumstances that require such a sacrifice of black men. (McKay 1992, 282)

Crenshaw also pointed to the expectation of "reflexive solidarity," which drove a large part of the internal nastiness that developed in the black community. She concluded that part of the tragedy of the Hill–Thomas phenomenon was that a substantial fragment of the black community would end up supporting a man who was at odds with the policy preferences of well over 85 percent of the black community in the misplaced, mystical, mythical hope that he would return the racial solidarity which helped put him on the highest bench most probably for several decades (Crenshaw 1992).

Nell Painter and Kimberle Crenshaw pointed out several problems with how Anita Hill's case was framed that illustrated the liabilities that black women and other women of color face when attempting to make claims highlighting the intersection of race and gender. Painter (1992) pointed out that the historic stereotyping suffered by black women as Jezebels, welfare cheats, scorned women, and so on, made it more difficult for a positive framing of Hill to be constructed. A century ago, Ida B. Wells was neither the first nor last woman of color to have her character assassinated when making claims on the national and international stage. Crenshaw argued that by framing the problematic as one of race versus gender instead of one where Hill represented the intersection of race and gender, the women's movement seriously damaged Hill's case among both blacks and white women. Similarly, the unthinking call for racial solidarity on the part of many blacks was only possible if one's definition of the black racial agenda was built solely on the needs of powerful black men. The same dynamics repeated themselves four years later with the controversy that surrounded the Million Man March. The difficulties which have confronted black feminists over the past several years have led to an internal debate among members of the movement about whether it is more appropriate to characterize themselves as part of the feminist movement or as part of a more indigenous tradition of black women's activism.

Black Feminism and Womanism

Patricia Hill Collins has compared the nuances in the differences between black feminism and womanism (Collins 1996). The social bases of both sets of women, Collins claimed, was relatively privileged. The differences in the two rest to a significant degree on how they saw their relationship to both the worldwide feminist movement and to white feminists within the United States.

Black Feminism

Black feminism, Collins asserted, was part of worldwide women's movement but was also seen as the property of white women in the United States, despite the long struggle of black woman against white women's exclusionary practices. To wit, "Using the term 'black feminism' disrupts the racism inherent in presenting feminism as a for-whites-only ideology and political movement. Inserting the adjective 'black' challenges the assumed whiteness of feminism and disrupts the false universal of this term for both white and black women. Since many white women think that black women lack feminist consciousness, the term 'black feminist' both highlights the contradictions underlying the assumed whiteness of feminism and serves to remind white women that they comprise neither the only nor the normative 'feminists'" (Collins 1996, 13). There is, however, a price for the use of the term: "But the term 'black feminist' also makes many black women uncomfortable because it challenges black women to confront their own views on sexism and women's oppression" (Collins 1996, 13).

Black feminists walk a careful and often treacherous line in trying to build ties with other progressive women while maintaining working ties to progressive black men and women, often facing hostility in both camps over their refusal to give priority to gender, race, class, or sexuality over the other categories. Further, as both hooks and Cohen have noted, feminism is connected to homophobia in many blacks' minds (Cohen 1994; hooks 1984). Cohen, Lorde, and other black feminists have argued that black feminists must fight against homophobia at the same time that they fight against patriarchy and racism (Cohen 1994; Lorde 1984). Collins claimed that one difference between the womanist tradition and those who label themselves black feminists is a reduced emphasis on sexuality.

E. Frances White made an additional point. She argued that black feminists and womanists who are too quick to embrace Afrocentric and nationalist models underestimate the problems inherent in trying to graft an antipatriarchal movement and ideology onto a movement that, while strongly antiracist, also contains deeply embedded patriarchal norms and practices (White 1990). Collins has come to agree with this viewpoint: "The term 'black feminist' also disrupts a longstanding and largely un-questioned reliance on black racial solidarity as a deep tap root in black po-litical philosophies and especially black nationalist and cultural pluralist frameworks" Thus challenging that issues of gender are 'lesser' than those of race" (Collins 1996, 13).

Womanism

The author Alice Walker (1993) is credited with popularizing the use of the term *womanism*. She defined a womanist as "a woman who loves women, a black feminist, or feminist of color. Committed to survival and wholeness of the entire people, male *and* female. Not a separatist, except periodically, for health. Traditionally universalist" (Walker 1993, 722). The term itself, Walker tells us, comes from southern black women who would describe women as "womanish" when they were acting seriously. As with most of her essays and fiction, there is a strong spiritual compo-nent to the definition of womanism. That the term is created in part to differentiate black women from white feminists is evident in her compari-son of Virginia Woolf's dictum that women need a room of their own to the condition of Phillis Wheatley, who did not even own herself. The lack of property, self-ownership, or assessment of worth has plagued creative blacks, particularly but not exclusively black women. Just as Wheatley had to prove that she was indeed the author of her poetry, and Sojourner Truth had to prove she was a woman, Benjamin Banneker could not prove to Jef-ferson that he was the architect and inventor of the first rank. African-

American women had to assert their ability to be creative even when living under oppressive circumstances.

Collins argued that womanist ideology has the problem of being less likely to be connected to global women's movements but the benefit of being more likely to be embraced by black women. Brown (1992) also connected the womanist movement to the lack of recognition of black women activists within the women's movement and their insistence on not having to prioritize either gender or racial issues. Brown, in contrast to Collins, argued that women of color around the globe have had this response to the Euro-American-dominated women's movement. Brown's work richly highlights the long historical tradition of black women's activism which she argues is consistent with womanist principles (Brown 1992; Brown 1995, 1989).

Core Components of Modern Black Feminism

Both womanists and black feminists—the same individuals have been known to use both terms—agree on a core set of principles that lie at the root of these ideologies. The need to understand the intersection of at least race and gender, and often sexuality and class, as a grounding for both theoretical and practical work is of course one core component common to both the womanist and black feminist traditions. The need to put community at the center of the theoretical and practical project is also a critical component of black feminism. A third key component is that the ideology that guides black women in their political and civil activities must be based on contemporary and historical experiences of black women. Knowledge is both personal and contextual; claims on behalf of the universal experience of either all women or all blacks are to be resisted. As Saville, Brown, Spillers, Lorde, and countless other activists and theoreticians have argued across generations, black feminism is a practical ideology that is centered on insurgency; black women must define themselves and their agenda not as separatists, but as vital members of multiple communities.

WHO ARE THE SUPPORTERS OF A BLACK FEMINIST AGENDA?

The following sections analyze the support for a black feminist agenda. Table A3.1 displays the four items that are used to gauge support for black feminist ideology among contemporary African Americans. All four questions represent core themes within modern black feminist thought. Before

I report on both the descriptive and causal analyses of the support for and the consequences of black feminism, I report on how support for black feminism is distributed within the African-American population. These analyses once again are based on data from the 1993–1994 National Black Politics Study. Full specification and reporting of the analyses can be found in the appendix.

The attempt to model a scale of modern black feminism similar to the one modeled for community nationalism faced severe complications. First, when the model was estimated for men and women separately, there was clearly a different structure for black men and women regarding how these items were cognitively organized. Second, there is a low level of inter-item correlation for these items—they do not cohere well. Thus while LISREL scales can be built from several of the core components that fit the data well, these scales have low reliability (see table A3.2). Despite the reasonable fit of theoretical models of black feminism to the data, the low level of inter-item correlation is indicative of several potential obstacles to the modeling of black feminism in the black mass public. First, part of the problem is probably due to measures which inadequately tap the core components of black feminism. For comparison, over half of the black autonomy/black nationalism measures have been tested at least once over the course of three previous surveys. All of the black feminism items are being tested for the first time. Second, however, there are a few methodological and stronger substantive reasons to believe that these preliminary results, if confirmed in future studies, are symptomatic of a lesser degree of dispersion of black feminist orientations than black nationalist orientations within black public opinion.

Several factors lead to this preliminary inference. First, while counterelites, intellectuals, and activists are responsible for shaping these two black ideologies (as elites are often critical for shaping ideology), nationalist activists have historically had and continue to have much greater access to institutional, cultural, organizational, and media channels into the black community. Black nationalist newspapers with relatively wide circulation have been available weekly on the street corners of inner cities for decades. Cable television in large cities generally has nationalist-oriented public affairs programs. Nationalist organizations have had a steady presence in many black communities and several college campuses since the 1960s. Popular artists such as Public Enemy, Sister Souljah, Ice Cube, and X-Clan have identified themselves with black nationalism and to various degrees incorporated nationalist viewpoints into their artistic products.

Further, in the current period, the visibility of nationalists and their program is heightened by the mainstream white media's increased coverage of nationalists ranging from Afrocentrist scholars such as Molefi Asante to the leaders of the Nation of Islam. While the black community *is* strongly divided over nationalist strategy and programs, the *views and programs* of black nationalists are relatively visible and understood.

On the other hand, while the black feminist or womanist tradition has a long history, the codification of black feminism is relatively recent.[3] Further, organizations such as the black church and the major civil rights organizations, which have strong patriarchal norms (Payne 1989), have been much less willing to provide a forum for black feminist views than for proponents of black nationalism. While a few popular female artists such as Queen Latifah have presented material consistent with black feminism, in terms of measures such as air-time, sales volume, and the like they are much less visible than nationalist-oriented hip-hop performers. The organizational presence of black feminists as black feminists is currently less widespread in black communities and more confined to the academy. The obstacles that black feminists face in disseminating their program and ideology are greater than for the other ideological tendencies (including that of black Marxism). It should not be surprising that in this period there is a weaker and less cohesive presence of black feminism in black public opinion. The historical contingency of such a statement should not be underemphasized. Evidence presented later suggests that black Marxism is also weakly present in the black mass public. However, during other periods, black Marxism has been prominent in the black community, and although deep divisions existed about what status should be accorded black Marxists and their programs, knowledge of black radical programs and concepts was relatively widespread.

The "best" feminist scale is composed of the four items presented in table A3.2, which were at the core of how both black women and black men cognitively organized the indicators of black feminism. All four items are also at the core of how activists describe the black feminist project. While the reliability of this scale is still low, even this relatively weak indicator of black feminist orientations allows us to compare the effects of these three ideologies for shaping black public opinion.

---

3. "A Black Feminist Statement" from the Combahee River Collective (1979), published in 1977 is considered a foundational text for modern black feminism and discusses the major themes that black feminists would further develop during the 1970s, 1980s, and 1990s.

Figure 4.1   Smoothed Black Feminism distribution using normal and
Epanechinikov estimators

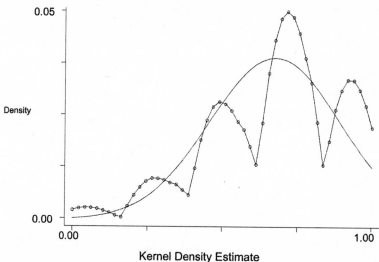

Kernel Density Estimate

	Observations	Mean	Std. Deviation	Minimum	Maximum
Black Feminism	1,174	0.70	0.24	0	1

Source: 1993–1994 National Black Politics Survey

Figure 4.1 shows the distribution of the Black Feminist scale. Black
feminism displays a distinct multipolar distribution. While a strong pro-
feminist mean is present at .70, about 20 percent of the sample oppose
black feminism. The lack of single peakedness of the distribution helps to
explain the vociferousness of the conflict that swirls around the position
and role of black women in the community and in the struggle for black
social justice.

THE ANTECEDENTS AND CONSEQUENCES
OF MODERN BLACK FEMINISM

What factors lead to the adoption of a black feminist agenda? The sets
of variables described earlier for measuring the structural factors of social

location, spatial situation, and ties to black information networks with regard to black nationalism are all included again.

Antecedents of Support for a Black Feminist Agenda

Those who believe their fate is linked to that of other blacks, who believe that blacks are economically worse off than whites, and have more educational and economic resources are supportive of black feminist orientations (see table A2.1 in the appendix for details of the estimation). Not surprisingly, women were somewhat more likely to support a black feminist agenda than were men. Age was a weak predictor of black feminist orientations—younger African Americans were more likely to support a black feminist agenda.[4] Further, those tied into black information networks were also more likely to have a positive view of feminist ideology. Economic class has the greatest effect—indeed, the only significant effect—on support for black feminist ideology. By and large, support for the other ideologies is not predicated on one's economic and educational resources; however, those with more resources are greater supporters of black feminism. On the other hand, even after all of the individual-level controls are included, those who live in neighborhoods with high levels of concentrated poverty are more likely to reject black feminist positions. Some of these social structural effects on feminist ideology are understated, since indirect effects are not shown in these analyses. For example, living in a very poor neighborhood decreases the likelihood of feeling that one's fate is tied to that of black women, which suggests that concentrated poverty has an indirect role in reducing support for black feminism. An interesting general finding is that concentrated poverty, which leads to social isolation, serves as a conservative structural force for shaping black public opinion, while integration into black information networks serves as a radicalizing force. Thus, black feminists would have the hardest time organizing among poor blacks living in the poorest neighborhoods. Individual poverty and the effects of poor neighborhoods reinforce each other as conservative influences in the realm of gender politics.

Finally, in line with my speculation earlier in the chapter, we once again see that only support for community nationalism is strengthened by

---

4. The relationship between gender and support for feminist orientation is more complicated than portrayed here. The relationship is strongly suppressed when the perception that one's fate is linked to that of black women is included in the equation. Gender strongly predicts, in turn, the perception that one's fate is linked to that of black women.

belonging to a black organization. No relationship is detected between black feminism and organizational membership. On one hand perceptions of black economic subordination, how strongly one feels linked to the race, and being embedded within these networks all lead to the strengthening of black feminism. It is the lack of organizational connectedness that differentiates black feminism from community nationalism. We will come back to the antecedents of black feminism later in this chapter when we consider the linkages between gender, identity, and ideology.

We saw in the last chapter that support for black nationalism was also strengthened by exposure to rap music. Does exposure to rap negatively affect support for a black feminist agenda? Critics of rap have fiercely argued that one of the most detrimental aspects of rap music is that it loudly, crudely, and constantly promotes violence against women and other forms of misogyny. Even politically oriented rap, it is argued, supports the patriarchal view of a subservient role for women in the struggle for black liberation espoused by many nationalists. Frequent references to "ho," "bitches," "punks," and "faggots" do give a consistent misogynistic and homophobic cast to rap that is not confined to gangsta rap. Some rappers have explicitly attacked feminism as a foreign ideology detrimental to the black community.

Rap music has a discernible but mixed effect on attitudes toward black feminists and feminist issues, and many of the findings are opposed to what was anticipated. Those who appreciate rap are no less warm toward black feminists than other African Americans. Indeed, when asked whether black feminists divided the black community or made positive contributions to the black community, those who approve of rap were 12 percent more likely to answer that black feminists made positive contributions. Those who appreciate rap are no more or less likely to believe that controversial black women leaders such as Lani Guinier and Jocelyn Elders are troublemakers than other blacks. Supporters of rap are also equally likely to believe that the problems of racism, sexism, and poverty are linked, as many black feminists have argued. However, even given the crude measures we have available to us in this study, it is clear that, on average, those who appreciate rap are colder toward gays and lesbians in the black community than other blacks.

While very little rap music attacks gay bashing (the song by the Disposable Heroes of Hiphoprisy "Language of Violence" is an exception), many female and a few male rappers have made strong efforts to counteract the misogyny of rap. Queen Latifah has led the way; her music criticizes the sexism of everyday life in the black community and in the music business, and also provides a positive model of gender relations in the black community. Consequently, the multiple messages regarding the role of women in the black community may counteract the dominance of the more brutal aspects of rap. Unfortunately, as expected, given the constant attacks against black gays and lesbians in rap lyrics, both exposure to rap and the belief that rap provides a legitimate source of information within the black community contribute to negative attitudes toward gays and lesbians (see appendix table A2.19 for details). Rap music contributes to black homophobia. While the size of the effects is relatively small, rap does significantly contribute to making black opinion toward the black queer community even more negative. I must point out that we don't have the best measures for assessing the effect of rap on attitudes toward black women; better measures to test this question would have included attitudes toward violence against women, and whether women are less trustworthy than men. Both of these themes are often cited by the critics of rap as some of the most destructive themes within rap. But the results do suggest that rap does contribute toward black hostility to the black gay and lesbian community, as predicted.

Black feminists have also claimed that black religious ideology is implicated in both resistance to black feminism and hostility toward the black gay and lesbian communities (Cohen 1994; Collins 1996). There is some basis for this viewpoint. As table A2.11 shows, those active in church are somewhat less likely to support a black feminist agenda. A greater role of religious guidance in one's day-to-day life also leads one to be more hostile toward both black gays and lesbians (table A2.12). On the other hand, feminism does directly affect one area of beliefs about the structure of the black church: not surprisingly, those who support a black feminist identity also support greater numbers of black women in the clergy (table A2.13).

Effects of Black Feminism on Black Public Opinion

How does black feminism shape black public opinion (see table A2.5). While not having as broad an impact as black nationalism, black feminism substantially contributes to the shaping of black public opinion (tables A2.6–A2.8). Not surprisingly, feminist orientation has a consistent effect in shaping black orientations toward questions of gender in the black community. Blacks with black feminist orientations are more likely to support a prochoice position on abortion and slightly more likely to feel affective warmth toward Anita Hill. On the other hand, black conservatives were somewhat more likely to believe that such women were merely "troublemakers." It may be surprising that those oriented toward community nationalism had more warmth for Hill than those who were not so oriented.

Adherents of black autonomy clashed with the adherents of black feminism over the question of whether AIDS is the result of an antiblack conspiracy. Those oriented toward community nationalism believed this was true, while those with feminist positions were more likely to see AIDS as resulting from tragic natural causes. Exposure to rap (in an analysis not displayed in table A2.19) does not contribute to the belief, held by one quarter of our sample of blacks, that the ravages of AIDS in the black community are the result of an antiblack conspiracy.[5] It is the case however, that those who have a positive orientation toward rap are 10 percent more likely to oppose abortion under any circumstances than other blacks. Again, consistent with black nationalist ideology, political rappers have with few exceptions been hostile to abortions within the black community.

With one exception, black feminism has a weak effect on indicators of black nationalism. In contrast to supporters of community nationalism, those with black feminist orientations are more likely to reject the view that the status of African Americans should be characterized as that of a nation within a nation or that a separate nation should be supported. Not surprisingly, given the clashes between black feminists and some nationalist leaders, those supporting a feminist agenda were somewhat more hostile toward Minister Farrakhan of the Nation of Islam than other African Americans. Black feminists were more likely to reach out to other groups in order to form coalitions, while those oriented toward autonomy were more likely to reject the idea that immigrants should have an equal chance at jobs. Black conservatives upheld immigrants' right to obtain jobs on an equal basis with everyone else. Those who supported black autonomy, as reported earlier, were also more likely to see America's large corporations as unfair to blacks. Those with feminist orientations disagreed.

In the last chapter we saw that black public opinion has undergone large shifts, particularly in the domain of nationalism. What would happen if the support for feminism changed as much as the hypothesized shift in nationalism? Shifts in black feminism generally have both a less broad and smaller effect on black opinion, but they do have modest but important effects on blacks' perception of the desirability of political alliances (as displayed in the appendix).

---

5. This is not quite accurate; exposure to rap does contribute a small amount to the belief that the ravages of AIDS in the black community are the result of an antiblack conspiracy indirectly through the large effect that support for community nationalism has on that variable.

Black feminism's impact is greatest on the domain of gender relations within the black community. In the next section we investigate more deeply how black feminist ideology interacts with both feminist identity and various versions of racial identity.

IDENTITY AND BLACK FEMINIST IDEOLOGY

Cohen, in her work on the role of black lesbian and gay identities for understanding the black community's response to AIDS, challenges us—as many black feminists have for the past two decades—to rethink both our understanding of what we see as political, and the political content of group identities (Cohen 1999). She also challenges the notion of undifferentiated racial and gender identities. She argues that we need to explore fully the "multiple positions within any" of these group's group identity. Cohen argues that we need to be able to differentiate among the role of gender, often seen by some as an essentialist construct; how one sees one's fate linked to that of various racial and gender groups (an extension of the concept of linked fate that I explored in my earlier work on black identity and black interests); and ideology, which we have seen in the last two chapters to be a powerful and coherent force shaping black public opinion.

This viewpoint challenges two political views that are commonly found in the black community. First, the degree to which one can assume that there is an undifferentiated black identity that is the same for black men and women is assumed to be an empirical question that has political consequences. Is there a gender content to black identity(ies)? Nationalists have often asserted both the need for a single "black" agenda and the need to subordinate the concerns of black women in the interests of the "progress of the black community." Thus, some see feminism, including its black feminist and womanist forms, as a foreign ideology that at best diverges from the main goals of African Americans.

This leads to the second challenge of this work. Some modern black activists have long held the view that identity as a black women or black feminist detracts from one's "black" identity. To a similar degree, many black feminists have argued that white feminists are often inattentive to the connections between race and gender and the concerns of black women. Debbie Robinson in her excellent dissertation, "The Effect of Multiple Group Identity among Black Women on Race Consciousness," convincingly demonstrates that "the charge that black women's involvement with women's issues detracts from their involvement with black issues has little basis in fact." Part of the goal of the following analysis is to further clarify how gender, identification with racial and gender groups, and black feminist ideology affect black public opinion and preferences.

This set of debates is increasingly at the center of both interracial and intraracial conflict. For example, in some quarters of the black community, some black feminists who raised questions about the subordinate role of black women in the context of the Million Man March were vehemently denounced. These internal conflicts will probably grow in the coming years. The combination of shifts in the political economy, shifts that can be viewed as earthquakes in terms of their implications for American society, and a consolidation of the stranglehold of the Right over political discourse have had grave consequences for blacks specifically and the disadvantaged more generally. One result has been that the meaning of being "black," who is "allowed" to be black, and the content of "black" agendas are even more fiercely contested within the black community than in the past. Essentialist notions of "blackness" themselves are under (deserved) attack by those who point to the social construction of black identity and by materialists who argue that there has been sufficient diversion in interests, not only along lines of class but also along gender lines, to make the concept of a unified set of "black interests" minimally a historical anachronism and at worst nonsensical. Toni Morrison eloquently captures this sentiment when she states, "It is clear to the most reductionist intellect that black people think differently from one another; it is also clear that the time for undiscriminating racial unity has passed" (Morrison 1992a, xxx). Many disagree. Charles Henry, for one, argues for the need to rebuild black unity and identity: "Is the loss of a national black identity a bad thing? I think it is, unless we believe that this country as a whole currently embodies those values and goals we seek to be identified with. If it does not, then we must seek to present alternative values and goals as forcefully as possible. This struggle is not new . . . " (Henry 1992, 41).

Both Morrison's and Henry's sentiments are based on the view that at some time in the recent past a "black" identity has existed that was sufficiently shared by people of African descent to forge a potent political unity as to goals, values, and ideas. In Morrison's opinion such a unity is not only unrecoverable but, to the degree that it is "undiscriminating," it is undesirable. Henry believes that it is imperative to recover such a unity because the goals and values of African Americans are sufficiently different from those of the nation as a whole as to require not only a separate political agenda but also sufficient political unity to achieve this agenda. Part of the bases of the tension produced by Morrison's and Henry's views can be determined in various forms of empirical research. Questions such as the degree to which fundamental social cleavages exist within the black community and how African Americans perceive shared interests versus intragroup conflict can to a significant degree be analyzed and answered. The tension between Morrison's and Henry's views raises important normative questions about the nature of debate among African Americans, the existence and nature of democratic institutions within the black community to facilitate democratic debate, and the nature of the dialectical relationship between debate within the black community and debate between African Americans and other communities about the relationship between race and American democracy. Further, the tension between the views of Morrison and Henry has at its roots conflicting conceptualizations of "black identity" and whether such an identity can exist to the degree necessary to facilitate the forging of a single black agenda.

For many in the black community, debates over black identities and gender have painful consequences. McKay in her testimony discusses how many like her father would have been angered by Thomas's actions but would have been ashamed of their own daughters if they had publicly revealed harassment at the hands of black men (McKay 1992). For many black feminists like McKay, a key issue that black men and white women must politically confront is that unity must be built on the basis of the acknowledgment of differences—differences with political, economic, and social roots as well as consequences. As we will see, black feminist ideology among black women is least tied to feelings of fate linked to white women. However, blacks who support a black feminist ideology are most likely to support coalitions with those outside of the black community. Black feminists in the black community argue that such unity must be based on a political recognition of hierarchies of power that structure the positions of and the relationships between black women, white women, and black men.

The following set of analyses focuses on the interrelationship of feminist identification, linked fates, and black feminist ideology. When thinking about how gender influences identity and politics in the black community, it is important to consider how these factors affect the development of feminist identity and feminist ideology among black women. We need to be somewhat careful in analyzing ideological labels and their connection to specific ideological clusters in the black community. For example, only a third of African Americans identify themselves as liberal; yet, with regard to policy, vote preference, views of the state, and the economy, blacks remain overwhelmingly the most liberal group in the polity. On the other hand, we also know that black ideologies such as nationalism and black feminism are powerful forces shaping black public opinion. When we look at feminist identification among black women, we find that (1) 54 percent either identify as feminist or are not opposed to such an identification; (2) 36 percent identify as feminists; and (3) 17 percent identify as strong feminists.

Here we reanalyze the determinants of support for black feminism among only black women in order to answer the following question: What are the links between the strength of belief among black women that their fate is tied to that of various racial and gender groups and the adoption of the label feminist? After controlling for the usual control factors, no links were found. This finding becomes strongly reversed, however, when we turn to what factors predict black feminist ideology. What does predict feminist identification? It is less systematically related to either structural, socioeconomic, or political outlook than the ideological constructs.

There is, however, a strong relationship between the versions of linked fate that included the intersection of gender and race and support for feminist ideology (the relevant table is A2.14). A clear hierarchy exists in the relationships between the groups to which black women feel linked and the predictive power for black feminist ideology. The main finding is that the interaction between gender and racial links predicts support for black feminism among black women. Neither feeling linked to blacks nor to white women in general helps us predict strength of support for black women. Indeed, feeling linked to white women is the weakest predictor of support for black women. Feeling linked to women in general only very marginally predicts support for black feminism. Feeling linked to nonwhite women or to black men both predict increased support for black feminism. It is interesting that the gendered versions of linked fate are more effective than the general racial versions, even when it is men that are being invoked. And the punch line is, of course, that by far the best predictor of black feminist ideology is how strongly black women feel linked to other black women. As hooks noted in 1984, empirical evidence shows that black women perceive that the intersection of race and gender produces different experiences among women. These different experiences in turn produce different strengths of linkages between black women and other racial and gender groups.

Other key determinants of black feminist ideology are whether one lives in poor neighborhoods (a negative factor even after controlling for individual socioeconomic attributes), higher levels of education, and the degree to which one sees whites faring better than blacks economically. Age and income do not predict support for a black feminist program among black women, even though age does predict adoption of the *label* "feminist."

For over a century and a half, black feminist activists and theorists have argued that racial oppression alone or gender oppression alone could explain neither the identity black women held nor the problems black women faced. Here we have strong evidence that the intersecting identities of race and gender forge the critical identity for encouraging support for black feminism among black women.

Conclusion: The Challenges Facing Black Feminism

Black feminism faces multiple challenges at the beginning of the new century that arose in the 1990s: theoretical challenges, challenges from within both the black and white feminist movements, and policy challenges from the government and its intellectual allies who oppose the policy agenda of black feminists. Theoretical challenges come from several directions. Some black feminists, such as Deborah McDowell, have argued for the recognition of the multiple faces of black feminism, including black feminist writings outside of political fields of endeavor and discourse. Contributions to the development of black feminism come from such diverse sources as critical legal studies, literary theory, the social sciences, political theory, and the practical work of organizers and activists from around the country. An area of theorizing less prominent than in the early 1980s is how to situate the status of black women both empirically and theoretically within the structures of advanced capitalism. This is partly due to the increased attention given by many black feminists over the past two decades to questions of intersecting and conflicting identities. The anti-essentialist stance of many black feminists has led them into direct conflict with some white feminists as well as some black activists from other camps as these feminists argue against a primary, uninterrogated status for race or gender when trying to understand black women's social location and their ensuing identities.

This strand of black feminist thought has generated serious challenges in the form of an antidifference backlash from some white feminists. White feminists such as Catherine MacKinnon and Susan Moller Okin have come to believe that feminism suffers from an "excessive amount of deference to differences among women" (Okin 1998, 663). MacKinnon bitterly complains that women share space in a hierarchy within which they are oppressed by men. Quoting Dworkin, MacKinnon urges feminists to rigorously theorize about "women as women" (MacKinnon 1991). Black feminists agree with MacKinnon when she argues that women are subjected to rape and domestic battering, that they are given unequal pay and are employed in disproportionately disrespected jobs, and that they are under assault in multiple policy arenas, particularly those that involve reproduction rights (MacKinnon 1991). As figure 4.2 shows, MacKinnon is correct when she claims that white women's income is, on average, less than that of black men (although she doesn't mention that it is substantially better than that of black women or the enormous gulf between white men and everyone else). The problem that many black feminists have with the new drive to subordinate racial differences among feminists specifically, and women more generally, is that, as Patricia Hill Collins states, white women have a difficult time seeing themselves as white (Collins 1998).

Angela Harris recounts that at a meeting of West Coast feminist critics, all of the women of color but none of the white women used ethnic descriptors in the two or three words of self-description that each participant was asked to give (Harris 1994). Many black feminists claim that the lack of attention to racial differences on the part of white feminists leads black women to disappear and narratives of oppression to shift (Collins 1998; Harris 1993; hooks 1991). Political consequences can be severe. Black and white feminists supported raped inmate Joanne Little in her fight against unjust prosecution when she defended herself against a rapacious prison guard. White feminists did not respond, however, when Little organized a drive after being freed to fight for black men who had been falsely accused of rape (Harris 1993). When the storytellers are white, Harris argues, narratives of the oppression of women are harmed by a pervasive "white solipsism." This solipsism leads, as Collins argues, to naive talk of sisterhood, which in turn can distract from the hard task of building women's unity across segregated communities. White feminist critique of standpoint theory comes in part from frustration with the difficulties of building unity and from their lack of understanding of their own placement (Collins 1998).

Even if they do not explicitly embrace standpoint theory and do explicitly reject essentialist understandings of the concept of groups, many modern theorists of group oppression, including black feminists, black Marxists, and black nationalists, as well as many others, have tended to embrace structuralist accounts of group formation and consciousness. Some, such as Iris Marion Young (1997) in her work on seriality, take an approach similar to the one outlined in the first chapter. The tendency for (in this case) American society to treat some people worse systematically due to ascriptive status is seen as the basis for either loose collectivities from which some

Figure 4.2   Historical median income for individuals by race and gender, 1953–1997 (in 1997 dollars)

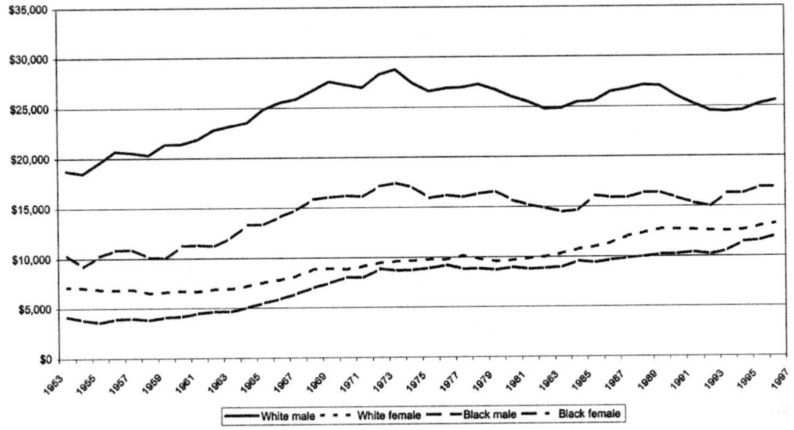

Sources: U.S. Bureau of the Census; U.S. Department of Commerce, Income Statistics Branch/HHES Division; March 1998 Current Population Survey, table P-2.

members work together from time to time (what Young, borrowing from Sartre, calls "serial collectivities") or more self-reflexive groups which share, at least for a time, common projects. One implication of this view, as black feminists have emphasized, is that intersecting structures may help determine one's social location, influence one's self-understood identity in any given context, *and* make it more difficult to organize within groups. Collins (1998) emphasizes, for example, that a barrier to the organizing of women around "women's" concerns in the United States is precisely the fact that they live in segregated communities, and thus their experience as women is highly racialized (the reverse is also true, of course). While black women and white women share some critical gender constraints (repro-duction and the sexual division of labor are prominent in feminist writ-ings), the experiences of black women and white women, or those of black women themselves (whose experiences are further structured by class and sexuality), cannot be substituted for each other. As Dorothy Roberts (1997) abundantly attests, even in an area such as reproduction, black and white women's experiences are substantially different due to the impact of race on stereotypes, American culture, and public policy.

Indeed, the state plays a major role in shaping structures such as gen-der, race, and class, as well as their intersection. The state helps define racial, ethnic, and gender categories through the census and other instruments. For example, the U.S. census originally had the categories of family head, number of free white males over age 16, number of free white females, other free persons, and the number of slaves (Collins 1998). This and other examples lead Collins to argue, "These [census] questions established a series of foundational categories that shaped American notions of public and private as well as American national identity. For free white men and women, gender emerged as one important feature that framed their status in the new nation-state. . . . The status of free white women was linked to that of men of their economic class" (Collins 1998, 15). The American state and American markets fundamentally determined how the institution of slavery would structure the intersections of gender, race, class, and sexuality. Many black feminists see as a continuing part of their political and theoretical task the need to focus critical attention on the way that differences among women arising from race provide both obstacles to unifying women and opportunities for building progressive coalitions.

Draconian public policies are another challenge taken up by many contemporary black feminists. "Reforms" in arenas ranging from reproduction to welfare are viewed by theorists such as Collins as part of an increasingly aggressive state policy of "containment" aimed at circumscribing and policing the behavior and bodies of black women (Collins 1998). This is argued to be a continuation of the status of black women when they were first workers in slave households and later domestic servants. The status of black women as what Collins labels "outsiders-within" led to black women being policed within their own homes, in their communities, on the street, and within white women's houses. While black women were able to assert some influence, Collins argues, within black civil society, they were unable to exercise power within white spheres of influence (including arenas such as white homes, where white women dominated black women) and had to struggle as well against patriarchal attempts within black communities and households to limit their roles.

Today the new policies of containment and increasing class differences among African-American women provide new challenges. On one hand, middle-class black women such as Bari-Ellen Roberts (who filed the suit against Texaco which led to the unveiling of their corporate leaders' racist behavior) face the intersection of gender and racial discrimination at relatively high levels in the workplace (Collins 1998). On the other hand, poor black women are facing increasingly severe regulation over their reproductive behavior. While *"regulating black women's reproductive decisions has [always] been a central aspect of racial oppression in America,"* the regulation of their behavior combined with their lack of access to the most advanced fertility and contraceptive aids routinely available to other middle-class women represents a serious affront to democratic justice according to black feminists such as Dorothy Roberts (1997, 6; emphasis in the original).

Another continuing challenge that faces black feminists and their allies is how to refute claims that a black feminist agenda is either secondary, unrelated, or hostile to "the" black agenda. This is the other side of the same historical coin discussed in the previous section. Black feminists continue to argue against patriarchal attempts to normalize "male" concerns as the true black agenda while also emphasizing that race is experienced differentially due to the way gender structures race. Roberts describes, for example, being "assailed" by a black man who claimed that the concerns she raised about black women's reproductive rights were not part of the black agenda, that reproductive rights were "a white woman's issue" (Roberts 1997, 5). As noted earlier, the mutual distrust and suspicion between black feminists and nationalists continues in many communities and on many campuses.

These challenges face black feminism at a time when black feminists are taking increasingly diverging directions. As Deborah McDowell and others outline, the result has been a proliferation of approaches to black feminism; some are rooted in political economy and some in cultural studies; some are heavily theoretical, while others rely on practice and are suspicious of overly theoretical black feminisms (Collins 1996, 1998; hooks 1991; McDowell 1995). Yet as Elsa Barkley Brown, Kimberle Crenshaw, Nellie McKay, Audre Lorde, bell hooks, and many other black feminists have argued, what remains decisive for understanding the ideological orientations of black women and their identities is the intersection of race and gender. Brown argues as follows in her essay on "Womanist Consciousness":

> Most feminist theory poses opposites in exclusionary and hostile ways: one is black and female, and these are contradictory/problematical statuses. This either/or approach classifies phenomena in such a way that everything falls into one category or another, but cannot belong to more than one category at the same time. It is precisely this kind of thinking that makes it difficult to see race, sex, and class as forming one consciousness and the resistance [to] race, sex, and class oppression as forming one struggle. (Brown 1992, 195)

The importance of this viewpoint is borne out in results which convincingly show that the links black women perceive to other black women are more powerful than other linkages in predicting black feminist ideology, itself a powerful shaper of black public opinion. Feminist ideology proved to shape the political attitudes of both black men and black women toward a variety of gender issues and a smaller set of other issues of critical importance to the black community.

Finally, we should note that while the differences between black feminism and black nationalism at the mass level are sometimes overstated, the results suggest continued conflict within the black community between black feminists and nationalists (as well as other ideological forces, as shown in subsequent chapters). While we found that, in general, support for black feminism did not deterministically lead to intense hostility toward a community nationalist orientation, there were important areas of difference between black feminists and black nationalists. Both community nationalism and black feminism share majority support, but they hold severely conflicting views on coalitions, the applicability of characterizing blacks as a nation within a nation, and their attitudes toward immigrant groups in the United States. The outcome of the debate between black nationalists and black feminists has serious implications for the rest of the nation. The ideology that becomes dominant will influence not only what types of coalitions blacks may enter into in the future, but even whether blacks engage in coalitional activity at all with any degree of regularity. For black feminists to have more *political* influence within the black community, they must reach the goal that so many of them have striven for—they must move much farther beyond academic communities as black feminists than they have done so far (Collins 1998; McDowell 1995). Black feminists have historically been found in nationalist, communist, and liberal formations, and today they can be found in a myriad of organizing efforts. But to compete in the ideological marketplace, a more independent presence in the community would seem warranted.

Given the ideological differences within the black community, we must heed Morrison's call and not empirically or theoretically assume that we can take for granted an undifferentiated, ungendered black community or that, for black women at least, there is a contradiction between their intersecting identities as both women and blacks. Unity between black women and others will come best with the acknowledgment of difference and respect for the multiple positions which have led to a gendered racial identity. This means that if the black community is to make any significant progress on its political agenda, the patriarchal exclusions of the past and present must be permanently relegated to the past. Crenshaw's anger was justified after the Million Man March when she responded to those who would call anyone criticizing the march a traitor: "No one seems to notice that the gender exclusion is just as much of a problem as what everybody in the march wanted to talk about, which is racism. . . . A unity that is purchased through the exclusion of the interests of specific obstacles facing 50% of the community is ill begotten unity" (Mays 1996).

Black feminists had made similar pleas for principled criticism and debate when they were labeled traitors for supporting an appointment to the Supreme Court which black commentators have retrospectively labeled as disastrous for the black community. It is past time to heed Toni Morrison's advice when she argued in the aftermath of the firestorm that surrounded the Clarence Thomas–Anita Hill hearings, "In matters of race and gender, it is now possible and necessary, as it seemed never to have been before, to speak about these matters without the barriers, the silences, the embarrassing gaps in discourse" (Morrison 1992a, xxx).

Revolution is discussed, but it is the successful revolution of white folk
and not the unsuccessful revolution of black soldiers.

W. E. B. Du Bois

What I demand of Marxism and Communism is that they serve
the black peoples, not that the black peoples serve Marxism and
Communism.

Aime Cesaire

CHAPTER 5

Black and Red: Black Marxism and Black Liberation

In their masterwork, *Black Metropolis*, St. Clair Drake and Horace Cayton
describe why Chicago's black community began to embrace the Communist Party of the United States during the Depression. A "few hundred"
blacks in Chicago joined the communists, and even wider tactical support
was gained because "with the Depression, 'the Reds' emerged as leaders—
fighting against evictions, leading demonstrations for more adequate relief,
campaigning to free the Scottsboro Boys. Their reservoir of good will was
filled to overflowing" (Drake and Cayton 1962, 735). Though communists
had been active in large urban centers, especially New York, in the previous decade, Drake and Cayton argue that the black/white unity that the
Communist Party urged was treated with great distrust by African Americans during the 1920s because "those were the days when black America
had no use for anything led by white people—its memory of the [severe

antiblack] race riots and of the wartime jobs now lost was too fresh" (Drake and Cayton 1962, 735). Not surprisingly, in the late teens and the 1920s black Marxism was dominated by black nationalists, especially those of Garvey's UNIA. The dilemma that communists generally felt during the 1920s was felt especially keenly by black communists inside and out of the Communist Party. Animosity on the part of whites, particularly white workers, toward blacks, and the perception that the political economy was racialized and racist made "traditional" socialist organizing extremely ineffective among blacks. This was especially true since those organizing from this perspective viewed racial oppression as merely a residual effect of capitalism that was better ignored until "after the revolution."

The American Communist Party never sustained a high level of support in the black community nor a consistent approach to working within the black struggle for equality, justice, and self-determination. Indeed, as the Civil Rights movement began its transformation into the Black Power movement of the 1960s, the Communist Party of the United States (CPUSA) was not a major player in the nonviolent and violent black rebellions that were rocking America from the rural hamlets of the Mississippi Delta to the angry metropolises of the North and West. But in the fires of these revolts, the seeds of a new generation of black Marxists were sown. Once again numerous Marxist cadres had their roots in what would appear to be the unlikeliest of sources—the black nationalist movements and organizations that were present in virtually every city with even a moderate population of African Americans. Once again these black Marxists would struggle through the contradictions of race and class as they tried to build a political movement based on both the racial oppression of African Americans and their concentration at the bottom of economic ladder of American society. Once again they would rail against those they saw as part of a traitorous and relatively privileged black leadership stratum in the black community. Once again, in at least a few places, local black communities would embrace the fledgling efforts of these cadres. But once again the concerns of black women would be largely absent from the agenda of this movement and its key constituent organizations. And once again the combination of dogmatic internal "struggle" against the "impure" and state repression would sweep black Marxists off the stage as major players in the black community.

Black Marxism has its roots in the history and culture which developed out of African Americans' resistance first to slavery and then to the decades of economic, political, and social subordination that followed the defeat of what Du Bois called Black Reconstruction (Du Bois 1979; Kelley 1990,

1994; Robinson 1983). Despite the claims of those such as Genovese that black radicalism was a twentieth-century phenomenon which owed its roots to white radicals, the history of black radicalism can be found in the autonomous efforts of black organizations to analyze and fight black subordination. I agree with Cedric Robinson, who argues that each generation has had to rediscover (reinvent) the tradition of black radicalism (Robinson 1983; see also Franklin 1995; Kelley 1990, 1994).

Each generation "rediscovers" Marxism under the influence of multiple pressures. First, the theoretical issue of trying to reconcile the interrelationship between race and class led activists—both nationalists and disillusioned liberals—to Marxism as a way to understand the ravages of capitalism and colonialism upon blacks throughout the Diaspora, and the class contradictions within the black community. For liberals in particular, Marxism seemed to offer a vehicle for understanding the apparent inability of capitalism to incorporate economically the most disadvantaged sectors of the black community. Former liberals, and some nationalists, saw nationalism as either utopian or, more often, as defeatist. Blacks had earned a claim to the riches of the United States. On the other hand, both former nationalists and former liberals saw liberalism as providing false hope to blacks in the United States. Both believed that neither full democratic rights nor economic incorporation would be won by blacks under American capitalism. From this perspective, both democracy and economic advancement for working-class and middle-class whites were built on black exclusion and economic superexploitation. Second, liberals and nationalists alike were inspired by successful overseas revolutions and liberation struggles. Just as black slaves in the United States had been inspired by the Haitian revolutionaries of the early nineteenth century, early-twentieth-century black activists and intellectuals were inspired by the Russian revolution and midcentury black activists were inspired by the Chinese revolution and the national liberation struggles that occurred throughout Latin America, Asia, and particularly Africa. Third, black activists, both nationalists and disillusioned liberals, pragmatically turned to Marxism as a way to identify potentially progressive allies outside of the black community.

The collision between the black radical tradition and Enlightenment-derived Marxism left both transformed. Marxism, in the same way as many world religious traditions, was transformed by the historical and cultural matrix of each group that adopted it. Robinson (1983) argues in his massive work *Black Marxism* that Marxism has a European origin but has been altered by the cultural experiences of each group that has appropriated it. Black Marxism's European origin, according to Robinson, has led some

Euro-descended Marxists to confuse their experience with "world-historic" experience, thus have leaving largely unexamined how Marxism is situated within their own, European, cultural matrix. This in turn leaves unexamined how racialism has shaped European Marxism (Robinson 1983). While Robinson concentrated much of his book on the clash between traditions as evidenced by the confrontation between Marxism and the black traditions of resistance through the analyses of the works of key black intellectuals such as Du Bois, Robin Kelley has concentrated on showing how the activists of the first half of the twentieth century brought black culture and black traditions of struggle into the Communist Party with unpredictable and occasionally explosive results. The two long-standing traditions did not mix easily, according to Robinson, and not only because of the racism and racial blinders of cadres grounded in the Euro-American Marxist tradition. Black activism had its own long history, its own sets of epistemic and metaphysical assumptions and contradictions—it was a *different* tradition:

> Black radicalism, consequently cannot be understood within the particular context of its genesis. It is not a variant of Western radicalism whose proponents happen to be Black. Rather, it is a specifically African response to an oppression emergent from the immediate determinants of European development in the modern era and framed by orders of human exploitation woven into the interstices of European social life from the inception of Western civilization. (Robinson 1983, 96–97)

This chapter explores the historical and contemporary clashes that have occurred when concerns about race and class are fused into a single ideology. While the suggestion of some historians that black radicalism is a movement inspired by whites and that black Marxism has no indigenous roots is clearly false, analyses are complicated by the historical fact that black organizations rarely remained primarily black after making the transition to Marxism. Like many black liberals, black Marxists usually worked within interracial organizations. Unlike many liberals, however, they often found the transition difficult because they came out of organizations organized around race. Black Marxists would in the end join organizations that roughly fell into two different categories. Some joined socialist organizations which had little or no interest in organizing blacks as blacks, but which saw blacks as part of a general working class. Some of these organizations found it only marginally important to fight racism. Organizations such as the Socialist Party early in the century saw such a struggle as distracting from the main fight for worker emancipation. So although the great black labor leader A. Philip Randolph joined the Socialist Party during this period, he and others in succeeding generations would continue working to build black organizations at some remove from their activities in socialist organizations. Black radicals to some degree in the 1920s, but particularly in the 1930s and the 1970s, had multiple options. Some, like Randolph, joined organizations such as the Democratic Socialists of America of a later era, which did not emphasize an approach to the status of blacks that centered on autonomous traditions of black activism. Others would remain independent as black radicals, as Bunche did early in his career or Du Bois did in the middle of his. Still others would either join or already belonged to black organizations that transformed themselves into organizations which simultaneously attempted to pursue doctrinaire Marxism (often Leninism), with an approach to black organizing centered within African-American historical and cultural traditions. Kelley characterizes this approach as bringing black nationalism within the Communist movement. I trace this ideological trend in particular in this chapter because its adherents sought, as Cesaire suggested, to transform Marxism into an ideology "that serve[s] the black peoples." (Robinson 1983, 260).

First, I sketch the development of black radical ideology, focusing on the tensions within the CPUSA and the transition to Marxism that many black nationalists followed during the 1960s and 1970s. I look briefly at the black organization that was a precursor to the CPUSA and the social democratic "successors" of the black radical tradition in the 1990s. Then I detail the level of support for the core concerns of the black Marxist tradition within contemporary African-American public opinion. In the conclusion, I sketch some theoretical questions that remain unanswered by activists within the black radical tradition. These questions center around what a newly transformed black radical analysis might look like, given a radically transformed global economy, the development of various social schisms among African Americans, and the most conservative political climate in the United States in possibly a century.

EARLY HISTORY

In 1923 several black sharecroppers were killed by the Ku Klux Klan near Elaine, Arkansas. When blacks fought back in self-defense, killing two of the terrorists, they were arrested for murder and sentenced to death (Lynn 1993). When the Supreme Court reversed the convictions, the defendants were summarily lynched. Such incidents helped to convince Conrad Lynn, a young, black law student, to dedicate his life to a radicalism which he and others saw as the only possible road for black liberation in a country where blacks were brutally oppressed, where the guarantees of a liberal constitution were nearly meaningless, and where blacks were badly outnumbered, thus rendering any nationalistic political solution problematic.

A few years earlier, another future leading black radical had a series of experiences that culminated in the violent streets of Chicago during the Red Summer of 1919. It was a time of turmoil for black America, a time in which the violent hostility of whites was fueling calls for new, militant leadership in the black community. Hill describes the context for the rise of nationalist and socialist revolutionaries during this period:

> A consequence of this era of violence against blacks, starting with the East St. Louis race riot [July 1917] and culminating in 1919 with the infamous "Red Summer" [major race riots in Chicago and many other cities], was not only the emergence of a new generation of radical black spokesmen (the generation of 1917), but the creation of a popular constituency ready and willing to support a different kind of black leadership than that which had previously existed. As one of the New Negro spokesman was to explain the desire for new leadership, "The [East] St. Louis riot demonstrated to every Negro that the lackey, cringing, and conservative spirit was not a help to him, but a decided hindrance." (Hill 1987, xii)

Harry Haywood, a Chicagoan for much of his early adult life, was profoundly shaped by the events that shook black communities within the United States during the early decades of the twentieth century. A veteran of World War I, Haywood was powerfully influenced by the war. The hospitality of the French, the vile racism of the American commanders, the inability of blacks to defend themselves from racists such as those who had driven his family from Omaha after badly beating his father, all convinced the young Haywood that militant activism was African Americans' only hope. Haywood was also influenced by the oral traditions of black political militancy and self-determination that were an active part of his family's history. His father was a follower of Booker T. Washington, but his mother passed on the traditions and stories of earlier, Reconstruction-era militants (Franklin 1995).

After returning from World War I, Haywood landed in the middle of a Chicago riot in which armed whites attacked the black community. According to Franklin, Haywood went to see some of his veteran friends who were organizing to defend the community (Franklin 1995). Haywood describes what happened on the street while he was on another assignment guarding black residences: "When the whites on the truck came through, they pulled behind and opened up with a machine gun. The truck crashed into a telephone pole at Thirty-ninth Street; most of the men in the truck had been shot down, and the others fled. Among them were several Chicago police officers—'off duty,' of course" (Haywood 1978, 82). Haywood described the impact these events had on his and other African Americans' political outlook.

> The Chicago rebellion of 1919 was a pivotal point in my life. Always
> I had been hot-tempered and never took any insults lying down. This
> was even more true after the war. I had walked out of a number of jobs
> because of my refusal to take any crap from anyone. My experiences
> abroad in the Army and at home with the police left me totally disillu-
> sioned about being able to find any solution to the racial problem
> through the help of the government; for I had seen that official agencies
> of the country were among the most racist and most dangerous to me
> and my people. (Haywood 1978, 83)

African Americans had responded to World War I in two different ways. Some, such as a (relatively) young Du Bois, had urged blacks to fight to prove their worth as citizens. This liberal strategy was similar to the demand made by Douglass and others half a century earlier that black troops be allowed to fight for their own freedom during the Civil War. Others, such as A. Philip Randolph, strongly argued that international socialist solidarity and democratic sensibilities demanded that blacks refrain—as workers and as a race which did not enjoy democracy at home—from participating in the war effort. Randolph and his newspaper, the *Messenger* (which he coedited with Chandler Owens), were solid advocates of the Socialist Party line within the black community until approximately the mid-1920s. Proud to claim that their paper was "The Only Radical Magazine Published by Negroes," the paper advocated socialist political views within the black community (Anderson 1972). Consistent with the Socialist Party line, which stated that the party had nothing extra to offer blacks, Randolph and Owen argued that black and white workers had common interests:

> First, as workers, black and white, we all have one common interest, viz.,
> the getting of more wages, shorter hours, and better working condi-
> tions. Black and white workers should combine for no other reason than

that for which individual workers should combine, viz. to increase their bargaining power, which will enable them to get their demands. Second, the history of the labor movement in America proves that the employing class recognize no race lines. They will exploit a white man as readily as a black man. (Randolph and Owen 1965, 67)

Randolph would argue in a *Messenger* article published the same year that "prejudice is a capitalist trick" (Randolph 1965, 74). His plea for black and white workers to unite fell mostly on deaf ears among the workers of both races. Cruse argues that this political line could never win mass black support: "As pioneering Negro Socialists, the *Messenger* intellectuals were just as unoriginal as the Negro Communists were to become during the 1920s. They took their political schemes from the whites, and thus did not grasp the fact that from the native American Negro point of view, neither politics, economics, nor culture took precedence over each other but were inseparable and had to function together" (Cruse 1967, 42). Eventually Randolph would abandon active agitational efforts for the socialists, and the *Messenger* became a different type of magazine by the end of the decade (Anderson 1972). Randolph would make his organizational reputation by successfully organizing railroad black workers into their own Brotherhood of Sleeping Car Porters.

Harry Haywood found a different route into black politics. While interested in the Garvey movement, he found Garvey's brand of nationalism both utopian and defeatist (Franklin 1995; Haywood 1978). The following passage from his autobiography highlights many themes: why he rejects nationalism, both pragmatically and on principle; why he is still sympathetic to the ends of nationalism; and the tactical failure to understand the mobilizing potential of black nationalism:

> Our Sunday discussion group underestimated the significance of the Garvey movement and the strength it was later to reveal. We regarded it as a transient phenomenon. We applauded some of the cultural aspects of the movement—Garvey's emphasis on race pride, dignity, self-reliance, his exultation of things Black. This was all to the good we felt. However, we rejected in its entirety the Back to Africa program as fantastic, unreal, and a dangerous diversion which could only lead to desertion of the struggle for our rights in the USA. This was our country, we strongly felt, and Blacks should not waive their just claims to equality and justice in the land to whose wealth and greatness we and our forefathers had made such great contributions. Finally we could not go

along with Garvey's idea about inherent racial antagonisms between Black and white. This to us seemed equivalent to ceding the racist enemy one of his main points. While it is true that I personally often wavered in the direction of race against race, I was not prepared to accept the idea as a philosophy. It did not jibe with my experience with whites. (Haywood 1978, 107)

In the end Haywood resisted the urge to join the Garvey movement and joined a very different sort of black nationalist organization—the African Blood Brotherhood.

The African Blood Brotherhood was founded by Cyril Briggs, an immigrant from the island of Nevis. Briggs also was the founding editor of the *Crusader*, an important New York newspaper. The *Crusader* combined "black nationalism with revolutionary socialism." (Hill 1987, vi). The magazine first appeared in August of 1917, the same month that Garvey's *Negro World* was first published (Hill 1987). Briggs, in the September issue, called for the formation of a separate black nation. This call was based on the same bleak assessment of blacks' plight in the United States that typified nationalists' motivations for separation:

Considering that the more we are outnumbered, the weaker we will get, and the weaker we get, the less respect, justice, or opportunity we will obtain, is it not time to consider a separate political existence? As one-tenth of the population, backed with many generations of unrequited toil and half a century of contribution as free men to American prosperity, we can with reason and justice demand our portion for purposes of self-government and the pursuit of happiness, one-tenth of the territory of the continental United States. (Hill 1987, xiii)

The African Blood Brotherhood for African Liberation and Redemption was founded by Briggs and other black radicals in New York in early 1919 according to Briggs (Hill 1987; but see Kelley 1994). The party combined socialism and black nationalism. It was an all-black organization aimed at organizing blacks in the United States and throughout the world. The *Crusader* published the following objectives of the Blood Brotherhood:

1. A Liberated Race
2. Absolute Race Equality
3. The Fostering of Racial Self-Respect
4. Organized and Uncompromising Opposition to the Ku Klux Klan

5. A United Negro Front
6. Industrial Development
7. Higher Wages for Negro Labor, Shorter Hours and Better Living conditions
8. Education
9. Cooperation with Other Darker Races and with the Class-Conscious White Workers

This combination of demands includes some which are consistent with black radical liberalism, others consistent with black nationalism, and still others consistent with black Marxism. These demands provided the prototype of demands that black worker and other radical organizations of the 1960s and 1970s would adopt. While different historiographies disagree about how independent the ABB was of the nascent Communist movement at its own inception (Hill 1987; Kelley 1994; Vincent 1973), the language of the organization's publications was much more consistent with black traditions of resistance than with the traditions of the predominantly white left of the period. In 1921, for example, Briggs explained the symbols and the name of the organization by making reference to the organic tie of blood between blacks in North America and on the African continent. Briggs brought this political perspective to Harlem through a variety of mechanisms; the most powerful was perhaps the paper of black New York—the *Amsterdam News*, of which he was an editor (until forced to resign).

The State Department was not amused by a black newspaper that combined nationalism and Bolshevism. State policy during World War I was to censor black publications, since any agitation for racial reform was seen as seditious. Using the language of American liberalism didn't allow them to escape the ire of the official censors. One noted "[T]hese colored editors have a certain talent for spreading a seditious feeling without uttering any actually seditious words." The *Amsterdam News*, he complained, "has a peculiar talent for saying the most fervently patriotic things in the most irritating, unpatriotic manner" (Hill 1987, xvi).[1] Government censorship of black papers intensified throughout the war. Briggs was called in twice, once for writing an article which documented that white officers were "neglecting wounded Negro-Americans on the field and in the hospitals and in giving prior aid to slightly wounded enemy prisoners over badly wounded Negro Heroes." This scrutiny continued well into the middle of

---

1. For a full account of the government attack on the black left during this period, see Kornweibel's 1998 volume, *Seeing Red.*

1919 as the state became even more worried about communism than Germans. As a Post Office agent argued, black Bolsheviks were a growing concern. He noted, "The purpose of this summary has entirely failed of its mark if it has not made clear the fact that the Negro is rapidly being made strongly race conscious and class conscious" (all quotations are from Hill 1987, xxiii).

The *Crusader* and its editor *were* becoming increasingly pro-Soviet. The anticolonial stance of the Soviet Union found fertile ground in a black left which had become increasingly preoccupied with anticolonial struggles in Africa and was increasingly disenchanted with Wilson's League of Nations as it became clear that the principle of "self-determination" was never meant to be applied to Africans. James (1998) argues that Briggs's nationalism led to his being attracted by the Bolsheviks. By the fall of 1919, the *Crusader* had become pro-Bolshevik. As Briggs would tell it in 1960, he became a communist, as would generations of black Marxists, not because of an abiding faith in socialism, but because of its program on racial issues. "I entered simply because the party had a program, even [though] not written, . . . on the Negro field; because of the solution of the national question in the Soviet Union, and because I was confident that the American party would in time take its lead on that question from its Soviet party, which is what it eventually did" (Hill 1987, xxvi).

As the ABB became more closely tied to the new Communist Party, it too, along with liberals such as Du Bois and more conventional socialists such as Randolph, joined the anti-Garvey "crusade" (Franklin 1995; Hill 1987). The tension between the two organizations culminated in a famous clash between its members, who were closely allied with the young CPUSA by this time, and Garvey at the UNIA convention during the summer of 1921. Though the ABB cadres were thrown out of the Garvey movement for their criticism of Garvey and Garveyism, they were joined by a number of defectors, including the Bishop of the organization, George McGuire, and the former secretary general of the organization (Hill 1987). As more young radicals, such as Harry Haywood, joined the ABB, it soon ceased to function as an independent organization. Blacks who wanted to join a socialist organization that at least on paper saw the struggle for black liberation as a struggle of enormous potential in its own right, one that could not be simply reduced to an appendage of the "class struggle," joined the Communist Party during the 1920s and most of the 1930s. As Hill shows, though Briggs eventually was pushed outside of the mainstream of the party for being too nationalist, as were many of the other early black cadres (this would happen in several waves over the ensuing decades), he continued to believe that it was possible to be a good communist while fighting for the national liberation of blacks: "To the end of his life, however, Briggs held fast to a black nationalist line within the party. In 1930 it caused him to be censured by party chief Earl Browder" (Hill 1987, xlviii). Briggs, like several other black pioneers in the party, was eventually expelled for promoting "nationalism" within the party. Their experience, as well as the work of the CPUSA itself, convinced the majority of the next generation of black Marxists of the need for organizations completely independent and highly critical of the Communist Party. This new generation would, however, face many of the same problems that Briggs's generation faced in the first quarter of the twentieth century. Before we turn to the 1960s, however, we need to review the experience and ideology of black cadres within the Communist Party.

THE CPUSA

The Communist Party proved to be the organizational vehicle for the most sustained organizational attempt by African Americans to develop an Afrocentric version of Marxism within a doctrinaire organization. Despite the ultimate failure of this attempt, the successes and failures of black cadres and the party itself would shape the black radical experience for the remainder of the century. The CPUSA was unable, however, to capitalize on its incorporation of the African Blood Brotherhood. While estimates vary, there is a strong consensus that during most of the 1920s black party membership was very small (Vincent estimates no more than a couple of dozen; Haywood estimates about fifty members), but there is also widespread acknowledgment that by the md-1930s party membership had mushroomed to more than ten thousand black members (Vincent 1973; Haywood 1978). The lack of membership growth during the 1920s can be traced to external factors such as the black suspicion of whites in general and white workers and leftists in particular. Further, during at least the first half of the decade, Garvey's UNIA continued to represent a viable alternative. Internal factors contributed to the lack of membership as well. Despite the presence of an articulate, reasonably experienced black cadre, the party did not emphasize specific work among African Americans.

As early as 1920 Lenin had invited discussion within the international Communist movement about the direction that work among African Americans should take (Haywood 1978). John Reed and other leading, white, American communists opposed any thesis which characterized black oppression as a national question. Willing to ignore the testimony of Garvey's successful mobilization of blacks in the United States, they maintained that nationalist movements such as Garvey's could/would enjoy "no success" among African Americans (Haywood 1978, 223). Most blacks in the party and the leadership of the Communist International (COMINTERN) wanted work among African Americans to receive a much higher priority and wanted to engage in such work in a manner that made it clear that it had a revolutionary significance of its own. The black cadre, however, disagreed about the best way to do this. Haywood's brother, among others, opposed, stating that African Americans were an oppressed nation in the South and that their experience did not reflect such a "reality," but he wanted to increase the antiracism work within the party. Others, such as Haywood, who (with the possible exception of Briggs) was the first black cadre to embrace a black nation thesis within the party, sought powerful allies in the COMINTERN and embraced the black-belt-nation thesis — a thesis that was embraced much later in the century by both nationalist and Marxist forces (Haywood 1978).

By 1928, the COMINTERN, augmented by a number of American cadres, including Haywood and his brother, had launched a full debate on the "Negro National Question" (COMINTERN 1975). The 1928 resolution called for self-determination, but nowhere were African Americans characterized as an oppressed nation. Indeed, the main form of work among African Americans that was emphasized in the 1928 resolution was trade-union organizing. While black women were explicitly targeted as a "powerful potential force for Negro emancipation," the analysis was shallow and never emphasized by the American party (COMINTERN 1975, 19). By the 1930 resolutions, which would in theory govern the CPUSA for years to come, self-determination was expressly tied to a black-belt nation in the South that had the right to "governmental autonomy" (COMINTERN 1975, 30). Organizing among blacks in the North was to operate under the slogan "equal rights" for blacks. In either case there was still an anti-autonomy line in the 1930 resolutions. They explicitly argued, "It is advisable for the Communist Party in the North to abstain from the establishment of any special Negro organizations, and in place of this to bring the black and white workers together in common organizations of struggle and joint action." (COMINTERN 1975, 27). The international and American Communist movements still did not recognize the legitimacy of the black demand for autonomy or the special character of black oppression, even in the North. Ironically, the 1928, resolution, which spoke of self-determination for African Americans without specifying the nature or existence of a black "nation," was much closer to the formulation of the

Panthers and a myriad of other black organizations during the 1960s. Across the ideological spectrum, many nationalist and quasi-Marxist black organizations adopted the principle of self-determination for African Americans substantially before they became doctrinaire Leninists in the 1970s.

While the great majority of white and some black communists opposed the COMINTERN resolution, for "black Communists, particularly those in the urban North, the resolution on black self-determination indirectly confirmed what they had long believed: African Americans had their own unique revolutionary tradition. . . . Black Communists published dozens of articles in the party press supporting the idea that African Americans have their own identifiable, autonomous, traditions of radicalism" (Kelley 1994, 109). Many black cadres rejected the black nation thesis because it was inconsistent with their understanding of American conditions. Conrad Lynn's rejection of the line was not atypical. He argued,

> I could hardly contain my amusement when we discussed this proposition at the YCL meeting. My contacts with the Deep South were close; in fact, my emotional affinity for Southern blacks was far stronger than for their Northern cousins. In all my reading of Southern Negro expression, and in conversations with acute black thinkers from that region, I had never heard of any demand for a separate black nation in the American South. I was particularly familiar with the strongest blacknationalist movement this nation has produced—Garvey's Universal Negro Improvement Association. Yet Garvey demanded only that blacks return to Africa as their spiritual, political, and physical homeland. None of the passionate, even angry voices of the Negro Renaissance had raised [James] Allen's thesis. The party leaders were obdurate. Stalin, through Allen, had furnished the key. (Lynn 1993, 50)

Many black cadres such as Haywood, however, fully supported, in fact helped create, the new line. The definition of a nation that was adopted was of course Stalin's. Stalin defined a nation as "a historically evolved, stable community of language, territory, economic life, and psychological make-up manifested in a community of culture" (Van Zanten 1967, 137–38). Lenin's characterization of blacks as an oppressed nation, which was extended by Stalin's COMINTERN, was then used by black cadres as a way to gain textual authority in party debates. Consistent with this move, Haywood characterized blacks as an internal colony. "Blacks had paid for the right to control the land with their sweat, toil, and blood." (Hutchinson 1995, 52). The official line on the national question, as Kelley, Haywood,

Briggs, and others have argued, provided an ideological space for black communists to seek black liberation with allies while providing a platform for combating reformist elements within the black community. I agree with Kelley that "by the late 1920s and early 1930s, black nationalism(s)—especially as expressed in culture—had much more in common with American communism than most scholars have admitted" (Kelley 1994, 105). Haywood describes the political importance of the new line to the black cadre of the CPUSA:

> This new line established that the Black freedom struggle is a revolutionary movement in its own right, directed against the very foundations of U.S. imperialism, with its own dynamic pace and momentum, resulting from the unfinished democratic and land revolutions in the South. It places the Black liberation movement and the class struggle of U.S. workers in their proper relationship as two aspects of the fight against the common enemy—U.S. capitalism. It elevates the Black movement to a position of equality in that battle. The new theory destroys forever the white racist theory traditional among class-conscious white workers which had relegated the struggle of Blacks to a subsidiary position in the revolutionary movement. (Haywood 1978, 234)

This emphasis on the independent political importance of black emancipatory movements is what attracted black communists of both the 1930s and 1970s to the Leninist/Stalinist version of the black national question, not strong support for the concept of a black-belt nation. Part of the problem was that the debate during both periods occurred entirely within Leninism; thus, the only two positions which could be supported internal to the paradigm were self-determination, which could only mean supporting the black nation thesis, or a position which "liquidates" the national question, (i.e., the position found then and now which says that the oppression of blacks is secondary and can wait). This is the binary opposition that the Panthers, among others, rejected. They insisted that one could support the right to self-determination without buying into the "fantasy" of a black struggle for secession.

The CPUSA in the 1930s succeeded where the Socialist Party failed, despite the best efforts of A. Philip Randolph and Chandler Owens, because of its rejection of the Socialists' (and its own) earlier line of absolute insistence on the unimportance of the special demands of African Americans (Kelley 1994). Black nationalism was a consistent theme in black communist exhortations in the 1920s and 1930s, and the importance of the salvation of the race is another theme that flows from black communists of the period. Both themes were usually resisted by the leadership and the white cadre. These themes were especially central from the period of the mid 1920s to the mid-thirties, after which we see the first of the great purges of the racially oriented black cadre.

Communist work among African Americans proceeded in both the North and the South. The party in the South was both black and red, Kelley explains,

> They became Communists out of their concern for black people and thus had much in common with the black elite whose leadership they challenged. The Communist Party was such a unique vehicle for black working-class opposition because it encouraged interracial unity without completely compromising racial politics. Irrespective of Comintern directives or official pronouncements, the Alabama CP was resilient enough conform to black cultural traditions but taut enough to remain Marxist at the core. (Kelley 1990, 116)

Black activists in the South during the Depression were ready for alliances, ready for "war." Black farmers found themselves in a deadly situation where activism had to be underground, politically motivated terrorism was common, and the Klan, police, and white elites operated in close cooperation. Black southern traditions were grounded in black resistance, often armed, of the Civil War and Reconstruction eras. They were looking, according to Kelley, for white allies to help "finish the job" begun during the titanic struggles of the Reconstruction era (Kelley 1990, 99).

One hallmark of the work in both the South and the North were the black communist attacks on black elites. As in the often violent struggles of sharecroppers (in the Sharecroppers Union) and in the Alabama steel mills, they had to take on the black elites who were often, but not always, fervently anticommunist. Kelley argues that "the Party's critique of the black petite bourgeoisie often resulted in unrestrained intraracial class conflict" (Kelley 1990, 111). Black steelworkers, sharecroppers, and other working people of the black South supported the party's activities in their organizing drives in urban and rural Alabama and in the campaign to free the young black men falsely accused of rape whom the world would come to know as the Scottsboro Boys.

Scottsboro was instrumental in helping to build the reputation of the Communist Party among grassroots African Americans. The case received enormous attention in the black community; it was the top news story between 1931 and 1935 in the black press (Vincent 1973). At the time, it caused great debate and criticism among black elites. The NAACP, which entered the case late and was forced out by the CPUSA, consistently accused the communists of opportunistically sacrificing the lives of the young defendants in order to build the party's reputation. Even left-leaning black elites such as Langston Hughes, who at the time wrote a play supporting the party's work in the case, would denounce the party's efforts in later years (Murray 1967). Yet the CPUSA just as vigorously argued that it was the NAACP which was opportunistically trying to enter the case to recover their mass base and that only a mass, worldwide campaign to free the brothers would succeed in saving their lives. One observer several decades later argued that indeed the NAACP entered late and that the Communists "saved the lives of nine young boys and opened new avenues of protest to Negroes" (Murray 1967, 287). Conrad Lynn, himself one of those purged for being too nationalist, and neutral on the merits of Communist Party activity, believed that Scottsboro represented Communist Party work at its best and indeed was instrumental in preventing the execution of the black youths (Lynn 1993). Franklin believed that the Scottsboro case, as well as their sharecropper work, marked the real breakthrough for Communist Party organizing in the black community. They out-organized the NAACP by building worldwide support for the falsely accused black boys on trial for their lives in Alabama (Franklin 1995).

The sharecropper organizing in Alabama also built the party's reputation among African Americans. As detailed in *All God's Dangers*, sharecropper work was built around the defense of black farmers trying to protect their families and property (Rosengarten 1994). Similarly, the lone position of the Communist Party in defending blacks against police brutality in urban areas also won them support, as did the rent strike and unemployment council work in urban areas. The National Urban League in 1931, then as now not the most radical of African-American organizations, reflected on why blacks would join communist organizing efforts and join or support the Sharecroppers Union in Alabama. Elmer Carter spoke for the organization when he wrote that blacks were not being attracted by Marxist philosophy. But, he argued, the SCU's demands were not exorbitant, and he went on as follows:

> These things they know. They know of grinding toil at miserably inadequate wages. They know of endless years of debt. They know of two and three months of school. They know of forced labor and peonage. When the sheriff and his deputies invaded the Negro church and broke up

the meeting of the Share Croppers Union, they were guilty of a flagrant violation of one of the basic guarantees of American Democracy. The right of peaceful assembly for the purpose of discussing grievances is so fundamental that its abrogation anywhere must be abhorrent to every right thinking individual. The threat of Communism among black tenant farmers in the South will not disappear through repression and force, for on these it feeds and grows. Rather, it will diminish in proportion to the efforts which the enlightened South puts forth to end the deplorable conditions which prevail to such a large extent in its rural areas. (Aptheker 1973, 3: 693)

The grudging respect that black elites began to give the communists was matched by the more substantial support they garnered among grassroots African Americans in the North and the South. But southern black activists of that generation would be disappointed, as were their ancestors of the Reconstruction era. Once again their allies would retreat as they decided that white allies in the South and North were more important than militant black activists. We will get to that story after discussing the briefly successful communist organizing in North.

In 1932 the editor of the black newspaper, the *Baltimore Afro-American*, stated, "The Communists appear to be the only Party going our way" (Vincent 1973, 203). A year earlier, Joseph Bibb, the editor of the *Chicago Whip*, had reported:

When thousands of colored men and women gather every night of the week at the open-air forums held by these radical groups in the park and on the street corners of nearly all of our large cities to listen with rapt attention and enthusiasm to doctrines of a radical reorganization of our political and economic organization, the evidence to the contrary of the declaration that "Negroes will never take to Communist [*sic*]" is too strong to be ignored. . . . The rottenness, the injustice, the grim brutality, and cold unconcern of our present system has become too irksome to the man farthest down to be longer endured in silence and pacifism. . . . The Communists have framed a program of social remedies which cannot but fail to appeal to the hungry and jobless millions, who live in barren want, while everywhere about them is evidence of restricted plenty in the greedy hands of the few. (Vincent 1973, 200)

The early 1930s saw growing black support in northern urban areas for the Communist Party. At the grassroots level, marches of "several thousand" took to the streets in Harlem under communist leadership around economic issues. Cultural elites such as the great Duke Ellington volunteered their services at party fund raisers.

This level of support in black communities such as Chicago and Harlem was based on a number of different communist-led activities. Mark Naison traced the growth of mass influence in Harlem to communist work on the Scottsboro case, work with the unemployed, the courage with which white communists physically defended black communists, and work on health and housing issues. This set of activities garnered massive community support, and united front work with black elites paid off during the 1930s (Naison 1983). One particularly critical event that occurred was the Yokinen "trial." This 1931 trail was held publicly in Harlem to deal with a Finnish immigrant cadre who didn't want to let blacks into a worker's dance. Major black newspapers such as the *Afro-American* in Baltimore (28 February 1931) covered the Yokinen trial with a glee that doesn't match a cynical analysis which questions the wisdom of an antiracist campaign being conducted among party members during this period (Aptheker 1973; Hutchinson 1995). The spectacle of a predominantly white organization trying one of its own members for racist actions and then sentencing him to work on behalf of blacks was covered favorably within the black community. One disastrous result, however, amidst a number of positive results, was that the party's policy of encouraging race-mixing and assimilation in all social and political situations led to the expulsion of a number of a black cadres who opposed the policy (Franklin 1995).

The Communist Party's northern work was uneven when it came to the questions of culture. On one hand, they were able to involve many of the leading cultural, intellectual, and artistic leaders of black America in their activities. Thus Richard Wright, Langston Hughes, Duke Ellington, and many others either donated artistic performances or more directly worked on party-sponsored publications. On the other hand, the spectacle of black cadres dressed like Russian peasants attacking the church in a black Chicago park struck many black residents of these communities as at least ludicrous if not offensive (Franklin 1995; Wright 1966).

Initially the main vehicles for the work among African Americans outside of the South was the American Negro Labor Congress (ANLC), formed in 1925. The ANLC was supposed to be the main vehicle for united front work among African Americans, bringing black and white workers together to fight against racial, social, and economic oppression. The enemy was "white ruling-class terrorism," according to the founding documents (Aptheker 1973, 657). Enemies also included (white) labor bureaucrats and "treacherous" black, middle-class leaders (Aptheker 1973). As Baraka and other black Marxists would argue half a century later, the black struggle must be led by black toilers (workers and farmers). The emphasis on class struggle as opposed to black liberation can be found in the argument that the black struggle is "essentially a class struggle, and not as [petit bourgeois blacks] pretend, a purely racial struggle" (Aptheker 1973, 663). Thus working-class struggle is needed both because the black middle class is not "courageous" enough and because the working class should lead what is in essence a working-class struggle. The view that black struggle is aimed at national liberation is never fully developed in the founding ANLC documents. The program itself was a liberal one; equal rights, antidiscrimination work, and extension of public services to black neighborhoods are among the outlined demands (Aptheker 1973).

The ANLC never got off the ground; its line reflected the pre-COMINTERN resolutions' approach to communist work among blacks. Its successor organization, the League of Struggle for Negro Rights, was founded in 1930 (Naison 1983). It worked against lynching, around the Scottsboro case (here the International Labor Defense, the ILD, took the lead for the communists), around unemployment, employment discrimination, and for equality. The party's membership in New York grew slowly, while its influence (as it did around the country) grew rapidly during the early 1930s (Kelley 1990, 1994; Naison 1983). By mid-1930 in New York and elsewhere in urban black America, communists were major players. Their ideological influence far exceeded their numbers, as their work especially influenced intellectual and cultural elites.

Problems in their work grew on multiple fronts. Race-baiting was a standard tactic that both white elites and white workers systematically used to undermine the party's influence among whites. White workers in 1932 Atlanta were organized in terrorist "Black Shirt" groups to preserve the racial order in labor markets. Earl Ofari Hutchinson reports that "their slogan was . . . No Jobs for Niggers Until Every White Man Has a Job" (Hutchinson 1995, 55). Further, as the party tried to develop black leadership, its detractors labeled the communists as a black party, as the Republicans were labeled during Reconstruction and the Democrats from the 1970s on—a framing that remains deadly in American politics (Dawson 1994; Hutchinson 1993).

The Central Committee was worried both by what they saw as the nationalist trend developing in the Harlem branch (allegedly under the leadership of former ABB cadres such as Richard Moore and Cyril Briggs), as well as by the problem of garnering white allies who wouldn't be offended by the work among blacks (Kelley 1990; Naison 1983; Hutchinson 1995). These cadres had an independent political base due to their long residence and history of agitation as respected members of Harlem's black community (Kelley 1994; Naison 1983). The party's leadership sabotaged the efforts of Briggs and other black communists in 1930s to build the League of Struggle for Negro Rights, and its newspaper the *Liberator* (of which Briggs was the editor) into instruments for black liberation and black organizations. The Central Committee explicitly condemned attempts to turn one into "a Negro organization" and the other into a "Negro paper." (Kelley 1994). More nationalist-oriented cadres were never able to convince the party hierarchy that blacks should be given the same group status and protection that European ethnic groups had been (Cruse 1967). Black attempts at forming black organizations were treated differently and more stringently. Not surprisingly given this orientation, the leadership believed that the Harlem branch was much too responsive to the community's political views (Naison 1983). They brought in a communist member of the black elite, James Ford, to take control of the Harlem work (Naison 1983).

Concretely, the Central Committee opposed campaigns aimed at community control, opposed boycotts of Harlem stores that didn't hire black workers, opposed policies conducted by the Harlem branch with other African Americans that led to displacement of white workers, and argued that the anti-discrimination campaign should be a citywide struggle, not a campaign intended specifically to control employment in a "segregated district" like Harlem. Moore opposed this change in policy, because it put the "burden" on black not white workers. In July of 1933 Moore made the following argument: "Why all this talk about antagonizing white workers. . . . Are not these white workers in Negro neighborhoods living on the backs of the Negro masses? Are they not occupying jobs that rightly belong to Negroes?" (Naison 1983, 101–2).

Moore's views were labeled as black nationalist by the Central Committee and condemned (Naison 1983). His views, however, were quite consistent with those of black leftists outside of the party during the same period. Du Bois argued in 1933 that white workers, including immigrants, rose up the ladder on the backs of blacks. So a Marxist analysis would suggest that "colored labor has no common ground with white labor." (Du Bois 1973, 214). A few years earlier Ralph Bunche had argued that white workers got a psychic boost from caste exploitation of blacks (Bunche 1995b). The party was unmovable on this question, however, and the old Harlem leadership was dismantled. In October 1933, Ford removed Briggs from the editorship of the *Liberator*, and in 1934, Moore was replaced as the head of the League of Struggle for Negro Rights by Haywood, who was religiously following the party "antinationalist" line. By 1934, Kelley argues, the League was defunct.

The work in the South follows an even more rapid denouement, and, unlike the work with northern blacks, it was not as adaptable to changes in party line. The work among blacks in the South was destroyed by both external attacks and internal changes in policy. For example, strikes by black workers were broken with appeals to white interests. In 1936 a strike by black Birmingham women was attacked by the White Legion with the appeal to white women that "there are too many Negroes in the industry" (Kelley 1990, 121). The strike didn't receive labor support and was quickly put down, despite communist efforts (Kelley 1990). By the second half of the 1930s, black membership was dropping in Alabama. Kelley argues that the party was trading black membership for white membership and the desire to have southern white liberal leadership—a stratum that was openly racist. The situation deteriorated to the point that "progressive" lyrics were written for the "great" racist anthem "Dixie," and the term "comrade Nigger" became common (Kelley 1990, 137). These changes all occurred in the name of an unprincipled and ultimately racist unity that was common during the united front period.

By the mid-1930s, charges of nationalism were being used to silence blacks who were charging white cadres with racism. Conrad Lynn, with many other black intellectuals (he claims), was purged from the party in 1937 for protesting the lack of party support for Trinidadian oil workers who had been fired on by British warships. He pointed out the hypocritical nature of the party's stance when they supported Cuban revolutionaries in 1934 but now couldn't support black oil workers. He claimed the anti-"nationalist" purges began before the first National Negro Congress meeting in 1936. Part of the problem for Lynn and many other black communists was that they viewed the main enemy of black people to be in the United States, not overseas (which is why some black radicals joined the merchant marine rather than join American armed forces during World War II; see Lynn 1993).

On the other hand, mass organizations such as the International Workers Order (IWO) were making good "headway" with blacks because of their relief services (such as support for sick members) and their sponsoring of cultural activities, including a thirteen-city tour which featured the renowned black poet Langston Hughes. Despite problems with racism within the organization, it did break down barriers between blacks and white ethnic workers (Hutchinson 1995). During this period African-American work had built links to trade unions, and, as united front work became central during the mid-1930s, the party's work moved into the mainstream of black politics, particularly in New York City (Naison 1983). The main vehicle for united front work was the National Negro Congress (NNC). The NNC policy deemphasized communist leadership, but emphasized building as wide a front as possible. For example, communists did not push their own cadres for elected positions in the NNC, and A. Philip Randolph was elected president of the organization. Formed in 1936, the National Negro Congress attracted the Howard radicals such as Bunche, Harris, and Frazier, as well as Randolph (Franklin 1993). Its goals were both international (supporting Ethiopia) and domestic (the CIO's organizing drive and black equality in the trade unions). During this period the dividing line between party and sympathizers grew dim. Skeptics like Randolph and Carter Woodson were favorably impressed, while even the NAACP moderated its policies against the CPUSA (Naison 1983). Although the party rejected racial politics in favor of interracial action, it did not (and could not) stifle the creative contributions of black radicals. On the contrary, during this period African-American culture created a home for itself in communist circles because of the growing presence of black working people (Kelley 1994).

Still, black disenchantment with the CPUSA grew rapidly during this period. Black progressives, especially black communists, were angered by the party's refusal to remain staunch in the face of atrocities such as the Fascist invasion of Ethiopia or, as Lynn detailed, the British massacre of striking dock workers in Trinidad. Some, Kelley argued, didn't leave the party but expressed what he called "Black Internationalism" through participation in the Spanish Civil War. He quotes one black cadre as saying, "This ain't Ethiopia, but it'll do" (Kelley 1994, 123). An independent working-class, college educated, black cadre from Chicago was always in trouble because of his alleged nationalism and a knowledge of black history and Marxist theory that some of the leadership found "threatening." While white southern cadres were routinely addressing blacks as "Comrade Nigger," he got into trouble for referring to black folks as "my people" (Kelley 1994, 127). The invasion of Ethiopia, the one independent African state, mobilized the black community as much as the Spanish Civil War a year later mobilized white progressives. Indeed, the mobilization and breadth of feeling in the black community exceeded the breadth and depth of support among whites for the Royalist forces in Spain.

As Earl Browder and his colleagues become more entrenched in the Communist Party's leadership, African-American and antiracist work declined in both importance and quality. By World War II, the retreat on the centrality of black liberation was so pronounced that the Sharecroppers Union was dissolved since "it was an obstacle to unity between southern black and white farmers" (Franklin 1995, 181). Once again unity had to be on whites' terms. At approximately the same time, Browder urged that the slogan of "self-determination" for blacks in the South be eliminated as an official position of the party. Browder in 1944 argued that blacks had already opted for full integration and that the American system was quite capable of granting blacks "full equality" (Mouledous 1964, 80). During the war, black veterans, including Spanish Civil War veterans and a wide range of other black organizations and leaders (including once again the newspaper editors), launched the famed (and once again seditious, according to the War Department) "Double V" campaign against Fascism overseas and racism at home. The campaign was not only opposed by the state in this World War, but also by the Communist Party, which considered it too militant (Kelley 1994). Blacks who had been allied with the party felt abandoned.

Despite temporary appearances of a revival in African-American work after war when Browder's faction was defeated, the party continued to be increasingly inhospitable to cadres who wanted to adapt the theory and practice of Marxism to black liberation. Once again calls to end support for black self-determination came from the party's leadership. In the early 1950s, things got so bad that a memorandum by Doxy Wilkerson was issued which argued that "race and racial characteristics had nothing to do with the special oppression of Afro-Americans" (Haywood 1978, 594–95). Haywood and others protested a line that they saw as both false and disastrous. Their rebuttals were squashed, but a year later, in 1952, they were partially co-opted into the party line. A couple of years before the Montgomery bus boycott, but during the period of Tampa and Baton Rouge boycotts, the CPUSA's leadership had lost touch with the anger that was building among southern blacks. Party leader James Jackson wrote, "To the Negro masses in the South who have yet to win their elementary democratic right to vote, to remove the Jim Crow pale in the street cars, to sit in the public parks—such a slogan of action would be rejected, considered "utopian" (Haywood 1978, 600). He went on to argue for the liquidation of the party's independent work in the Civil Rights movement. Not surprisingly, organizations within which the party's work had been instrumental were dissolved; among them were the Council of African Affairs, which involved Du Bois and Robeson, among others; the National Negro Labor Council; and dozens of similar organizations (Haywood 1978).

Davis recommended in 1956 that the party should abandon the slogan of self-determination because the national question was at root a peasant question, which had been solved by black migration to the North. Consistent with this view was the continued attack on nationalist forces, with particular emphasis on the Nation of Islam. By 1958, black and Puerto Rican cadres were being quickly pushed out of party. Briggs was attacked in late 1950s (as were Haywood and James Jackson) for arguing that progressive nationalist movements were about to become once again important. In 1959 he argued, "There is occurring today a veritable mushrooming of Negro nationalist groups. . . . It is necessary that we give serious thought to the nationalist trend in the Negro movement" (Hutchinson 1995, 237). He was dismissed as a "bitter and disillusioned old man whom the times had passed by" (Hutchinson 1995, 237).

By the seventeenth National Convention of the CPUSA in 1959, the downgrading of the status of the black freedom struggle had come to a head. Black communists were particularly concerned with this trend (Van Zanten, 1967). According to Haywood, these debates were occurring at the time of increasing racial conflicts, such as the confrontation around the schools of Little Rock, Arkansas, in the fall of 1957. But even during this period, the CPUSA's top leadership was arguing that the focus of activity should be on the NAACP and that no work should focus on the independent left (Haywood 1977). In a document prepared for internal debate, Haywood ultimately loses the following argument:

> We, Negro Communists, do not accept the status of "aliens" to which the Negro Resolution relegates us. We are an integral part of the Negro movement, embodying the great revolutionary traditions of Nat Turner, Frederick Douglass, Harriet Tubman, etc. We do not become "foreigners" when we become Communists. It is, therefore, not only the right, but the duty of Negro Communists to project forms and methods of struggle consistent with the great revolutionary traditions of the Negro people. As true patriots, we call for a consistent fight against U.S. imperialism as the main enemy of the Negro people. We call for an alliance with the white working class based upon common revolutionary aims. We call for international solidarity with the heroic struggles for national liberation, peace, and socialism which embrace the vast majority of mankind. (Haywood 1977, 38)

It would take another generation of black communists who also refused to sacrifice their black identity on the altar of socialist solidarity to take up Haywood's call. Haywood was expelled in 1958 for his "nationalist" position on the black national question (Franklin 1995).

Haywood argued that the CPUSA went from leading the black fight for equality, a clear overstatement, to opposing the black revolutionary movement: "The CPSUA did not even attempt to mobilize labor support for the black struggle, and the labor aristocracy maintained hegemony over the workers' movement" (Haywood 1978, 630). The optimism of the 1960s exhibited by both liberals and the CPUSA was a partial result of misanalyzing the potential for the economic and social integration of African Americans into American civil society. The CPUSA's optimism was such that on the eve of the March on Washington, the party declared Kennedy a "friend." They had, Hutchinson argued, seriously misjudged the amount of anger in urban black communities (Hutchinson 1995, 247). In contrast, black communists in the late 1960s would rely on an analysis which saw the superprofits that derived from the perceived superexploitation of blacks as being the foundation on which the social peace between white workers and the ruling class was built and maintained. The leadership of the CPUSA also did not recognize that Malcolm X was changing and continued to attack him in the middle 1960s, even after his death (Hutchinson 1995). The CPUSA's leadership was isolated from any understanding of the political and social dynamics within black America, even though it still had dedicated black cadres active in the black movement. The party's official blindness was stunning. Even by 1966, General Secretary Gus Hall could still write, "The Negro freedom struggle [was] a specialized part of the general class struggle" (Hutchinson 1995, 252).

By the late 1960s, the CPUSA started paying more attention to black militancy, even as it denounced the Panthers and others, because it recognized the depth of nationalist sentiment in the black community. For example, 21 percent of blacks in a *Newsweek* poll found a separate nation "desirable." The party called the demand for reparation issued by the former Student Nonviolent Coordinating Committee (SNCC) activists a "just" demand (Hutchinson 1995, 260). The "Free Angela" work (the popular, revolutionary, black college professor and CPUSA leader who was falsely arrested and tried for murder in California during the early 1970s) built a true mass movement that brought blacks and whites together, but the party was unable to translate this success into long-range improvement in African-American work (Hutchinson 1995). The CPUSA was largely outside of the black movement and discredited by the late 1960s, when black nationalists and other experienced black activists, leaders, and organizations once again started turning toward a "black" version of Marxism. Both Moscow's needs in the Sino-Soviet split and the CPUSA's complete misreading and dismissal of the black liberation movement (except the Free Angela movement and some trade-union work) would more or less isolate the party from the black radical movement which soon exploded in the midst of the urban uprisings of the 1960s.

BLACK RADICALISM AND THE BLACK POWER MOVEMENT

You're supposed to represent the American way of life, and I believed
in you for the job ahead and agreed with you mostly because I see what
you see . . . but when you settle for a weak Civil rights Bill, we part
company. . . . I do know that the masses of black people are very much
displeased with your action . . . to back down from what you believed
and what I thought you believed in—Freedom for all. How long
Mr. President will my people have to wait in bondage? Do you not see
what revolution can do to a country? The Negro today are not waiting
any longer for excuses. We want action and we want it now. Not word,
Mr. President. Action! Or the massive force of the black Revolution will
soon turn to *RED* in *these* United States. I pray for your good health.
From a letter in the Kennedy Presidential Archives dated
November 1963 from a black, New York city male

Lifelong black radical lawyer Conrad Lynn described an incident in New York City in April of 1964 in which a black youth was viciously beaten by a special tactical police squad. When neighborhood men protested the beating, all hell broke loose. The police proceeded to break the nose of a Puerto Rican seaman and gouged out the eye of Frank Stafford, who wasn't taken to the hospital for nineteen hours. Other community activists were arrested and became known as the Harlem Six. The mothers of the six were turned away by the NAACP, and there was no International Labor Defense to go to bat for them in the 1960s. It wasn't until the early 1970s that the determined efforts of Lynn and fellow radical attorney William Kunstler were able to win a new trial for the last of the six to remain incarcerated. The anger generated by incidents like this during the mid-1960s led directly to the long hot summers in places such as Harlem, Watts, and Detroit, and, what is more important, led to the rise of a black-power-oriented, urban black movement that would dominate the politics of the black community for a decade and had a strong institutional presence in the military of the Vietnam era, on virtually every college campus that had even a modest number of black students, and in many of America's workplaces.

The most militant of the organizations which emerged from the massive organizing that was occurring in urban black communities and on college campuses during this period were, as the most prescient black cadre of the CPUSA predicted, ideologically oriented around black nationalism. Just as Malcolm X moved to a position of revolutionary nationalism after his trip to Mecca, such diverse organizations as the Student National Coordinating Committee (SNCC), the League of Revolutionary Black Workers, the Congress of Afrikan Peoples, and the Black Panther Party would move from black nationalism to a variation of black Marxism. These organizations had influence on dozens of college campuses, participated in successful electoral coalitions, had the capability and will to shut down production at key Detroit auto factories, had relations with several foreign governments, many on very poor terms with the American state, and, along with other nationalists, mounted the most serious ideological challenge to black liberal hegemony in theory and practice since the height of the Garvey movement.

These organizations often did not represent a seamless tradition with their contemporaries and predecessors in the CPUSA. They did, however, face many of the same organizational and ideological problems. They also faced the criminal lack of understanding of race and nationality within large segments of the predominantly white left. With the "liquidation" of the national question by the Browder-led CPUSA during the 1940s, the new generation of black radicals looked once again overseas, turning to Africa and Asia for ideological inspiration.

This section examines the ideological development of three of these organizations for which the relationship between theory and practice was particularly critical. In theory these organizations self-consciously moved from revolutionary nationalism to Leninism. In practice, the story is much more complicated. At the time, each of the organizations took great pains to distinguish itself from the other. Two were oriented around building a movement within the black community. The third, at least initially, was focused on organizing black workers at the point of production. Despite great differences in geographic location, rhetorical style, (and even style of dress), they shared a great many similarities in ideological development that helped define the development of a particularly "black" radicalism as the twentieth century emerged from the depths of Cold War politics and into the era of national liberation. The three organizations whose ideological orientations I examine are the League of Revolutionary Black Workers, the Black Panther Party, as represented by some of its later writings, and the Congress of Afrikan Peoples, represented in the writings of Amiri Baraka, as it transitioned from cultural to revolutionary nationalism and ultimately to Leninism. We start at the point of production with an analysis of the ideology of Detroit's League of Revolutionary Black Workers.[2]

Our Thing Is DRUM! The Dodge Revolutionary Union Movement and the League of Revolutionary Black Workers

Dare to fight! Dare to Win!
Fight, Fail,
Fight Again, Fail Again,
Fight on to Victory.

DRUM chant

By the 1960s, blacks in Detroit had had significant exposure to Marxism. Not only did "black auto workers come to identify Marxism with people willing to fight for black causes. This identification was spread to the larger community during the late forties" (Geschwender 1977, 80). Several types of Marxism were available; there was the CPUSA, and the great black Trotskyite intellectual C. L. R. James "spent much of World War II" in Detroit. James and Grace Lee Boggs were both active among black auto workers as well. Marxists had a long history of struggle both in and out of the auto industry, in and out of the union, and in and out of the CPUSA. Boggs, a Detroit auto worker, and his philosopher wife, Grace Lee Boggs, were very influential in the black radical circles of Detroit auto workers and community activists. Through a series of articles, they produced a body of work (much of which was collected in the 1970 volume *Racism and the Class Struggle*) whose influence went beyond Detroit's black radicals. Their works

2. One important organization which unfortunately is not reviewed here is the African Liberation Support Committee. Primarily a coalition of black nationalist, black Marxist, and black community organizations to support the armed liberation struggles of Southern Africa, it also did extensive work in many communities for many years during the 1970s around issues of blacks within the United States. More important for our purposes, it provided the key forum for ideological debate within the black movement. At several key conferences, issues of nationalism versus Marxism were debated, and it was through this forum that we can document the shift from nationalism to Marxism. This history is, however, largely undocumented, while the memories of state repression, red (and black) baiting, and violent internal conflicts remain fresh despite the assurances of a "democratic liberal" state that those days are past.

were standard fare in black study groups, in worker circles, and among student activists from New York to California. Their most direct influence, however, was on the group of young black activists and auto workers who became the core of the League of Revolutionary Black Workers.

A consistent theme of their work, one that Bunche and Du Bois had emphasized a generation earlier, and one that would be repeated by black Marxists of their generation even in its Leninist incarnations during the 1960s and 1970s, was that white workers were *not* the natural allies of African Americans seeking justice. Boggs's main critique of contemporary Marxists was their lack of "scientific" analysis of the relative position of white and black workers in any progressive struggle:

> The Marxists recognize that a revolution is involved in the Negro struggle, but still they want the Negroes to depend upon the white worker being with them. The Negro worker who works in the shop knows that if he is going to depend upon the white worker, he will never get anywhere. The average white worker isn't joining any liberal organizations or radical organizations. If he is joining anything, he is joining racist organizations. (Boggs 1970b, 30)

White workers, in the main, constitute part of the enemy because the white working and middle classes benefit economically from the superexploitation of blacks. The black power movement must stay independent, and progressive whites, regardless of class, can support black liberation by organizing among themselves (Boggs 1970c). The reason that whites are unlikely allies was that the American economic system was constructed on the superexploitation of black labor, and the extra profits were used to "bribe" a portion of white workers:

> Economic development has been the reason for the super-exploitation of blacks at every stage, and the super-exploitation of blacks has in turn accelerated economic development. Thus the American way of life has been created, a life of expanding comfort and social mobility for whites, based upon servitude and lack of freedom for blacks. This in turn has encouraged everyone to look upon everyone else as a steppingstone to personal advancement. (Boggs 1970a, 167)

Unlike some other black activists of the period, but in close agreement with the political views of the Black Panthers of the early 1970s, Boggs forecast that black labor was becoming superfluous. Because blacks were becoming "expendable" to the economy, a social revolution, a black revolution, was necessary (Boggs and Boggs 1970). The political consequences for the Boggses were clear—as black people, "[We] can't escape our destiny. Our destiny is right in this country" (Boggs 1970d). Thus the land over which blacks should fight for control is the land of the cities of America (Boggs and Boggs 1970). Community control of the economic and political power of black communities has to be the goal of black activists. But, like many revolutionary nationalists and black Marxists from that period (as well as black activists from the United Kingdom), they had an expansive definition for the term *black*, which was meant to include other people of color as well as African Americans (Boggs and Boggs 1970).

Thus Boggs's revolutionary nationalism, like that of the Panthers, contained an internationalist element, as it was meant explicitly to include those other than whites who did not share the wealth generated by an exploitative capitalist economy. Also like the Panthers, Boggs viewed cultural approaches to black liberation and reliance on a "mythical" African past at best as distractions to the real work of winning black power (Boggs 1970d). Thus by 1970 Boggs was arguing that black nationalism could be progressive but was limited: "Black nationalism has been progressive because it has bound black people together and given them strength, but black nationalism in and of itself is not a sufficient answer to the problems of black people" (Boggs 1970a, 72). Like all of the revolutionary organizations of the time, Boggs explicitly argued that revolution is the only road to black salvation. The liberal road must be rejected:

> The key to the future lies in being able to resist the temptation to reform the system so that it can work. It is not difficult to recognize that a system is in trouble. What is difficult is to recognize this and at the same time recognize that all attempts to reform the system will in the end only create more bitterness and conflict with those forces already in motion, forces which can only survive by transforming the system from top to bottom. (Boggs 1970a, 167)

The young activists who participated in the study circles with the Boggses would put much of this ideological extension of black radicalism into practice in Detroit, which had been shaken by the most severe race rebellion to occur in a series of summers of racial disturbances.

The industrial buildup for World War II saw a huge influx of blacks into Detroit, especially in the auto industry, leading to massive racial tensions that resulted in the World War II Detroit race riot. Chrysler's number of black workers alone went from 0 in 1941 to 5,000 by 1945 (Georgakas and Surkin 1975). Many of these jobs were lost in the downturn that followed the war. The supervisory and better-paid jobs were reserved for whites through collusion between the company and the UAW to protect "white" jobs. This set of circumstances was directly responsible for encouraging the formation of black revolutionary worker organizations such as the Dodge Revolutionary Union Movement (DRUM) in 1968, one year after the 1967 conflagration. DRUM's formation was announced with a massive wildcat strike on May 2, 1968, which succeeded in shutting down Dodge Main. The cadre at the *Inner City Voice* (a radical black newspaper) and General Baker, a young black auto worker, were instrumental in forming DRUM and the other RUM chapters that quickly followed. The *Inner City Voice* was a popular newspaper in Detroit's black community that emphasized black liberation at home and an anti-imperialist political viewpoint in its analyses of foreign affairs. It was seen as enough of a threat to incur the active hostility of the state and white vigilante groups. FBI and vigilantes put tremendous pressure on the paper; its production facilities were eventually driven out of Detroit, and it had to be printed by the same firm in Chicago that printed the Nation of Islam's *Muhammad's Speaks* (Georgakas and Surkin 1975).

The League of Revolutionary Black Workers was formed to unite the RUMs in June of 1969. The most important work was in-plant organizing, led by General Baker and Chuck Wooten. Chapters were formed at Dodge Main, Eldon Avenue, Ford River Rouge, Chrysler Jefferson Avenue, the Mack Avenue plant, the Cadillac Fleetwood plant, and at other plants, including chapters at hospital and UPS work sites (Georgakas and Surkin 1975). They received strong black community support. Students often worked with them and took on picketing and leafleting duties when workers in the plant were under severe management, union, and police pressure. Eventually they were able to seize control of the Wayne State University student newspaper, *The South End.* One reason for the strong community support was the idiocy of management during this period, as reflected in a GM vice president's view of the life of a "typical" auto worker:

> He's got a hell of a nice home, two-car garage. He has two cars. He's got a trailer that he hooks on the back of one of those cars, and he hauls his boat up north, and he's got a hell of a big outboard motor on the back of that. . . . And he probably has a summer place up north. . . . In the wintertime, he puts a couple of snowmobiles on that trailer and hauls them

up there. He leaves Friday night while you and I work. (Georgakas and Surkin 1975, 126)

But it was not only an exploitative and racist corporate management that the league targeted as the enemies of black workers and the black community. The UAW was considered part of the system of black oppression, as the following statement from the league illustrates: "The UAW with its bogus bureaucracy is unable, has been unable, and is in many cases unwilling to press forward the demands and aspirations of black workers" (Georgakas and Surkin 1975, 21). The league saw itself as an explicitly revolutionary organization: "The League of Revolutionary Black Workers is dedicated to waging a relentless struggle against racism, capitalism, and imperialism. We are struggling for the liberation of black people in the confines of the United States as well as to play a major revolutionary role in the liberation of all oppressed people in the world" (Geschwender 1977, 127). The league argued that all whites benefited from "white skin privilege," and that these material benefits kept white workers from allying with black workers (Geschwender 1977, 128). A common theme in black radical thought, both Marxist and nationalist, was that white interests led white identity to be focused on race, not class:

> As long as white workers think of themselves as white workers or white middle or lower class, they will be counter to the struggle, and will retain white consciousness as opposed to class consciousness. To think in those terms means a struggle for the decaying privileges that buttress the system of racism and exploitation instead for the liberation of all working people. It is without question that white labor will be forced to shift gears. Currently, however, the liberation struggle of blacks is moving at a quickening pace. It is our contention that the key to the black liberation struggles lies with the black workers. (Geschwender 1977, 129; from the *Inner City Voice*, February 1971)

The league theoretically justified its concentration on black workers by arguing that they were concentrated "at the point of production" and in the lowest, hardest, and worst-paid sectors of the industrial hierarchy." The point of black workers' struggle should be to "control the point of production" (Geschwender 1977, 129,130).

Their line on the national question was somewhat undefined. What emerged was a view which rejected both non-working-class rule in any type of state and what was seen as utopian nationalism. Like Boggs, they viewed any nationalism which posited a separate black state while U.S. capitalism and imperialism remained intact as utopian. This was explicitly stated in an interview with one of the league's leaders, John Watson: "We are no more for integrated capitalism than for segregated capitalism. Neither are we in favor of a separate state, based on the same class lines as this society. We are against a separate state in which a black capitalist class exploits a black proletariat. We are opposed to all sorts of haphazard talk which doesn't tell us what to do with the United States, capitalism, and imperialism" (Georgakas and Surkin 1975, 71). White workers and, more generally, progressive whites had a role to play, to struggle; primarily they should struggle against racism and help build a black workers' movement. Black workers were to be revolutionary examples who could serve to energize and mobilize progressive white workers. Black workers were understood as more likely to be class conscious due to their superexploitation. Embedded in this view was the same colonial model that we find in Baraka, the Panthers, and others from this period. The black bourgeoisie was viewed as reactionary, as were programs which promoted black capitalism. They saw the black bourgeoisie as performing the same neo-colonial role for white elites that Fanon described the bourgeoisie of colonized countries playing for imperialism and the former colonizers.

Their alliance policy toward whites was very similar to that of the Panthers. In the 1969 documentary film, *Finally Got the News*, they described the reason for their policy as follows: "White workers came to support us. Some wanted to work with us. But we found out that management knew how to divide the whites. We decided that we could work best by organizing alone. We told whites to do the same thing. Once they did that, we could work with them on a coalition basis" (Georgakas and Surkin 1975, 48). Not surprisingly they also had working alliances, although usually short-lived, with other black nationalist forces. There was a brief alliance between the Panthers and DRUM. There were a number of dual memberships during 1968. Differences over line, and the desire of the Oakland-based Panthers to have tight control over the Detroit branch led to the ending of league involvement in the Detroit branch.

Tensions around the national question grew within the organization. The line in practice toward white workers was different from that of stated policy. The official line is outlined by Watson again in the documentary:

> The white workers face the same contradictions in production and life as blacks do. If they work harder, they think the enemy is 'the nigger.' If life is worse, the problem is 'crime in the streets.' . . . [George] Wallace

raps the money barons and the niggers; and these white workers love to hear it. . . . Many white workers end up being counter-revolutionary in the face of a daily oppression which should make them the staunchest of revolutionaries. . . . We are calling for the uplifting of the working class as a whole. (Georgakas and Surkin, 1975, 142)

Nationalism among cadres continued to be a problem in 1969 during a series of actions at the Eldon Avenue plant which had horrendous working conditions. Some black cadres, for example, refused to give their leaflets to white workers. The tensions within the leadership and among the cadres were also tied to what Georgakas and Surkin call "hostile ELRUM attitude toward white participation and working with nonrevolutionary blacks" (1975, 122).

The seeds for the later split were sown when one faction of the leadership wanted to emphasize the plant work and subordinate the other work to the needs of the plant units. The other faction was busily recruiting students, professionals, and generally building community-wide networks and support. They argued equally strongly that while the working class should lead, community and workplace organizing went hand in hand, and that much of the community organizing was being conducted and led by workers around working-class issues. The scope of activities was spectacular. A Black Student United Front had branches in twenty-two high schools and had its own citywide newspaper. They were influential in a coalition called Parents and Students for Community Control that worked on school issues. They also became involved in local electoral campaigns (Georgakas and Surkin 1975).

This faction of the league was also instrumental in reparations work and worked in a Black Economic Development Conference (BEDC) in 1969 (spring) that called for black socialism. This pulled them closer to former SNCC national leader, James Forman, who under BEDC auspices was demanding reparations from predominantly white church congregations during this period. The "Black Manifesto" called for $500 million dollars to be paid to aid in a wide variety of projects, ranging from a Southern Land Bank a to technical job skills training program in large urban areas. This set of activities was opposed by the plant-based cadre and leadership, who saw it as a diversion from what should be the main thrust of the League. (Georgakas and Surkin 1975).

The black middle class was involved through a series of book discussion clubs which grew to a membership of several hundred. It provided a forum for political discussion and persuasion, filling a function not unlike

Habermas's salons. His bourgeois public spheres were rooted in the institutional milieu of salons, barbershops, and other sites of critical discourse (Habermas 1989). The multitude of League and other black radical activity in Detroit created a cross-class, active, black public sphere that provided an arena for both the critical debate of the key political, economic, social, and cultural issues facing Black Detroit as well a base for political work ranging from strike work at the plants to united fronts that would be instrumental in electing Detroit's first black mayor in 1973. (It is no coincidence that former Mayor Coleman Young was a more responsive mayor during his first administration when there was active radical and public scrutiny than during later administrations when the mass movement and the left were largely dismantled).

Another cause of tension within the organization, the Black United Front work, especially among the leadership, was growing tension over the role of gender in society, as a theoretical analytical category, and the role of women in black liberation. The League had an extremely underdeveloped line on "the woman question." They viewed black women as subject to sexual and economic abuse, but did not organize separately around black women's issues and had few black women cadres and leaders (Georgakas and Surkin 1975). Their sexism was even more blatant than their anti-white attitudes. ELRUM, for example, failed to incorporate women into their organizing, even though two of the workers killed on the job were black women, and there was rampant sexist abuse from foremen directed toward black women on the shop floor. Many in the main leadership body of the League thought that paying attention to women's issues would be bowing down to "the white woman's movement." (Georgakas and Surkin 1975, 171). Not surprisingly this faction of the League saw women's issues as divisive.

The tensions within the organization over the scope of united front work (with both whites and blacks not concentrated at the point of production), the role of nationalism in the organization, and the role of women in both the League and black liberation generally came to a head as the organization, or at least one leadership faction, was preparing to form a nationwide revolutionary black workers' organization—the Black Workers Congress. Early documents outlined the purpose of the BWC as follows: "Workers' control of their places of work—the factories, mines, fields, offices, transportation services, and communication facilities—so that the exploitation of labor will cease and no person or corporations will get rich off the labor of another person, but all people will work for the collective benefit of humanity" (Georgakas and Surkin 1975, 139).

There was general agreement on the need to build a national, black, Marxist-Leninist organization, but disagreement about whether the League should take the lead. The basic tension existed between what some characterized as more nationalist local work and more Marxist-oriented national work. Disagreement over whether issues such as sexism and imperialism should be targeted also contributed to the split. The faction calling itself the Marxist-Leninist faction argued that the following three groups existed within the leadership: (1) those who saw themselves as proletarian revolutionaries trying to build a multiracial revolutionary movement; (2) petit bourgeois opportunists who portrayed themselves as Leninist revolutionaries but did not engage in real work and who had a disdain for "the people"; (3) undisciplined nationalists who had an abusive work style, no vision, and "tailed" behind the masses on questions of sexism and working with whites, among other issues. Their basic political outlook was outlined in a document which describes their side of the split:

> We saw the fundamental contradiction in the world and the U.S. as existing between capital and labor, nonetheless recognizing that the color-caste nature of U.S. society gives a national character to the oppression of blacks within this society. Consequently, we felt that, of all the forces in the U.S. proletariat, the black working class constitutes, by dint of its peculiarly acute oppression and a conscious history of relentless opposition to this oppression, the objective vanguard of the proletarian-led struggle to defeat imperialism and build socialism as a necessary step in creating a new world free of imperialist aggression and the degradation of the masses that accompanies the maintenance of the imperialist system. (Geschwender 1977, 156)

There is no mention of a black nation, but black oppression had a national character. Also note that black workers were considered the vanguard of the coming revolution. As in the Black Panthers (see chapter 3), many cadres had what this faction saw as an unacceptable disdain for working with whites either at the plant or in coalitions. This group had no love for nationalism: "We observe that the history of reactionary nationalism . . . is a history of bankrupt politics and policies, laced with such idealistic perversities as astrology, mysticism, infantile militarism, and adventurism. For years past, such elements around the country and locally were continually involved in 'clandestine plots' to 'get it on,' or to start the revolution through some dramatic act of violence" (Geschwender 1977, 157).

The opposition, of course, didn't share this characterization of the split. They argued that the base was the "basic black worker" who was in the plants fighting racism. They saw the national question as fundamental. They saw themselves as Leninists oriented toward the national question as opposed to Watson et al., who were viewed as ignoring the national question:

> The major and fundamental problem in the leadership of the Marxist-Leninist group was the national question. This was the problem that had not been discussed. Some of us saw the form that Black people were taking obviously led to the recognition of independent nationhood. We also recognized this as a necessary struggle and that capitalism et al. must be liquidated in order to achieve this. The other sector viewed the Black struggle as a present form becoming subsumed at a later stage in a multiracial party ruling America. At one point this faction saw the multiracial party subsequent to the dictatorship of the Black proletariat ruling America until whites proved themselves by their practice and entered the multiracial party. However, this position has been voted out in favor of the involvement of Third World peoples, poor whites, and Blacks making up the multiracial party in America. This faction also saw that nationalism was in essence reactionary, and Ken Cockrel, Mike Hamlin, and John Watson . . . indicated that they would purge themselves of all nationalism. (Geschwender 1977, 159)

The dictatorship of the *black* proletariat is a much more nationalist formulation than usually found even in black Marxist circles. While the formulation was unusual, the debates were not. The black Marxist movement would be debating these very questions for most of the next decade. Unfortunately for that movement, this debate was accompanied by the abandonment of most community and plant organizing. The first faction was also charged by the "nationalist" faction with "elevating the problems of women on par with capitalism by calling it sexism" (Geschwender 1977, 159). The "nationalist" faction ended up in the Communist League, while the first went on to form the Black Workers Congress (BWC). The League of Revolutionary Black Workers split in June 1971 (Geschwender 1977).

The BWC was formed after the League split in 1971. Its manifesto had "thirty-two objectives, mostly concerned with workers' demands, the elimination of racism, the liberation of women, and foreign-policy questions" (Geschwender 1977, 160). One-third of the founding convention in

September 1971 were women, and there was significant representation from other activists of color. Both groups represented a conscious break with past League practice and line. Eventually the BWC fragmented, and most of its remnants joined the movement to build a new Communist Party, a movement that would eventually incorporate most of the organizations that made the transition from nationalism to Marxism (with the notable exception of the Black Panther Party).

One reason the League was successful, according to Geschwender, is that there was a rise among black activists of Marxist rhetoric from a variety of sources. Marxist ideology was a viable influence within the black public sphere of Detroit. Indeed, Marxist ideology, at least the black variant of it, was influential in a wide variety of communities, workplaces, and college campuses with a significant concentration of African Americans. Geschwender argues that the reason, at least in part, was the resistance of white workers. It wasn't even clear if black and white workers shared a common language. State *and* union hostility was another major problem for the League. Its activists were under constant attack, notably by the state and auto companies, but also by the UAW and other AFL-CIO unions. There was also an ideological base for the split (in addition to the numerous organizational difficulties not mentioned here). Black workers had to deal with both racism and class exploitation, and the balance was not usually clear, although even class oppression is often racialized or experienced as racialized.

The world that black workers face today is very different from the world that existed when the League reached its height. The point of production has shifted out from beneath black workers. While the following quotation might be exaggerated, it was far truer when Watson stated it in 1969 in *Finally Got the News* than it is now, over thirty years later:

> You get a long list of arguments that black people are not numerous enough in America to revolt, that they will be wiped out. This neglects our economic position. . . . There are groups that can make the whole system cease functioning. These are auto workers, bus drivers, postal workers, steel workers, and others who play a crucial role in the money flow, the flow of materials, the creation of production. By and large, black people are overwhelmingly in those kinds of jobs. (Georgakas and Surkin 1975, 139)

The League of Revolutionary Black Workers went further than any other black organization in combining the classical Marxist concern to organize workers and the ideology of black workers. The result was that for a very few years in one major black community, the working class was leading the movement for black liberation and was also influential in the metropolitan-wide workers' movement. The black working class was also instrumental in shaping the public discourse that flowed between Detroit's oppositional counterpublics. The exponential growth of automated manufacturing processes and the information technology revolution have transformed the industrial heartland. This transformation has turned many large factory complexes into acres of brown fields. With the move of heavy industry outside of the United States, a reinvigorated black workers' movement would have to have a very different character in the twenty-first century.

Moving Toward Black Marxism? The Later Writings of the Black Panthers

One of the issues underlying the split in the League of Revolutionary Black Workers was disagreement about the advisability of growing from a disciplined (barely, in the eyes of some of the leadership) local organization to a nationwide organization that would attempt to lead the black liberation movement. Ideological cohesion, some leadership factions believed, could not be maintained if the organization became nationwide, and they pointed to what they perceived as both the lack of discipline and lack of ideological cohesion in the Black Panther Party as *the* prime example of what could go wrong when an organization expanded too fast. Indeed ideological disunity (as detailed in chapter 3) was a hallmark of the Panthers even at the local level.

But the writings of Black Panther leader Huey Newton showed that segments of the Panther leadership were beginning a more systematic study of Marxism, trying to adapt the ideology to the conditions black people faced. At a press conference in August of 1970, Newton makes this point directly:

> History has bestowed upon the Black Panther Party the obligation to take these steps and thereby advance Marxism-Leninism to an even higher level along the path to a socialist state. . . . We have the historical obligation to take the concept of internationalism to its final conclusion—the destruction of statehood itself. (Newton 1970a)

One way in which the Panthers delineated how they viewed the application of Marxism to black liberation was the outlining of their differences with nationalist forces, particularly with Stokely Carmichael (now known as Kwame Toure), former SNCC leader and, for a very short time, a member of the Panther leadership. In a press conference during September 1970, Newton argued that Pan-Africanism (Carmichael's avowed ideology) was the "highest expression of cultural nationalism"; as always, this idea was resolutely rejected by the Black Panthers (Newton 1970b). The Panthers, Newton stated, were internationalists. He further argued that African governments that had adopted Pan-Africanism were the allies of U.S. imperialism—the main enemy of the world's people. Further, African Americans' destiny was to be found within the United States. In a major adjustment of the original line on self-determination, Newton argued that black people should not and could not choose self-determination:

> Self-determination and national independence cannot really exist while United States imperialism is alive. That's why we don't support nationalism as our goal. In some instances we might support nationalism as a strategy; we call this revolutionary nationalism. The motives are internationalist, because the revolutionaries are attempting to secure liberated territory in order to choke imperialism by cutting them off from the countryside. (Newton 1970b, 6)

He continued his criticism by rejecting Carmichael's view of what constituted the roots of black oppression in the United States.

> He [Carmichael] said that socialism is not the question, economics is not the question, but it's entirely a question of racism. We take issue with this; we realize that the United States is a racist country, but we also realize the roots of the racism . . . is [*sic*] based upon the profit motive and capitalism. So we would like to start with the cause and then later on handle the effects of it. We believe that while socialism will not wipe out racism completely, we believe that a foundation will be laid. When we change the structure of bourgeois society; when we transform the structure into a socialist society, then we're one step toward changing attitudes. . . . We know that the concept of cultural lag will probably run true to form; while the structure changes, the attitudes will lag behind, because values take some time to change. But we say that the only way to start changing the racist nature of the society is to revolutionize their institutions, or transform the institutions. (Newton 1970b, 3)

This was a remarkably orthodox Marxist view for an organization that began as self-consciously nationalist, and—as with the League of Revolutionary Black Workers, the Congress of Afrikan Peoples, and dozens of other nationalist organizations, collectives, and study groups—the move toward a more orthodox even if recognizably "black" Marxism led some cadres to leave the organization.

By 1972 the Panther leadership in Oakland was presenting an ideological orientation that substantially reduced the importance of race as an aspect of black oppression. On one hand, a strong critique persisted of what was seen as the CPUSA's abandonment of people in color in general and of black liberation in particular. On the other hand, they argued that just because "white" communist parties could not get it right, that was no reason for people of color to abandon Marxism:

> Can we conclude, from such a point, because a Russian Communist Party, a Communist Party of America failed to fully support any of the people of color, that racism is the prime characteristic of Black and other oppression? Can we then further conclude that if the colonized Blacks only united, sharing among themselves all their wealth, this will resolve the oppression; and if we say that on what territory shall U.S. Blacks unite? . . . There was certainly the betrayal by silence by the American communists of the Blacks at the crucial point when the United States rose above the imperialist crowd. The essential question here, through analytical summation of such events and analysis of the real conditions of today, is how shall the liberation of Blacks in the United Sates, or Blacks in Africa, or people of color throughout the world, or of the world's oppressed be effected? The second essential question is what does liberation mean? (Newton 1972, 2–4)

The answer is one that nationalists and many black Marxists would reject out of hand. Newton argues, "U.S. Blacks can lay no real claim to U.S. territory or Africa's" (Newton 1972, 4). The answer for the Panthers no longer lay in black liberation but in world revolution. The deemphasis on race was much more reminiscent of a black Trotskyism than traditional black Marxism:

> Let us return, however, to the basic, functional definitions. If it is agreed that the fundamental nature of oppression is economic, then the first assault, or the prime assault, by the oppressed must be to wrest economic

control from the hands of the oppressors. If we define the prime character of the oppression of Blacks, either in Africa or the United States, as
racial, then the situation of economic exploitation of human beings can
be continued if performed by Blacks of Blacks or Blacks of whites or
others. If, however, we are speaking of eliminating exploitation and
oppression, in general, then it would seem feasible, with our analysis
clearly in mind, that the oppressed begin with a united, worldwide
thrust, along the lines of oppressed versus oppressor, to seize the ma-
chinery of power and through the unity of struggle begin the task of
redistributing the world's wealth. (Newton 1972, 5)

Nationalists, of course, rejected the viewpoint that the fundamental nature of oppression is economic, and even later black Marxists would not
have gone this far in reducing the role of race in the oppression of African
Americans. The Oakland-led branch of the Black Panthers was never able
to fully implement the new position. Violent confrontations with the other
side of the split (which had largely opted for an urban guerrilla warfare
strategy), continued legal and violent confrontations with various police
agencies, and the continued dropout of disillusioned and burnt out cadres,
all took their toll. By the time the next wave of radical black organizing was
launched in the early 1970s, the Black Panther Party was no longer a national force in the black movement.

From Cultural Nationalism to Marxism-Leninism: The Congress of Afrikan Peoples

The Congress of Afrikan Peoples (CAP) was a central East Coast, nationalist organization that was involved in numerous activities, ranging
from involvement in electing one of the first black mayors in the country
(Kenneth Gibson of Newark) to widely promoting African-American culture, serving as one of the major East Coast centers of cultural nationalism
(playing a role similar to that of Karenga's U.S. organization in California),
and eventually becoming one of the major organizations to be involved in
African Liberation Support activities (through the African Liberation Support Committee—ALSC).

The CAP's visibility was enhanced by having as its primary leader the
award-winning playwright, poet, and essayist Amiri Baraka (Leroi Jones).
In a series of articles starting in 1974 and continuing to the early 1980s, as
a member of a multiracial Leninist organization, Baraka documents the

transition from nationalism to hardcore Marxism which a significant portion of the nationalist movement made.

The first stage of this transition is marked in a 1974 article by Baraka, "Toward Ideological Clarity: Nationalism, Pan-Africanism, Socialism." It starts with a fairly "nationalistic" application of Lenin's writings on imperialism as a way to explain the slave trade and its effects on both Africa and African Americans as well as the development of racism. Racism is more than just plain ethnocentrism but "must be backed up by an actual demonstration of superiority. In other words, the racist must have the power to enforce that superiority in the objective world" (Baraka 1974, 26). He extends this analysis to institutional racism which is the institutionalization of racism through capitalism. As Baraka, quoting the influential West Indian radical, Walter Rodney, argued:

> Racism was not the trailing edge of Imperialism, it was its form. It appeared as racial oppression, national oppression, and cultural aggression, though its reproductive means and ultimate reason for being was, and remains, essentially economic. It is a method of economic exploitation, meant to benefit the imperialists, but it also in a broader sense was meant to confirm and establish for all times the superiority and supremacy of the cultures it issued from. (Baraka 1974, 27)

Because of the continued centrality of race and racism during this period, Marxism and socialism were important, but African cultural identity needed to be maintained. Not surprisingly, given both CAP's cultural nationalist roots and Baraka's stature as one of the cultural giants among twentieth-century black artists, there was more emphasis on the political importance of culture than is found in many radical political organizations. Arguing that "Black people's struggle . . . [must be] the organized political expression of our culture," Baraka used the writings of Amilcar Cabral (the slain leader of the national liberation struggle of Guinea Bissau, who was enormously influential in both nationalist and black Marxist circles) to support his call for a "dynamic synthesis of the material and spiritual condition of our society" (Baraka 1974, 31).

The primary struggle is viewed as being against imperialism, not capitalism. Certain consequences derive from this point: "It seems evident that Imperialism has oppressed us nationally, racially, and culturally, in order to make a profit, but also as a result of the reproduction of racist systems and institutions, philosophies, and way of life, which perpetuate it with no specific thought of the profit motive, although that is its base" (Baraka 1974, 31). Therefore, the way out is national liberation: "The struggle against racial oppression in the United States is basically a struggle for national liberation, and in its pre–civil rights movement aspects it took on the character against colonialism, because of the segregated, South Afrikan–style social relations which existed in the United States previous to the fifties" (Baraka 1974, 32). Baraka grounded his analysis in Boggs's writings on the superexploitation faced by black workers at "the point of production." Thus Baraka's writings on the need for national liberation and class struggle are similar to those of Haywood in 1957 and of the Detroit black radicals a few years earlier.

Black struggle was a dual struggle; while the principle contradiction was viewed as being between the proletariat and the bourgeoisie, the nature of black struggle according to Baraka was both national (which he labels "racial and cultural") and against capital (class). Thus, while he again argued very much as Cornel West would later for a nonreductionist treatment of black struggle, he had not yet embraced the Leninist formula for understanding the essence of national oppression—nationhood and national liberation. Baraka's view was much closer historically to that of most black Marxists than to the orthodox Stalinist view. At the time, Baraka argued for a synthesis of Pan-Africanism and socialism, but this synthesis proved to be a transitional ideology. CAP soon embraced a conventional, black Leninist model. This transition was accelerated by the participation of CAP and other nationalists in the ALSC, which Baraka saw as critical for bringing together many of the nationalists who would become the new black Marxists. At the time of this essay, however, the ALSC was characterized as a nationalist organization, even given its united front and anti-imperialist nature.

For Baraka, blacks represented the vanguard of an American revolutionary movement, and a black united front was needed to pull together the progressive elements of the black community to struggle for national liberation. He also argued that a vanguard revolutionary party must "be the spearhead of the Black Liberation movement." The call for a black revolutionary party in 1974 would evolve, as CAP evolved into the Revolutionary Communist League, into a call for building a new vanguard Communist Party. Baraka concluded with a call for party building and ideological debate: "It is a time of ideology, and it is a time of organization" (Baraka 1974, 95). By 1975, the transition foreseen in the 1974 piece was complete: CAP was calling for a multinational Communist Party, with party building as the key task (Baraka 1975).

As noted earlier, large differences separated CAP, the League of Revolutionary Black Workers, and the Black Panther Party. We should not, however, forget the similarities between the three organizations. All three had self-determination of blacks as a central concern, and none initially tied self-determination to a specific land-mass such as the black-belt South. All three were *black* organizations and, as the Panthers noted, they were nationalist in form. And all became—at least in theory—socialist in action. The internal tensions that the "nationalist in form, socialist in action" paradigm engendered eventually led each organization to split or lose substantial parts of its membership. The tensions over the race-class (and, more silently, gender) divide(s) led to uneven development among the cadres. Splits occurred not only between different regions and among the leadership, but also between the leadership and the rank-and-file. None of the three organizations would survive unscathed as the black movement moved into its next phase. The Panthers had ceased to exist as a strong leading organization by the mid-1970s. The Black Workers Congress and the Congress of Afrikan Peoples, however, would join with organizations that were to some degree the counterparts of the Panthers in the Puerto Rican, Chicano, and Asian-American movements to take up the call to build a new Communist Party in the United States—a party that would not make what was in their estimation the fatal mistake of the CPUSA. These new Marxist organizations vowed not to underestimate the progressive potential of nonwhite people in general and of African Americans in particular.

The New Black Left

Elements from the ALSC, several major East Coast student and youth organizations, CAP, the BWC, and independent local collectives from around the country took up the call to build a new Communist Party. While one major wing of the successor organizations from SDS (the major, anti-imperialist, predominantly white, antiwar group, Students for a Democratic Society) became part of this movement, the white new left and the black new left remained mostly separated. The democratic socialist movement and the major new left organizations, which eventually combined into the Democratic Socialists of America, remained largely unattractive to the various Third World left organizations that had come out of the urban community and the college campus struggles of the late 1960s and early 1970s. To many activists of color, the line of the new social democratic movement was every bit as dismissive of the importance of racial oppression in the United States as was the old Socialist Party; unlike the old Socialist

Party, however, the new social democrats lacked a strong focus on the most economically disadvantaged sectors of American society, making them even less relevant. The more Leninist sectors of the remnants of the new left, unlike the social democratic factions, did incorporate positions on the black national question similar to that of Haywood, but they were equally unable to attract cadres of color and remained predominantly white. The one relatively influential, predominantly white successor to the SDS which was openly hostile toward viewing movements of people of color as having any revolutionary potential was the Revolutionary Communist Party (RCP). They were utterly rejected by Third World Marxist organizations when the RCP marched with the Ku Klux Klan and other racist forces in Boston's antibussing movement during the middle 1970s.

The black Marxists who emerged out of the Black Power movement adopted a set of ideological positions that were similar to the Haywood line within the CPUSA. The handful of organizations which incorporated many of the black Marxists who remained active had serious differences with each other, but ideologically their profiles were very similar. The evolution from revolutionary (indeed, cultural) nationalism to Leninism is well documented in Baraka's writings from the early 1980s. The 1981 essay "Black Struggle in the 1980s" and the 1982 essay "Nationalism and Self-Determination" show significant evolution (more properly characterized as changes) in ideology from the late CAP period of the middle of the previous decade.

Baraka characterized black struggle as a national democratic struggle for equality, self-determination, and national liberation. But this struggle could be harmed by certain class elements—by "the various electoral political figures and cultural and academic personalities who at one point were identified with the struggles of the black majority, who later clearly isolated themselves from the masses in selfish pursuit of the limited goals of the black middle class. Too often, once they got elected, or appointed to top token positions or similar roles, their real connection with Black people was over, in any positive way" (Baraka 1981, 2). According to Baraka, a national black united front, led by the black working class, was needed to carry out the democratic struggle for African Americans. Even the black middle class was oppressed by racism, but, according to many black Marxists of the time, the selfishness of the black middle class and its self-doubt necessitated working-class leadership. Thus the goals that Baraka emphasizes for the Black United Front (which was both a concept and an actual national organization that many black Marxists, nationalists, and unaffiliated community activists worked within for a short while) would be, according to this view, "Self-Determination, Land, Political Power, Economic Self-Sufficiency, Democracy, and Equality" (Baraka 1981, 3). All of these goals (particularly if you interpret the demand for land, with Boggs and other black radicals, as a demand for community control over the land and institutions of the black community) receive massive support in black public opinion, as we saw in chapter 2.

This version of black Marxism still differs from "standard" Marxist fare because this perspective still focuses on the racialization of oppression. When describing the worsening conditions that disadvantaged Americans experienced in the early 1980s, Baraka argued, "But obviously Blacks and other oppressed nationalities will be hit first and worst" (Baraka 1981, 3). Thus blacks and other people of color suffer most, and the suffering of the working classes among these ethnic and racial groups is the absolute worst. The extension that black feminists of this period were writing about—that women of color were at the absolute bottom of the economic ladder—was not incorporated into this version of black Marxism. Indeed gender was not considered an analytical category worthy of serious attention by the black Marxist movement of this and earlier periods.

The move to the right highlighted by the election of Ronald Reagan, Baraka continued, was accompanied by an intensification of repression and exploitation of blacks. Baraka was writing during a period when unemployment rates for blacks (the official ones) were soaring over 20 percent in highly industrial states such as Illinois and Michigan, twice the white rate, as bad as they were (Dawson 1994a, chapter 7 in particular). Baraka concludes, as have black Marxists of every previous generation, that in the end only socialism would bring about black equality.

This ideological perspective is extended in the article on "Nationalism, Self-Determination, and Socialist Revolution." (Baraka 1982). One major modification from the black Marxism of a decade earlier was the belief that only a small sector of the white working class and petite bourgeoisie were bribed as opposed to the entire white working class benefiting from the exploitation of black workers (Baraka 1982). The white left has been plagued by the idiocy of those such as the RCP, who were screaming "smash busing" while marching with the Klan in Boston, while other leftists, according to Baraka, protested the activities of the Black United Front. White left racism helped to fuel black nationalism and led to a situation where the communist movement was not giving leadership to the mass struggles of African Americans. The left, Baraka believed, should learn from the mistakes of the CPUSA and fight against chauvinism and for self-determination for the Afro-American nation (Baraka 1982). Marxists must

fight white supremacy and support the nationalism of the oppressed only
to the degree that nationalist forces battle against the forces which oppress
blacks. Nationalism was viewed as the ideology of the bourgeoisie, which
served to divide the workers of different nationalities from each other. This
was a much more negative assessment of nationalism than black Marxists
of this tradition had had even five years earlier, but it was common among
the many former nationalists who had joined or formed Leninist organizations. By this time, Baraka was arguing that white workers would support
the struggles of the oppressed nations. Why? Black and white workers had
the same main enemy, he argued, even if white workers did not acknowledge this fact. Like the great majority of black Marxists during this period,
Baraka argued that the main tasks were building a new Communist Party
and waging the struggle against nationalism. This political viewpoint accelerated the withdrawal of veteran activists from trade unions and from
community, campus, and cultural organizing. The simultaneous drop in
the activity of non-Islamic black nationalists left the black radical movement at its lowest point in half a century (Dawson 1994b).

Coda

By 1988 Baraka's formal affiliation with the organizations of the
Leninist left was coming to an end (Baraka 1991c). Jesse Jackson's 1988
campaign for the Democratic nomination for president gave Baraka and
others the opportunity to reflect on the nature of a progressive black agenda.
Like Reed, Marable, and several other progressive black writers of the period, Baraka was sharply critical of Jackson's action during the campaign
(Marable 1995; Reed 1986). Baraka was also sensitive to what the Jackson
campaign could *potentially* mean for black progressive mass mobilization.
Baraka in particular criticized deferring to what he saw as the corporate
and reactionary forces of the Democratic Leadership Council (DLC) and
Dukakis-led Democratic party. Jackson's strategy, Baraka argued, eliminated any possibility for turning the movement being built around his electoral campaign into an independent political movement. Baraka's analysis
centers on the fact that Jackson's capitulation, as signified by his abandonment of his longtime colleagues and advisors in the Black Liberation
Movement in favor of "slick," white, "hustling" campaign professionals,
was part of his giving up self-determination as a key aspect of his movement. For Baraka, this capitulation was also signified by the fact that rightists like Texas senator Bentsen, who supported contra aid and Savimbi (of
Angola's rightist rebel movement, UNITA) and opposed DC statehood,

were "calling the shots" (Baraka 1991c, 468). Baraka still argued that what blacks want remains self-determination and equality. The tragedy of Jackson's betrayal for Baraka was that "we want democracy in America; we want equality. Jesse represented our desire for Self-Determination, the shaping of our own lives with the same opportunity possessed by any other American." (Baraka 1991c, 480). With both electoral politics and the organized left proving to be dead ends for black radicals, new directions were needed if the black radical tradition was not to become totally moribund.

BLACK SOCIAL DEMOCRACY IN THE 1990s: TRUE HEIRS OF A RADICAL TRADITION?

The black radical tradition lost much of its mass character in the 1990s and can be found mainly in the academy, in newspaper columns, on radio talk shows, and other venues that make up the limited, contemporary, black counterpublic. The black radical tradition has also moved to the right toward a more social democratic orientation. Two of the more visible black radicals as the twentieth century came to a close were Cornel West and Manning Marable. While intimately familiar with the black radical tradition, each attempts to move the tradition into a different trajectory. Both have been prominently associated with democratic socialist organizations for a number of years, and both have tried theoretically and pragmatically to outline areas where the analyses of the race-class intersection which has occupied the attention of black radicals for much of the twentieth century needs to be made more complex. We start with the moralistic approach to radicalism proposed by Cornel West.

Cornel West

West can be located within the black radical tradition due to his emphasis on the need to understand simultaneously an irreducible racial element in the African American condition and how that condition is both shaped (mostly detrimentally) by and has shaped the development of American capitalism. Like every generation of twentieth-century black radicals and nationalists, West identifies "white supremacy" as a worldwide problem (West 1988, 17). West solidifies his place within the black Marxist tradition when he claims, "In short, the time has passed when the so-called race question, or Negro question, can be relegated to secondary or tertiary *theoretical* significance in bourgeois or Marxist discourses" (West 1988, 18; emphasis in the original). But unlike those who represent the main trends within the activist traditions of the 1930s and 1970s, West rejects theoretically characterizing the black condition as a "national" question in favor of the formulation "racial problematic" (West 1988, 17). West correctly argues that the "black nation" thesis adopted by the orthodox, black Marxist tradition was too static (West 1988). He also argues that while any analysis of black oppression must analytically place capitalism at its center, his approach demands that the theoretical and practical privileging of the mode of production, or class oppression, should end. He uses the metaphor of the historical bloc from Gramsci to emphasize the complexity of black oppression. Blacks are fighting a war of position in which "the complex interaction of economic, political, cultural, and ideological regions in social formations of Marxist theory . . . does not permit a priori privileging of the economic region within this structural feature." (West 1988, 25). Therefore, elements of new Marxist analyses must include (1) historical analysis of "discursive conditions for the possibility of the hegemonic European supremacist logics operative in various epochs in the West and the counterhegemonic possibilities available"; (2) localized analyses of the "mechanisms" that inscribe these "logics" into everyday black oppression (West 1988, 22), including cultural and psychological mechanisms for domination as well as counterhegemonic possibilities; and (3) macrostructural analyses which focus on the analysis of class and political oppression.

West's Marxism, which is clearly more social democratic than communist in nature, opposes either the demonization or deification of any class or social grouping (West 1993c). Marxism has theoretical and pragmatic limits. Adopting Marxism is a moral choice in that West sides with those the current society degrades, and existential in that it helps him understand the reality of the existence of those who are degraded and his own place in such a society: "Marxism helps me keep track of and account for structural and institutional life-denying forces like degradation, oppression, and exploitation, and though I believe that the complexities of racism, sexism, and homophobia cannot be fully grasped in light of Marxism, they surely cannot be understood without it" (West 1993c, 181). Adopting Marxism is a necessary moral choice, given the ills fostered by societies governed by advanced capitalism:

> It seems to me that to be a socialist means, if anything, to keep track of the wasted energies, the spiritual sterility, the exhausted potential left by the rule of capital—that set of interlocking elites, the banks, corporations, the political elites. If we as socialists cannot highlight the trail left

by the rule of capital across national boundaries, across racial boundaries, across gender boundaries, then there is no future for a socialist
Left in the United States, and it will dissolve and degenerate into a
micropolitics of single issues and identity politics. (West 1993e, 240)

To attack the crisis that the left finds itself in facing the massive forces
that are tearing our communities apart, the left must rebuild the public
spheres of civil society to provide a space where critical exchange can occur. This is a step in combating the market morality which is directly responsible for the erosion of public and private morality as well as the degradation of the moral and spiritual bases of individuals' lives. Morality must
be both a foundation and a goal in fighting a capitalism that has run amok
(West 1993a).

The social democratic sensibilities of West are a long way from Boggs's
dictatorship of the black proletariat of the 1960s and Baraka's stern Leninism of the early 1980s. West celebrates a philosophical and pragmatic democratic faith that he sees in the spirit and tradition of Walt Whitman, John
Dewey, and the early Du Bois. West's radicalism is more in the tradition of
A. Philip Randolph than his early twentieth-century contemporary Cyril
Briggs. A contemporary of West who attempts to bridge the social democratic tradition and the activist-oriented black radical tradition is Manning
Marable.

Manning Marable

Like West, Marable argues that the intersection of white supremacy
and capitalist oppression has to be the starting point for understanding
not only black oppression, but the condition of the disadvantaged in the
late-twentieth-century United States. Marable proclaims, "The hegemonic
ideology of 'whiteness' is absolutely central in rationalizing and justifying the gross inequalities of race, gender, and class, experienced by millions
of Americans relegated to the politically peripheral status of 'Others'"
(Marable 1995d, 185). Unlike West, however, Marable *does* privilege one
mode of oppression. Quoting C. R. L. James, Marable argues for the pre-
eminent role of class for analyzing disadvantage, "The race question is sub-
sidiary to the class question in politics, and to think of imperialism in terms
of race is disastrous. But to neglect the racial factor as merely incidental is
an error only less grave than to make it fundamental." (quoted in Marable
1995a, 229).

Marable sees corporate greed and the massive redistribution of wealth and resources in recent years from the bottom to the top as responsible for the "levels of misery" found in American civil society, especially in the cities (Marable 1995a). A radical impulse is needed to fight the evils of civil society, but Marable believes this impulse is weak:

> The cultural politics of the transformative vision have been grounded in anti-imperialism and internationalism. The assumption here is that colonialism abroad is inextricably connected with capitalism at home, and that race as a social category cannot be deconstructed by relying on liberal solutions. . . . Yet, at this historical moment, the transformation-ist current's organizational and institutional base is weaker than it has been since the depths of the Cold War, when Robeson and Du Bois were silenced, and thousands of radicals were purged or imprisoned. (Marable and Mullings 1995, 213)

Still, he sees some progressive potential for various social and electoral movements. The Washington campaign for mayor of Chicago in 1983, the Jackson primary campaigns for the Democratic nomination for president, and the anti-apartheid campaign all represented the potential (and weak-ness) of the radical impulse during the 1980s. To strengthen this radical im-pulse, black activists must move beyond the model of "competitive group empowerment" implied by the pluralist model of politics to one where the left and the black community build a movement whose goal is multicultural democracy (Marable 1995d, 190). The new bases for unity will be

> the disproportionately high percentages of Latino and African-American workers [who] will be trapped within this second tier of the labor market. Black, Latino, Asian-American, and low-income white workers all share a stake in fighting for a new social contract relation to work and social benefits: the right to a good job should be guaranteed in the same way as the human right to vote; the right to high-quality health care should be as secure as the freedom of speech. The radical changes within the domestic economy require that black leadership reaches out to other oppressed sectors of the society. (Marable 1995d, 201)

Marable urges us to construct coalitions of the disadvantaged, partic-ularly among people of color, which identify the common interests possessed by all groups. He correctly points out that progress was made in the 1960s and 1970s toward this end, but the interests of elected officials, agency heads, and the like led those involved to emphasize racial group competition instead of cooperation. To achieve the end of intergroup progressive cooperation, Marable argues, we need new "cultural and political" identities. These identities would be based on the new realities of an emerging "multicultural democratic milieu" (Marable 1995d, 194). This is a formidable task because Americans' perceptions of economic gain and loss remain firmly rooted in perceived racial group interests. While the major division is between whites and people of color in terms of the intersection of policy preferences and perceived racial interests, significant differences divide people of color as well (Dawson 1997). Marable points to some of the potential for building such coalitions while also outlining the obstacles. Blacks tend to be electoral internationalists, when voting overwhelmingly for a black liberal candidate, blacks also vote overwhelmingly for the white and other liberals on the same electoral tickets. Whites will racially split their vote, voting for the white candidate (regardless of ideology) when confronted with a black candidate, and voting their ideology when choosing between white candidates (Marable and Mullings 1995).

Marable, like Baraka, believes that while tactically useful at times, electoral strategies are ultimately limited in their progressive potential. He is particularly critical of what he saw as the antidemocratic actions of Jesse Jackson, who, he argued, systematically removed all democratic controls within the Rainbow coalition while dismantling the mass aspects of the coalition during the 1988 primary campaign (Marable 1995b, 1995c). The black radical movement should learn from the Jackson campaigns that any electoral campaign must include both mass mobilization and electoral mobilization, and reject blind loyalty to the Democratic party (Marable 1995c). Blind loyalty to the Democratic party ultimately for Marable means cooptation by the forces of economic globalization and corporate greed. Indeed, the one good thing that came out of the "destruction" of the Rainbow coalition was that it allowed more space for progressive forces to organize. Marable argues, "The only positive impact of the DLC-Clinton 'political coup' is that the ideological and organizational 'space' for a left alternative to both major parties has grown dramatically in the past year" (Marable 1995c, 61).

To rebuild the black movement, black radicals must become dedicated to building a multicultural movement. Blacks must go beyond simple "black" identities. To be more precise, black identity itself must change in this new economic and political era. The very meaning of black radicalism must change, according to Marable:

> In short, we must go beyond black and white, seeking power in a world which is increasingly characterized by broad diversity in ethnic and social groupings, but structured hierarchically in terms of privilege and social inequality. We must go beyond black and white, but never at the price of forgetting the bitter lessons of our collective struggles and history, never failing to appreciate our unique cultural and aesthetic gifts or lacking an awareness of our common destiny with others of African descent. We must find a language that clearly identifies the role of class as central to the theoretical and programmatic critique of contemporary society. And we must do this in a manner which reaches out to the newer voices and colors of U.S. society—Latinos, Asian Americans, Pacific Island Americans, Middle East Americans, American Indians, and others. We have entered a period in which our traditional definitions of what it has meant to be "black" must be transformed. (Marable 1995, 226)

Marable is as concerned as any of his predecessors with maintaining and extending the black radical tradition. But Marable and West both argue that a radically different radicalism is necessary for the next century, one that may not even be recognizably "black." Whether black Marxism will survive into the next century remains—as with all the other ideologies— an open question.

CORE PRINCIPLES

What constitutes the ideological core of modern black radicalism, given the transformation in both the black movement and the country? The following sets of concepts have been historically at the core of the black Marxist tradition.

The National Question

While one main tradition of black Marxism has consistently argued that there is a black nation physically located in the South, and other groups have argued that blacks have the right of self-determination even if such a nation does not exist. "The national question" is less central to black radicalism in the 1990s than at any time since the 1920s. Consequently, no current consensus exists on the "national question" beyond a strong viewpoint that racial subordination is not reducible to class or to any other phenomenon. Black radicals also continue to argue that liberal democracy has yet to come close to solving the problem of systematic racial disadvantage.

Superexploitation and the Racial Nature of Capitalism

A constant theme in black radical ideology is the belief that capitalism systematically disadvantages African Americans, workers, and the poor. A consequence of this view is that the intersection of race and class often serves to place blacks at the bottom of the socioeconomic ladder. More controversial even within black radical circles is the ideological claim that some of the profits from the superexploitation of black workers have been used historically used to buy off sectors of the white working and middle classes. More orthodox black Marxists have tended to either reject this point of view or argue that it is a relatively minor phenomenon.

Class Conflict and Black United Fronts

Another feature of the black Marxist tradition is the belief that at best the black middle and upper classes are unreliable allies for the black working class. While the great majority of black radicals believe that the racial oppression of most blacks provides a material base for the tactical unity of many segments of the black community, they also believe that if affluent blacks lead such movements, they will be aimed at satisfying the class interests of more advantaged African Americans. Further, the rapidly increasing inequality that is occurring in black communities has led to increasing skepticism that a single black agenda can speak to the myriad of interests that exist within the black community.

Gender

Historically, at best, the black Marxist tradition has subordinated claims about gender, much as orthodox Marxists have subordinated claims about race. For both black and white radical movements, the proletariat was masculine. There was an "equation of literary and political vitality with masculinity" within the CPUSA from the 1930s on (Rabinowitz 1987, 4). Contemporary black Marxists who strongly argue for an antisexist agenda which incorporates the demands of black women also argue that the intersection of race and class is especially critical (Marable and Mullings 1995).

Angela Davis is one of the few prominent black Marxists who has strongly urged that radical movements with a progressive agenda must take seriously the intersections of race, gender, and class. Where many black feminists, particularly in recent years, emphasize race and gender (although some also still emphasize class) and black Marxists emphasize race and class, Davis argues for emphasizing all three. She argues that a progressive agenda, whether centered on feminism or other issues, must not only include the concerns of black women and other women of color, but also embrace the fight against anti-immigration policies and politics. This is of course an uphill fight in the black community (Davis 1990b). The goal is still to "forge a new socialist order," but this can only be done by recognizing that "in the aftermath of the Reagan era, it should be clear that there are forces in our society that reap enormous benefits from the persistent, deepening oppression of women. Members of the Reagan administration include advocates for the most racist, anti–working class, and sexist circles of contemporary monopoly capitalism." (Davis 1990b, 13–14). Consequently, progressive movements should sharply challenge perspectives that ignore class and racial divisions within progressive movements such as the feminist movement. Just as black-centered movements must be challenged to incorporate an antisexist orientation, some white women are privileged and can achieve "their goals" without bringing appreciable relief to women of color or working-class white women (Davis 1990a). How strongly Davis's perspective has taken root within black radical circles is not clear, although it is clearly a stronger perspective than during the 1960s and 1970s.

Alliances with Nonblacks

A hallmark value of black Marxist ideology is that allies exist for the black community. In particular within the United States other nonwhite progressives are considered strong potential candidates, but most black Marxists have also believed that in the long run a portion of the white working class can be won to a progressive agenda. This tradition differs from that of orthodox Marxists, black and white, in believing that whites are best organized by other whites, perhaps even in separate organizations.

Africa, Pan-Africanism, and Anti-Imperialism

Historically, the black Marxist and radical tradition has strongly identified with the anticolonial and national liberation struggles of the Third World, particularly those in Africa and the Caribbean. At the same time, black Marxists have also strongly argued for the position that *African Americans'* destiny, by right and historical circumstance, lies within the borders of the United States.

Culture

The black Marxist tradition has had a split personality when it comes to its views on culture. As Kelley persuasively demonstrates, black cadres have brought African-American cultural traditions into Marxist organizations such as the CPUSA. Because of the strong alignment of the black artists' movement of the 1960s with the black power movement, many of the organizations that became part of the new black Marxist movement of the 1970s had strong roots in black cultural work. Some black Marxists have remained worried that cultural work can become a substitute for organizing and mobilizing the black community.

Nationalists

Finally, while they often emerged from black nationalist movements and organizations, black Marxists became frequent opponents and only occasional tactical allies of black nationalists. Nationalists, as we saw in chapter 3, believe that black Marxists are essentially the agents of the enemy within the black community (as are the liberals and feminists), while black Marxists argue that at best the black nationalists represent the most backward and privileged sections of the black community. Even when they find themselves tactical allies in radical, black united fronts, representatives of the two ideological tendencies tend to have very cool relations with each other.

THE ANTECEDENTS AND CONSEQUENCES OF BLACK MARXISM

The black radical tradition has a long and storied history. It has attracted as supporters and active participants some of America's greatest intellectuals and artists of the twentieth century. Leading American intellectuals such as Ralph Bunche and W. E. B. Du Bois saw themselves at various points of their careers as both sympathetic critics as well as independent participants. Black Marxists and their organizations were a vital component of the black power movements of the 1960s and 1970s and had some local influence in the early 1980s. Several observers of black politics have argued, however, as

I have, that the influence of Black Marxism during the 1990s has reached a twentieth-century nadir. As for the other ideologies, the questions I ask in this section are, (1) To what degree are the core concepts of black Marxism supported by African Americans? (2) Who are the supporters and opponents of black Marxism? (3) How strongly does black Marxism shape black public opinion?

Measurement and Distribution of Black Marxism

A black Marxism scale was constructed out of variables that are proxies for critical core components of black Marxism. Modern black Marxism has reached consensus on the destruction that corporations inflict on the black community, the unfairness of the American economic system, the differences in interests between the black middle class and less affluent blacks, and the increasing political salience of class divisions within the black community. Consensus has not been reached on the black national question, the role of gender in shaping society, and the role of political movements. Further, at various times in the past, black Marxists have emphasized exclusively black socialist organizations, while at other times they have emphasized the need to build multiracial political organizations. Consequently, the following four sets of statements were used as the core for a black Marxism scale:

1. Economic divisions in the black community have grown so much that black people as a group no longer share common interests, OR, Black people still have important things in common.
2. America's big corporations are a powerful source of economic growth that benefits the black community, OR, Big corporations are unfair to the black community.
3. America's economic system is fair to everyone, OR, America's economic system is unfair to poor people.
4. Please tell me whether you strongly agree, somewhat agree, somewhat disagree, or strongly disagree with the following statement: Black people who have made it are doing a lot to improve the social and economic position of poor blacks. (Four-point scale: 0 = strongly disagree; 4 = strongly agree.

As with the previous ideologies, three measures of black Marxism were set up using these variables. One was a scale using the four items. This measure is designed to be consistent with the definitions of ideology found in public opinion research, and should give us some estimate of how well the core ideas cohere among grassroots African Americans. The second measure is once again a simple one that indicates whether individual respondents agree with all of the key components of the ideology, and the third measure provides an indicator of whether someone disagrees with all of the components. The latter two measures provide indicators of potential support and opposition within the black community. As with the other ideological scales, the LISREL model fits the data adequately (see table A3.1).

While table 2.8 indicates that black Marxism shared about the same combination of a substantial number of supporters with few opponents, which all other ideologies except black conservatism enjoy, it does not cohere well as an ideology in this period.[3] Like black feminism, the public presence of black Marxism as an ideology is extremely low—even lower than that of black feminism during this period. Where black feminists have been usually willing to identify themselves as either feminists or womanists, black Marxists have been generally unwilling to label themselves Marxists since the late 1980s, the defeat of the Soviet Union, and the shattering of the black radical movement during the 1970s and the early 1980s. Thus, while the ideology's key tenets are supported, they are not widely connected in African Americans' minds as a coherent ideology.

The degree of potential support can be seen in the distribution of the black Marxism scale displayed in figure 5.1. The distribution of black Marxism is roughly normal, with a moderately pro-radical mean of 0.69. Black Marxism, like black feminism and black nationalism, has the moderate support of a wide segment of the black community. In the next section I probe further into the nature of support (and opposition) to black Marxism.

Antecedents

Who is most likely to support the black Marxist ideology? By far the best predictor of support is the belief that blacks are economically subordinate to whites.[4] African Americans are nearly 20 percent more likely to support black Marxism than those who believe blacks are doing economically better than whites. Perception of racial economic interest drives support for black Marxism. As the intersection between gender and race drove black women's support for a black feminist agenda, perceptions of

---

3. The alpha statistic is a low .34.

4. The same set of controls is used in all regressions that were discussed in the chapters on black nationalism and black feminism. The tables are in part 3 of the appendix.

Figure 5.1   Smoothed Black Marxism distribution using normal and Epanechinikov
estimators

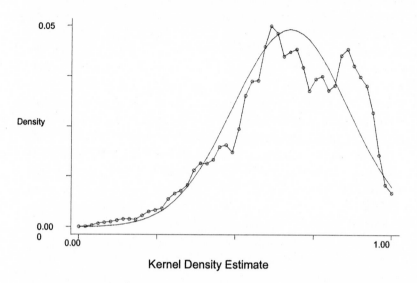

Kernel Density Estimate

	Observations	Mean	Std. Deviation	Minimum	Maximum
Black Marxism	1,184	0.69	0.20	0	1

Source: 1993–1994 National Black Politics Survey

the intersection between race and class substantially increase support for a
black radical agenda. We can more fully appreciate the importance of this
perception to support for a black radical agenda when we realize that 71
percent of African Americans in the sample believed that blacks were economically disadvantaged as compared to whites.

Another strong predictor of support for black Marxism is the perception that the interviewer is black. African Americans' support for a black
Marxist position is more likely to be expressed when the conversation is
perceived as being within the community than when "outsiders" are present. This finding is consistent with Sanders's arguments and sets of results
that interracial settings are likely to moderate each race's political stances
(Sanders 1995a, 1995b).

Consistent with what we have found in previous chapters, living in a
poor neighborhood has a weak but significant antiradical effect, reducing

support for black Marxism. On the other hand, a traditional indicator of opposition to Marxism, the financial resources of an individual's family, has a weak effect. While not significant at traditional levels of evaluation, black Marxism is the only ideology besides black feminism which shows some degree of structuring by the combined indicators of social class (see the F-Test section of table A2.1). Greater black family income slightly reduces the probability of supporting a black Marxist position.

Black Marxists have also often claimed that religion was the enemy of black progressive movements. A wide range of religious variables, such as the degree of respondent religiosity and church attendance, do not predict support or opposition to black Marxism.[5] In addition, Black Marxism is the only ideology which is not tied to how one views one's connection to the race. Support for black Marxism is driven by the economic component of black identity.

The depth of the decline in black Marxism's ties to the institutions and networks of black civil society is apparent in several areas. Like black feminism, but unlike black nationalism, embeddedness within black organizations has no effect on support for a radical agenda. Unlike both black feminism and black nationalism, black Marxism is not affected by embeddedness within black information networks. Finally, unlike the feminist or nationalist agenda, the black radical agenda has been neither helped nor harmed by the artistic force of popular music. Exposure to rap does not make one more or less open to a black radical ideological orientation. Nor does exposure to rap affect whether one believes America's corporations aid or harm the black community. Adherents of rap are also no more or less likely to believe that blacks have common interests or have too many social divisors for a common agenda. Support for black Marxism is shaped by one's social location and the degree that one perceives blacks to be racially disadvantaged in the economy, not by the institutions and networks of black civil society. In the next section I analyze how strongly support for black Marxism shapes black public opinion.

Consequences

Black Marxism modestly shapes black public opinion. It has neither the force or breadth of impact that black nationalism has in shaping black public opinion. While a large majority of blacks are pessimistic about the possibility of racial progress in the United States (nearly two-thirds believed

5. Tables are available from the author on request.

that racial equality will either not be achieved in their lifetime or at all within the United States), black Marxists are more likely than others to believe in a bleak future. The nationalist component of black radicalism also comes through. Black radicals are both more likely to feel slightly more negative toward whites than other blacks and also more supportive of the formation of an independent, black political party. Only the nationalists believe more strongly than the Marxists that white elected officials cannot represent blacks as well as black representatives. Black Marxists still believe—though less strongly than either the radical egalitarians, disillusioned liberals, or nationalists—that blacks should have a shot at jobs before immigrants. A black Marxist orientation in the 1990s is heavily racialized. Perceptions of racial economic subordination and class conflict among blacks lead them to have a more racialized view of the political economy. This set of orientations helps explain black support for radical agendas that have components built around both race and economic redistribution. Supporters of black Marxists in the 1990s remain as suspicious of a "unite and fight" strategy as many of their predecessors earlier in the twentieth century.

Black radical ideology does not, however, influence attitudes on questions of gender in the black community. More surprisingly, and perhaps reflective of the black Marxist experience in the 1980s (see Baraka 1991c, for example), those with a black Marxist orientation are not more likely to support blacks seeking allies outside of the black community than other African Americans. Those who support black feminism are the members of the black community most receptive to outside alliances, as is consistent with modern black feminist ideology. Having a black Marxist orientation does substantially shape how African Americans evaluate politics *within* the black community. Disillusioned liberals and those with a black Marxist orientation are the only ones to think that neither Democrats nor Republicans work hard on "black" issues (across the board, all of the ideologies think that the Republicans do not work hard on black issues). Throughout the twentieth century, black Marxists (along with the revolutionary nationalists) have been the political force within the black community most consistently critical of *both* major political parties.

In summary, having a black Marxist ideology influences how political and class divisions are perceived within the black community, not one's religious values. Neither the strength of one's religious faith nor how frequently one engages in prayer are affected by having a black Marxist orientation. Religiosity and black Marxism are not related to each other among grassroots African Americans. Not surprisingly, given the lack of gender analyses by black Marxists, black Marxist ideologues are no more or less likely than other blacks to support issues of concern to black feminists. Black Marxists are more critical of whites than other African Americans. This result is not surprising when we remember that black Marxists, unlike orthodox Marxists in the United States, incorporated the concept of white supremacy to explain both the economic position of blacks at the bottom of the economic order and the remarkable lack of enthusiasm exhibited by white workers over the decades to unite with their nonwhite cousins. Black Marxists, at least among the African-American grassroots, are not particularly hostile to many of the central tenets of the community nationalist paradigm outlined in chapter 3. Black Marxists are more likely (if not quite as likely as black nationalists) than other African Americans to support local control of both the political and economic institutions of black communities. "True believers" are somewhat more likely to believe that blacks constitute a nation within a nation. Black Marxists, however, are as unlikely as other blacks to support a separate black nation. Black Marxists in the grassroots are no more likely than other blacks to condemn Minister Farrakhan. Black Marxists, like black nationalists, are not ambivalent about forming an independent black political party—they strongly support that idea. The pendulum has swung back to the early 1970s when young activists of color with a Marxist orientation overwhelmingly supported the formation of independent, racially based political organizations and movements.

Black Marxists also have strong views on the electoral system and its efficacy for African Americans. They are more likely to believe that blacks represent the interests of African Americans better than white officials. As mentioned above, the black Marxist racialized view of black *political* subordination is further demonstrated by the sets of results which show that both true believers and those with a black Marxist orientation are substantially more likely to believe that *neither* the Democratic nor Republican parties are working hard in the interests of blacks. And the skepticism about Jesse Jackson as a viable alternative for African Americans expressed in the writings of Reed, Baraka, and Marable is also found among grassroots black Marxists (Baraka 1991c; Marable 1995a; Reed 1986). Black Marxists see both the economic and political orders as racialized with pernicious consequences for African Americans.

Black Marxism does shape black public opinion but neither as systematically nor as deeply as does black nationalism. What is clear is that beliefs remain embedded within the black grassroots which connect a racialized political and economic order to perceptions of political and economic divisions within the black community. The lack of a black Marxist presence in black communities has led to an ideology that more weakly coheres among blacks than either black feminism or black liberalism. To once again become a public force, black Marxists would have to return to the streets.

CONCLUSION

At the onslaught of the Great Depression, when black and white workers were suffering from the capitalist crisis that Marxists had so fervently predicted, white workers in Atlanta were forming "Black Shirt" committees which organized around the slogan "No Jobs for Niggers Until Every White Man Has a Job" (Hutchinson 1995, 59). In the summer of 1995, *Washington Post* data showed once again that whites, unlike blacks, Latinos, and Asian-Americans, believed that they were threatened by antidiscrimination efforts in employment (Dawson 1997). On the other hand, blacks, Latinos, and whites—every group except Asian-Americans—felt further from the American Dream in 1995 than they did a decade earlier (Dawson 1997). Can the type of progressive unity that Marable and others advocate become the basis for a new form of movement? Or is economic anxiety likely to spark the type of movement that plagued Atlanta in the 1930s when Black Shirts took to the streets to strip blacks of the few jobs they held.

Today, black Marxism is not a mass force. Not surprisingly, black Marxism coheres poorly as an ideology among grassroots blacks. In general, this is true of all other black ideologies except nationalism, whether within the liberal tradition or as challengers of liberalism. But as with black feminism, significant changes would have to occur within black politics for black Marxism to become a mass force. Black Marxism, the analyses demonstrate, has the potential to shape black public opinion within a broad range. Even now the ideology has some influence on how African Americans perceive both divisions within the black community and the American political process.

Black radicalism as a tradition could build on its history of analytical alertness when it comes to the class tensions within the black community. It provides a useful corrective to both liberal and orthodox radical tendencies which attempt to reduce racial conflict within the United States to a phenomenon of secondary importance at best. When most influential, black Marxists emphasized the central importance of both race and class as systems of oppression in the United States. Perhaps most important, as West details, black Marxism can provide the critical analytical force for critiquing the depredations of capitalism, particularly as the intersection of class and race systematically assigns some groups of Americans to the bottom of the ladder. At its best, black Marxism provides a vital and critical voice within the black counterpublic.

Black Marxism also has a significant amount of history to overcome if it is once again to become a major ideological force within the black community. Black Marxists will have to take gender as an analytical category and their own sexism seriously for the first time. New labor markets are fundamentally gendered, right-wing movements based on patriarchal public policies are making it extremely difficult to organize for progressive political change, and black nationalists are attempting to rebuild their own movement based on a severe gender hierarchy that would limit the life chances of black women. Black radicals in this period would find their most natural allies, on the basis of similarity of ideology, among black feminists, not among most black nationalists.

Black Marxism has also been historically hurt by subservience to foreign, often brutally repressive, Marxist regimes, whether it was the domination of Moscow in the 1930s or the ideological dependence on Third World Marxists in China and North Korea during the 1970s. This ideological dependence has rightly alienated black Marxist organizations from the black community at different points over the past three-quarters of a century. This dependence contributed to the dogmatism which wrecked nearly all organizations that had significant black Marxist participation from the 1930s on. Finally, ideological dependence on foreign models had the effect of minimizing efforts to analyze concretely the contemporary conditions and historical patterns found within both the black community and American society.

To be successful, black Marxism figure out how to unite with those outside the black community while holding onto their base. To solve that puzzle, black Marxists of this generation must determine how they view the intersection of race, class, and gender in this historical era. Equally fundamental is the need to analyze the meaning of black liberation when democratic rights have been largely gained through the Civil Rights movement, and the nature of capitalism in the era of globalization. The heirs to the black radical tradition need to remember that theory can provide only a partial answer to these questions. The validity of the answers obtained can be tested only through local and national public organizing. If these questions are not satisfactorily answered, black Marxism is likely to remain primarily an academic phenomenon.

[The Negro] asks nothing from the society except that it consider
him as a full-fledged citizen, vested with all of the rights and
privileges granted to every citizen; that the charter of liberties
of the Constitution apply to the black as to all other men.

Ralph J. Bunche, 1939

Here at home, my heart is with the continuing struggles of my own
people, to achieve complete liberation from racist domination and to
gain for all black Americans and the other minority groups not only
equal rights, but an equal share.

Paul Robeson, 1975

CHAPTER 6

A Vision of Freedom Larger Than America Is Prepared to Accept? The Diverse Shades of Black Liberalism

THE AMERICAN LIBERAL TRADITION AND BLACK LIBERALISM

Has the American liberal tradition failed African Americans? Is liberalism in any form, black or white, woefully inadequate for providing a framework through which racial justice can be achieved in America? Every black ideology has had to address that question, as have every generation's black activists and leaders. Black nationalists and black Marxists have passionately claimed across generations that American liberalism is a bankrupt ideology which serves more to enslave than empower African Americans. Black feminists, some of whom have moved into the black liberal tradition, remain profoundly suspicious of liberalism's capacity to eliminate oppressive hierarchies. In this chapter I explore three questions. First, how does black liberalism differ from the liberalisms that dominate American political practice? Second, how does black liberalism differ from other black ideologies? In the conclusion I return to the question posed by many activists: Does liberalism as an ideology provide a viable ideological alternative for the future of African Americans?

There are many reasons for black ideologue and activist suspicion of the practiced version of American liberalism. Nationalists especially, and thoughtful black progressives as well, feel that, of all of the enlightenment-derived ideologies, liberalism is the most open to the charge of being what Charles Mills has provocatively, if often accurately, called a *Herrenvolk* ideology (Mills 1997). Mills and many other black theorists, activists, and ideologues have charged that ideologies such as liberalism, Marxism, and feminism incorporate the hierarchies of white supremacy within them in their explicit theoretical premises, their implicit theoretical and historical blind spots, as well as their actual instantiation within constitutions, institutions, and social movements. The claim, to use Mills's term, is that a *racial contract* is implicit in these ideologies.

This contract is understood differently by black nationalists on one hand, and by most black liberals, feminists, and Marxists on the other. Nationalists often claim that each of these ideologies is *inherently* racialized and racist. They claim that the history of liberalism, for example, is inextricably intertwined with the colonization of the nonwhite world by Europeans, and that within societies such as the United States, the founders and their descendants excluded blacks and other nonwhites in theory and practice from both the polity and the full benefits of being members of a liberal civil society.[1]

Adherents of the other ideologies argue that liberalism is not inherently racist, nor are Marxism and feminism, but that, given the historical epochs within which each emerged and the racist political cultures of modern Western polities, we should not be surprised that their practitioners betray the universal principles of these ideologies when they marry the "ideology" to white supremacy. This is not the same argument that some commentators such as Rogers Smith and Alan Brinkley make about separate traditions within polities such as the United States; they argue that liberal,

---

1. Jefferson's *Notes on the State of Virginia* provides perhaps the most prominent of early arguments about the unsuitability of blacks' participation in any aspect of "American" civil society or the polity. Similar sentiments can be found in Lincoln's writings as well. Chapter 1 provides some examples from the late nineteenth through mid-twentieth centuries.

egalitarian, antiracist—or at least nonracist—traditions exist alongside racist and parochial antiliberal historical traditions. Black defenders of feminism, Marxism, and liberalism generally have little patience with claims that these ideologies, particularly liberalism, are incompatible with white supremacy. Their argument is simply that this need not be the case.

But most black liberals have an even more difficult set of claims to defend. They must not only argue that liberalism need not be connected to white supremacy, but that liberalism provides the best philosophical and moral framework for blacks' desire for equality and justice. To be sure, African-American liberalism differs substantially from traditional American liberalism, particularly, as we shall see, from the thin liberalism that has become so popular with many academics. Black liberalism, black liberals, and the great majority of African Americans, have demanded equality. Black liberals' conception of equality includes equal shares of the fruits of the nation as well as equal opportunity. In particular, black liberals' belief that liberal egalitarianism should encompass the economic as well as the social and political realms separates them from most other American liberals. This separation has not gone unnoticed by either grassroots African Americans or activists. Malcolm X told SNCC workers in Selma, Alabama, just before he was murdered in 1965, that he was worried that though they were struggling for a just cause, America would turn its back on them: "I don't want to make you do anything you wouldn't do. . . . I disagree with nonviolence, but I respect the fact that you're on the front lines and you're down here suffering for *a version of freedom larger than America's prepared to accept.* (from an interview with Taylor Branch; National Public Radio Transcript, Saturday, April 4, 1998). Over thirty years later, a professor at an elite university who teaches public law, a former socialist who remains very liberal, reluctantly came to the conclusion that Martin Luther King Jr. was not a liberal because his version of freedom was one that was too large for America. Specifically, he argued that King's and other black liberals' view of economic equality was not consistent with liberalism. Black liberals have had the difficult task of convincing African Americans (mostly, but not always, successfully) that their collective vision of freedom was achievable within America, while at the same time trying to convince the rest of the country (much less successfully) that only by embracing the widest vision of freedom and equality could America both fulfill its obligation to its black citizens and, by doing so, redeem itself.

In this chapter I probe the challenges that black liberals face both in confronting the American liberal tradition and when making their case to the black community. Just as there is more than one liberal tradition within the American polity, I argue that multiple liberal traditions exist within the black community. Some are militantly egalitarian, one is radically disillusioned, and the one with the weakest grassroots support borders on radical libertarianism. Before examining the different shades of black liberalism, we outline the occasionally tortured relationship between black liberalism and the American liberal tradition and then briefly examine the American liberal tradition.

THE PRAGMATIC TRIUMPH OF THE INDIVIDUAL AND THE AMERICAN CREED

Liberalism permeates American political culture, nearly monopolizes the attention of students of American political thought, and presents a challenge to the adherents of each black ideology. The triumphant reign of hegemonic liberalism is celebrated by many authors and decried by a few. To a significant degree, this tradition of scholarship was shaped by Louis Hartz in his seminal book *The Liberal Tradition in America*. In the opening discussion Hartz argues that "the American community is a liberal community" (Hartz 1955, 3). He asserts that the degree of consensus around liberalism in the United States is so deep that it approaches "moral unanimity" (Hartz 1955, 6). J. David Greenstone agrees with the first part of the argument that "at its core American political culture is pervasively liberal" (Greenstone 1993, 6), but he disagrees with the second part about the degree of consensus, arguing that liberalism in the United States is contested. The United States, according to Greenstone,

> is pervasively liberal but not consensually so; that although American liberalism excludes nonliberal alternatives, it is nevertheless fundamentally divided, philosophically as well as politically. It is divided by an opposition between what I have called reform liberals, who were concerned primarily, with the development of the faculties of individuals, and what I have called humanist liberals, who were concerned primarily with the satisfaction of the preferences of individuals. (Greenstone 1993, 6)

But even commentators like Greenstone and Rogers Smith, who point to the multiple traditions in American political thought, concede that liberalism dominates American political culture. Liberalism is hegemonic. As

Anne Norton argues, "The force of a political idea lies in its capacity to transcend thought and make itself part of everyday life in the material world. Liberalism has become the common sense of the American people, a set of principles unconsciously adhered to, a set of conventions so deeply held that they appear (when they appear at all) to be no more than common sense" (Norton 1993, 1).[2] She continues that liberalism's power to guide our actions is multiplied because it is "taken for granted." Indeed, both black and white liberalisms have an enormous advantage in that "their primacy is [not] aggressively asserted but . . . they go unquestioned" (Norton 1993, 1). This is an important advantage when compared to black nationalism, Marxism or feminism. Nationalism *must be* aggressively promoted as must any serious challenge to the liberal hegemony. Not only are you trying to combat an usually hostile ideology, but one so grounded that it has the force of common sense. Norton concludes, and I agree, that for Americans "liberalism is a way of life" (Norton 1993, 7).

Liberalism is pervasive, it is consensual, and it is unconscious. It can also be, Hartz argues, an irrational force during some periods within the United States: "Locke has a hidden conformitarian germ to begin with, since natural law tells equal people equal things, but when this germ is fed by the explosive power of modern nationalism, it mushrooms into something pretty remarkable" (Hartz 1955, 11). Or pretty grim, as he makes clear in his discussion of the role of liberal ideology during the McCarthy era. Hartz is, however, more concerned with unanimity than majority tyranny. Black liberals, as the trenchant passage quoted earlier from Dahl reminds us, must be concerned with majority tyranny because the collective nature of blacks' liberal claims flies in the face of one of the key pillars of American liberalism—the privileged position of the individual citizen and *his* rights. A key contention, then, is that many aspects of the dominant liberalism practiced in the United States are viewed as problematic, if not outright hostile to the interests of African Americans.

Recent developments in modern political philosophy, including liberal philosophy, would also have caused the classic, egalitarian-oriented, black liberals significant concern. The philosophical emphasis on "thin" liberalism, that is, "minimal" grounds for justifying a liberal political order, would be treated with suspicion (for examples and discussion, see Larmore 1996;

---

2. Norton also argues in that passage that the quotidian nature of American liberalism allows it to have transformed itself from being an ideology. I would argue that liberalism still has the aspects of ideology as defined in the first two chapters, despite its everyday nature.

Rawls 1993; Sposito 1998). There are several points here. As Sposito argued, the point of a search for minimal grounds for justification is that
"reasonable people" in a diverse society are likely to disagree about what
constitutes the "good life." Thus it is necessary to find a consensus about
which "reasonable" citizens can agree in order to insure political neutrality, a neutrality that will not favor one form of the liberal "good life" over
another (Larmore 1996; Sposito 1998). Other liberals, such as Holmes,
Herzog, Waldron, and many others, can justifiably argue that the forms of
liberalism they favor can easily encompass a generous welfare state, and
that such a state can be justified on the basis of the historical claims of classic as well as modern liberals. As Holmes argues, liberalism is not equal
to libertarianism; liberalism, despite what some argue, is consistent with
both democracy and the welfare state, as well as justice (Holmes 1995). But
Rawls, Larmore, and other proponents of a thin liberalism argue that there
can be many conceptions of liberalism, and therefore the principle of political neutrality entails that we need not favor a liberalism which encom-
passes a generous welfare state over one which has a more draconian, libertarian conception of welfare (Larmore 1996; Rawls 1993). Larmore
argues, for example, that we can construct a politically neutral liberal order
on the twin principles of equal respect for persons and rational dialogue
(Larmore 1996).

But there is a substantive edge to Larmore's quest for a minimal conception of the justification for liberalism. He states quite clearly that one
reason for this moral minimalism is that "to avoid the oppressive use of
state power, the liberal goal has therefore been to define the common good
of political association by means of *a minimal moral conception*" (Larmore
1996, 123; emphasis in the original). Black liberals would find several problems with Larmore's conceptualizations. First, they would object, as both
King and Du Bois do, as much to the concentration of private power as to
state power. Larmore's formulation is similar to Holmes's when the latter
argued that "the most obvious superiority of liberal over Marxist thought
stems from liberalism's persistent concern for—and Marxism's infamous
blindness to—abuses of accumulated political power" (Holmes 1995, 18).
But earlier in the same passage Holmes argued that "the essence of liberalism, from this perspective, lay in techniques for taming absolute power"
(Holmes 1995). This formulation, unlike the earlier one and Larmore's, is
one with which many black ideologues could be comfortable. The *desire* of
black liberals, feminists, and Marxists for a strong central state has much to
do with African Americans' historical experience with concentrated *economic*

power. Much of the accumulated power in the hands of racists, whether blacks were chattel slaves or mid-career corporate executives, has been in private hands. Even black liberals believe that a strong state is necessary to discipline racist power in private hands which, they argue, continues to operate through employment, real estate, loan, and retail markets, as well as less visibly through private organizations ranging from elite social clubs to churches. African Americans believe that the state is needed to discipline racism in civil society. Thus black liberals' concern with the egalitarian aspects of liberalism—even if limited to mean equal opportunity—drives them to seek a much stronger state than other American liberals.

Historically, Holmes and Larmore are right in the American case. As Shklar has reminded us, American liberalism was instantiated by practitioners who believed "the best government is that which governs least" (Shklar 1998, 117). Holmes, unlike Larmore, clearly details the liberal concern with both private and public accumulation of power, but in the wake of the Cold War and its aftermath, even Holmes is more fixated on the dangers of public power, while the black experience has made the dangers of both private power and a tyrannical, permanent governing majority manifest. Thus Larmore's political neutrality is not in the least neutral; it favors a conception of the good life and state which privileges controls on state power rather than one which is at least equally concerned with controls on power in private hands.

The principle of equal respect, by which Larmore quite rightly means, among other things, not treating people as ends, is on the surface quite reasonable and one that a wide range of black ideologues would support. But even here there are problems. Black liberals (as always with the exception of black conservatives), black feminists, black Marxists, and many black nationalists would all question the ability to maintain "equal respect for persons" without significant limitations on private power. Indeed, it is precisely the failure of liberal states, especially the United States, to curb private power in order to bring about equal respect for persons which Du Bois and King identify as both the failure and hypocrisy of liberalism as instantiated in this society.

Similarly, from the standpoint of most black liberals, there are problems as well with the principle of rational dialogue. Two problems stand out from the standpoint of African Americans' historical conception. The first is that, historically, blacks, like women, were considered incapable of rational dialogue. Charles Mills makes this point when he argues, "European liberalism restricts 'egalitarianism to equality among equals,' and blacks and others are ontologically excluded by race from the promise of 'the liberal project of modernity'" (Mills 1997, 56). For most of American history, therefore, the principle of rational dialogue did not apply, because whites, most explicitly the political and civil elite of the nation, did not believe blacks were capable of functioning as citizens. As Mills documents, this was not just a peculiarity of a racist United States, but was a widespread belief among the classic liberal theorists. Kant (who had a particularly vile view of blacks' intelligence), Hobbes, and Locke also wrote about the unsuitability of the liberal order and liberal rights for the darker races. Indeed, J. S. Mill argued that the lack of intellectual and cognitive ability of blacks and other nonwhite races, led to his "judgement that 'those races in their nonage' were fit only for despotism" (Mills 1997, 60). Given the embeddedness of racism in these liberal theorists' works and the trajectory of American history as seen through many black eyes, it is not useful, black ideologues argue, to separate the founders as democratic liberals from the exact same men who, like John Adams, believed that "Negroes, Indians, and [Kaffirs] cannot bear democracy" (Mills 1997, 57). The contemporary legacy of this common attitude in the history of both continental and American liberal theory as well as political leaders has led novelist Toni Morrison to conclude, "American means white, and Africanist people struggle to make the term applicable to themselves with ethnicity and hyphen after hyphen after hyphen. Americans did not have a profligate, predatory nobility from which to wrest an identity of national virtue while continuing to covet aristocratic license and luxury. The American nation negotiated both its disdain and its envy in the same way Dunbar did: through a self-reflexive contemplation of fabricated, mythological Africanism" (Morrison 1992b, 47). For most of American history, entering into rational dialogue was not an option.

There is a contemporary as well as a historical problem with the principle of rational dialogue. Even in the twentieth century, great disparities of power exist even among those who are "oppressed." For example, there were conflicts between "communist" maids and their "communist" women employers (Jones 1995). Black feminists have often commented on the disparities of power they face with regard to both white women and black men when attempting to engage in a discourse among equals. Black workers in Detroit formed the Revolutionary Union Movement because their speech and their set of interests were not acknowledged by the UAW. Liberal theorists would logically argue that they are arguing and proposing principles at the level of the abstract, and therefore these disparities and accidents of history need not invalidate the principles of minimal liberalism. Mills responds,

> My suggestion is that by looking at the *actual*, historically dominant, moral/political consciousness and the *actual*, historically dominant, moral/political ideals we are better enabled to prescribe for society than by starting from ahistorical abstractions. In other words, the point is not to endorse this deficient consciousness and these repugnant ideals but, by recognizing their past and current influence and power and identifying their sources, to correct for them. Realizing a better future requires not merely admitting the ugly truth of the past—and present—but understanding the ways in which these realities were made invisible, acceptable to the white populations. We want to know—both to describe and to explain—the circumstances that actually blocked achievement of the ideal raceless ideals and promoted instead the naturalized, nonideal racial ideals. We want to know what went wrong in the past, is going wrong now, and is likely to *continue* to go wrong in the future if we do not guard against it. (Mills 1997, 92)

Ultimately both equal respect and rational dialogue are reasonable principles that fail black activists' pragmatic test. Equal respect requires for most black ideologues greater state involvement and therefore negates Larmore's and others' goal of a minimal state. Rational dialogue among reasonable citizens is problematic when those with power determine both who is reasonable and with what weight their dialogue is accepted. Rawls appeals to the "common sense" of a given political culture for the "justifications" needed by a liberal order for legitimacy (Rawls 1993, 224). But the common sense of a historically racist political culture becomes suspect as ground for the foundations of political neutrality. Thin liberalism is a version of liberalism that most black liberal ideologues would have to reject on multiple grounds.

Michael Sandel provides a useful summary of the key tenets of the American liberal tradition that black liberals have historically found problematic:

> The political philosophy by which we live is a certain version of liberal political theory. Its central idea is that government should be neutral toward the moral and religious views its citizens espouse. Since people disagree about the best way to live, government should not affirm in law any particular vision of the good life. Instead, it should provide a frame-

work of rights that respects persons as free and independent selves, capable of choosing their own values and ends. Since this liberalism asserts the priority of fair procedures over particular ends, the public life it informs might be called the procedural republic. . . . [This tradition] emphasizes toleration and respect for individual rights." (Sandel 1996, 6)

Sandel concurs with Hartz, Greenstone, and Norton that liberalism dominates American political debates. He contends, "The public philosophy of contemporary American politics is a version of this liberal tradition of thought, and most of our debates proceed within its terms" (Sandel 1996, 5). While the public philosophy might be liberalism, it is not a strand of liberalism with which most black liberals feel comfortable. Even so, black liberals do believe that their brand of liberalism provides the best hope for race and country.

BLACK LIBERALISM: TAKE 1

Historically, the majority of black activists have argued that the just demands of African Americans are fully consistent with the broad principles of American democracy. In 1935 Ralph Bunche made this point while bitterly arguing for the utility of a more Marxist analysis of black liberation:

> In general, the objectives which minority groups traditionally struggle for are the tenets of social justice embraced by eighteenth-century liberalism, with its democratic creed of liberty, equality, and fraternity. This liberalism purported to guarantee the individual's economic and political freedom. Economic freedom for the individual assumed his right to protection of the state in the acquisition and use of his property for his private benefit and profit. . . . In the United States the presence of the frontier, with the free land it offered and its rich natural resources, vitalized the American Dream that every energetic and thrifty American could win economic independence. The American frontier, however, was never widely open to the Negro population. (Bunche 1995c, 53)

The black population was denied, Bunche continues, "[the] political freedom for the individual [which] assumed his right to equality before the law, the right to freedom of speech, press, religion, assemblage, and movement, and to the democratic participation in the government through the unabridged use of the ballot" (Bunche 1995c, 53).

Ralph Bunche's career as black activist and American civic leader followed a path opposite of that of many of this century's greatest black liberals. For Dr. King, the activists of the Student Nonviolent Coordinating Committee, and many others, the path was a hard one, marked by a journey from hope to despair. At the end of their journey, they became convinced of the nation's recalcitrance; they believed racism was entrenched within the American psyche as well as American social, political, and economic structures. Indeed, Bunche's contemporary and one-time friend, W. E. B. Du Bois, is perhaps the best example of an activist who traveled this dark road. Bunche followed a pattern in the mid-twentieth century which has often been repeated since the 1970s. He began his career as a militant Marxist, Harvard-trained, Howard-based political scientist. Writing path-breaking works on both black politics in the United States and colonialism in Africa, Bunche was a key colleague and researcher of Gunnar Myrdal, providing much of the research and thinking for the still seminal work on American race relations written in the 1940s, *An American Dilemma.* But Bunche gradually abandoned his militancy and began a long career as part of the American intelligence community during World War II and as a major leader in the United Nations after the war. As an international diplomat, Bunche became known simultaneously for his advocacy of black rights and support for the Civil Rights movement, his stand for human rights, his racial moderation, and his defense of Western democracy and liberal ideology. The latter stances led to an estrangement from his contemporaries such as Du Bois and from the younger activists of the Black Power era. Thus Bunche in his role as CIA officer, State Department diplomat, and high-ranking UN official prefigures the careers of Colin Powell a generation and a half later and of other progressive, black elected officials who had early careers as racial militants before joining Congress. Bobby Rush, John Lewis, and Ron Dellums were strong critics of liberalism and American democracy in their activist youth who sought social justice through the electoral system and the state later in life. Trained in political theory, Bunche directly confronted the attractions and pitfalls of liberalism both from the inside and from the standpoint of an activist. Near the time of his death, he too began to worry about whether American liberalism and democracy were at all capable of providing a framework for enduring black justice.

Bunche had earlier argued, as had many others, including Du Bois in his great autobiography, *Dusk of Dawn*, that the promise liberalism offered blacks was a sham. Du Bois would never again fully embrace liberalism, while Bunche would become one of liberalism's leading champions while remaining a critic of both racism and much of the black movement during his twilight years.

During this early period of his career, Bunche captured widespread black concern with the inadequacies of liberal democracies when discussing America's most sacred document, the Constitution:

> In other words, this charter of the black man's liberties can never be more than what our legislatures and, in the final analysis, our courts wish it to be. And what these worthy institutions wish it to be can never be more than what American public opinion wishes it to be. Unfortunately, so much of American public opinion is seldom enlightened, sympathetic, tolerant, or humanitarian. Too often it resembles mob violence. (Bunche 1995c, 57)

Many liberals in the 1990s, both black and white, would respond that Bunche was writing at the point in the twentieth century where the situation of blacks, and perhaps the nation, had reached its nadir. Unfortunately, data from the 1990 General Social Survey show that 54 percent of whites still believe that blacks are less intelligent than whites.[3] A majority of white Americans also believe that blacks are more prone to violence and more prone to prefer welfare than whites. Nearly half of all whites believe that blacks are less patriotic. A group of people who are believed to be less intelligent, violent, abusers of public funds, and less committed to the nation is hardly a group on which one would confer the duties and rights of citizenship. When a member of such a group is savagely beaten by police in the name of law and order, one may not be sympathetic. After all, many would argue, "order and control" are important to impose on a group which is *alleged* to hold the above traits. We should not be surprised when members of this group are called "niggers" over the public intercom system and otherwise harassed on a regular basis at factories owned by some of America's largest corporations, such as the Miller Brewing Company and Ford Motors (Janofsky 1993). The Texaco tapes demonstrate that similar language can be found at the top level of the American corporate structure. After all, they neither deserve their jobs nor the constitutional rights granted first-class citizens of the nation. We should not be surprised if these people are systematically excluded not only from the "official" public spheres of civil society but from oppositional counterpublics as well.

---

3. Data compiled by author from the 1990 General Social Survey.

In this racial context, liberalism presents several challenges to black activists and ideologies. Liberalism provides some guarantees that blacks might find attractive, as when Bunche points to the American "high regard for the . . . rights of the individual" (Bunche 1995f, 93). Liberalism also provides a set of dangers which concern African-American theorists. First, liberal democratic polities always confront "despised minorities" with the potential disaster of the tyranny of the majority. One astute observer of the United States of the middle 1950s, for example, described the political system as being open to everyone except "Negroes and communists" (Dahl 1956). In essence, Dahl equated the political status of blacks with that of communists during the height of the McCarthy era. Hostile white majorities have historically led black liberal activists and theoreticians to emphasize liberal rights as a matter of group protection.

Libertarian-oriented theorists and political leaders present a different perceived danger to non-conservative black liberal leaders. Representatives from this tradition continue to lead fierce assaults against the expansion of the state-sanctioned liberal rights that Kantian-oriented liberal theorists argue are crucial for protecting disliked minorities (Boxill 1992; Epstein 1992; Nozick 1974; Sandel 1996). A particularly broad assault on the legacy of rights that were won as a result of the Civil Rights and Black Power movements comes from a University of Chicago Law Professor, Richard Epstein, in his book, *Forbidden Grounds*. Epstein simply argues, "The entire apparatus of anti-discrimination laws in Title VII should be repealed in so far as it applies to private employers. . . . My view is quite categorical: it is meant to apply to criteria of race, sex, religion, national origin, age, and handicap" (Epstein 1992, 9). Epstein's vision of a world where discrimination is permissible is based neither on a "moral statement" nor on "historical injustices," as black conservative Thomas Sowell states in a laudatory review (Sowell 1992). Instead, Epstein argues that society is better off because economic rationality insures that societal payoffs are maximized when employers are allowed to discriminate rationally. Further, it is morally permissible to do so because "employment discrimination laws were an unjustified limitation on the principle of freedom of contract notwithstanding the overwhelming social consensus in their favor" (Epstein 1992, xii). Why? Because in his reductionist version of the Lockean contract and "natural law," liberal democracy is reduced to the absurd proposition that the efficiency and profits of firms are a greater good than equality before the law and in employment markets. These attacks undermine the very foundation of rights based black liberalism. The attacks come from another direction as well. Just as the libertarians relentlessly attack the conceptual foundations of black liberalism by attacking concepts such as equality and rights, theorists such as Storing attack the moral foundations of radical egalitarianism in particular and all other activist-oriented black ideologies.

Storing argues that even at its height the Civil Rights movement lacked a defensible moral foundation:

> The circumstances of the Negro in America, under slavery and after
> the Civil War, taught Frederick Douglass a lesson which many whites at
> that time and many whites and blacks today have forgotten: that a fun-
> damentally decent and just civil society, in which men are protected and
> encouraged in the pursuit of happiness, is a rare and precious thing. . . .
> Injustice can be protested and private conscience gratified from a
> protest march or a jail cell, but the positive demands of justice cannot
> be served there. (Storing 1995, 258)

Storing goes on to say that the philosophy of civil disobedience which pro-vided much of the action orientation of black liberals provided only a "false morality" (Storing 1995, 257). One should be sure to support the laws of a just nation; to undermine them is immoral. How should blacks advance? "The Negro's duty was to make himself fit" (Storing 1995, 188). He con-tinues by stating that "the hardships and injustice faced by the Negro in America are not tragic or even exceptional" (Storing 1995, 204). Blacks have to prove themselves in order to be granted full citizenship rights. Black liberal demands are misguided, impolite, and ultimately immoral. While black conservatives such Glenn Loury celebrate Storing's perspec-tive, other black liberals have reminded these white theorists and their black cohorts from Booker T. Washington to Loury that there is a minor theoretical and pragmatic problem, for when it comes to the status of Af-rican Americans, America *has* behaved in any manner but that of a just polity and society (Loury 1995, 71). While black liberals from Du Bois to King grew extremely angry in the face of such attacks, the reaction of both black Marxists and nationalists was to say, "I told you so" while preparing, at least figuratively, for war.

Attacks such as these on the basic framework of the equality-based, antidiscrimination movement provided the context for black leaders such as Martin Luther King Jr., at the end of his life, to become increasingly skeptical about the capacity of a society dominated by liberal ideology to address the needs of its most disadvantaged citizens. And as black activists have repeatedly seen, liberal democratic polities during some historical periods are quite capable of succumbing to a nationalist fervor that insists on a stultifying, indeed terrifying, conformity.

Despite these dangers, the great majority of progressive black liberals, while cognizant of these dangers, still insist that liberalism provides the best ideological hope, even with all of its flaws, in theory and practice, for black justice. Indeed by 1941 Bunche argues precisely this point:

> The entire constitutional history of the nation has reflected this compromise in the quixotic tendency to sanctify its democratic creeds while stubbornly retaining its racial bigotries. Paradoxical as it may seem in the light of the historical record, however, the fact remains that the Constitution did lay the basis for the most broad ideological pattern of individual human equality, human liberty, and human rights that the modern world has known. (Bunche 1995f, 93)

Black liberals claim that blacks' only option for advancing both American democracy and black social justice is to finally redeem the promise of America (Howard-Pitney 1990; King 1986i; Du Bois 1969). Black liberals base their claim on pragmatic (in both the practical and philosophical meanings of the word), theoretical, and moral grounds. The moral claims are often particularly complicated, as they usually entail claims about the dignity of individuals, the earning of the rights and duties of citizenship, and a recognition of the need to be accepted within civil society on a morally equal basis. Black liberals argue not only that, with all of its flaws, American liberalism is the best philosophical and pragmatic system for achieving justice for blacks, but that America can only redeem itself by finally becoming a society where blacks have gained justice and equality. Many remember Martin Luther King's eloquence when he shared his vision of a world, an America where the content of one's character was the sole criteria by which citizens were evaluated. Many either have never heard or have forgotten his earlier condemnation of America's racist legacy in the same "I Have a Dream" speech. In this segment of his "March on Washington" speech, King forcefully repeats the theme that America owes blacks for past wrongs and current injustices and inequalities:

> But one hundred years later, the Negro still is not free; one hundred years later, the life of the Negro is still sadly crippled by the manacles of segregation and the chains of discrimination; one hundred years later, the Negro lives on a lonely island of poverty in the midst of a vast ocean

need is the ability to try and control your feelings when people who strike you as irredeemably different show up at City Hall, or the greengrocer, or the bazaar. When this happens, you smile a lot, make the best deals you can, and, after a hard day's haggling, retreat to your club. There you will be comforted by the companionship of your moral equals. (Rorty 1991, 209; emphasis in original)

But the frequency in black life of racist abuse suffered at the hand of those who don't consider blacks *their* moral equals leads me to agree with Charles Taylor (1992) and others when they argue that a prerequisite for democratic debate as well as for the survival of democratic societies is precisely the recognition of the humanity and dignity of all individuals within a political community.

Black liberals do not, despite the allegations of some of their critics, reject the ethnocentric and cultural nationalist visions of Rorty and Walzer, or of the black nationalists for that matter, because they favor assimilation. Most black liberals ground their claims in racial pride and uplift (Gaines 1996; Wells 1970). Ida B. Wells, Frederick Douglass, and Martin Luther King Jr., among many others, all advocated not only black racial pride, but also the need for blacks to form autonomous, black, social, economic, and political organizations (Boxill 1992; Du Bois 1986; King 1986h; Wells 1970). Racial pride was strongly encouraged by black liberals of all periods. Uplift ideology, as Gaines explains, is a phenomenon associated with black middle-class liberalism. Acceptance into the mainstream of American society will be predicated on blacks lifting themselves up as a race (Gaines 1996). This is not just the aggressively promoted viewpoint of the conservative strand of black liberalism; it appeared in the works of progressive liberal activists such as Du Bois and Wells a century ago, as well as in the works of the seminal black conservative, Booker T. Washington. Today, black liberals such as Jesse Jackson and Henry Louis Gates Jr. speak of racial uplift as part of a tradition that can be traced back to Du Bois and Wells, as does the work of contemporary supporters of Washington such as the conservative economist, Glenn Loury. The uplift ideology is one of the most criticized aspects of black liberal philosophy. Black Marxists, along with many black feminists and nationalists, find it at least moderately paternalistic for the black middle class to appoint itself the bearer of standards for the rest of the race in the name of some Du Boisian "talented tenth" (Gaines 1996; Reed 1997).

Paternalistic or not, black liberals have historically struggled—by emphasizing the need for racial uplift, the potential of the American Creed to

of material prosperity; one hundred years later, the Negro is still lan-
guished [*sic*] in the corners of American society and find [*sic*] himself in
exile in his own land. So we've come here to dramatize a shameful condition. In a sense we've come to our nation's capital to cash a check.
When the architects of our republic wrote the magnificent words of the
Constitution and the Declaration of Independence, they were signing a
promissory note to which every American was to fall heir. This note was
the promise that all men, yes, black men as well as white men, would be
guaranteed the unalienable rights of life, liberty, and the pursuit of happiness. It is obvious today that America has defaulted on this promissory
note in so far as her citizens of color are concerned. Instead of honoring
this sacred obligation, America has given the Negro people a bad check;
a check that has come back marked "insufficient funds." We refuse to
believe that there are insufficient funds in the great vaults of opportunity of this nation. And so we've come to cash this check, a check that
will give us upon demand the riches of freedom and the security of
justice. (King 1986i, 217)

This theme of American redemption through the achievement of bl;
justice is a powerful, recurring jeremiad according to David Howard-Pit
(Howard-Pitney 1990). Ultimately, black liberals of all stripes argue t.
blacks and whites have an identity of interests. But most black liberals
further and argue that since most whites have "false consciousness" a
don't recognize the identity of interests between blacks and whites (bl;
Marxists and some black feminists also often argue that the relevant grou
of whites have false consciousness, often to the glee of black nationalis
state enforcement of a strong set of rights is necessary. While desiring m
tual acceptance, black radical egalitarians would settle for a strong, righ
enforcing, redistributive central state.

Some contemporary political theorists and philosophers such as Ric
ard Rorty and Michael Walzer downplay the need for mutual acceptan
by the citizens of a liberal polity or for a strong central state. All one nee
are procedural rights and laws which guarantee equal treatment within
minimal state, although norms of "politeness" are useful, it is implied, f
transacting business. Rorty make this argument explicitly:

You cannot have an old-timey *Gemeinschaft* unless everybody pretty well
agrees on who counts as a decent human being and who does not. But
you *can* have a civil society of the bourgeois democratic sort. All you

provide a just democratic society, and the need for America to redeem itself through rectifying its long history of antiliberal, antidemocratic practices—to place themselves squarely within the mainstream of American liberal debates. They have not always been successful. Those outside the black community have often turned a deaf ear toward black liberal pleas, and many inside the black community have been suspicious of liberal discourse and practices.

BLACK LIBERALISM, TAKE 2: THE DIFFERENT FLAVOR OF MAINSTREAM BLACK LIBERALISM

As I have demonstrated, many black debates *do not proceed* within liberalism's terms. This is particularly true of the ideologies we considered earlier that view themselves as outside of the traditional liberal camp. But even most black liberal ideologies also vary tremendously from the American Creed. Both radical egalitarianism and disillusioned liberalism differ substantially from the American Creed. American liberalism is centered around individualism. Self-determination is defined for the individual, while blacks and others such as Native Americans tend to define it for the group. The republican (the philosophy, not the party) view of self-determination is closer to the views of most blacks. The advancement of the self, the liberation of the self, is a meaningless concept outside the context of one's community. Elsa Barkley Brown (1989) argues that the black world view is grounded in "autonomy" and "communalism." Both Brown and Saville point to the political practices of black communities during the era of Reconstruction to show the collective nature of black politics: even the most individual of liberal political acts, the casting of a vote, was embedded in community relationships (Brown 1989; Saville 1994b). Black autonomy, Brown argues, is not the moral autonomy of a possessive individual but is grounded in the moral autonomy of free black communities. Historians of black politics starting with their studies of the Reconstruction era and continuing through Redemption, the Great Depression, and the Civil Rights era have repeatedly demonstrated the communal nature of the theory and practice of black politics (Brown 1989; Dawson 1994a; Foner 1984; Holt 1982a; Lewis 1991; Saville 1994a, 1994b). Such a communal orientation is not only at odds with the liberalism advocated by liberals with libertarian leanings, but with the liberalism of liberals such as Holmes, who support a strong welfare state but nevertheless argue that individualism, not communitarianism, provides the best hope of disadvantaged minorities for achieving equality and inclusion (Holmes 1995).

Certain aspects of the communitarian society envisioned by theorists such as Sandel, however, distinctly make African-American liberal theorists nervous. Standards of neutrality and diversity appeal to those who often find themselves in a minority position no matter how attractive the concept of forging a common understanding of the common good may appear in the abstract. Black liberal theorists have historically walked a knife edge by combining some republican concepts of community with Kantian concepts of rights.

Blacks of all ideologies would have problems with some Kantian versions of the liberal self—a self so alienated from community as to achieve full realization only when it is a self of and for itself. Black feminists, nationalists, and Marxists all fundamentally believe in community and reject the view of the "liberal conception of the person as free and independent selves [*sic*], unbounded by prior moral ties, capable of choosing our ends for ourselves" (Sandel 1996, 12). While supporters of liberal ideology may with good reason reject Sandel's characterization, American political discourse has often emphasized such themes. Historically, during periods such as that of the Reconstruction era after the Civil War, there were important political consequences that resulted from the black emphasis on community. How one was buried, whether one could remain a minister of a black church, and the peacefulness of domestic relations all hinged on whether members of the black community were perceived as acting politically in the interests of the common good. This standard of correct community political behavior has in this era been blasted by black conservatives such as Loury even as they bemoan the lack of black political conformity with the *white* mainstream (Loury 1993, 1995). On the other hand, black liberals, feminists, and Marxists have all had *their* blackness questioned by the nationalists. A norm of community still governs black politics even as the norm becomes contested on multiple fronts.

While most black liberals reject the fully autonomous, isolated, liberal individual, they do embrace Kantian notions of basic rights as advanced by modern theorists such as Rawls (Boxill 1992). None, however, except for the black conservatives, has any sympathy for libertarian-oriented versions of liberal "rights." Libertarian views such as those of Nozick and Epstein, who argue that any set of state-guaranteed rights other than the right to make and enforce contracts and be free from coercion is a violation of liberal morality, are utterly rejected by black liberals who not only hold community at the center of their versions of liberalism, but see a strong central state as necessary for enforcing minority rights (Nozick 1974; Epstein 1992).

Finally, nearly all forms of liberalism consistent with the American Creed posit strong liberal separation between the public and private spheres. Arendt, though not a liberal herself, makes this argument, with which many liberals agree. There must be a sharp separation of the two spheres: "A life spent entirely in public, in the presence of others, becomes, as we would say, shallow" (Arendt 1958, 71). The dark side, Arendt argues, remains hidden in the private sphere. But both black and feminist theorists, who belong to groups which at various times in American history have been treated as property—sometimes by law, sometimes by custom—and who have been assigned an inferior status in civil society, have called for the state to scrutinize and regulate many aspects of the private sphere. The dark side of the private sphere has in American history hidden the violent oppression of entire peoples and groups. Agreeing with Arendt, many contemporary political and legal theorists, however, ranging from libertarians like Richard Epstein to more progressive democratic theorists like Michael Walzer and Richard Rorty, wish to maintain and strengthen these barriers.

Democratic theorists such as Rorty and Walzer wish to emphasize that the best way for liberalism to flourish in racially diverse societies would be to embrace a liberalism which they cheerfully and approvingly call cultural nationalist (Walzer) and ethnocentric (Rorty). Their version of bourgeois democratic societies would allow and celebrate ethnic particularism and clubbiness in civil society while minimizing the centrality of the state and citizenship. Indeed, Walzer argues for the state to play an active role in encouraging such particularistic civil associations. They are both explicitly optimistic about the ability of both racial minorities and the liberal state to flourish. We have already heard from Rorty; Walzer's view is similar: "The United States is a political nation of cultural nationalists. Citizenship is separated from every sort of particularism: The state is nationally, ethnically, racially, and religiously neutral. At least, this is true in principle, and whenever neutrality is violated, there is likely to be a principled fight against the violation. The expression of difference is confined to civil society" (Walzer 1992, 9). Walzer explicitly states his optimism about the unproblematic nature of race relations within the United States:

> How are we, in the United States, to embrace difference and maintain a common life? I am less nervous about this question than many contemporary writers and critics. There are more important and harder questions that Americans have to answer, having to do with economic decline, growing inequality, the condition of the underclass. This is a good

time to reassert the twin American values of a singular citizenship and a
radically pluralist civil society. (Walzer 1992, 17)

Black liberals, with the important exception of the black conservatives, have historically been and continue to be skeptical about such claims
(Dawson 1995). Black liberals have generally favored a strong central state.
As David Greenstone has argued, Americans fear a strong central state
(Greenstone 1993). Blacks on the other hand, have found more to fear in
markets and at the subnational levels of government than from the central
state (Dawson 1994a). Further, where Emerson and much of the pragmatic
philosophical tradition that underlies the American Creed would question
whether we bear responsibility for the disadvantaged of society, black liberals have argued that indeed we are obligated toward each other, and the
state is the proper instrument for ensuring minimum guarantees of opportunities to live a productive, autonomous life as part of a supportive community (West 1989). Black liberal theorists for the most part are also radically egalitarian and want the state to have the capacity and responsibility
not only to insure racial fairness, but also to provide economic opportunity
for all of its citizens. Black theorists have agreed with theorists ranging
from Rousseau to modern democratic theorists such as Waldron who have
argued that economic equality, the ability to find useful work, is a necessary
aspect of being a dignified, autonomous citizen (Rousseau 1978; Shklar
1995, 1998; Waldron 1993). Let me be clear, as Holmes, Waldron, Shklar,
and others demonstrate in their analyses of the history of the liberal tradition: There is no necessary contradiction between the liberal tradition in
theory and black liberalism. The contradiction exists between black liberalism and how liberalism has come to be understood in practice within the
American context. The differences between black and American Creed
versions of liberalism stretch across all but one category of black liberalism.
These differences are starkest, however, when one considers what is historically the most supported black ideology—radical egalitarianism.

RADICAL EGALITARIANISM

Without struggle, there is no progress.

—Frederick Douglass

The ideology of radical egalitarianism is sufficiently to the left of the
American mainstream that one might ask the question, Is it still liberalism?
Well into the 1980s, its practitioners have been denounced as communists

by political leaders ranging from Mayor Daley (the first) to Strom Thurmond. It is indeed a form of liberalism, one that would be recognized as such in most Western democracies outside of the United States, although it may have more in common with Swedish social democracy than the American Creed. Adherents believe in procedural justice, and there is a strong theme of individual uplift consistent with Emersonian and Du Boisian pragmatism. The theme of individual uplift can be found in the writings and work of radical egalitarians from Ida B. Wells to Jesse Jackson. Radical egalitarians generally support a highly regulated capitalism, though certainly the working class is not favored over other classes of blacks. Revolution is generally rejected, and socialism is considered to have its good aspects, but to be deeply flawed on democratic grounds. They do believe, however, in political, social, and economic struggle waged morally, through the electoral process, and in the streets.

Activism in Radical Egalitarianism

In 1857, Frederick Douglass described why activism is a core feature of egalitarian ideology:

> The whole history of the progress of human liberty shows that all
> concessions yet made to her august claims have been born of earnest
> struggle. The conflict has been exciting, agitating, all-absorbing, and for
> the time being, putting all other tumults to silence. It must do this or it
> does nothing. If there is no struggle, there is no progress. Those who
> profess to favor freedom and yet deprecate agitation are men who want
> crops without plowing up the ground, they want rain without thunder
> and lightening. They want the ocean without the awful roar of its
> mighty waters. . . . The struggle may be a moral one, or it may be a
> physical one, and it may be both moral and physical, but it must be a
> struggle. Power concedes nothing without a demand. It never did and it
> never will. Find out just what any people will quietly submit to, and you
> will have found out the exact measure of injustice and wrong which will
> be imposed upon them, and these will continue till they are resisted
> with either word, blows, or both. The limits of tyrants are prescribed by
> the endurance of those whom they oppress. (Martin 1990, 277)

Without activism, there can be no progress; without activism to emancipate themselves, blacks don't *deserve* freedom; and activism yields results, where its opposite yields only shame and despair. Indeed, ideologues of this liberal tradition consider progressive activism to be necessary for the society as a whole, not just for blacks, if the country's racial travails are ever to be surmounted. Bunche makes exactly this argument over a century after Douglass's pre–Civil War speech:

> In my view, the United States can pull through this crisis and avert
> domestic disaster only by a huge amount of heavy thinking by a vast
> number of people, by good sense and goodwill in tremendous volume,
> by determination and resources on a war-scale. Indeed, this is a war, a
> domestic war, that must be waged—against racism, against rejection,
> against poverty, against slums, against the betrayal of the rich promise of
> America, inexcusably unfulfilled for black men. (Bunche 1995i, 301)

The idea that we are at war with racism and its consequences is a common theme that radical egalitarians use to justify not only their own militant action, but militant action by the state on behalf of African Americans and their supporters. Activism is important because one needs to prove one's worth as a citizen and that one can emancipate oneself, that one deserves freedom. It is no coincidence that war and its aftermath is often the context for both high levels of black activism and the most impassioned pleas by radical egalitarians for black social, economic, and political justice. These ideologues argue that black actions during war constitute the repeated proof necessary to demonstrate black worthiness for full economic, social, and political equality and participation in American society. Du Bois highlights this theme in the important, if understudied, second chapter of *The Souls of Black Folks*: "But to me neither soldier nor fugitive speaks with so deep a meaning as that dark human cloud that clung like remorse on the rear of those swift columns, swelling at times to half their size, almost engulfing and choking them. In vain they were ordered back" (Du Bois 1969, 59). The *Union government and army* did everything possible to discourage slaves' desire to free themselves. But blacks were determined to be free.

This is a force King was convinced was necessary for African Americans to wield. He argued that "the most powerful force that is breaking down the barriers of segregation is the new determination of the Negro himself" (King 1986j, 101). This is very different than Rorty's view that author Harriet Beecher Stowe, modern news reporters, and anthropologists like Clifford Geertz are the agents most responsible for social change on topics ranging from slavery during Stowe's era to the modern concern about raped Bosnian women or the plight of Native Americans (Rorty

1989, 1991, 1993).[4] For Rorty, the main mechanism for social change is at the elite level, and therefore the key battleground is the hearts and minds of the nation's elite.

King's view is somewhat different: "We know, from my experiences in past, that the nation does not move on questions involving genuine equality for the black man unless something is done to bring pressure to bear on Congress, and to appeal to the conscience and the self-interest of the nation" (King 1986h, 672). For King and for the entire category of radical egalitarianism from the time of Douglass, the decisive social force that sparks social change is the pressure generated from below, from those who would be free.

Protest is necessary to combat the racist practices that Bunche describes and to address the systematic injustice and inequality inflicted on African Americans, even if politicians and theorists working within the official tradition of the American Creed decry the use of civil disobedience, protests and calls for expansion of state capacity:

> There are twenty-two million black Americans whose constitutional rights are being violated flagrantly and persistently. But the black veteran from Vietnam, like all other blacks, is not permitted to do very much about that. He cannot "disturb the peace" and must respect "law and order," although white citizens are not compelled to respect the law of the Constitution where its application to black citizens is concerned. The black veteran, along with all others, may in some places even be denied permission to demonstrate or to march peacefully in protestation against racism and racial injustice. The government requires black citizens to fight for the South Vietnamese but will not even empower the issuance of a cease and desist order to white employers who flagrantly deny employment to black men and women wholly on grounds of race. That, in the eyes of the senator from Abraham Lincoln's state, Everett Dirksen, would be intolerable "harassment" of business. (Bunche 1995j, 312)

Radical egalitarian ideologues and their legions of followers have historically been convinced that protest and agitation are effective tactics for

---

4. Public opinion specialists have also emphasized the leading role of elites in bring about major changes in racial policy. One version of this can be found in Carmines and Stimson's (1989) work on issue evolution. Lee (1997) shows, however, consistent with the research of Civil Rights movement historians, that public opinion shifted as a result of the mass movement and not in response to changes among party elites.

winning black justice. Wells documents that the agitation in which she and numerous others were involved was instrumental in leading to the decline of lynching beginning in 1893, as both national and international protest began to affect the practice in America. The process Wells describes was not dissimilar to the dialectical interaction between domestic protest and international pressure that led to black majority triumph in South Africa a century later. When an Illinois community organized several years later with her leadership over the objections of those whom she labeled "ubiquitous Uncle Toms," the result, despite great danger and initial resistance, was the end of lynching in Illinois in 1909 (Wells 1970). The *Chicago Defender* lamented while praising her efforts, "If we only had a few men with the backbone of Mrs. Barnett," lynching would soon be ended (Wells 1970, 320).

In every era the "American Creed" is invoked to oppose either protest movements for racial justice, the enforcement of antidiscrimination legislation, or the quest for political, economic, and social equality (see Bunche1995j for Senator Dirksen's views; Storing 1995; Epstein 1992). But grassroots blacks have generally agreed with egalitarian ideologues that protest was a worthy and principled tool for gaining justice. In Chicago in the early 1920s, blacks urged the following action to stop the (still existing, if now illegal) practice of restrictive covenants which help maintain segregated residential neighborhoods:

> The colored people residing on the South Side should assemble together in a great convention and select two hundred men and women to form a delegation and let it march or call on L. M. Smith, President of the Chicago Real Estate Board, and the other high officials of the Grand Boulevard District Property Owners Association, and plainly inform them, that unless they refrain from attempting to boycott or black list them that they will endeavor to land them behind the prison bars at Joliet, Illinois, for conspiracy. (Vincent 1973, 55)

Similarly, Civil Rights movement activist Charles Sims explained why he became a movement activist:

> I went to World [War] II. I helped train a thousand men to kill . . . and I didn't know what the hell I was teaching 'em for. Went in behind the Civil Rights Act, I know what the hell I was fightin'; I was fightin' for equal rights that Roosevelt promised us before he died. Didn't do a

damn thing about it. Truman he promised . . . He didn't do a damn
thing. (Lipsitz 1988, 95)

Du Bois summarized the principle of activism, a principle well entrenched among generations of African Americans, a principle only questioned by black conservative ideologues, when he declared, "Whenever I
meet personal discrimination on account of my race and color, I shall
protest. . . . I shall deem it my duty to make may grievances known, to bring
it before the organs of public opinion" (Boxill 1992, 187). Why take such
and uncompromising stance, one that comes at so great a cost? Du Bois
again represents the sentiments of the radical egalitarians when he prays,
"May God forgive me if . . . I ever weakly admit to myself or the world that
wrong is not wrong, that insult is not insult, or that color discrimination is
anything but an inhuman and damnable shame" (Boxill 1992, 189).

Radical Egalitarianism as State-Centered

A great difference between black radical egalitarianism and the American Creed is the great emphasis that these black theorists, almost always with high levels of mass support, place on a strong central state.
These theorists demand with great regularity that the national government
intervene in subnational governments, regulate markets, enact national
economic policies that are highly redistributive, and regulate behavior in
civil society more generally. Blacks well into the 1990s remain the nation's
only strong supporters of a centralized, powerful state (Dawson 1994a,
1997). Thus black historians and their allies tend to analyze the failure of
the post–Civil War southern Reconstruction as a failure of the national
government to do enough on behalf of the former slaves, and not, as mainstream historians have analyzed this set of events, as a case of failed federal
intrusion into state prerogatives. Du Bois, in his role as historian, argues
as early as 1903 that it was not that the national government and the Freedman's Bureau, a state within a state, did too much but that they did too
little:

> The Freedmen's Bureau, . . . summed up in brief, may be epitomized
> thus: for some fifteen million dollars, beside the sums spent before 1865,
> and the dole of the benevolent societies, this Bureau set going a system of
> free labor, established a beginning of peasant proprietorship, secured the
> recognition of black freedmen before courts of law, and founded the free
> common school in the South. On the other hand, it failed to begin the

establishment of goodwill between ex-masters and freedmen, to guard
its work wholly from paternalistic methods which discouraged self-
reliance, and to carry out to any considerable extent its implied promises to furnish the freedmen with land. Its successes were the result of
hard work, supplemented by the aid of philanthropists and the eager
striving of black men. Its failures were the result of bad local agents,
the inherent difficulties of the work, and national neglect. (Du Bois
1969, 74)

More than fifty years later, Du Bois the activist demanded federal action
to stop white terrorism aimed at blacks and, like thousands of blacks before
him, decried the great injustice caused by federal officials' "justification"
for inaction—the refuge of states "rights." In a case where a mother of
fourteen children and her two eldest sons were sentenced to death after she
was beaten nearly senseless by an armed white farmer, Du Bois and several
other black leaders from across the ideological spectrum pleaded the case
to the newly formed United Nations in 1949:

A boy of sixteen struck an armed white man who was attacking his
mother. The mother and two teen-age sons were tried by a jury of
hostile whites, with no representative of their race. Their meager property was seized, and the children are today subsisting on charity. The
federal government has made no move; the governor of Georgia has
done nothing. The President of the United States, when approached by
a delegation from eight states, would not talk to them and through
his secretary said he had never heard of the case. The Chief of the
Civil Rights Division of the United States Department of Justice, A. A.
Rosen, said, "This sort of thing is in the papers every week. It's shocking to me personally, but it is a matter to be settled internally by
the State." He pleaded lack of jurisdiction and no available funds.
(Du Bois 1985b, 262)

It was precisely this type of outrage and state inaction that led to the generation of the militant mass movements that raged across America from the
mid-1950s through much of the 1970s (although the latter period's black
activism went unreported and therefore is unknown both to whites of all
generations and younger African Americans). It was also this combination
of outrage and inaction that led black leaders such as Ida B. Wells, Du Bois,
Malcolm X, and Martin Luther King Jr. to attempt to internationalize
the plight of African Americans, always with the unfailing hostility of the

American state. Such internationalization led the State Department to file a "friend of the court" brief on behalf of the black plaintiffs in *Brown vs. the Board of Education of Topeka, Kansas.* The State Department argued that the United States was losing face in the international arena because the world saw it as a great hypocrisy that the so-called champion of democracy was allowing the constant brutalization of a substantial part of its population (Van Woodward 1966).

With the passage of another quarter-century, black demands for state action had shifted to include demands that the state act to insure black inclusion in politics, the economy, and civil society. In 1962, King argued that a just America necessitated "an expanded federal government program of vigorous law enforcement" and a greatly expanded regulatory function for all cabinet departments on matters of race and economics (King 1986k, 110). In a 1961 article entitled "Equality Now: The President Has the Power," King argued that the president as national leader had the utmost responsibility to mobilize the state on behalf of blacks (King 1986c, 153). When discussing the "American Dream" in the same year, he bluntly stated what many blacks "know" and even more whites deny is that state legislation is needed to regulate behavior:

> Now, people will say, "You can't legislate morals." Well, that may be true. Even though morality may not be legislated, behavior can be regulated. And this is very important. We need religion and education to change attitudes and to change the hearts of men. We need legislation and federal action to control behavior. It may be true that the law can't make a man love me, but it can keep him from lynching me, and I think that's pretty important too. (King 1986d, 213)

And King and black radical egalitarians across the decades also think it's pretty important for the state to regulate interstate commerce, employment practices, and other arenas in civil society and the private sphere in which blacks perceive that they face systematic discrimination. King isn't joking when he states, "The law cannot make an employer love me, but it can keep him from refusing to hire me because of the color of my skin" (King 1986l, 473). The idea advanced by Epstein and others that some racial discrimination is rational and moral would be anathema to black liberals as well as some black conservatives. Radical egalitarians (and their disillusioned cousins) do not hesitate to demand that the state step in and enforce racial equality and racial justice. And these concerns also flow from these ideologues' extreme skepticism about the perfectibility of or the justice derived from "free" markets. Most African Americans, regardless of ideology, take seriously the talk of U.S. senators such as the late Everett Dirksen, esteemed professors of law such as Richard Epstein, and several philosophers and economists whose construction of rights makes it rational and moral to discriminate against blacks. When combined with public opinion evidence that the majority of whites still consider blacks to be their inferiors in many ways, it is understandable why a strong central state becomes a priority for black egalitarians despite (or maybe because of) the long American tradition of hostility toward an effective central government. Blacks have not forgotten that once they were property and that in the current era even affluent blacks lack the wealth of lower middle-class whites (Oliver and Shapiro 1995).

Black focus on a strong state derives not only from justifiable fear of subnational governments and white citizen hostility, but also from a positive outlook which demands that we take collective responsibility for our fellow citizens. This view is captured in the discussion of welfare reform by a black women worker in the 1970s:

> I guess I just wouldn't make it possible for people to live in a way that was too degrading for me. But I know that might mean that some people who are living better than they should would have to have a little less. I wouldn't just give people any old thing and say that I was helping them. These tarts are made with frozen blackberries. Well, if I didn't think that they were a lot better than no tarts, I wouldn't have given you any. Now, we all know that they would be better if they were made with the fresh berries. Well, that's what I mean. Maybe some people might have to give up the fresh blackberries so that we could all have the next best thing together. But it's not right that some of us should have fresh blackberries whenever we want and the rest have imitation blackberries that are not fit for people to eat. (Janet McCrae, quoted in Gwaltney 1980, 125)

McCrae's sentiments on redistribution would necessitate more direct intervention in the economy than even "liberal republicans" like Cass Sunstein (1988) or welfare-state liberals (Holmes 1995) would countenance. This communitarian view of our mutual obligations complements black radical egalitarians' view of the necessity for full equality, an equality which it will take state action to achieve.

Equality and Radical Egalitarianism

From Douglass to King, black liberals have demanded real equality. Public opinion work by Rokeach in the 1960s and 1970s, for example, showed that of all American "values," blacks ranked equality at the top and liberty toward the bottom, while whites did the opposite (Rokeach 1976, 1979). Blacks' views that whites are hypocritical on questions of equality is a constant theme in black political thought. As King argued in 1967,

> There is not even a common language when the term "equality" is used. Negro and white have a fundamentally different definition. Negroes have proceeded from a premise that equality means what it says, and have taken white Americans at their word when they talked of it as an objective. But most whites in America in 1967, including many persons of goodwill, proceed from a premise that equality is a loose expression for improvement. White America is not even psychologically organized to close the gap—essentially it seeks only to make it less painful and less obvious but in most respects to retain it. Most of the abrasions between Negroes and white liberals arise from this fact. (King 1986f, 560)

Other radical egalitarians agree with King that equality is the only answer. Equality is mandated by and a hallmark of democracy. America, once again, cannot fulfill its democratic promise until blacks gain full equality. Bunche declared in 1951, "Full equality is the answer. There is no other. In a democracy there can be no substitute for equality. The Negro can never be content with less. I am sure you agree with me that we shall carry on this fight until we achieve full equality; until, Americans, we are all free and equal" (Bunche 1995g, 248). Bunche continues that the quest for equality is one which brooks no compromise:

> Equality is all the Negro citizen demands, and I am positive that the Negro will never give up this struggle until he achieves it. I am equally positive that he can and will achieve it, the hysterical antics of the racial bigots and demagogues notwithstanding. I am categorical about this because I have a deep faith in democracy. The force of democracy is inexorable, and democracy is on the march in American society. It is the driving force of our society, and if it should ever be lost, it will be not only the Negro citizen who will suffer the loss of his freedom and individual liberty. (Bunche 1995g, 246)

The demand for equality is extremely reasonable, one any fair citizen should not only accept but embrace and encourage.

Du Bois in the 1940s also argued for a program of full equality for blacks that included both social and economic components. There was a need for

> a movement to increase the income of Negroes by giving them opportunity to work according to ability and to receive higher wages for their work. Labor unionization, trade apprenticeship, together with consumer organization will help here. But the decisive aid will come as Negroes are integrated in a new organization of industry which, discarding the assumption that unrestrained private initiative and private profit always make for the public welfare, demands that the public welfare be the first object of industry and that individual income neither rise above nor fall below the interests of the public good. (Du Bois 1985a, 219)

For radical egalitarians, full equality meant that one was both equal before the law and also participated fully in civil society. Equality of opportunity should be reflected in equality in outcomes. How does one achieve full equality in a liberal democracy? The answer is tied to why radical egalitarians favor a strong state. The programmatic agenda black egalitarians deem necessary to achieve equality, while still consistent, at least in their view, with liberal democracy, necessitates a political and economic program that can only be considered radical by the standards of the theory and practice of the American Creed.

A Radical Agenda?

The agendas designed by Du Bois in the 1940s and King in the late 1960s to ensure full equality for blacks despite their reformist rhetoric were sufficiently radical to necessitate a revolutionary restructuring of the American state, its relation to civil society, and (white) American values. In the same passage, for example, in which Du Bois calls for profit to be limited, he also calls for "social medicine and public hospitalization, on a national scale with security against age, sickness, and unemployment" (Du Bois 1985a, 225). "Liberals" in the 1990s could not even manage a state guarantee of full hospitalization, let alone a guarantee of employment.

Radical egalitarians have been aware of the radical nature of their programmatic agendas. King at the end of his life called for revolution, but a nonviolent revolution: "The dispossessed of this nation—the poor, both white and Negro—live in a cruelly unjust society. They must organize a revolution against that injustice, not against the lives of the persons who are their fellow citizens, but against the structures through which the society is refusing to take means which have been called for, and which are at hand, to lift the load of poverty" (King 1986f, 650).

While the non-nationalist black movements of the 1960s had their doctrinaire left wing as well as a more social democratic, radical egalitarian element, even the beliefs of the latter were viciously attacked by adherents of the tenets of mainstream (i.e., "white") American liberalism. Lee reports that "Truman alleged that communists were 'engineering the student sit-downs at lunch counters in the South.' When asked to provide details to back up such allegations, Truman demurred with the reply, 'I know that usually when trouble hits the country, the Kremlin is behind it.'" (Lee 1997a, 22). Lee also shows that in letters to the president from southern whites two critical themes were states' rights and the communist nature of the movement. Leaders such as Mayor Daley of Chicago during the 1960s as well as grassroots whites attacked the Civil Rights movement as being both anti-American and communist-inspired.

As the following passage from King's last presidential speech to the SCLC demonstrates, relatively moderate black leaders, even in the face of such hostility, have tended to place demands on the state and limits on property that stretched the boundaries of liberalism:

> We [must] honestly face the fact that the movement must address itself to the question of restructuring the whole of American society. There are forty million poor people here. And one day we must ask the question, 'Why are there forty million poor people in America?' And when you begin to ask that question, you are raising questions about the economic system, about a broader distribution of wealth. When you ask that question, you begin to question the capitalistic economy. And I'm simply saying that more and more, we've got to begin to ask questions about the whole society. We are called upon to help the discouraged beggars in life's marketplace. But one day we must come to see that an edifice which produces beggars needs restructuring. . . . What I'm saying to you this morning is that communism forgets that life is individual. Capitalism forgets that life is social, and the kingdom of brotherhood is found neither in the thesis of communism nor the antithesis of capitalism but in a higher synthesis. It is found in a higher synthesis that combines the truths of both. Now, when I say question the whole society, it means ultimately coming to see that the problem of racism, the problem

of economic exploitation, and the problem of war are all tied together. These are the triple evils that are interrelated. (King 1986f, 250)

Such a radical program is necessary to build a polity which could support "a program that will drive the nation to a guaranteed annual income." Such a guarantee was necessary because "we've come a long way in our understanding of human motivation, of the blind operation of our economic system. Now we realize that dislocations in the market operations of our economy and prevalence of discrimination thrust people into idleness and bind them in constant or frequent unemployment against their will" (King 1986f, 247).

Jesse Jackson continued the tradition of radical egalitarian questioning of the privileges of wealth and power in his 1988 presidential campaign. In an issue brief entitled "A Corporate Code of Conduct," Jackson demands that corporations be accountable "not just to their shareholders, but to all their 'stakeholders'—their workers, their communities, and their nation" (Jackson 1989, 107). Jackson continues that he would require corporations to give long notice before closing plants, require extensive monitoring and negotiations between corporate officials and local communities over a variety of issues, and require higher wages both internationally and domestically. Many other requirements appeared in Jackson's position paper, but the main point is that the Jackson campaign represented a concrete implementation of the radical economic restructuring within the framework of capitalism that radical egalitarians have been urging for the entire twentieth century, which enjoys enormous popular black support.

Black liberal egalitarians are not, however, Marxists. While (at their best) they are passionately committed to eliminating poverty and building a movement to end systemic disadvantage of all types, there is tendency that can be found explicitly both in Du Bois and Wells toward a leading role not for the proletariat but for the black middle class, the "talented tenth." Modern theorists who see themselves as the inheritors of this tradition emphasize what they see as the need for continued elite leadership of the African-American community:

This new Talented Tenth, then, while remaining an elite, a vanguard, is acutely aware of its social and ethical obligations to the larger group, its members keenly aware that their privileged positions stem not from their own inherent nobility of mind and spirit but from "opportunity." There but for the grace of God, Du Bois maintains, pointing to the plight of the black lower classes, goes even the Talented Tenth. (Gates 1996, 132)

As Gates and West declare in their preface, "Dr. King did not die so that *half* of us would 'make it,' and *half* of us perish, forever tarnishing two centuries of struggle and agitation for our equal rights. We, the members of Du Bois's Talented Tenth, must accept our historical responsibility and live under King's credo that none of us is free until each of us is free" (Gates and West 1996, xvii). Their sentiment is very much in the tradition of egalitarians such as Bunche, who declared in 1951, "In my view, no Negro, however high he may think he has risen, no matter how much wealth he has amassed, is worth very much if he forgets his own people and holds himself aloof from the unrelenting struggle for full Negro emancipation" (Bunche 1995g, 245).

But King, Du Bois, and others have repeatedly worried about the possibility that the black middle class would forget less affluent black classes as it made economic and political progress. He explicitly stated this concern in 1967:

> But many middle-class Negroes have forgotten their roots and are more concerned about 'conspicuous consumption' than about the cause of justice. Instead, they seek to sit in some serene and passionless realm of isolation, untouched and unmoved by the agonies and struggles of their underprivileged brothers. This kind of selfish detachment has caused the masses of Negroes to feel alienated not only from white society but also from the Negro middle class. They feel that the average middle-class Negro has no concern for their plight. The feeling is often corroborated by the hard facts of experience. How many Negroes who have achieved educational and economic security have forgotten that they are where they are because of the support of faceless, unlettered and unheralded Negroes who did ordinary jobs in an extraordinary way. (King 1967, 131–32)

More worrisome, however, for most radical egalitarians, including King, than the short memories of the black middle class is the perceived intransigence of white Americans. As Du Bois did before him, King begins to consider temporary segregation as a tactical option at the end of his life: "What is necessary now is to see integration in political terms where there is sharing of power. When we see integration in political terms, then we must recognize that there are times when we must see segregation as a temporary way-station to a truly integrated society. . . . There are points at which I see the necessity for temporary segregation in order to get to the integrated society" (King 1986h, 666). As this perception grows, radical egalitarians not only consider the possibility that temporary segregation is a necessary tactic which must be incorporated within black planning, but they become more concerned with the attainment of black political and economic power. King argues for black power, even if he still refused to call it by that name, during the month that immediately preceded his assassination:

> In every city, we have a dual society. This dualism runs in the economic
> market. In every city, we have two economies. In every city, we have
> two housing markets. In every city, we have two school systems. This
> duality has brought about a great deal of injustice, and I don't need to go
> into all that because we are all familiar with it. In every city, to deal with
> this unjust dualism, we must constantly work toward the goal of a truly
> integrated society while at the same time we enrich the ghetto. We must
> seek to enrich the ghetto immediately in the sense of improving the
> conditions, improving the schools in the ghetto, improving the economic
> conditions. At the same time, we must be working to open the housing
> market so there will be one housing market only. We must work on two
> levels. (King 1986h, 667)

These observations are not meant to deny that indeed there is a strong liberal theme within radical egalitarian thought. The last writings by King, at the height of his radicalism, still contain strong liberal elements. American liberalism, however is usually defined in such a way as to privilege the autonomy and liberty of the individual and the sanctity of private property while maintaining a deep skepticism of central state power (Greenstone 1993; Oakes 1992; Waldron 1993). In summary, however, any sustained examination of this most influential of black ideologies demonstrates how strongly black political thought challenges the boundaries and the core tenets of the American Creed.

Black Autonomy and Radical Egalitarianism

An internal criticism of radical egalitarianism, usually issued from the nationalist camp, is that radical egalitarians are shameless assimilationists who lack sufficient black pride to invest in building the institutions and culture of the black community. Certainly some from this camp prefer a goal where race becomes an unimportant marker in American society. But even Douglass thought that no one had the right to force blacks to assimilate; it should be a matter of choice not coercion. He also strongly argued that black organizations were absolutely necessary to achieve black progress. He somewhat apologetically explained this position: "Although it may seem to conflict with our views of human brotherhood, we shall undoubtedly for many years be compelled to have institutions of a complexional character, in order to obtain the very idea of human brotherhood" (Boxill 1992, 174). Ida B. Wells believed that it was mandatory that blacks provide the institutions necessary for self-development, particularly if they were not available to blacks in the general society. She had little patience for some middle-class blacks who did not want to build these institutions for fear that they and their families could not one day join "integrated" institutions: "To say that I was surprised does not begin to express my feeling. Here were people so afraid of the color line that they did not want to do anything to help supply the needs of their own people. The reason was that it would be better to let our children be neglected and do without the kindergarten service than to supply the needs of our own" (Wells 1970, 249–50).

Often increased attention to questions of autonomy was motivated by the beginning of a despair generated by growing suspicions that the promise of liberal, democratic America would not and possibly could not be met. Blacks of all ideologies have concluded during almost all historical periods (including the current one) that King's check would remain unredeemed. Racial equality, however, remains a central concept within black political thought. What happens when and if black liberals no longer believe it to be achievable? Where do they find an ideological home?

FROM HOPE TO DESPAIR: DISILLUSIONED LIBERALISM AND THE GREAT BETRAYAL

Now, after a long-enduring faith and patience, without parallel, I think, in human history, the black citizen has lost his patience—and his fear-and is, I am afraid, also losing his faith in the American establishment and system insofar as their promises to him are concerned. He is demanding, not appealing, nowadays, and his demands begin to take unexpected courses—courses which could only be born out of profound frustration and complete disillusionment.

—Ralph J. Bunche

It's—it's fr—it's really frustrating. It's—I'm sure I'll go to my grave— god, and I hate to sound pessimistic—but I'll go to my grave not having

seen a real improvement in race relations. Jeez, and that's—boy, that's
scary. I even hate to say that.
> —From a 1997 Tom Brokaw interview on NBC's *Dateline* with
> Mr. Murphy, whose white neighbor refused to talk with him

We may wonder what happens when you come to the position that
Bunche reached in 1969 and King reached in 1968 when he stated, "Let me
say that we have failed to say something to America enough. I'm very
happy that the Kerner Commission had the courage to say it. However
difficult it is to hear, we've got to face the fact that racism still occupies the
throne of our nation. I don't think we will ultimately solve the problem of
racial injustice until this is recognized, and until this is worked on" (King
1986h, 676).

W. E. B. Du Bois and Martin Luther King Jr. both moved from relatively optimistic analyses of America's bitter racial conflicts to evaluations
that were more tempered by despair than hope. Their optimism was much
more critical than that of most theorists from outside of the tradition of
black political thought, and their critiques of America during their period
of despair were brutal.

The work of Du Bois and King exemplifies a long tradition of African-
American political thought which has critically analyzed the fundamental
nature of American society, state, and citizenship. This tradition has been
largely ignored, or occasionally ghettoized, because much of the study of the
history of American political thought has often treated phenomena such as
slavery, the Civil War, and race riots (both black and the even bloodier
white ones) as either non-events or anomalies in a history remarkably
shaped by consensus. This tradition is also ignored because its major practitioners, such as Du Bois and King, have more often than not been activists as well as intellectuals. This narrowness of vision about "where"
democratic theory is created robs us of the insights to be gained from studying the work of those who thought deeply about many of the fundamental
flaws of American democracy and responded, as King did in his "Letter
from a Birmingham Jail," to those who attacked black radical egalitarianism for being undemocratic, un-American, and destructively radical. It
leaves us with unsatisfying and even hypocritical homilies of those such as
Herbert Storing, who argued that, even with America's history of racial oppression, American democracy was basically sound and good.

During significant parts of their careers, both Du Bois and King believed that it was possible to transform America into a sound and good

democracy. However, their work exhibits deep and profound shifts in their analyses of the state of American race relations, their emotional moods, and their evaluations of American democracy. Many have argued that these shifts reflect either a disturbing departure from the sound philosophies they had advocated earlier in their careers or at least a lack of rigor in their thinking. The shift in King's and Du Bois's thinking is actually relatively common in black political thought and activism, and can be dramatically demonstrated in the work of Du Bois. These shifts have caused some problems for commentators who wish to impose a unified analytical framework on these authors' work. For example, the multiple and totally contrary interpretations of Du Bois's work are striking.[5] The great majority of these analysts correctly view his work as central to understanding the development of black political discourse within the United States. A perceptive few also realize that Du Bois's work is central to understanding the development of American political thought in the twentieth century (Reed 1997).[6] What is striking is how little agreement there is on how to categorize his political thought.

A more useful interpretation of the same materials, one that is hardly original with me, is that Du Bois moved from hope to despair. This view struck me as particularly useful because it highlights a pattern of development that also appears in King's thought. Many activists from the civil rights movement made this journey as they became increasingly disillusioned with American society and skeptical about the prospect of winning racial justice in their lifetimes. What shifts, I argue, as African-American activists, intellectuals, and citizens move from hope to despair are the evaluation of white willingness to "accept" black equality, the evaluation of the nature of American society, and the assessment of prospects for gaining full democratic citizenship.

It is a bitter shift for Du Bois, Bunche, King, the activists of the Student Nonviolent Coordinating Committee (SNCC, who, as a result of their disillusionment, substituted "National" for "Nonviolent"), and thousands of black activists across the years who had been deeply committed to

5. Wilson Moses is one scholar who castigates Du Bois for monumental inconsistencies in his scholarship (Holt 1990).

6. Reed, with some cautions, follows Skinner (1988) in his critique of Du Bois's analysts. He argues that black political thought both generally and specifically has to be understood in the context of American political discourse, and that Du Bois in particular must be placed within the discourse community of the turn-of-the-century pragmatist philosophers (Reed 1992). West (1989) also places Du Bois squarely within the pragmatist tradition. Others place Du Bois within various black-centered discourse communities; see Stuckey (1987) for one example.

achieving the full promise of American democracy. The bitterness of King, Du Bois, and the SNCC activists is palpable. Du Bois argued,

> I had been brought up with the democratic idea that this general welfare was the object of democratic action in the state, of allowing the governed a voice in government. But through the crimson illumination of war, I realized and, afterward, by travel around the world, saw even more clearly that so-called democracy today was allowing the mass of people to have only limited voice in government; that democratic control of what are at present the most important functions of men: work and earning a living and distributing goods and services; that here we did not have democracy; we had oligarchy, and oligarchy based on monopoly and income; and this oligarchy was determined to deny democracy in industry as it had once been determined to deny democracy in legislation and choice of officials. (Du Bois 1986, 762)

Du Bois sadly concludes that the optimism of his early years was unsupported by the facts, a result of his youthful inexperience:

> First and natural to the emergence of colder and more mature manhood from hot youth, I saw that the color bar could not be broken by a series of brilliant, immediate assaults. Secondly, I saw defending this bar not simply ignorance and ill will; these to be sure; but also certain more powerful motives less open to reason or appeal. There were economic motives, urges to build wealth on the backs of black slaves and colored serfs; there followed those unconscious acts and irrational reactions, unpierced by reason, whose current form depended on the long history of reason, whose current form depended on the long history of relation and contact between thought and idea. (Du Bois 1986, 557)

A brutal lynching had convinced Du Bois that he was wrong when he had believed "it was axiomatic that the world wanted to learn the truth, and if the truth was sought with even approximate accuracy and painstaking devotion, the world would gladly support the effort. This was, of course, but a young man's idealism, not by any means false, but also never universally true" (Du Bois 1986, 602–3).

King reached a similar disillusionment about American society. By 1967 he was also arguing that white Americans never wanted true racial equality:

These are the deepest causes for contemporary abrasions between the races. Loose and easy language about equality, resonant resolutions about brotherhood fall pleasantly on the ear, but for the Negro there is a credibility gap he cannot overlook. He remembers that with each modest advance the white population promptly raises the argument that the Negro has come far enough. Each step forward accents an ever-present tendency to backlash. This characterization is necessarily general. It would be grossly unfair to omit recognition of a minority of whites who genuinely want authentic equality. Their commitment is real, sincere, and is expressed in a thousand deeds. But they are balanced at the other end of the pole by the unregenerate segregationists who have declared that democracy is not worth having if it involves equality. . . . The great majority of Americans are suspended between these opposing attitudes. They are uneasy with injustice but unwilling yet to pay a significant price to eradicate it. The persistence of racism in depth and the dawning awareness that Negro demands will necessitate structural changes in society have generated a new phase of white resistance in North and South. Based on the cruel judgment that Negroes have come far enough, there is a strong mood to bring the civil rights movement to a halt or reduce it to a crawl. Negro demands that yesterday evoked admiration and support, today—to many—have become tiresome, unwarranted, and a disturbance to the enjoyment of life. Cries of Black Power and riots are not the causes of white resistance, they are the consequences of it. (King 1967, 11–12)

King believed that black political and economic power were necessary to achieve true equality. He argues that when blacks demand equality, they mean what they say: just outcomes are equal outcomes. And King was quite willing to stretch public policy beyond the mainstream white norms to achieve this equality. His disillusionment had led him to modify the view he held in 1958 that the state should enforce antidiscrimination laws to ensure that equal outcomes in employment were achieved. King supported equality of outcomes, and by implication, affirmative action and quotas: "The decision on the number of jobs requested is usually based on population figures. For instance, if a city has a 30 percent Negro population, then it is logical to assume that Negroes should have at least 30 percent of the jobs in any particular company, and jobs in all categories rather than only in menial areas, as the case almost always happens to be" (King 1967, 144). King's and Du Bois's disillusionment pushed them both to the left, and eventually, if slowly for Du Bois, completely outside of the camp of black liberals. However, King's disillusionment comes from a somewhat different source than Du Bois's. It is the insufficiency of moral suasion as a force that dismays King in the few years before his death. Neither the Kantian rationalism of Du Bois or King's Rorty-like emphasis on sentimental education had been able to overcome centuries of whites viewing blacks stereotypically as the inferior other.

One might believe that the tactical problem that faced Du Bois was more embittering than that which faced King during the last two years of his life. When Du Bois wrote *Dusk of Dawn*, the United States was still in the midst of a depression, fascism was dragging the world into yet another bloody cataclysm, and the Roosevelt administration, while taking some grudging steps toward economically aiding blacks as part of its poverty programs, was still refusing to implement any serious program for racial justice. Despite the slow progress the NAACP was making in the courts, and the promise a year after the publication of *Dusk of Dawn* of the effectiveness of the threat of mass action demonstrated by A. Philip Randolph's moderate victory in winning the creation of the Fair Employment Practices Commission (FEPC), Du Bois's bitterness would lead him to turn increasingly to communism and Africa in the remaining decades of his life.

However, King's bitterness was of a different order, and perhaps in some ways his bitterness is more frightening than Du Bois's. King saw all too clearly the developing racial polarization in American society. King became most embittered after he saw the victories that the Civil Rights movement achieved, in the midst of the longest ongoing economic expansion at the time in American history and after the nation, or at least its leading public officials at the time, had made a public commitment to full *political* equality for African Americans. He lived long enough to see capable rightists such as Ronald Reagan and former racial "moderates" such as Richard Nixon (re)-build political careers by capitalizing on white racial resentment. He lived long enough to see that *economic* justice was not considered part of the package of American citizenship rights, even during periods of unprecedented prosperity. He lived long enough to see that public opinion surveys which showed increasing racial tolerance on the part of whites were mere gloss on a more despairing reality in which northerners proved every bit as violent as southern segregationists in fighting to maintain the racial "purity" of their neighborhoods. He lived long enough to prophesize that the increasingly large chasm between the races would not only continue to grow but act as a cancer tearing at the moral, social, and political fabric of the nation.

In retrospect, we should not be surprised that the intellectual prowess of Du Bois, the moral fervor of King, and the power of the black movements of the 1960s proved insufficient to overcome the stereotypes which undermine black inclusion in both the polity and civil society. Public opinion studies continue to show at the end of the twentieth century that centuries-old racist stereotypes of blacks remain well embedded among white Americans (Bobo and Kluegel 1997; Dawson 1997; Gilliam and Iyengar 2000). The responses to disillusionment include for King, Du Bois, the SNCC activists, and many blacks today self-segregation and an increased perception of the need to acquire black political power. As we saw, by 1968 King was talking about the need to build political and economic power within the ghetto. The acquisition of power was necessitated by the dawning realization that "segregation is a temporary way-station" on the road to true integration. Given the unsettled state of disillusioned liberalism, it is not surprising to see shifts from the liberal camp to nationalism, Marxism, feminism, and occasionally conservatism. Even more common is complete withdrawal from activism.

Radicalization was the most common response among those who remained active, with the majority of disillusioned liberals moving toward Marxism, nationalism, or some combination of both. Reasonably typical in trajectory if not visibility is the career of Amiri Baraka. In the early 1960s, as a winner of the Pulitzer Prize for poetry and a playwright, he described himself as a "bohemian liberal" (Baraka 1991a, 19). By 1967 he was a committed nationalist, and by the mid-1970s, a committed Leninist. This was a route traveled at least in part by thousands of black activists across the country. Clay Carson reports on how Coretta Scott King described King's disillusionment at the end of his life. While still deeply critical of communism (at least as critical of communism as he was of capitalism), he was becoming clearly more radical:

> Coretta Scott King has insisted that "Martin firmly agreed with certain aspects of the program that Malcolm X advocated," particularly the need for racial pride and black access to power. She surmised that "at some point the two would have come closer together and would have been a very strong force in the total struggle for liberation and self-determination of black people in our society." (Carson 1991, 47–48)

The disillusionment that produced an ambivalence about America in King and had him moving toward political positions that Malcolm X had reached at the end of *his* life persists in the deep disillusionment among grassroots African Americans. Blacks continue to believe that they live in a country that is fundamentally racially unjust. No matter how the question is worded, 75–85 percent of black adults support this view. For example, 83 percent of blacks say that the legal system is not fair to blacks, 82 percent say that about American society in general, and 74 percent say the same about American corporations. An overwhelming 86 percent say that the American economic system is unfair to poor people. Sixty-five percent of blacks believe that racial equality will either not be achieved during their lifetime or at all in America. Bunche, in the prelude to the quotation that opened this section, predicted that current levels of black distrust would be reached if racial tensions continued to increase:

> The estrangement between white and black Americans intensifies and becomes increasingly disruptive and dangerous. It could reach catastrophic proportions. The core of the problem is the glaring disparity between the theory and practice of American democracy. The attitudes and actions of white Americans do not, and many begin to feel cannot, correspond to the ideals and promises of the American Constitution and system. This is not merely because some Americans are hard-bitten racists who oppose bitterly and openly the very idea of integration and equality in rights and opportunities for the black American. The harsh fact is that most white Americans, many without realizing it, harbor in themselves, as an inheritance from the society's history and mores, some degree of racism or bigotry. (Bunche 1995j, 312)

Now there is little sign of a vibrant mass movement, and clearly there are high levels of disillusionment in the black community about race relations in America. As always, particularly with the collapse of the left and the isolation of the feminists, the nationalists are waiting in the wings. As the Million Man March graphically demonstrated, and public opinion data show, the level of disillusionment in the black community provides an opening for nationalist forces such as the Nation of Islam. And as is common in periods marked by high levels of racial despair, disillusioned liberals face the current situation with deep ambivalence. Even less likely to turn to Marxism than in the past, and with many remaining skeptical of feminism (as the debates around Clarence Thomas's nomination and the Million Man March highlight), where do they turn? The nationalists have one answer. The black conservatives, who are as unencumbered by ambivalence as the nationalists, have another.

THE STRANGE CAREER OF BLACK CONSERVATISM

Blacks are disadvantaged because of government intervention.
—Walter Williams

Black conservatism presents both its adherents and its opponents with a number of intriguing and critical paradoxes. Black conservatives are the most visible black ideologues in mainstream (white) American media and cultural outlets, but they have remarkably little mass support (see Kilson 1993). Not only are their major policy positions on race and economics rejected, black conservative candidates are routinely shunned at the polls. Their electoral failures are a bitter source of bafflement to black conservatives. They believe, and there is *some* evidence to support their view, that the black community supports their socially conservative positions on a number of issues ranging from school prayer to hostility toward gay and lesbian communities. Their bafflement is deepened by the fact that in this historical era they are the most influential set of ideological elites in the halls of power—as they once were when Booker T. Washington attempted to rule black America with an iron fist. They argue that black America is squandering its chance to have a voice in corridors of power by slavishly following liberal leaders and supporting the Democratic party.

A more political, and philosophical, paradox also afflicts black conservatives. On the one hand, they constantly attack other black elites and ideologues for always playing the race card—a practice they find enormously destructive of the mores and values of both the black community and individual African Americans. Similarly, they bemoan what could be called the "authenticity game," through which they claim that black nationalists, "liberals," and feminists attack conservative positions specifically and moral stances more generally by claiming that either the espoused practice ("acting respectfully toward whites") or its advocates (black conservatives) are not part of black culture or the black community. Yet they use the "authenticity" derived from their own blackness to be particularly acute and visible critics of practices, values, ideologies, and leaders which they claim are damaging to black community.

Yet another paradox flows from black conservatives' appropriation of a variety of icons from black political history. This appropriation is not the root of the paradox; the followers of virtually every ideology make similar appropriations—often of the same iconographic historical figures. What is paradoxical is the manner and subject of their appropriation. Black conservatives such as Glenn Loury, Armstrong Williams, and even Supreme Court Justice Thomas, one of the most conservative justices on the nation's highest court, have evoked the spirit of Malcolm X, if not the core of his teachings, in support of their conservative program. Malcolm X during all phases of his political career represented political forces that were not only substantially outside of the boundaries of the American Creed, but which also pushed the acceptable limits of black political thought. To the outside observer, hearing Clarence Thomas praise Malcolm X during his confirmation was a good prescription for generating substantial cognitive dissonance. Well-established, respected leaders such as Martin Luther King Jr., are less often evoked, or are minimalized, or reduced to a pale reflection of their true beliefs, even though they are part of the same liberal tradition as black conservatives. Indeed, on the ground, within black politics, black conservatives are more likely to find allies among black nationalists who resolutely reject the West and its ideological products than among adherents of other ideologies who share a common enlightenment heritage with black conservatives.

Black conservatives view themselves as the fiercest defenders of the poor and disadvantaged of the black community—warriors who attack middle-class complacency, smugness, and abandonment of the black poor. At the same time they are the proud advocates of libertarian capitalism. Because much of the organized black left has abandoned day-to-day organizing, black conservatives are increasingly unchallenged when they portray themselves as both the best hope for the "truly" disadvantaged and black political thought's most consistent champions of unfettered capitalism. This pairing of positions reverses the historic pairing in black political thought which attacked capitalism in the name of defending those disadvantaged by both race and class. They are lauded as the courageous harbingers of a new maturity in black politics by powerful white media and government elites in several different historical eras while often held in contempt by their fellow black ideologues. Their situation presents a major puzzle, if not a paradox: despite the predictions of social theories ranging from social choice to Marxism and pluralist theory and of black and white political prognosticators of the left and right—all of which predict an increase in support for black conservatives, given the rapid increase in the size and financial maturity of the black middle class—support for black conservatives is extraordinarily low. Despite the support some aspects of their social program receive in the black community, black conservative ideology has little grassroots support.

I propose now to evaluate these sets of claims. Although black con-servatives are no more a homogenous group than the other ideological formations, they did share a common heritage in the twentieth cen-tury. We start with a brief review of the controversies that surrounded the most influential black conservative of the twentieth century—Booker T. Washington.

The Legacy of Booker T. Washington

Booker T. Washington at the turn of the century was the hegemonic ruler of black elites, the gatekeeper who counted Theodore Roosevelt and Andrew Carnegie among his patrons, and the great nemesis of W. E. B. Du Bois and other black elites dedicated to the cause of black equality. His controversial career finds supporters among black conservatives, black na-tionalists who appreciate his concern to build the independent economic base of the black community (Garvey originally came to this country to work with Washington but did not manage to arrive before the latter's death), and those who argue that Washington's accommodationist stance was the only one tactically plausible for blacks in a deeply hostile and vio-lent South. His detractors charge that Washington never really cared for poor black people but cared only for enhancing his own power and pres-tige; that he was by no means the only black leader who was concerned with either building autonomous black institutions or black economic life; that he was a dictator who ruthlessly tried to crush possible rivals; and that in the end he was a traitor to his race.

Despite the claims of some of his supporters, the difference between Washington and his critics was not that he emphasized pragmatic eco-nomic development while his detractors did not, nor that he emphasized racial uplift as a strategy. Nor did Washington differ from critics such as Wells and Trotter in urging that the black community build autonomous black institutions. Both Washington's legacy to modern black conserva-tives as well as the differences between him and his contemporaries can be found in his seminal "Address to the Atlanta Cotton Exposition of 1895."

Racial uplift *is* the central theme of both the speech and his autobiog-raphy, *Up from Slavery* (Stepto 1991). In the address he argues that since the black man is "ignorant and inexperienced," he must be told, "cast down your bucket where you are" (Washington 1995). Putting down roots where you are for Washington meant concentrating on industrial, mechanical, vocational, and primarily agricultural pursuits through which one could prove both individually and as a race that blacks were fit to join a nation of citizen-producers. In order to achieve such an end, one had to guard against the following:

> Our greatest danger is that in the great leap from slavery to freedom we may overlook the fact that the masses of us are to live by the productions of our hands, and fail to keep in mind that we shall prosper in proportion as we learn to dignify and glorify common labor and put brains and skill into the common occupations of life; we shall prosper in proportion as we learn to draw the line between the superficial and the substantial, the ornamental gegaws of life and useful. . . . Nor should we permit our grievances to overshadow our opportunities. (Washington 1995, 244)

What Du Bois and like-minded colleagues objected to was not the emphasis on the necessity for, and the dignity of, common labor. What was much more problematic was that it was counterposed to the life of the mind and a cultural education, which Washington dismissed as useless. Even more dangerous to Du Bois, Wells, and their colleagues was the minimization of "our grievances." The historical context is critical here; he was *not*, as are today's black conservatives, writing in the period after the victories of the Civil Rights and Black Power movements, but during a period when entrenched, racist hostility was manifested extremely violently in thousands of murderous lynchings and in waves of violence from the Ku Klux Klan and other unofficial and official racist terrorists, and during a period when the black populations of cities such as Atlanta in 1906 were subjected to deadly mob violence. Thus his advice to beware of those "who underestimate the importance of cultivating friendly relations with the southern white man" (Washington 1995, 243) carries a much different resonance than the plea heard from contemporary black conservatives that blacks should pursue closer relations with the Republican party. Thus the charge of "traitor" carried a different valence during Washington's era, when black lives were constantly at risk. Thus the following advice sounds less like good sense in his historic era and more like cowardice to Trotter, Lewis Douglass (Frederick's activist son), and their compatriots: "We began at the top instead of at the bottom; . . . a seat in Congress or the state legislature was more sought than real estate or industrial skill; . . . the political convention or stump speaking had more attractions than starting a dairy farm or truck garden" (Washington 1995, 243).

What Ida B. Wells and others argued was that one could not separate political and social struggle from economic advancement. The narratives of sharecropper Nate Shaw, Richard Wright, Ida B. Wells, and numerous others make the case that when southern blacks did cast down their buckets and managed to accumulate property, either the state or terrorist arms of white supremacy (in some cases one and the same) would expropriate black property, the owners sometimes finding themselves at the wrong end of the barrel of a gun. While Du Bois, Douglass, and hundreds of other were protesting the violent attacks on Atlanta's black community during the 1906 riot, Washington, in a much criticized series of statements, called for "law and order" and for the black community to be "calm" while condemning rape. He also made the following plea to the black community: "I would especially urge the colored people in Atlanta and elsewhere to exercise self-control and not make the fatal mistake of retaliation" (Aptheker 1979, 867). But Wells's and Du Bois's point was that antiblack violence was seldom about attacks on white women; in the Georgia case it was part of the campaign to disenfranchise Georgia's black citizens, and in the case of the Memphis lynchings that Wells describes, it was about economic expropriation. She made the following bitter observations about the 1892 Memphis lynchings:

> But Thomas Moss, Calvin McDowell, and Lee Stewart had been lynched in Memphis, one of the leading cities of the South, in which no lynching had taken place before, with just as much brutality as other victims of the mob; and they had committed no crime against white women. This is what opened my eyes to what lynching really was. An excuse to get rid of Negroes who were acquiring wealth and property and thus keep the race terrorized and 'keep the nigger down.' (Wells 1970, 64)

Thus Wells, Du Bois, and thousands of African Americans of this and succeeding generations argued that it was not possible for blacks to separate political from economic development. One could not acquire property and wealth if the state and the leading forces of civil society denied you not only property rights, but an even more basic right guaranteed by the liberal state since the time of Locke—the safety of one's own person (Holmes 1995).

In this context it is easier to understand both the bitterness which greeted Washington from the black community and the eagerness with which he was greeted by both northern and southern elites when he counseled that blacks should abandon not only politics, but any desire for social equality: "The wisest among my race understand that the agitation of questions of social equality is the extremest folly, and that progress in the enjoyment of all the privileges that will come to us must be the result of severe and constant struggle rather than of artificial forcing. No race that has anything to contribute to the markets of the world is long in any degree ostracized" (Washington 1995, 245).

This passage is lauded by both black and white conservative theorists such as Loury and Herbert Storing (Loury 1995; Storing 1995). Markets are the mechanism through which social equality is gained, and producers will be granted citizenship rights. This view not only runs counter to the basic tenets of liberal democratic equality, but seems to mark only the most dangerous hypocrisy as blacks functioned in markets in which their lives were in danger if they attempted to participate successfully, let alone equally.

As many black conservatives argue today, Washington argued that the older generation of black leadership must be denigrated if his program was to have a chance to take hold (Stepto 1991). The following passage is echoed in many of the texts of modern black conservatives:

> Mr. Douglass's great life-work had been in the political agitation that led to the destruction of slavery. He had been the great defender of the race, and [a leader] in the struggle to win from Congress and from the country at large the recognition of the Negro's rights. But the long and bitter political struggle in which he had engaged against slavery had not prepared Mr. Douglass to take up the equally difficult task of fitting the Negro for the opportunities and responsibilities of freedom. The same was true to a large extent of other Negro leaders. (Stepto 1991, 48)

It is hardly surprising that black activists committed to equality, such as Ida B. Wells, Du Bois, and influential nationalist leader Monroe Trotter, bitterly objected to Washington's philosophy, his attempts (largely successful) to dominate black discourse and institutional life, and his deadly attacks on their characters and initiatives. Black elites have very little monopoly over leadership conflicts that emerge due to jealousy, personal rivalry, and ideological principle. More indicative perhaps of the contemporary black opinion regarding Washington's ideological and pragmatic program are the comments of a black Alabama contemporary of his, who lived and worked close to Washington's center at Tuskegee. Sharecropper Nate Shaw made the following observations:

> And I seed Booker Washington—after I was grown and got big enough. . . . They gived him piles of money to run this school business here in the state of Alabama. But I wouldn't boost Booker Washington

today up to everything that was industrious and right. Why? He was
a nigger of this state and well known and everything, but here's what
his trouble was, to a great extent: he didn't feel for and didn't respect
his race of people enough to go to the bottom with 'em. He leaned
too much to the white people that controlled the money—lookin' out
for what was his worth, that's what he was lookin' for. (Rosengarten
1974, 542–43)

Today Washington's black conservative heirs are attempting to reha-
bilitate his legacy. Like the other contemporary ideologues, many of their
most visible representatives are found within the academy. But black conservatives can also be found in the ranks of government (a legacy largely of
the Reagan-Bush regime), business, to an exceptional extent in the media,
and in the cabinet of George W. Bush. One of their number was considered a serious candidate for president. They are also somewhat diverse politically. Part of the their legacy from Washington, however, is that they
have inherited a common set of central themes that constitute the core of
modern black conservatism.

Racial Uplift

Washington's ideological heirs have also embraced the theme of uplift,
but unlike other black liberals and black nationalists, black conservatives
seek to sever the link between racial uplift and white racism commonly
found in other black ideological narratives. The need for black racial uplift
is a central theme in Glenn Loury's argument that African Americans
would be much better off if they followed the path of Booker T. Washington as opposed to that of Du Bois.[7] The problem, argues Loury, is not the
racist attitudes of whites, for "blacks' problems lie not in the heads of white
people but rather in the wasted and incompletely fulfilled lives of too many
black people" (Loury 1995, 45). Loury, like Washington, believes that
blacks need to prove to whites that they are fit citizens worthy of all the
benefits of American society. Loury explicitly argues that Washington's
strategy of a century ago is still relevant as he "advocates . . . a conservative
philosophy for advancement based on direct empowerment of the poor, re-
lying significantly on self-help, and dubious about the ability of government

---

7. Loury's views are evolving, as I briefly discuss in the conclusion; see Loury's 1998 volume,
"Selected Clips." Even there, however, he describes himself as a black conservative.

programs to resolve the deepest problems afflicting black society" (Loury 1995, 65). Concentrating on racial uplift is necessary because equality comes from contesting dysfunctional behavior. Civil rights leaders and strategies provide no help in improving the quality of life for the black poor. What is necessary, according to Loury, is the recognition that "further progress toward the attainment of equality for black Americans, correctly understood, depends most crucially at this juncture on the acknowledgment and rectification of the dysfunctional behaviors that plague black communities, and that so often threaten others" (Loury 1995, 72).

Loury and his conservative comrades argue that two things must occur before the black poor—indeed, the entire black community—can make such progress. First, blacks must abandon their dysfunctional, pathological concentration on justice in this era. Loury, unlike many of his compatriots, freely admits that blacks suffered horribly under racism and may indeed face some racism in the current period. Lack of progress, however, is due to problems arising primarily within black communities and attitudes, not as a result of white hostility:

> The point on which Booker T. Washington is clear, and his critics seemed not to be, is that progress such as this must be earned, and not simply demanded. . . . It is of no moment that historic wrongs may have caused current deprivation, for justice is not the issue here. The issues are honor, dignity, respect, and self-respect, all of which are preconditions for true equality between any peoples. The classic interplay between the aggrieved black and the guilty white, in which the former demands (and the latter conveys) a recognition of the historical injustice is, quite simply, not an exchange among equals. (Loury 1995, 73)

Du Bois, King, and other activists in the black liberal tradition would argue that first Washington and now Loury profoundly misunderstand both black history and the morality of justice. They would argue that dignity comes from the quest for justice, that citizenship is earned by the demonstrated desire to participate in all aspects of the life of the polity and civil society. They would also argue that when one side has systematically structured a polity and civil society for its own benefit, then power is necessary to ensure that a level playing field is attainable in the public and private spheres.

This utter rejection of Washington's stance on the part of the great majority of black leaders, activists, and ideologues is well understood by Loury and forms the basis for black conservatives' second point (which I will soon explain in more depth): the current generation of black leaders and their ideas must be defeated. But Loury is optimistic. He believes that soon the black community will come to its senses and increasingly turn to the teachings of Booker T. Washington: "But there are signs that a new era is dawning, and that in the contemporary struggle over which ideas will inform efforts to improve the black condition into the twenty-first century, the principles laid down by Booker T. Washington will be rediscovered and play an important role. I intend to urge that this be so" (Loury 1995, 66). Only when the black community turns to such ideas will it succeed in "securing the sympathetic support of the rest of the political community. It is essential to establishing in the minds of whites what is true, which is that the bulk of poor blacks are deserving of the help they so desperately need" (Loury 1995, 80).

Racism's Legacy

Black conservatives have a very different view of the legacy of American racism than other black liberals. They also disagree widely among themselves. Loury is fairly atypical in believing that there actually is a legacy of racism which has current negative consequences for African Americans. Loury explains,

> Now blacks have in fact been constrained by a history of racism and limited opportunity. Some of these effects continue to manifest themselves into the current day. Yet now that greater opportunity exists, taking advantage of it requires that we accept personal responsibility for our own fate, even though the effects of this past remain with us in part. But emphasis on this personal responsibility of blacks takes the political pressure off those outside the black community, who also have a responsibility, as citizens of this republic, to be actively engaged in trying to change the structures that constrain the black poor in such a way that they can more effectively assume responsibility for themselves and exercise their inherent and morally required capacity to choose. That is, an inherent link exists between these two sides the "responsibility" coin: between acceptance among blacks of personal responsibility for our actions and acceptance among all Americans of their social responsibilities as citizens. (Loury 1995, 29)

Loury argues that the legacy of racism does mean that the nation bears some responsibility for the plight of disadvantaged blacks. But other black conservatives such as fellow economists Thomas Sowell and Walter Williams question whether racism has had any major effect on blacks either historically or in the current era. They follow the main strategy adopted by black conservatives to deny the importance of racism for understanding and explaining contemporary black social and economic outcomes. Williams argues, and Sowell would agree, that racism cannot possibly be the reason that blacks are disadvantaged, since other groups throughout both world and American history have been systematically persecuted:

> Clearly, the experience of Orientals, Jews, and West Indians calls into question the hypothesis that racial bigotry can be a complete explanation of the difficulties that blacks face in America. The point is that if racial discrimination is not the most important cause, then economic and political resources need to be reallocated to address the more important causes of the disadvantages faced by many blacks. There was in the past gross denial of basic rights of and gross discrimination against blacks in the United States. Residual discrimination remains. But the basic premise of this book is that racial bigotry and discrimination is neither a complete nor a satisfactory explanation for the current condition of many blacks in America. (Williams 1982, xvi)

They disagree about the main causal factor that explains the plight of black communities. Sowell insists that culture determines the outcomes that both peoples and civilizations experience. Further, culture is the main determinant in world history; it explains intergroup differences and intra-civilization differences—all are products of cultural differences (Sowell 1994). Culture travels with people and across generations, so Sowell states that U.S. military success from early in its history through the Gulf War can be explained by the high proportion of American generals of German extraction: "Cultures are not erased by crossing a political border, or even an ocean, nor do they necessarily disappear in later generations which adopt the language, dress, and outward lifestyle of a country" (Sowell 1994, 4). Thus, for Sowell, what explains group outcomes are the ancient cultures that travel with a group, not contemporary or even relatively "recent" persecution.

This theory of culture as a universal explanation for social and economic outcomes tends to ignore evidence such as the ability of different peoples with "ancient" cultures to quickly change the trajectory of their societies. (For example, it provides little basis within Sowell's framework for understanding how or why the national economies of "backwards" Asian cultures grew extremely rapidly and gave both the Japanese and the Koreans a run for their money.) Black conservatives such as Sowell and Walter Williams also dismiss solid statistical evidence of racial discrimination in earnings, employment, loan and housing markets, and which also demonstrates continued high levels of racial animosity aimed at African Americans. Williams (1982) argues, for example, that it is impossible to use statistical models successfully to assess the importance of race in determining group outcomes—a somewhat unusual stance for a modern economist.

The propensity to dismiss broad classes of evidence allows cultural theorists such as Sowell to make sweeping claims such as "Indians, blacks, and South Americans concentrate too much on easy subjects like ethnic studies, law and medicine and not enough on hard ones like math, science, and economics. Thus they are only prepared for shuffling paper as clerks, bureaucrats, or disgruntled ethnic politicians," or that Latin American elites have a "disdain for commerce and industry" (Sowell 1994, 23, 25). Evidence such as the mushrooming of the software industry on the Indian subcontinent is also ignored.

Similar inconsistencies can be found in the treatment of black cultural patterns. On one hand, when discussing his definition of culture, Sowell dismisses artistic accomplishments as evidence of cultural expertise (an area in which African Americans have excelled on the world stage), but two hundred pages later he states, "Edison, Einstein, or Beethoven were not mere creatures of their environments—nevertheless their genius required a major cultural foundation on which to build" (Sowell 1994, 233). The genius of John Coltrane or Duke Ellington, however, is not provided as evidence of African-American cultural strength. Culture is an internal attribute of a group. Historic shocks such as colonialism or slavery are dismissed as explanations for the historical development of groups. If culture and other internal pathologies are the causes of disadvantage in black communities, what remedies should African Americans seek?

First, African Americans should concentrate on winning the "right" type of equality. Loury defines true equality as follows: "By 'true equality' I mean more than an approximately equal material provision. Also crucial, I maintain, is equal respect in the eyes of one's fellow citizens. Yet much of the current advocacy of blacks' interests seems inconsistent with achieving equal respect for black Americans" (Loury 1995, 22).

Gaining respect also means not harping on "voluntary" segregation or "rational" discrimination, or on forcing society to assume the "burdens" of the increased costs of antidiscrimination policies. Walter Williams argues that segregation is perhaps tolerable, if voluntary: "Many people assume that the existence of homogenous association is evidence of racial injustice or racial exclusion. This point of view implicitly assumes that, in the absence of racial injustice or exclusion, voluntary individual actions would not produce today's pattern of homogenous groupings by race" (Williams 1982, 7). Of course middle-class blacks are prevented from exercising their preferences through the housing market by violence, restrictive covenants, and other mechanisms to preserve white preferences (Massey and Denton 1993).

Sowell makes a slightly different point. Employment segregation costs potential black employees, but may be rational. *Preventing* discrimination imposes a burden on employers:

> Group segregation as a deliberate policy or action by employers is a very old and widespread phenomenon. . . . What job segregation of this sort does imply is that there are higher costs of employing mixed groups of incompatible workers, whether those costs originate in language differences, lifestyle differences, or intergroup animosities. In other words, *the higher costs are inherent.* There are no "solutions" to this "problem" that will make it disappear without incurring other costs. (Sowell 1994, 84–85; emphasis in original)

Sowell does not consider equality before the law a fundamental feature of any liberal democracy. The principles around which such a democracy is organized do impose costs if we are to have a society which cherishes the basic values of equality before the law and even the minimum standard of equal opportunity for all citizens. If we really want equal opportunity for individuals, his "let them discriminate" viewpoint would really lead to the balkanization with which he is so concerned. For example, he "justifies" discrimination in loan markets by arguing that lenders should not be forced by law to bear the increased costs of loaning to minorities because they lack sufficient information to make profitable loans at the same rate they can for whites. A liberal, commonsense solution would be to argue that is precisely a good business reason to hire a more diverse set of loan officers.

Armstrong Williams speaks for his fellow black conservatives when he argues that blacks need to take advantage of the opportunities provided by America and stop acting as victims, as well as victimizing the nation. The advice he gives a young black hoodlum that he is attempting to straighten out is similar to the advice that black conservatives as a group have for black America:

Here you are, a young black man with a criminal record, a lousy education, and no real experience, and I know plenty of people who would give you a second chance at a job and a career, a second chance at an education, even a second chance at building a reputation. Even now I can say with confidence that you can go as far in America as your abilities will take you. You may not realize it, but the whole American system is structured to give people like you a second, third, and even a fourth chance. (Williams 1995, 21)

Martin Kilson, in an essay which analyzes the roots and programs of modern black conservatives, replies as would many black liberals from the non-conservative camp:

The notion of a color-blind American society is never tested against typical racist practices blacks experience every day—like being charged more than whites when purchasing an automobile, being denied a job in one-third of instances during undercover tests where a black and white person who are equally qualified apply for the job, and encountering massive discrimination in housing markets and residential choice. (Kilson 1993, 8–9)

Black conservatives call for blacks to abandon what they see as cultural pathologies. They also are united in their belief that a pathological reliance on the state is a major barrier to black advancement.

The Evil State

Self-reliance and advancement through taking advantage of the market are the preferred strategies of the black conservatives. The state provides a seductive but ultimately destructive avenue for black progress. Even for a black conservative such as Glenn Loury, who is nearly unique in believing that the "federal government can play a critical role" in the process leading to black advancement, agrees with his conservative compatriots that the cultural pathologies found in the black community are best addressed through nongovernmental avenues: "It makes sense to call for greater self-reliance at this time because some of what needs to be done cannot, in the nature of the case, be undertaken by government. Dealing with behavioral problems; with community values; with attitudes and beliefs of black youngsters about responsibility, work, family, and schooling are not things government is well suited to do" (Loury 1995, 22). He goes on to say that this task is best left to families, churches, and various civil associations. Walter Williams, however, is more typical of black conservatives in his scathing attack on the relationship between blacks and the state. His thesis is well captured in the title of his book, *The State against Blacks* (Williams 1982).

The state represents a massive barrier to black progress: "There are numerous laws, regulations, and ordinances that have reduced or eliminated avenues of upward mobility for blacks" (Williams 1982, 144). Like Williams, Sowell also argues that government regulations allowing unionization, mandating a minimum wage, requiring licenses of service workers, and banning discrimination in labor, loan, and housing markets all hold blacks back (Sowell 1994; Williams 1982). Williams further explains this viewpoint, which many black activists and ideologues find bizarre at first hearing:

> Herein lies the power of the market. People can offset some of their handicaps by offering a higher price for what they buy or a lower price for what they sell. Many well-meaning people are morally outraged by such a necessity. But the fact of business is that if handicapped people are not permitted to use price as a bargaining tool, they may very well end up with none of what they want as opposed to some. (Williams 1982, 143)

Other black ideologues would argue that this viewpoint virtually abandons the centuries-long quest for black equality by acquiescing to a citizenship status for blacks that can only be viewed as second-class at best.

State intervention also exacerbates race relations by encouraging "exaggerated" group consciousness and the formation of "new" ethnic groups such as Hispanics, according to Sowell. These groups form merely to "capitalize on government grants and appropriations (Sowell 1994, 144). This encouragement of racial consciousness on the part of the state also encourages another pathological tendency, according to black conservatives. They attack as debilitating what they see as the excessive concern of blacks for racial authenticity.

Authenticity

The pressure to conform, to be authentically black, exacts a dire cost, according to black conservatives. It exacts both a personal cost as well as costs to the entire community. Loury makes the following observations about the costs of racial authenticity:

I now understand how this desire to be regarded as genuinely black, to be seen as a "regular brother," has dramatically altered my life. It narrowed the range of my earliest intellectual pursuits, distorted my relationships with other people, censored my political thought and expression, informed the way I dressed and spoke, and shaped my cultural interests. Some of this was inevitable, and not all of it was bad, but in my experience the need to be affirmed by one's racial peers can take on a pathological dimension. (Loury 1995, 5–6)

Those that conform to the pathology of conformity risk their "individuality and their dignity" (Loury 1995, 181).

There is a political cost as well. Blacks feel compelled to support flawed policies, argue the black conservatives, so that the political strength of black conservatives is underestimated, while support for policies such as affirmative action is alleged to be overestimated. Black conservatives believe they pay a personal cost because their leaders are continually castigated by the rest of the black community. The result, Loury in particular argues, is an unhealthy self-censorship and the silencing of conservative viewpoints which might have something valuable to offer. Loury asks, "Do the ideas of Booker T. Washington, as I have tried to elaborate them here, really have no place in the deliberations of the Supreme Court?" (Loury 1995, 81). His answer, of course, is an emphatic no. Star Parker makes the same point about the "unfair" treatment Justice Thomas received at the hands of the black community:

If you're black, it's taboo to speak out against affirmative action, even if you oppose it. Consequently, Thomas has been a whipping boy for black leftists ever since his nomination to the high court. How do they get away with this? The black community has been wimped into a code of silence. Consequently, it has become just another special interest group controlled by liberal Democrats. Black civil rights leaders know how to keep their sheep in line. Anyone who speaks up is called a racist if he's white and a sellout or a traitor if he's black. (Parker 1997, 149)

The result, according to the Los Angeles media figure, is the silencing not of just a few black conservative elites, but of a vast segment of the black community. She believes, but offers little evidence for, the following proposition: "I know millions of blacks believe as I do, so it doesn't bother me when I cross a few who don't" (Parker 1997, 202). Her belief in significant support for the conservative position in the black community has a sharp edge, and that edge is based on class interests. According to Parker, upper-income blacks should be particularly ready to abandon failed government programs which expropriate their wealth through taxes:

> All along, poverty has been increasing, and quite frankly, I'm sick of wasting my money on failed government programs. Hey, there are a million black folks in America making over $50,000 a year, and they ought to be sick of it, too. There are an overwhelming number of black conservatives in this country, but many are still in the closet because they don't want to show white America that there's a break in the ranks. I've broken the code of silence, and some folks are angry with me about that. But how can we continue to promote ourselves as victims of racism when despite our long, hard journey through slavery, Jim Crow, and the civil rights era, we now boast a population that circulates more than $400 billion annually in the United States? I can't cry racism when such success has occurred against all the odds. Capitalism is the answer. (Parker 1997, 201)

The joys of capitalism are not appreciated because corrupt black leadership, Sowell agrees, misleads the black community by overemphasizing ethnic identity and reliance on government programs:

> The implicit agreement of contending leaders [in an ethnic group] that leadership is important is too inherently self-serving to prove very much, but the most diverse political leaders share a common interest in exaggerating the importance of political leadership. Even ethnic minority leaders, with no realistic hope of acquiring decisive national power, have an incentive to join in the general promotion of the "leadership" concept, as that offers them individually their best chance of gaining whatever political positions may be available to them. (Sowell 1994, 145)

The way to counter the corrupt leadership of the black community is by replacing it with the moral leadership of black conservatives dedicated to the truth, not to a misplaced emphasis on racial authenticity.

The Need for Conservative Moral Leadership

There are two critical aspects to moral leadership, according to black conservatives. First is the need for black leaders to speak the truth and guide the black community away from the destructive and self-interested policies of current mainstream black leaderships. Further, the writings of Loury, Parker, and Armstrong Williams emphasize the need for the black community to turn toward evangelical Christianity. The current generation of black leaders fails because, the black conservatives believe, they embrace the role of victim. This role not only has "unacceptable costs" but is also "undignified and demeaning" (Loury 1995, 20). Black leadership refuses to abandon such a bankrupt approach because it is not in their selfish self-interest:

> There are few things more valuable in the competition for government largess than the clearly perceived status of victim. Blacks "enjoy" that status by dint of many years of systematic exclusion from a just place in American life. A substantial source of influence thus derives from the fact that blacks are perceived as having been unjustly wronged and hence worthy of consideration. The single most important symbol of this injustice is the large, inner-city ghetto, with its population of poor blacks. These masses and their miserable condition sustain the political capital that all blacks enjoy because of their historical status as victims. (Loury 1995, 46)

According to Armstrong Williams, it is not just the self-interested behavior of other, nonconservative leaders that is the problem, but their ideologies as well. He explains to the young black criminal that he's trying to reform, "I also believed that the self-defeating ideology of many black leaders prevents young men like you from learning how to take advantage of them" (Williams 1995, 20). These ideologies, Loury explains, prevent black leadership from confronting the dire problem of crime that plagues black communities. When discussing the fact that the NAACP was concerned about the injustice in incarceration and sentencing by race, he argued, "This kind of intellectual perspective clearly precludes any serious discussion by black leaders of the problem of criminal behavior." He continued, "There are worse things than blaming the victim" (Loury 1995, 41).

Black feminists are particularly singled out for vilification by black conservatives. Black feminism is blamed for everything from encouraging the destruction of the black family to encouraging black welfare dependency. The warped view of black feminism held by some black conservatives can be seen in the following passage from Armstrong Williams: "Brad's views of women are better described as those of a superradicalized male feminist. He has absolutely no doubt that women are as capable as men, and he lives that view. Whether in business dealings or sex, Brad almost never even thinks about treating 'females,' as he calls them, any differently than he does men—with little concern and no respect" (Williams 1995, 100). Contrast this view with view that "Brad" expresses several pages later. Williams first explains that the young man "seem[s] to view women in much the same way you view Big Macs: when you are hungry you have one, and then you toss the wrapper on the street without giving it another thought. As you bluntly explained about these women, "I don't respect them much" (Williams 1995, 59). There is absolutely nothing vaguely feminist about Brad's views. Why does Williams feel compelled to label Brad's views "feminist?" Well, first, there is the implication in the first passage that being "a superradicalized male feminist" is part and parcel of the extraordinary pathological—indeed, murderous—mindset and behavior of the young criminal. Thus feminism is scurrilously attached to Brad's murderous pathologies. Black feminists would argue that Brad's misogynistic attitudes are indeed part of his criminal pathologies.

Black conservatives believe, like their progenitor, Booker T. Washington, that is necessary to destroy or discredit alternative black leaders and their ideologies in order to lead the black community to a more advantageous, economically centered future. Like their predecessor, however, black conservatives have had notably little success in gaining mass support.

American Politics, Black Leaders, and the Black Rejection of the Republican Party

Black conservatives blame several actors for their lack of political support, but the most important culprits are, of course, those in the mainstream black leadership. This leadership's sins include not only those discussed so far, but also the sin of being to the left of both their constituency and the mainstream of white public opinion. The first is patently false. On the core issues of race and economics, mainstream black leaders tend to be placed squarely within the mainstream of black public opinion and may be slightly to the right on economic issues (Dawson 1994a, 1994b; Hamilton 1982). Black leaders as well as the black grassroots find themselves considerably to the left of the mainstream of white opinion (Dawson 1994a, 1997; Kinder and Sanders 1996). Nevertheless, despite more than a decade of survey evidence and the harder evidence that black preferences are liberal, as expressed in their electoral behavior, black conservatives (and their white conservative allies) continue to insist that black leaders are way to the left:

But of all the actors in this drama, black leaders play the most important role, and the most problematic. The prevailing ideological cast of many prominent black leaders and intellectuals is considerably to the left of the national mainstream and often of the black community itself. Because of the long history of racist exclusion, many blacks place group solidarity above mere philosophical differences when deciding whom to support. (Loury 1995, 560)

The answer for Loury and his fellow travelers is to substitute a conformity with white opinion for what they see as a conformity with black opinion. Blacks need to take into account white sensibilities on issues of race, economics, and preference for presidential candidates and change their behavior and preferences to be more in line with white preferences. This is the same view that Washington held a century earlier. The following passage from Loury is typical of this ideological mindset:

If whites reject racial preferences as unfair to them, and if politicians campaign on the issue, the problem is construed as a lack of restraint by unscrupulous candidates who are willing to use divisive tactics to achieve their ends. Today's orthodoxy holds in contempt the need to express concern for and acknowledge the legitimacy of the sensibilities of whites when they run up against the presumed interests of blacks. (Loury 1995, 74)

Not surprisingly, given this perspective, the blame for the racial divisions is assigned clearly to the leadership and political attitudes of the black community. For example, in a campaign where his white opponent used the most vile racist leaflets while he campaigned for votes in every community in stark contrast to his opponent, Harold Washington is the one accused of racializing his campaign for mayor of Chicago (Loury 1995). Star Parker condemns the entire class of black politicians as criminals. Those who are not yet in jail, should be:

Liberal black politicians who have avoided state prison hide behind the same cloak of deception. These elitist whores claim their mission in life is to squelch bigotry, when they are in fact racists themselves. It's not that they hate whites, but they frequently accuse them of hating blacks and judge every issue through race-colored glasses. They are the projectionists of the black cause, and every word they utter and every political move they make is predicated on one thing: skin color. (Parker 1997, 143)

The right and the Republicans do bear some responsibility for the estrangement between African Americans and whites. Loury points to several examples from the Reagan administration which he believes were hostile to the black community. Star Parker also believes that the early history of GOP opposition to civil rights and black concerns a generation ago was a "tactical blunder" which gave the Democrats an opening and made it more difficult for the right to make headway within the black community. Nevertheless, black conservatives believe that with proper leadership, the black community would correct its course and move in a conservative direction.

The Future of Black Conservatism

African Americans have not, much to the consternation of Sowell, Loury, and their colleagues, chosen the path of Booker T. Washington. It takes a very unusual perspective to claim as Sowell does that Washington was successful. Loury's more thoughtful analysis of the debate between Washington and Du Bois partially explains the dilemma of black conservatives who seek to win over a political community that is programmatically and ideologically committed to a leftist economic agenda and a progressive racial agenda. They seek to have a voice within a black community which Loury understands remains unpersuaded of the viability of black conservatism. At least as of the 2000 presidential elections, black conservatives' political position within the black community remained tenuous. Not only did black voters reject Republican candidate George W. Bush at near record levels, an immense amount of bitterness erupted as the charges of voter intimidation aimed at minority voters in Florida and elsewhere swept black communities across the nation. Indeed, the anticonservative backlash was so intense that the popularity of the most popular black conservative, Colin Powell, declined after the election when it became known that he would become a member in President George W. Bush's cabinet. Even with prominent black conservatives once again associated with a Republican administration, winning support for black conservative policy programs will be difficult, given the wide initial gap between blacks and the Bush administration on key policy issues.[8]

8. Data that support these comments was compiled by the author with data from the Harvard University W. E. B. Du Bois Institute/University of Chicago Center for the Study of Race, Politics, and Culture 2000 Presidential Election Study. The postelection component of the study was conducted December 1 through 15, 2000, and includes 605 black adults and 724 white adults. The principle investigators were Lawrence Bobo of Harvard University and Michael Dawson of the University of Chicago. The data was collected by Knowledge Networks. The sampling error for the black

Martin Kilson believes that there is another reason that should be considered when trying to understand the conservatives' lack of support. He argues that modern black conservatives have bought respectability and don't have organic roots in the black community (Kilson 1993). This is a common charge found in the black literature which analyzes black conservatism. It is true that they owe much of their current prominence to governmental, commercial, and media attention, given their lack of support within the black community. But it is also true that ideologically their beliefs and programs are consistent with a black ideological tradition which can be traced back at least to Booker T. Washington.

The same cannot be true of potentially the most powerful of the contemporary black conservatives—Colin Powell. His political stance is very different from that of other black conservatives. He supports both affirmative action and a women's right to choose (Gates 1997). Indeed, many consider him too left for the Republican party, despite the attractiveness his candidacy may offer. He described this tension in an interview with Skip Gates:

> One of my Republican friends had the nerve to send me one of their newsletters a few weeks ago saying that we had to get rid of affirmative action because we couldn't keep putting these programs in place for allegations of "vague and ancient wrongs." I almost went crazy. I said, "Vague? Vague? Denny's wouldn't serve four black Secret Service agents guarding the President of the United States." The Chicago Federal Reserve Bank just told us something that any black could have told you—that it's harder to get a loan if you're black than if you're white. (Gates 1997, 95)

This is not the viewpoint expressed by either Williams, Sowell, or even Loury. Yet he is still a fiscal conservative whose economic and foreign policy perspectives are considerably to the right of those of most African Americans. As important, perhaps—as both Jackson and Gates note—Powell does not ground himself in the symbols and icons of black culture as do most black conservatives. While he is a conservative, it is difficult to identify Powell as part of the black conservative ideological tradition.

---

sample is approximately $+/-$ 4.0 percentage points, and the sampling error for the white sample is approximately $+/-$ 3.6 percentage points. When comparing the two samples, we find that the sampling error is approximately $+/-5.4$ percentage points. Sampling error is only one form of potential error in public opinion surveys. Knowledge Networks employs a Random Digit Dialing (RRD) telephone methodology to develop a representative sample of households for participation in its panel.

Despite their identification with the iconic figures of black resistance and legend, black conservatives still substantially agree with much of the program of their white counterparts. Indeed, the more extreme, libertarian versions of black conservatism are not only significantly outside the mainstream of black public opinion, but also challenge basic tenets of the "American Creed." How far outside the mainstream of black opinion black conservatives find themselves is explored in the next section.

The Measure and Distribution of Black Liberalism

In this section I describe the distribution of the various black liberal ideologies within the black community. I go on to discuss the antecedents of traditional black liberalism and of disillusioned liberalism. Finally, I assess the impact of black liberal ideology on black public opinion. I start with a description of the measures of the various strands of black liberal ideology.

Measures

Given the limitations of this survey's data, as well as the structure of the survey instrumentation, radical egalitarians and black conservatives are modeled as the polar opposites of each other. Black respondents were asked to make a series of choices in describing their preferences across a wide variety of issue domains. For example, participants were asked whether "Poor people don't want to work" or "Poor people want to work but there are not enough jobs." Most black conservatives would choose the former, while most radical egalitarians would tend to choose the latter response. A similar pair of statements went into the construction of the combined radical egalitarian/black conservative scale; we asked respondents to choose either "There has been so much racial progress over the past several years that special programs for blacks are no longer needed" or "There is still so much discrimination that special programs to help blacks and minorities are needed." In both cases (as with the other items that make up the scales), the writings of the radical egalitarians and the black conservatives confirm that the two groups make the opposite choice within each pair. The radical egalitarian/black conservative scale models African Americans' attitudes toward the intersections of racial policies, economic policies, and the role of the state. Consequently, the scale is modeled as a combined radical egalitarian/conservative scale. The full set of items which make up this scale are displayed in table A3.1 in the appendix.

Before we discuss disillusioned liberalism, we need to model disillusionment. A model of racial disillusionment can be built easily from the four items that ask respondents for their evaluation of the racial and economic fairness of American society, the legal system, the fairness of American corporations and the overall fairness of the economic system. Finally, a scale for disillusioned liberalism can be built using the items from the radical egalitarianism/black conservative scale and the disillusioned scale. Both the disillusioned and disillusioned liberalism scales cohere well (see table A3.2 in the appendix), though the radical egalitarian/conservative scale does not for reasons similar to those discussed in chapters 4 and 5. Due to the particularly diffuse way in which liberal ideas permeate American society, we shall see that the tenets of both disillusioned liberalism and radical egalitarianism are widely embraced by African Americans. It is not surprising, given the extensive levels of black distrust, that the disillusioned liberalism scale coheres better than the radical egalitarian/black conservative scale does alone. There is a significant, if worrying, intersection of egalitarian attitudes and gloominess among grassroots African Americans.

Distributions

Examining the distributions of radical egalitarianism/conservatism, disillusionment, and then disillusioned liberalism helps to highlight the problems faced by both black conservatives and radical egalitarianism. Figures 6.1–6.3 display the distribution of the three scales. The center of the distribution of the radical egalitarian/black conservative scale is heavily shifted toward the radical egalitarian end of the spectrum. The largest clusters around positions on the scale represent moderate to very intense support for this ideology's position. There is another small cluster of opinion around the center of the distribution. There is some support for a moderate view of race, economics, and the state in the black community. As we suspected from the initial presentations of distributions in chapter 2, the black conservative position enjoys virtually no mass support, despite claims from those such as Star Parker that there are "millions" of black conservatives out there somewhere waiting to be led to a right-wing nirvana. The distribution of disillusionment shows, if anything, an even more extreme story. The largest cluster of blacks (the modal position) is concentrated at the end of the distribution that represents extreme perceptions of racial and economic unfairness across all domains within American society. No matter how the data are analyzed, whether the raw marginals are presented

Figure 6.1   Smoothed Radical Egalitarianism/Black Conservatism distribution using normal and Epanechinikov estimators

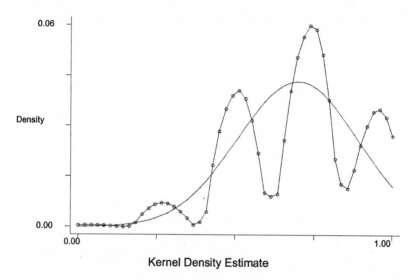

	Observations	Mean	Std. Deviation	Minimum	Maximum
Radical Egalitarianism/ Black Conservatism	1,187	0.72	0.21	0	1

Source: 1993–1994 National Black Politics Survey

or reasonably sophisticated scales are constructed, the answer is the same. Massive numbers of African Americans, well over three-quarters of the black population, continue to believe in the fundamental unfairness of this society. Finally, when we turn to the distribution of disillusioned liberalism among African Americans, we find that a very significant proportion of the population support both the radical egalitarians' view of the state and racial policies while holding a view of the United States as a fundamentally and racially unfair nation.

The entrenched nature of disillusioned liberalism is at least as much of a problem, if not more so, for the radical egalitarians as it is for black conservative ideologues. While black conservatives are clearly being rejected by the black community on the basis of their positions on racial and economic issues, radical egalitarians are having an equally hard time convinc-

Figure 6.2 Smoothed Black Disillusionment distribution using normal and
Epanechinikov estimators

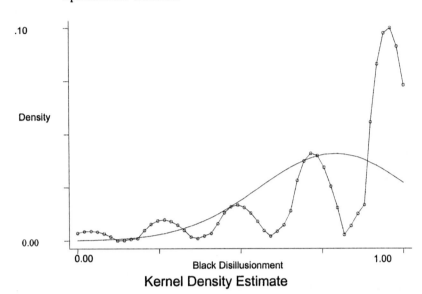

Kernel Density Estimate

	Observations	Mean	Std. Deviation	Minimum	Maximum
Black Disillusionment	1,045	0.81	0.25	0	1

Source: 1993–1994 National Black Politics Survey

ing this era's black community of the basic goodness of the polity that underlay both King's and Bunche's beliefs for most of their careers. During the period from 1960 to 1965, nearly 70 percent of all black letters to Presidents Johnson and Kennedy centered on the importance of winning justice through appeals made to the American principles of universal rights, democracy, and equality (Lee 1997b). It is doubtful that such high proportions of the black population would think such appeals would be successful today. With such extreme amounts of dissatisfaction with American society, we should not be surprised that support increased for those ideologies, particularly black nationalism, which explicitly argue that the nation is racist and mistreats blacks. Given the organizational weaknesses of both black feminists and socialists, it is easy to see why black nationalism is enjoying more grassroots success than it has had in three-quarters of a century.

Figure 6.3   Smoothed Disillusioned Liberalism distribution using normal and
Epanechinikov estimators

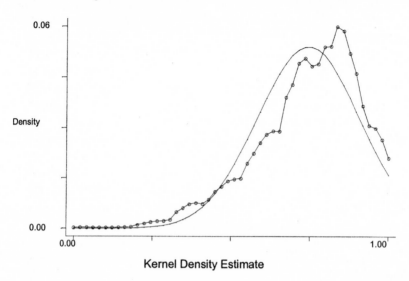

Kernel Density Estimate

	Observations	Mean	Std. Deviation	Minimum	Maximum
Disillusioned Liberalism	1,183	0.76	0.18	0	1

Source: 1993–1994 National Black Politics Survey

THE ANTECEDENTS AND THE
CONSEQUENCES OF BLACK LIBERALISMS

Who is more likely to support radical egalitarianism and oppose black conservatism? The same set of variables measuring the structural factors of social location, spatial situation, and ties to black information networks used
to model black ideologies in earlier chapters are once again included here.
The results are displayed in appendix table A2.1.

Antecedents

There is a small gender gap which helps predict support for radical
egalitarianism. As in other domains, black women on average are somewhat more progressive than black men (see Dawson 1994a for other ex-

amples). Those who believe their fate is linked to other blacks and those who believe that blacks fare less well economically than whites are both more likely to support the radical egalitarian policy agenda. Conversely, those who do not believe their fate is linked to that of the race are more likely to support the conservative end of the policy agenda. Support for radical liberalism is a product of a racialized world view. Neither one's individual social location, embeddedness in black information networks, education, nor age has any influence on one's level of support or rejection of black liberal ideologies. And radical egalitarianism is also not predicted by whether one is a member of black organizations. People's perception that their fate is tied to that of other black people and the economic status of blacks relative to whites is what drives black support for radical egalitarianism. Given both the high percentages of blacks who remain convinced that their fate is linked to that of the race as a whole and that whites are in a superior economic position, we should not be surprised by the strong support for the radical egalitarian agenda and the rejection of the black conservative platform.

Modeling disillusioned liberalism is considerably trickier. We must untangle the effects of disillusionment from those of racial progress. It seems reasonable to believe that one's perception of the possibility of gaining racial equality is related to one's belief in disillusioned liberalism. But what causal ordering should be used? My approach was to build a model in which each predicted the other (see table A2.15 for details). The standard set of control variables was used, but in addition I hypothesized that one's perception of how much racial progress has been or would be made also depended on whether one belonged to a black organization and whether one believed that the black movements of the 1960s had been helpful. Whether one believed that white people were inclined to see blacks get a break or be kept down, or whether they didn't care one way or the other was also used to predict how disillusioned one was. Not surprisingly, two of the strongest predictors of disillusioned liberalism were one's perception of relative black/white economic status and whether one felt one's fate was linked to that of the race. These are the same predictors that appeared earlier in the radical egalitarian/conservatism scale, a portion of which is incorporated in the disillusioned liberalism scale. One's assessment of white attitudes toward blacks also affects how disillusioned one is. The assessment of the likelihood of achieving racial equality within the United States, however, does not affect the likelihood of being a disillusioned liberal. On the other hand, being a disillusioned liberal greatly reduces the likelihood that one believes achieving racial equality in the United States is possible. Being a member of black organizations also leads one to have negative assessments.

As Sanders has predicted, those who perceive the interviewer to be black are more likely to voice disillusionment. Willingness to voice disillusionment is moderated by the racial context of the respondent. As the work of Harris-Lacewell (1999) predicts, discourse settings perceived as black produce anticonservative outcomes. According to Sanders, interracial settings produce moderation, while according to Harris-Lacewell, black settings produce anticonservatism. Both findings are supported by this research on disillusioned liberalism. Finally, more affluent blacks are likely to be pessimistic about the chances of winning racial equality in the United States.

This evidence suggests that the ideological orientation of disillusionment combined with egalitarian beliefs is largely responsible for driving many African Americans' pessimistic evaluations of the prospects for gaining racial justice. Social location has an indirect effect on perceptions of racial progress. More generally, however, the strongest direct effects leading to lack of faith in this nation's racial future flowed from a radical egalitarian ideology and embeddedness within black organizations, along with the presence of a strong racial consciousness.

Consequences

Black liberalisms have significantly less impact on public opinion and preferences than either black nationalism or black feminism. There are areas, however, where liberal ideology has broad, if moderate, impact. Where liberal ideology made a difference, black conservatives were likely to oppose the viewpoints of black feminists, while radical egalitarians were more likely to support the feminist position. For example, black conservatives were somewhat more likely to believe that women such as Jocelyn Elders and Lani Guinier were merely "troublemakers," while black feminists and egalitarians were more likely to believe that such black women leaders were being singled out. Black conservatives were also more likely to have negative feelings toward Anita Hill.

Black conservatives across the board opposed the views of black nationalists. They felt more warmly toward whites than other blacks, less warmth toward Minister Farrakhan of the Nation of Islam, and opposed the viewpoint that blacks should join black only organizations or form a separate political party. Further, black conservatives oppose both the nation-within-a nation and separate nation formulations discussed in chapter 3. The former is a particularly significant ideological effect, since 50 percent of the black community believe that blacks do indeed constitute a nation within the United States. Black conservatives are 20 percent less likely to support this view than radical egalitarians. Black conservatives are significantly more likely to reject nationalism than other blacks and more likely to feel more warmth towards whites than other blacks do. In political conflicts around black nationalism, conservatives and those who support independent black institutions are most likely to find themselves on opposite sides of the conflict.

Generally, though, black liberalism has a weak effect when compared to black nationalism or even black feminism in shaping blacks' general views toward American society. Black conservatives were more likely to uphold immigrants' right to obtain jobs on an equal basis with everyone else. In the last three chapters we saw that large shifts have occurred in black public opinion, particularly in the domain of nationalism. The simulations suggested that small to moderate shifts in support for black nationalism would have dramatic effects in reshaping black political attitudes and strategic orientations. Similar shifts in support for black feminist ideology would have much smaller though still noticeable effects. The same shifts, as displayed in Table A2.16, show that even large shifts in support on the radical egalitarian/black conservative spectrum would have minimal impact on many areas of black public opinion.

Are black liberals doomed to have a very small impact on the political preferences of the black community? No. But they would have to revamp their program and return to the grassroots to have a larger effect. Every other force is being out-organized by nationalist forces, although even they are having difficulty with long-range, sustained organizing efforts. The "victory" of radical egalitarians in public opinion polls, while substantial, misrepresents their ability to shape the contours of black politics. This major ideology, though widely supported, is least influential in shaping black opinion. Black nationalism powerfully shapes black opinion across domains, while feminism is a strong influence on black preferences within its own domain. Liberalism has become a weak force in shaping the politics of the black community, even though a large percentage of blacks support the radical egalitarian program. Radical egalitarians have lost control of the black agenda.

CONCLUSION: HAS LIBERALISM FAILED BLACKS?

What do we want? What is the thing we are after? As it was phrased last night, it has a certain truth: We want to be Americans, full-fledged Americans, with all the rights of other American citizens. But is that all? Do we simply want to be Americans? Once in a while through all of us

> there flashes some clairvoyance, some clear idea, of what America really
> is. We who are dark see America in a way that white Americans cannot.
> And seeing our country thus, are we satisfied with its present ideals?
>   —W. E. B. Du Bois, 1926

Black liberals face a variety of dilemmas as they look toward the racial politics of the twenty-first century. Their platform still enjoys more substantial support (at least the nonconservative branches) than any other ideology. As the enormous support for Jesse Jackson's platform in 1988 and
virtually all survey data demonstrate, African Americans still strongly support radical redistribution of wealth, they still see economic concerns as
central, they want to be able to function as full citizens, and black views
of citizenship include not only equal treatment before the law, which over
80 percent of blacks believe they do not receive, but economic rights as
well. Multiracial alliances are supported by the majority to gain these goals,
but at lower levels than in the 1980s. On the other hand, black nationalism is gaining adherents and political momentum. As important, perhaps,
the coherence of nationalism as an ideology strengthens its role in shaping black public opinion across a variety of domains. Levels of disillusionment are extremely high, and most blacks believe they are further from the
American Dream than they were a decade ago (Dawson 1997). More critical is the strong similarity in political preferences between disillusioned
liberals and community nationalists. Disillusionment stills seems to be a
marker of movement toward less liberal, more radical ideologies.

Liberalism itself has changed dramatically since its mid-century tri-
umphs. While we still have what Adolph Reed would argue is an over-
abundance of charismatic leaders, we have nothing approaching the level
of organizations that we have seen in the past. For perhaps the first time,
certainly for the first time since the height of the Garvey movement, black
nationalists are probably the best organized force in many black communities. The activism has gone out of radical egalitarianism. We have black
elected officials, black agency officials, and other elites who are in a medi-
ating position between the state and the black community, and while many
of them continue to embrace the values and political positions that have
made radical egalitarianism the most supported ideology, they are constrained by their positions, and the lack of an independent black or progressive movement.

At the same time as these political shifts have occurred, large sectors
of inner-city black communities have been devastated by the economic
shifts described in chapter 1 (see also Dawson 1994a, 1997). The economic

devastation of many black communities has profound political as well as social and economic implications. Cathy Cohen and I have shown that concentrated poverty is associated with a disastrous reduction in both mobilizational activity and organizational life in poor communities (Cohen and Dawson 1993). In some public housing projects in Chicago the employment rate has gone from a 10 percent unemployment rate in 1970 to a 25 percent unemployment rate in 1980 and a 4 percent *employment rate* in 1990 (Venkatesh 1993). In this set of projects the state and private institutions, including the black church, have withdrawn, and what remain are networks of mothers struggling to provide community childcare and fighting for tenants rights, and the gangs which provide employment and social services (including welfare and running the rec center). They constitute the real institutional power.

The liberalism of the mid-twentieth century is inadequate for the tasks at hand. While Bunche, King, Du Bois, and thousands of activists accurately portrayed the backlash that would occur, they did not foresee the size of the swing to the right, the devastation that globalization would wreak on the industrial and state sectors which provided the grounding for black economic stability, nor the rise of nihilistic forces of violence that would grow within the black community as a result of political and economic hope being dashed into the ground. They would certainly not have foreseen a situation where less than 1 percent of the offers to the 1997 class at the University of Texas Law School would be black and only another 2 percent would be Latino and in which no blacks would be present in the entering class.

And once again many white liberals and progressives are telling blacks to de-emphasize race. This is an argument that was made explicitly in 1992 on behalf of Clinton by several black politicians and intellectuals. But black liberals are faced not only with racial retrenchment but with the repudiation of the New Deal itself. This reminds too many blacks of that horrific period of American history between 1890 and 1935 when both racial and economic reaction reigned and when both political parties actively distanced themselves from blacks. Combine that with internal debates over gender issues and sexuality, new class divisions, and old divisions between black progressives and nationalists once again growing bitter and heated, and we can at least conclude that while liberalism may not have completely failed blacks, without a massive theoretical reworking, and equally massive organizational instantiation at the community level, radical liberalism will continue to lose political influence within the black community. Black radical liberalism will be seen as increasingly irrelevant to the future of black politics, while the American liberal tradition will be seen as increasingly hostile to the aspirations of blacks. Finally, radical egalitarians need to answer the question that Du Bois asked in 1926, which opens this section: What kind of Americans do they want to be? What kind of America do they want to offer the race and nation?

And the ranks of disillusioned liberals grow. Disillusioned liberalism has always been an unstable ideology. Its adherents, if they do not drop out, tend to move into one of the other ideological categories. There are fewer ideological choices, both abstractly and organizationally, than there were in the mid-1960s, when events ranging from the betrayal by the Democratic Party in 1964 to the firing of an assassin's bullet in April of 1968 drove many out of the camp of black liberalism. Various forms of black nationalism appear to provide increasingly attractive alternatives to the disillusioned. In a 1935 essay entitled "A Negro Nation within the Nation," Du Bois advocated a much more nationalist stance for African Americans because "the colored people of America are coming to face the fact quite calmly that white Americans do not like them, and are planning neither for their survival, nor for their definite future " (Du Bois 1971 [1935], 71). Sixty years later many disillusioned black liberals agreed with this somber assessment.

Black conservatives have even more of a problem than their radical (activist and disillusioned) cousins. African Americans' political behavior is still structured by their economic and racial preferences. In both arenas, blacks reject the black conservative agenda. No other ideology has such an abysmally low level of core supporters, nor such a dangerously high level of committed opponents. Some aspects of the black conservative agenda— the emphasis on self-reliance and some of the social conservatism—do have substantial mass support. But not only do most blacks rank racial and economic issues much higher than these in salience, even on these issues black conservatives must compete ideologically with a black nationalist ideology which is a more attractive package to many blacks is than black conservatism. More distressing for many black conservatives such as Glenn Loury and Robert Woodson, the conservative movement has taken a harsh, antiblack turn. When they have objected to this tendency within American conservatism, they have been viciously attacked by many of their former comrades (Loury 1998). Thus black conservatism may itself be dividing between an indigenous, even more isolated black wing populated by those such as Loury, Woodson, and perhaps Powell, and a staunchly libertarian wing led by those such as Sowell. Of the latter we can reasonably ask if there is anything distinguishably "black" about their conservatism. Given that their sometime allies in the Republican party are viewed by the great majority of blacks as extremely hostile to the interests of the black community (a factor that causes great distress to black conservatives), black conservatives of all stripes are the least likely ideologues to make major inroads in the immediate future.

Other black liberals need to ask themselves how can they regain the critical edge that propelled the proponents of radical egalitarianism and their organizations for so many decades. On the basis of their issue positions, black radical liberal leaders are by far closest to the remaining black socialists (most of whom have moved into the social democratic camp and should probably be viewed more as left liberals than Marxists) and black feminists. Both of these other ideological camps are more activist-oriented than the current mainstream of black radical egalitarians.

Jesse Jackson wondered if Colin Powell had taken too much "of the King's meat" to be still of the people (Gates 1997, 89). This is a question that all within the black liberal tradition need to ask themselves. What issues and interests could once again inclusively mobilize large segments of the black community? What are the policy recommendations and political strategies that will once again address the needs of those at the bottom of the ladder, not just those striving toward the top? The best radical egalitarians of the past were focused on building a movement around the needs of the despised and dispossessed. Are black liberals willing to do so once again?

Further, for the radical egalitarians to continue their leadership role, they must rethink their views on the role of gender in constructing a "black" agenda, alliances with other groups, the internal economic divisions within the black community, and what stance they are going to take regarding a global economy that is further dispossessing large segments of the black community. Perhaps most traumatically, black liberals' relationships to an increasingly conservative Democratic party would have to be put back on the agenda. The problems that face black liberals are similar to those that face all of the adherents to each of the ideologies analyzed here. If any of them are to become truly popular forces within the black community and the polity more generally, ideological reevaluation within the black community on a scale that has not been seen since the turn of the last century is a critical but necessary task.

I feel that for white America to understand the significance of the problem of the Negro will take a bigger and tougher America than any we have yet know. I feel that America's past is too shallow, her national character too superficially optimistic, her very morality too suffused with color hate for her to accomplish so vast and complex a task. Culturally the Negro presents a paradox: though he is an organic part of the nation, he is excluded by the entire tide and direction of American culture.

—Richard Wright

CHAPTER 7

Conclusion: The Future Evolution of Black Political Thought, Black Politics, and American Political Thought

Black ideological visions have structured black political discourse, invigorated oppositional black protest movements, and caused bitter internal conflicts throughout African-American history. The history of black political movements has been the rare one where "let a hundred flowers bloom, let a thousand schools of thought contend" has not been simply an abstract principle, but instead the practical norm. *Which* ideologies are influential in a given period changes radically across historical periods, though radical egalitarianism is generally the most strongly supported ideology. Black nationalism provides the most consistent challenge to liberal hegemony within the black community. Collectively, all black ideological visions except the weakly supported black conservatism have challenged the myth of the America as the "just and good" state in virtually all historical periods.

Black ideological visions continue to structure black public opinion and politics despite what public opinion theorists might predict. Black community nationalism most strongly structures black public opinion, although a disillusioned radical egalitarianism is the most heavily supported ideology. Each ideology is tied in different degrees to black informational networks and organizations. Black community nationalism is the ideology that has the strongest effect on black public opinion precisely because it is most strongly tied to black information networks and black organizations. The ties between black ideologies have also shifted somewhat, as seen in figure 7.1. Strong ties exist between radical egalitarianism and disillusioned liberalism, radical egalitarianism and black social democracy (formally black Marxism), and disillusioned liberalism and community nationalism (the most popular mass form of nationalism at the end of the twentieth century). But the paths out of disillusioned liberalism in this era most often lead to community nationalism or apathy in these times and less often to a more socialist or feminist alternative, as they had a generation earlier. The weak ties between community nationalism and black feminism are maintained mostly by black women who see themselves as "womanists," some of whom continue to work within nationalist-oriented organizations. The nationalist revival of the 1990s is reflected by the fact that the nationalists have at least some of their perspectives advanced by representatives of all of the ideological camps. What has not changed is the relative isolation of black conservatism.

Another change reflected in figure 7.1 is that both the black nationalist and black Marxist traditions have evolved into less militant, more pragmatic, and less ideologically "pure" versions. Neither a separate black state nor proletarian revolution are on the agenda of community nationalists or social democrats. The evolution has been more radical for the former black Marxist tradition to the degree that they should probably by and large be considered part of the liberal camp. But there are still significant differences between them and the radical egalitarians. The new black social democrats remain critical and suspicious of corporate power and the Democratic party, and they still put at the center of their program the championing of the economically dispossessed. The same cannot be said to be true of the radical egalitarians, whose leaders often sit on corporate boards, are often close to the elites of the Democratic party (even though they retain a critical stance toward the party), and champion the advancement of the interests of less and more affluent African Americans. Most of the ideological categories are weaker than they were in the early and middle decades of the twentieth century. This weakness is a result, in part, to the new conditions

Figure 7.1   Ties between black ideologies, 2000

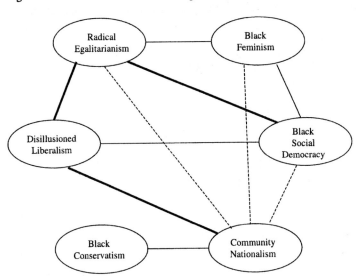

that black activists and ideologues have faced since the concluding decades of the twentieth century.

BLACK IDEOLOGICAL CHALLENGES
AT THE END OF THE TWENTIETH CENTURY

In his 1995 book, *Beyond Black and White*, Manning Marable lists some grim statistics which show the devastation suffered by some segments of the black population in the 1990s. Equally disturbing was that, on a number of indicators, black life chances had declined. Black male life expectancy has gone down, as has the percentage of high school graduates between the ages of nineteen and twenty-five who continue on to college. The number of young black males involved with the criminal justice system had become a catastrophe by the early 1990s. Marable and Mullings explain, "By 1992, 23 percent of all young African-American men between the ages of twenty and twenty-nine were in prison, on probation, parole, or awaiting trial. In New York City alone, the percentage of young black men within the penal and criminal justice system was 31 percent" (Marable and Mullings 1995, 204). Discrimination in a number of consumer markets reflected the intersection of racial and gender orders. Black women paid a thousand dollars more for a new car, audit studies show, than white men. Black men paid $400 less than black women though $300 more than white women, who paid

$200 more than white men. Marable understandably is most distressed about the situation in which we find black and Latino children. One in twelve black children will live in a homeless shelter over the next five years, according to Marable. Sixty percent of preschool children are not immunized, and there are only ninety-six nurses for the six hundred elementary schools in New York (Marable and Mullings 1995). On a variety of additional indicators, many blacks and Latinos are suffering increasing hardship.

Indeed, the similar social location of blacks and Latinos led a majority of these two groups to believe that not enough was being done to remedy the situation in which people of color found themselves, while at the same time half of whites thought their racial group was harmed by affirmative action. These findings by Marable parallel my own findings about how the racial order structures perceptions or racial interests, which in turn structure public opinion on racial policy (Dawson 1997; Marable 1995e). On these and other issues, blacks and Latinos find themselves closer to each other than to whites. On the other hand, Marable and others detail how many black and Latino elites see the relationship between blacks and Latinos as conflictual and zero-sum (what one group gets must come at the expense of the other). For reasons of their own self-interest and because of a narrow vision, each group's elites are failing to build the political coalitions that, to Marable at least, seem "natural." Certainly some black elites and many grassroots African Americans support job policies that favor native-born blacks over immigrants. The consequence is that in many locales blacks are in political conflict with those who would seem to have the most similar social location and political preferences.

An additional consequence of the conditions which face black activists is that most blacks still believe that Wright was bitterly prophetic when he stated (in the epigraph that opens the chapter) that America lacks commitment to racial equality. Remember that 65 percent of African Americans during the middle 1990s believed that racial progress in America would either not be achieved in their lifetime or would never be achieved at all. By late 2000 this percentage had climbed to 71 percent (from data compiled by the author). In the face of this level of disillusionment, black activists and ideologues face three additional extremely daunting problems. First, the changes in the political economy of the black community mean that conditions are dramatically worsening for some black Americans but improving for others. This has led not just to growing class divisions. As Cohen (1999) details, among others, these divisions are not confined to ones of class; black politics is fracturing along the many lines of social cleavage. The result, claims Marable (as I did in my earlier work), is that "many of the social, economic, and cultural linkages which previously connected various social classes and organizations began to erode" (Marable and Mullings 1995, 204; see also Dawson 1994a). These bridging organizations have been undermined in many cases by having to cope with a hostile political environment and occasionally by the self-interested strategies chosen by their leaders. Political unity, which has been achieved in the past even without ideological unity, will be increasingly difficult to achieve given the class, gender, and generational divisions that are becoming increasingly prominent. Second, the rest of country has moved much more profoundly to the right than the black community, leaving a political environment and establishment that is hostile even to just claims of either racial or economic redistribution and justice. Third, the growing magnitude of problems facing the black community and the simultaneous dwindling of political opportunities has led to widespread dissatisfaction with the racial status quo and significant dissatisfaction with the economic status quo. The result has been a resurgence in both nationalism and liberal disillusionment that makes it more difficult to build political movements and coalitions, both within the black community and between the black community and other communities.

DISCORD AND A SHARED HERITAGE:
BLACK IDEOLOGIES AND AMERICAN POLITICAL THOUGHT

Under these difficult conditions, which ideologies do African Americans support? Despite the protestations of the Thernstroms, black political thought as instantiated in today's black grassroots still stands in opposition to the current dominant understanding of the American Creed.[1] With all the ideological diversity to be found among African Americans, the small-government, free-market-oriented, libertarian-oriented society that dominates Washington as well as much of the electorate is decisively rejected. There is diffuse support for black liberalism, and strong support across ideologies for a jobs-based social safety net. There is also strong anticorporate sentiment among African Americans. The young are more likely to look toward black autonomy, while those with fewer resources are both more likely to view the world through a pro-autonomy as well as a radical, class-oriented, anticorporate lens. The poor are not feminists; both personal and community poverty reinforce antifeminist attitudes. Black consciousness,

---

1. See my review of the Thernstroms' book, *America in Black and White*, for a more thorough dissection of their views on America's racial history (Dawson 1998; Thernstrom and Thernstrom 1997).

however, as measured by how closely you feel your fate is tied to that of the race, does reinforce black feminism as well as community nationalism, black Marxism, and radical and disillusioned liberalism.

What this suggests is that the future of ideological conflict and cooperation within the black community is highly unstable. One of the most supported ideologies, disillusioned liberalism, is highly unstable and (at least in this period) has similar effects on public opinion as does community nationalism. If the nationalist resurgence continues, we can expect a more hostile orientation toward the police and immigrants, and support for building strong, independent political and civic black organizations. Certainly the organizers of the Million Man March wish to build ideological support in this direction. If, on the other hand, a broad coalition of black radicals, including black feminists, radical egalitarians, and some nationalists, is successfully built, then we could expect a progressive black community to aggressively seek alliances with other disadvantaged groups and generally support the building of strong, independent, black organizations. The organizers of the Black Radical Congress are attempting to build a movement around such a program. There was strong sentiment at their founding congress (June 1998) and in the debates that occurred both before and after to set aside ideological differences in order to build an inclusive, black, progressive movement. Like the Million Man March program (see chapter 3), which synthesized the strands of modern black nationalism, the program of the Black Radical Congress (BRC) represents a synthesis of several tendencies within modern black radicalism. The call from the Congress's Principles of Unity illustrates the diverse sources for this organizing trend and ideological combination:

> The Black Radical Congress will convene to establish a "center without walls" for transformative politics that will focus on the conditions of Black working and poor people. Recognizing contributions from diverse tendencies within Black Radicalism—including socialism, revolutionary nationalism, and feminism—we are united in opposition to all forms of oppression, including class exploitation, racism, patriarchy, homophobia, anti-immigration prejudice, and imperialism. (Black Radical Congress 1998, 1)

While its socialist roots are recognizable, the opposition to homophobia and patriarchy (which were not uncontroversial in the organizing that led to the meeting) and the openness to some nationalist tendencies mark a significant difference from the dogmatic black Marxism of the 1970s and early 1980s. On the other hand, just as many black feminists felt excluded by the Million Man March and its program, some nationalists felt excluded from the Black Radical Congress, even though serious attempts were made to include nationalists at both the local and national levels.

The least likely ideological possibility would be increased support for black conservatism, although growing class divisions and the increasing isolation of some segments of the middle class may enhance this possibility. There are some anecdotal accounts of growing conservatism among the new black middle class, but more evident than an ingrained conservatism is a widespread willingness to experiment in a search for alternatives to the perceived failure of the policies of *both* major political parties. This is particularly true in the realm of education, where the collapse of many urban public school systems has left black youth and their families severely disadvantaged in a global economy which places a heavy premium on the ability to manipulate, analyze, and acquire information and penalizes those who lack the necessary skills and resources. Even the electoral arena shows increasing evidence of black restlessness as support for the Democratic Party appears to be softening, and even local green candidates in cities such as Oakland are able to garner significant black support. If any of the ideologies are to gain support, their followers need to rebuild the black public sphere that was the grounding for the ideological flowering within black civil society for most of the twentieth century.

RECONSTRUCTING PUBLIC SPHERES: THE NEED FOR A DEMOCRATIC DEBATE ON RACE

There is a disjunction, however, between all of the ideologies and strong, mass institutional grounding in the black community, with the apparent exception of community nationalism. Only support for community nationalism is grounded in being tied to both black information networks and membership in black organizations. Black feminism and disillusioned liberalism are both grounded in black information networks, but not in organizational membership. Community nationalism, black radicalism, and radical egalitarianism all lead to greater political participation. While we might expect that being a disillusioned liberal does not encourage one's participation, it is surprising that a feminist orientation does not lead to greater participation (see appendix table A2.21). While leading representatives from *all* of the ideologies are committed to building a strong grassroots base, the radical egalitarians and the nationalists are in the best organizational position to do so.

But building a mass base is not sufficient. One of the planks from the BRC "Principles of Unity" included the following language: "We must be democratic and inclusive in our dealings with one another" (Black Radical Congress 1998). To do so, however, means rebuilding a black counterpublic that allows people to air differences of opinion honestly and vigorously without worrying about having their "blackness" questioned. To build a successful political movement requires more. It means building overlapping counterpublics and public spheres which reach across the racial and other divisions that plague the American political landscape. It will also take considerably more than black willingness to engage in democratic debate about the nature and future of the country. It will require two components that have been sadly lacking from the political landscape. First, political leaders must be willing to engage in a dialogue concerning race without either ducking and not engaging or resorting to race-baiting in order to gain votes. Second, white Americans in particular must be willing both to engage in such a debate and to seriously question the sources of their privilege as well as the legacy of white supremacy. As Martin Luther King Jr. remarked thirty years ago, black nationalist resurgence is a reaction to the lack of active goodwill on the part of white America when it comes to matters of race and economics.

We must finally ask whether African Americans can rely on a totalizing ideology to shape our visions of black justice and our future in America. My answer is no. I believe we need a more flexible approach than ideologies such as black Marxism, black nationalism, and at least the Cold War version of liberalism have allowed. We need a black critical theory that draws on and combines liberalism's concern with individual rights and autonomy, republican concerns with community, socialist concern with an egalitarian society and economic justice for all, feminist traditions such as resistance to suppressing intragroup differences in the name of a false and oppressive unity, and blends these with recognition of the need for autonomous organization and cultural pride. No single world view or ideology comfortably accommodates all of these. But a critical theory can—and such a theory must be *political*. We've had a black aesthetic, black power, and a plethora of black public policy pronouncements. But a black *political* theory has to embody a theory of the state, power, human nature, and the good life. And such a theory must be based on the hope for and potential of the improvement of human nature while recognizing the wickedness of the world. Kantian pronouncements about systems that can be governed by devils have led us to a world where ethnic strife and nuclear and other horrors proliferate. We must strive for something better, something democratic, something cosmopolitan, not in the elite sense but in the sense that, since homogeneity is a thing of the past, even within states, we must fall back on our basic humanness.

It is no coincidence that within American political thought this perspective appears most often in the black traditions and in black political thought, at least in the contemporary period—most often in the black feminist tradition. Thus the best legacy of black political ideologies for America is a tough, activist, inclusive democracy willing to challenge privileges of power and resources in the name of a grander vision which asserts that we are more than the mere aggregation of our individual preferences. Its morality, while democratic, would not be based on the latest consumer fad nor use the return to stockholders as the final arbiter of the public good. That we often fail in living up to our standards of justice within black activism as well as within America—that we are imperfect as individuals and as communities—does not mean, as King so eloquently demonstrated, that the vision itself is not a worthy goal. What black critical theory and each black ideology have demonstrated is that the doable, the mundane, incremental reform of the workings of American society is not enough; only the full promise of America has the potential to be truly liberating. Any other solution is not only unsatisfactory—it is likely to provoke the kind of deadly conflict most clearly seen in the Civil War but also seen today in the rapid upward spiral of political and personal violence which results as people measure their circumstances against what they see as the lies that fester at the center of the American Dream. A new, black, critical theory needs to retain one aspect of black ideological visions. At the heart of all of the black visions is a sense of pragmatic optimism combined with a steadfast determination to gain black justice. Both the optimism and the determination are needed now as ever to sustain the political projects and new visions of African Americans.

Epilogue

There has been a presidential election in the few years since I first wrote the conclusion to this chapter. This train wreck of an election once again brought to light the deep racial divisions that run through American politics. More than 90 percent of African Americans voted against the current sitting president—George W. Bush.[2] On a scale where 100 equals warmth

2. See chapter 6, note 6, for a description of the data analyzed by the author for this section.

and 0 equals cold, President-elect Bush was rated at a frigid 28 by African-American respondents. Of even more concern, 92 percent of African Americans believe that the president does not represent their interests, with fully a fifth believing that he is actively opposed to their interests. The depth of black pessimism as well as the depth of the division between black and white political attitudes often comes as a great shock to observers outside of the black community. This is partly because the levels of political pessimism and racial division *should* be found shocking by concerned citizens. But the surprising nature of the shock has roots in the fact that a good deal of black ideological politics lies both outside of the bounds of discourse and out of sight of "mainstream" American politics. Debates within the liberal family of ideologies may seem somewhat familiar to white Americans. Debates between the liberal camp and black nationalists, feminists, and social democrats are mostly unobserved. Thus we are likely to see political battles over issues such as reparations and voter intimidation intensify. Debates over reparations for African Americans are now part of the discourse on college campuses, in city councils, and in elite national discourse. At the time of the 2000 election, our survey data showed very deep racial divisions on this issue. Our data similarly showed deep racial divisions on the importance of perceived efforts to disenfranchise black voters This is an issue that is not only taking root in Florida and the South but also in Northern states such as Illinois.

What should not seem surprising is that at the turn of the century African Americans continue to believe that American democracy is broken—and the 2000 presidential elections did nothing to convince blacks that the nation was on the road to recovery. African Americans are still waiting for black visions of a just and egalitarian society to become American visions. It increasingly clear, though, that many African Americans fear that Malcolm X was right when he worried that blacks held a vision of freedom larger than America is prepared to accept.

This appendix provides documentation for the analyses done in the main text. It consists of three parts. The first is a brief disclaimer about two documents used in chapter 3. Part 2 provides a brief description of the study. Part 3 presents the tables that support the quantitative analyses. This section includes table A1.1, which provides a listing of question wording and coding for the variables used in the study. Tables A2.1–2.21 are the tables of estimation described in the text. Tables A3.1 and A3.2 describe the scale properties for the scales used in the estimation chapters. Finally, tables A4.1 and 4.2 compare the demographic data from the U.S. Census for blacks to the sample characteristics.

DOCUMENTS A AND B

Documents A and B are from two prominent nationalist organizations which participated in the National Black United Front during the late 1970s and early 1980s. They were not public documents. For purposes of confidentiality, identifying information has been removed.

THE DATA

The analyses that follow use survey responses from the 1993–1994 National Black Politics Study (NBPS). The data for the NBPS was obtained from a probability sample of all black households: 1,206 telephone interviews were completed, each one lasting approximately forty-five minutes. To be eligible, respondents had to be both black and eighteen years old or older. The survey was conducted between November 20, 1993, and

February 20, 1994. The response rate was 65 percent.[1] The two main substantive foci of the study were providing instrumentation for the analysis of the relationships between black ideologies and their determinants and consequences, and the relationship of black worship to black public opinion. A split-sample design was used to draw the sample. Half of the sample was drawn using random digit dial (RDD). The second half was drawn using high-quality, frequently updated lists of the African-American population residing in neighborhoods with at least a moderate concentration of blacks. Table A4.2 shows very strong evidence that the difference in subsamples did not affect the attitudinal distribution. The very low number of correlations found after pairwise correlations were taken of all of the attitudinal variables is what one would expect due to random patterns in the data. Also as expected, there were some differences between the census demographic profiles and that of each subsample. As usual in household surveys of non-institutionalized African Americans which use computer-aided telephone interviews (CATI), a disproportionate percentage of the sample is composed of women. The figure of 65 percent is consistent with that found in similar survey studies. Also, as is often the case with telephone studies, the sample population is older and better educated. As I have indicated in earlier work, telephone surveys of the African-American population tend to somewhat attenuate both the high and low ends of the income distribution (Dawson 1994a). Not surprisingly, the two subsamples differ slightly in that one is better at picking up the high end of the income distribution and the other the low end.

1. The principal investigators were Ronald Brown of Wayne State University and Michael Dawson of the University of Chicago. The study was administered through the University of Chicago. The Russell Sage Foundation provided a generous grant for the collection of the data. The data are now being processed for archiving.

THE TABLES

Table A1.1   Frequencies of Black Visions categorical variables

Variables	Value Label	Valid Percent
Gender	1 = Female	35.2
Valid cases 1,206 Missing cases 00	0 = Male	56.8
Tied to Black Organizations		
Are you a member of any organization	0 = No	70.2
working to improve the status of	1 = Yes	29.8
black Americans?		
Valid cases 1,203 Missing cases 03		
Interviewer		
Is interviewer perceived as white?	0 = No	78.5
Valid cases 1,190 Missing cases 16	1 = Yes	21.5
Black/White Economic Differences	1 = Much worse	37.2
Do you think blacks are economically	.75 = Somewhat worse	33.8
worse off than whites?	.5 = About same	24
	.25 = Somewhat better	3.6
Valid cases 1,170 Missing cases 36	0 = Much better	1.4
Black Linked Fate		
Do you think your fate is linked to	1 = Highly linked	36.2
that of black people?	.67 = Somewhat linked	31.7
	.33 = Barely linked	9.8
Valid cases 1,147 Missing cases 59	0 = Not linked	22.3
Separate Nation	0 = Strongly disagree	28.6
Black people should have their	.33 = Disagree	57.4
own separate nation?	.67 = Agree	9.0
Valid cases 1,168 Missing cases 38	0 = Strongly agree	5.0
Black Nation		
Black people form a nation within	0 = No	48.3
a nation?	1 = Yes	51.7
Valid cases 1,036 Missing cases 170		
Black-Only Organizations		
Blacks should participate in black-only	0 = Strongly disagree	8.8
organizations whenever possible?	.33 = Disagree	34.9
	.67 = Agree	35.8
Valid cases 1,185 Missing cases 21	1 = Strongly agree	20.6

Table A1.1 (continued)

Variables	Value Label	Valid Percent
Louis Farrakhan Positive		
Louis Farrakhan represents a positive viewpoint in the black community?	0 = No 1 = Yes	30.9 69.1
Valid cases 835 Missing cases 371		
Black Political Party		
Blacks should form their own political party?	0 = No 1 = Yes	50.0 50.0
Valid cases 1,129 Missing cases 77		
African Homeland		
Africa is a special homeland for all black people, including blacks in the U.S.?	0 = No 1 = Yes	68.7 31.3
Valid cases 1,085 Missing cases 121		
Abortion	1 = Yes	57.8
Support abortion?	.67 = When need established	7.5
	.33 = In extreme cases	23.8
Valid cases 1,181 Missing cases 25	0 = No	10.8
AIDS		
AIDS is a result of an antiblack conspiracy?	0 = No 1 = Yes	73.9 26.1
Valid cases 1,022 Missing cases 184		
Black Women Leaders Attacked		
There is a strong tendency in American society to attack and silence strong black women such as Attorney Anita Hill and Justice Department candidate Lani Guinier?	0 = No 1 = Yes	19.0 81.0
Valid cases 964 Missing cases 242		
Black Representation		
White officials elected from predominantly black communities represent black interests just as well as black elected officials?	1 = No 0 = Yes	64.7 35.3
Valid cases 1,049 Missing cases 157		

Variables	Value Label	Valid Percent
Corporations Unfair		
America's big corporations are unfair	0 = No	25.8
to the black community?	1 = Yes	74.2
Valid cases 1,068 Missing cases 138		
Political vs. Economic Rights		
Gaining political rights such as the	1 = No	52.2
vote have been most important for	0 = Yes	47.8
black progress?		
Valid cases 1,104 Missing cases 102		
Racial Equality	1 = No, and never will	23.2
Blacks have achieved racial equality?	.67 = No, not in my lifetime	41.7
	.33 = No, but will soon	30.5
Valid cases 1,157 Missing cases 49	0 = Yes	4.7
Problems Linked		
The problems of racism, poverty		
and sexual discrimination are all	0 = No	27.5
linked together and must be addressed	1 = Yes	72.5
by the black community?		
Valid cases 1,085 Missing cases 121		
Government Should Provide Job/Living		
Some people feel that the government		
in Washington should see to it that	0 = No	34.2
every person has a job and a good	1 = Yes	65.8
standard of living?		
Valid cases 1,147 Missing cases 59		
Political Allies		
Latinos, Asian-Americans, and other	1 = No	54.5
disadvantaged groups are potentially	0 = Yes	45.5
good political allies for blacks?		
Valid cases 1,027 Missing cases 179		
Immigrants		
Jobs should go first to blacks that		
are out of work and other Americans	0 = No	30.5
experiencing economic difficulty	1 = Yes	69.5
before they go to today's immigrants		
from places like Haiti, Mexico,		
and Korea?		
Valid cases 1,107 Missing cases 99		

Table A1.1   (continued)

Variables	Value Label	Valid Percent
Democratic Party	0 = Very hard	17.7
Democratic party works hard on	.33 = Fairly hard	50.6
black issues?	.67 = Not too hard	21.9
Valid cases 1,156 Missing cases 50	1 = Not hard at all	9.8
Republican Party	0 = Very hard	3.7
Republican party works hard on	.33 = Fairly hard	13.5
black issues?	.67 – Not too hard	34.2
Valid cases 1,129 Missing cases 77	1 = Not hard at all	48.6
Police		
The police are too much like	0 = No	48.8
just another gang to stop gang	1 = Yes	51.2
violence?		
Valid cases 1,082 Missing cases 124		
Active Church Member		
Aside from attending services,	No	45.2
are you an active member in your	Yes	54.8
place of worship?		
Valid cases 919 Missing cases 287		
Religiosity		
Does religion provide guidance in	Some	32.2
your life?	A great deal	67.8
Valid Cases 1,087 Missing cases 119		
Female Clergy		
Black churches should allow	0 = No	21.75
more women to become members	1 = Yes	78.25
of the clergy?		
Valid cases 1,140 Missing cases 66		
Black Male Linked Fate	1 = Highly linked	45.7
Do you think your fate is linked	.67 = Somewhat linked	22.8
to that of black men?	.33 = Barely linked	7.6
Valid cases 1,160 Missing cases 44	0 = Not linked	23.9
Black Women Linked Fate	1 = Highly linked	44.8
Do you think your fate is linked	.67 = Somewhat linked	26.1
to that of black women?	.33 = Barely linked	7.2
Valid cases 1,162 Missing cases 44	0 = Not linked	21.9

Variables	Value Label	Valid Percent
Non-White Women Linked Fate	1 = Highly linked	21.2
Do you think your fate is linked	.67 = Somewhat linked	35.8
to that of non-white women?	.33 = Barely linked	7.2
Valid cases 751 Missing cases 455	0 = Not linked	35.8
Women Linked Fate	1 = Highly linked	40.8
Do you think your fate is linked	.67 = Somewhat linked	33.2
to that of women?	.33 = Barely linked	7.3
Valid cases 763 Missing cases 443	0 = Not linked	18.7
White Women Linked Fate	1 = Highly linked	19.3
Do you think your fate is linked	.67 = Somewhat linked	32.9
to that of women?	.33 = Barely linked	6.9
Valid cases 755 Missing cases 451	0 = Not linked	40.9
Black Movement	0 = No	29.0
Black rights movement has	.33 = Not very much	5.2
influenced my life?	.67 = Some	23.4
Valid cases 1,181 Missing cases 125	1 = Yes, a lot	42.5
Exposure to Rap		
Have you in the past year listened	1 = No	52.3
to rap music?	0 = Yes	47.7
Valid cases 1,206 Missing cases 00		
Rap Destructive		
Rap music is a destructive force	1 = No	39.1
in the black community?	0 = Yes	60.9
Valid cases 961 Missing cases 245		
Black Women Divide		
Black feminist groups divide the	0 = No	30.9
black community?	1 = Yes	69.1
Valid cases 1,012 Missing cases 194		
African Language	1 = Strongly disagree	4.4
Black children should study an	.67 = Disagree	24.9
African language?	.33 = Agree	44.8
Valid cases 1,169 Missing cases 37	0 = Strongly agree	25.9
Academies	1 = Strongly disagree	8.8
Support black male academies?	.67 = Disagree	29.0
	.33 = Agree	36.5
Valid cases 1,144 Missing cases 62	0 = Strongly agree	25.7

Table A1.1   (continued)

Variables	Value Label	Valid Percent
Public Official or Agency		
Contacted a public official or agency?	0 = No	65.3
Valid Cases 1,205 Missing cases 01	1 = Yes	34.7
Protest Meeting/Demonstration		
Attended a protest meeting/	0 = No	70.8
demonstration?	1 = Yes	29.2
Valid cases 1,205 Missing cases 01		
Neighborhood March		
Taken part in a neighborhood march?	0 = No	77.1
Valid cases 1,204 Missing cases 02	1 = Yes	22.9
Petition I		
Signed a petition in support of/	0 = No	39.5
against something?	1 = Yes	60.5
Valid cases 1,204 Missing cases 02		
Talked about Political Issues		
Talked to family/friends about	0 = No	9.7
political issues?	1 = Yes	90.3
Valid cases 1,206 Missing Cases 00		
Registration Drive		
Helped in a voter registration drive?	0 = No	77.0
Valid cases 1,203 Missing cases 03	1 = Yes	23.0
Rides to Election Polls		
Gave people rides to election polls?	0 = No	74.8
Valid cases 1,203 Missing cases 02	1 = Yes	25.2
Gave Money		
Gave money to political candidates?	0 = No	75.8
Valid cases 1,202 Missing cases 02	1 = Yes	24.2
Fund-Raiser		
Attended a fund-raiser for a candidate?	0 = No	73.1
Valid cases 1,202 Missing cases 04	1 = Yes	26.9
Campaign Materials		
Distributed campaign materials?	0 = No	77.2
Valid cases 1,201 Missing cases 05	1 = Yes	22.8

Variables	Value Label	Valid Percent
Petition II		
Signed a petition supporting a candidate for office?	0 = No 1 = Yes	58.1 41.9
Valid cases 1,201 Missing cases 05		

Source: Compiled by M. Dawson from 1993–94 National Black Politics Survey. Estimates were derived using *Stata Statistical Software*.
Note: All Black Visions variables with values of 5 or less are presented in this table.

Table A2.1   Structure, racial identification, and black ideologies

	Ideological Orientation				
Variable	Autonomy Coefficient (SE)	Feminism Coefficient (SE)	Marxism Coefficient (SE)	Radical Egalitarianism (SE)	Disillusioned Liberalism (SE)
Do you think blacks are economically worse off than whites? (0 = no)	.08* (.03)	.10* (.03)	.18* (.02)	.07* (.03)	.18* (.03)
Do you think your fate is linked to that of black people? (0 = no)	.07* (.02)	.05* (.02)	—	.05* (.02)	.05* (.02)
Gender (0 = male)	—	.05* (.02)	—	.03* (.02)	.02* (.01)
Family income	—	.07* (.03)	−.04** (.02)	—	—
Age	−.08* (.03)	−.06** (.04)	—	—	—
Education	—	.01* (.00)	—	—	—
Tied to black information networks (0 = weak ties)	.14* (.03)	.08* (.04)	—	—	.08* (.03)

Table A2.1   (continued)

Variable	Autonomy Coefficient (SE)	Feminism Coefficient (SE)	Marxism Coefficient (SE)	Radical Egalitarianism (SE)	Disillusioned Liberalism (SE)
			Ideological Orientation		
Percentage of blacks in census tract	—	—	—	—	—
Census tract poverty	—	−.04** (.02)	−.04* (.02)	—	—
Is interviewer perceived as white? (0 = no)	−.03** (.02)	—	−.05* (.02)	—	−.07* (.01)
Tied to black organizations (0 = no)	.03* (.01)	—	—	—	—
Constant	.52* (.05)	.54* (.06)	.57* (.05)	.59* (.05)	.57* (.04)
n	946	936	938	936	936
adjusted R^2	0.108	0.083	0.067	0.026	0.126
Root MSE	0.186	0.231	0.191	0.210	0.167

F-tests of Social Location Variables

H_0 = Income = Education = Census Tract Poverty = 0^1

Ideological orientation	Autonomy	Feminism	Marxism	Radical Egalitarianism	Disillusioned Liberalism
F(d.f. denominator, d.f. numerator)	$F_{(3,924)}$ = 0.10	$F_{(3,924)}$ = 8.62	$F_{(3,926)}$ = 1.89	$F_{(3,924)}$ = 0.63	$F_{(3,924)}$ = 0.45
Prob > F	0.958	0.000	0.129	0.593	.719

Source: 1993–94 National Black Politics Survey. Estimates were derived using *Stata Statistical Software*.
[1]H_0, the null hypothesis, is rejected at the .05 level of significance. A rejection of the null hypothesis implies that the slope coefficients of the social location variables are not all simultaneously zero. Dash denotes not statistically significant at the .05 or .10 levels.
*Denotes statistically significant at the .05 level.
**Denotes statistically significant at the .10 level.

Table A2.2   **Determinants of support for conceptions of a black nation**

Variable	(Support Separate Nation? (0 = strongly disagree)		Blacks Form a Nation within a Nation (0 = no)	
Black autonomy	.38 (9.10)	◆	.24* (2.55)	◆
Do you think blacks are economically worse off than whites? (0 = no)	—	—	—	—
Do you think your fate is linked to that of black people? (0 = no)	—	—	—	—
Gender (0 = male)	−.06 (−3.73)	−.07 (−3.80)	—	—
Family income	−.09 (−2.99)	−.12 (−2.92)	−.17* (−2.75)	−.17* (−2.76)
Age	—	−.12 (−3.07)	—	—
Education	—	—	−.01* (−2.21)	−.01* (−2.22)
Tied to black information networks (0 = weak ties)	—	.07 (1.66)	.22* (2.52)	.25* (2.90)
Percentage of blacks in census tract	—	—	—	—
Census tract poverty	—	—	—	—
Is interviewer perceived as white? (0 = no)	—	−.04 (−1.87)	—	—
Tied to black organizations (0 = no)	.04 (2.32)	—	.12* (3.02)	.11* (2.81)

Table A2.2   (continued)

Variable	(Support Separate Nation? (0 = strongly disagree)		Blacks Form a Nation within a Nation (0 = no)	
Constant	.24	.44	−.09	.24
	(3.72)	(7.08)	(−0.24)	(0.73)
n	923	924	844	844
adjusted R^2/χ^2 (df)	0.121	0.043	46.15 (12)	39.62 (11)
Root MSE/Log likelihood	0.236	0.247	−560.08	−563.35

Source: Compiled by M. Dawson from 1993–94 National Black Politics Survey. Estimates were derived using *Stata Statistical Software*.

Note: Dash denotes coefficient was not statistically discernible from zero at the .10 level.

*Each unstarred cell contains an unstandardized OLS coefficient. Starred cells contain probabilities derived from probit estimates. These probabilities represent the percentage change in probability as one moves from the minimum value of the independent variable to the maximum value. In all cells, numbers within parentheses are the ratio of the unstandardized coefficient to the standard error.

♦ Cells containing this symbol indicate that the black autonomy measure is not included in the analysis for comparative purposes. The sets of structural and racial identity variables alone are employed as determinants.

Table A2.3   **The effects of structure and racial identification on support for economic nationalism**

Variable	Economic Nationalism
Do you think blacks are economically worse off than whites? (0 = no)	.49* (.12)
Do you think your fate is linked to that of black people? (0 = no)	.29* (.07)
Gender (0 = male)	—
Family income	.17** (.09)
Age	—
Education	—
Tied to black information networks (0 = weak ties)	.58* (.13)
Percentage of blacks in census tract	—
Census tract poverty	—
Variable	**Economic Nationalism**
Is interviewer perceived as white? (0 = no)	.12* (.06)
Tied to black organizations (0 = no)	.14* (.06)
Constant	.93* (.20)
n	947
adjusted R^2	0.12
Root MSE	0.790

Source: 1993–94 National Black Politics Survey. Estimates were derived using *Stata Statistical Software.*
*Denotes statistically significant at the .05 level.
**Denotes statistically significant at the .10 level.
Note: Dash denotes not statistically significant at the .05 or .10 levels.

Table A2.4   The effects of ideology on economic nationalism

Variable	Economic Nationalism
Black Autonomy	◆
Black Feminism	.27* (2.39)
Black Marxism	.36* (2.68)
Radical Egalitarianism	.38* (3.06)
Disillusioned Liberalism	.78* (5.18)

Source: Compiled by M. Dawson from 1993–94 National Black Politics Survey. Estimates were derived using *Stata Statistical Software*.

Note: A set of basic measures is used to model the effects of black ideologies on components of black public opinion. All of the right-hand side variables used in Table A2.1 are also used in this analysis. Each ideology variable is separately added to the sets of structural and racial identity variables used before. Instead of presenting the results for each of the individual analyses, this table summarizes the effects of ideologies for shaping black public opinion in the area of economic nationalism.

*Each cell contains an unstandardized OLS coefficient. Numbers within parentheses are the ratio of the unstandardized coefficient to the standard error. All coefficients are statistically significant at the .05 level.

◆ Cells containing this symbol indicate that the selected component of black public opinion is employed as an item within the predicting ideology variable; therefore, it cannot be used as a dependent variable.

Table A2.5   The effects of ideology on selected gender questions

	Support Abortion? (0 = Against Abortion)	Warmth for Anita Hill? (0 = not favorable)	Believe AIDS a Conspiracy? (0 = no)	Black Women Leaders Attacked? (0 = no)	Black Feminism
Black Autonomy[†]	—	.17 (3.60)	.28* (3.80)	—	.07 (1.68)
Black Feminism[†]	.22 (4.42)	.10 (2.50)	−.28* (−4.00)	—	◆
Black Marxism[†]	—	—	—	—	−.08 (−1.92)
Radical Egalitarianism[†]	—	.14 (3.33)	—	.21* (2.77)	—
Disillusioned Liberalism[†]	—	.14 (2.57)	—	.25* (2.64)	—

Source: Compiled by M. Dawson from 1993–94 National Black Politics Survey. Estimates were derived using *Stata Statistical Software*.

Note: Dash denotes the coefficient was not statistically discernible from zero at the .10 level.

[†]A set of basic measures is used to model the effects of black ideologies on components of black public opinion. All of the right-hand side variables used in table A2.1 are also used in this analysis. Each ideology variable is separately added to the sets of structural and racial identity variables used before. Instead of presenting the results for each of the individual analyses, this table summarizes the effects of ideologies for shaping black public opinion in the area of gender politics.

*Each unstarred cell contains an unstandardized OLS coefficient. Starred cells contain probabilities derived from probit estimates. These probabilities represent the percentage change in probability as one moves from opposition to an ideology to strong support for that ideological predisposition. In all cells, numbers within parentheses are the ratio of the unstandardized coefficient to the standard error.

◆Cells containing this symbol indicate that the selected component of black public opinion is employed as an item within the predicting ideology variable; therefore, it cannot be used as a dependent variable.

Table A2.6   The effects of ideology on indicators of Black Nationalism

Variable	Warmth for Whites (0 = favorable)	Warmth for Farrakhan (0 = not favorable)	Blacks Should Join Black-Only Organizations? (0 = strongly disagree)	Farrakhan Represents a Positive Viewpoint? (0 = no a dangerous extremist)	Support Separate Nation? (0 = strongly disagree)	Blacks Should Form an Independent Political party? (0 = no)	Africa Is a Special Homeland? (0 = no)	Blacks Form a Nation within a Nation? (0 = no)	Black Autonomy
Black Autonomy†	.17 (3.80)	.30 (5.77)	.66 (14.02)	.46* (4.49)	.38 (9.10)	.75* (9.37)	.30* (3.81)	.24* (2.55)	◆
Black Feminism†	—	-.08 (-1.85)	—	—	-.07 (-2.00)	—	—	-.19* (-2.56)	.04 (1.68)
Black Marxism†	.10 (2.30)	—	—	—	—	.16* (1.70)	—	—	.08 (2.35)

Ideology					
Radical†	—	.14 (2.95)	.19. (4.22)	.30* (3.26)	
Egalitarianism	—	.21* (2.52)	—	.21* (2.77)	.12 (4.00)
Disillusioned	.23 (4.59)	.19 (3.28)	.31 (5.41)	.37* (3.20)	
Liberalism†	.12 (2.48)	.38* (3.74)	—	.25* (2.64)	.23 (6.36)

Source: Compiled by M. Dawson from 1993–94 National Black Politics Survey. Estimates were derived using *Stata Statistical Software*.

Note: A dash denotes that the coefficient was not statistically discernible from zero at the .10 level.

†A set of basic measures is used to model the effects of black ideologies on components of black public opinion. All of the right-hand side variables used in table A2.1 are also used in this analysis. Each ideology variable is separately added to the sets of structural and racial identity variables used before. Instead of presenting the results for each of the individual analyses, this table summarizes the effects of ideologies for shaping black public opinion in the area of black nationalism.

*Each unstarred cell contains an unstandardized OLS coefficient. Starred cells contain probabilities derived from probit estimates. These probabilities represent the percentage change in probability as one moves from opposition to an ideology to strong support for that ideological predisposition. In all cells, numbers within parentheses are the ratio of the unstandardized coefficient to the standard error.

◆Cells containing this symbol indicate that the selected component of black public opinion is employed as an item within the predicting ideology variable; therefore, it cannot be used as a dependent variable.

Table A2.7   The effects of ideology on indicators of orientations toward American society

Variable	Whites Can Represent Blacks as Well as Blacks (0 = yes)	American Society Unfair? (0 = no)	Large Corporations Unfair to Blacks? (0 = no)	Political Rights More Important Than Economic Rights? (0 = political rights most important)	Blacks Have Achieved Racial Equality? (0 = yes)	Racism, Poverty and Sexism are Linked? (0 = not linked, emphasize race)	Government Should Provide Job and Living? (0 = no)	Black Marxism	Radical Egalitarianism	Dis-illusioned Liberalism
Black† Autonomy	.42* (4.58)	.27 (5.74)	.13* (1.62)	—	.12 (3.99)	.17* (1.96)	.20* (2.31)	.08 (2.35)	.15 (4.00)	.18 (6.36)
Black† Feminism	.17* (2.34)	—	-.15* (-2.51)	—	—	◆	—	-.05 (-1.92)	—	—
Black† Marxism	.28* (3.18)	.54 (12.55)	◆	—	.08 (2.65)	—	—	◆	.09 (2.45)	◆

| Radical Egalitarianism† | −.11* (−1.39) | .14 (3.26) | ◆ | — | — | — | ◆ | ◆ | .07 (2.45) | ◆ | ◆ |
| Disillusioned Liberalism† | .45* (4.52) | ◆ | ◆ | .28* (2.76) | .20 (3.80) | — | ◆ | ◆ | ◆ | ◆ | ◆ |

Source: Compiled by M. Dawson from 1993–94 National Black Politics Survey. Estimates were derived using *Stata Statistical Software.*

Note: Dash denotes the coefficient was not statistically discernible from zero at the .10 level.

†A set of basic measures is used to model the effects of black ideologies on components of back public opinion. All of the right-hand side variables used in table A2.1 are also used in this analysis. Each ideology variable is separately added to the sets of structural and racial identity variables used before. Instead of presenting the results for each of the individual analyses, this table summarizes the effects of ideologies for shaping black public opinion in the area of orientations toward American society.

*Each unstarred cell contains an unstandardized OLS coefficient. Starred cells contain probabilities derived from probit estimates. These probabilities represent the percentage change in probability as one moves from opposition to an ideology to strong support for that ideological predisposition. In all cells, numbers within parentheses are the ratio of the unstandardized coefficient to the standard error.

◆Cells containing this symbol indicate that an element of the selected component of black public opinion is employed as an item within the predicting ideology variable; therefore, it cannot be used as a dependent variable.

Table A2.8 The effects of ideology on attitudes toward selected groups and individuals

Variable	Other Minorities and Poor Make Good Allies? (0 = yes)	Immigrants should get jobs after blacks? (0 = no)	Warmth for Clarence Thomas? (0 = not favorable)	Warmth for Jesse Jackson? (0 = not favorable)	Democratic Party works hard on black issues? (0 = very hard)	Republican Party works hard on black issues? (0 = very hard)	Police contribute to problem of violence? (0 = no)
Black† Autonomy	—	.46* (5.31)	-.12 (-2.56)	.11 (2.78)	—	.17 (3.65)	.33* (3.64)
Black† Feminism	.34* (4.62)	—	-.06 (-1.70)	—	—	.15 (3.96)	-.13* (-1.74)
Black† Marxism	—	22* (2.61)	-.09 (-1.90)	—	.15 (3.16)	.17 (3.63)	—
Radical Egalitarianism†	—	.24* (3.09)	—	.09 (2.51)	—	.07 (1.67)	—
Disillusioned Liberalism	—	.48* (4.94)	-.21 (-4.03)	—	.12 (2.22)	.32 (6.23)	.32* (3.24)

Source: Compiled by M. Dawson from 1993–94 National Black Politics Survey. Estimates were derived using *Stata Statistical Software*.

Note: Dash denotes the coefficient was not statistically discernible from zero at the .10 level.

† A set of basic measures is used to model the effects of black ideologies on components of black public opinion. All of the right-hand side variables used in Table A2.1 are also used in this analysis. Each ideology variable is separately added to the sets of structural and racial identity variables used before. Instead of presenting the results for each of the individual analyses, this table summarizes the effects of ideologies for shaping black public opinion in the area of orientations toward American society. Each unstarred cell contains an unstandardized OLS coefficient. Starred cells contain probabilities derived from probit estimates. These probabilities represent the percentage change in probability as one moves from opposition to an ideology to strong support for that ideological predisposition. In all cells, numbers within parentheses are the ratio of the unstandardized coefficient to the standard error.

◆ Cells containing this symbol indicate that an element of the selected component of black public opinion is employed as an item within the predicting ideology variable; therefore, it cannot be used as a dependent variable.

Table A2.9   **Shifts in public opinion sample means induced by shifts in back autonomy**

Size of Shift in Black Autonomy	Selected Indicators of Black Public Opinion			
	Opposition to formation of Black Party	Immigrants should get jobs after blacks	Police part of problem of violence	Blacks comprise a nation within a nation
−1 Standard Deviation	.63	.64	.47	.49
No Shift	.48	.71	.52	.53
+ Standard Deviation	.32	.78	.57	.58

Source: Compiled by author from 1993–1994 National Black Politics Survey.
Note: Each cell contains the estimate proportion of the population that adheres to the opinion listed at the top of each column. These proportions were obtained by first estimating probit equations using the variables that produced the estimates in tables A2.5–2.8. Then the estimates (using the original probit coefficients) were recalculated after inducing a shift in black autonomy ranging from −1 to +1 standard deviations. The probabilities were then obtained using the cumulative distribution function. The program to implement this design was written by the author in Gauss-Markov.

Table A2.10   Shifts in public opinion sample means induced by shifts
in black feminism

	Selected Indicator of Black Public Opinion
Size of Shift	Other minorities and poor make poor allies?
−1 Standard Deviation	.50
No Shift	.43
+1 Standard Deviation	.36

Source: Compiled by author from 1993–1994 National Black Politics Survey.
Note: Each cell contains the estimated proportion of the population that adheres to the opinion listed at the top of each column. These proportions were obtained by first estimating probit equations using the variables that produced the estimates in tables A2.5–2.8. Then the estimates (using the original probit coefficients) were recalculated after inducing a shift in back autonomy ranging from −1 to +1 standard deviations. The probabilities were then obtained using the cumulative distribution function. The program to implement this design was written by the author in Gauss-Markov.

Table A2.11   Determinants of support for black feminist ideology

Variable	Black Feminism (SE)
Aside from attending services, are you an active member in your place of worship? (0 = no)	−.04* (.02)
Do you think blacks are economically worse off than whites? (0 = no)	.11* (.04)
Do you think your fate is linked to that of black people? (0 = no)	.05* (.02)
Gender (0 = male)	.07* (.02)
Family income	.08* (.03)
Age	−.08* (.04)
Education	.01* (.00)
Tied to black information networks (0 = weak ties)	—
Percentage of blacks in census tract	—
Census tract poverty	—
Is interviewer perceived as white? (0 = no)	—
Tied to black organizations (0 = no)	—
Constant	.49* (.07)
n	723
adjusted R^2	0.093
Root MSE	0.233

Source: 1993–94 National Black Politics Survey. Estimates were derived using *Stata Statistical Software.*
Note: Dash denotes not statistically significant at the .05 or .10 levels.
*Denotes statistically significant at the .05 level.
**Denotes statistically significant at the .10 level.

Table A2.12   **Determinants of feelings toward gays and lesbians**

Variable	Warmth for Gays (SE)	Warmth for Lesbians (SE)
Religion provides a great deal of guidance in daily life? (0 = no)	−.07* (.02)	−.08* (.02)
Do you think blacks are economically worse off than whites? (0 = no)	−.10* (.04)	−.09* (.04)
Do you think your fate is linked to that of black people? (0 = no)	—	.07* (.03)
Gender (0 = male)	.07* (.02)	—
Family income	—	—
Age	.11* (.05)	—
Education	.01* (.00)	.01* (.00)
Tied to black information networks (0 = weak ties)	.10* (.05)	.08** (.05)
Percentage of blacks in census tract	—	—
Census tract poverty	—	−.05** (.03)
Is interviewer perceived as white? (0 = no)	—	—
Tied to black organizations (0 = no)	—	—
Constant	.13** (.08)	.22* (.08)
n	838	827
adjusted R^2	0.047	0.051
Root MSE	0.286	0.285

Source: 1993–94 National Black Politics Survey. Estimates were derived using *Stata Statistical Software.*
Note: Dash denotes not statistically significant at the .05 or .10 levels.
*Denotes statistically significant at the .05 level.
**Denotes statistically significant at the .10 level.

Table A2.13 Effects of black feminist ideology on support for more female clergy in black churches

Variable	Black churches should allow more women to become members of the clergy (0 = Disagree)
Black Feminism	.31* (4.98)
Do you think blacks are economically worse off than whites? (0 = no)	−.14* (−2.66)
Do you think your fate is linked to that of black people? (0 = no)	.07* (2.05)
Gender (0 = male)	−.07* (−2.46)
Family income	—
Age	−.14* (−2.06)
Education	.01* (1.65)
Tied to black information networks (0 = weak ties)	.13* (2.00)
Percentage of blacks in census tract	—
Census tract poverty	—
Is interviewer perceived as white? (0 = no)	—
Tied to black organizations (0 = no)	—
Constant	—
n	896
χ^2 (df)	66.58 (12)
Log likelihood	−409.62

Source: Compiled by M. Dawson from 1993–94 National Black Politics Survey. Estimates were derived using *Stata Statistical Software*.
Note: Dash denotes the coefficient was not statistically discernible from zero at the .10 level.
*Starred cells contain probabilities derived from probit estimates. These probabilities represent the percentage change in probability as one moves from the minimum value of the independent variable to the maximum value. Unstarred cells contain unstandardized probit estimates. In all cells, numbers within parentheses are the ratio of the unstandardized coefficient to the standard error.

Table A2.14   The predictive power of linked fate on black feminist ideology
and feminist identity among black women

Variable	Black Feminist Ideology	Feminist Identity
Black linked fate	.05*	−.03
	(2.22)	(−0.85)
Black men linked fate	.08*	−.01
	(4.06)	(−0.39)
Black women linked fate	.09*	.02
	(4.57)	(0.69)
Nonwhite women linked fate	.04**	−.03
	(1.80)	(−1.01)
Women linked fate	.05*	.01
	(2.03)	(0.35)
White women linked fate	−.01	−.04
	(−0.44)	(−1.21)

Source: Compiled by M. Dawson from 1993–94 National Black Politics Survey. Estimates were derived using *Stata Statistical Software.*
Note: A set of basic measures is used to model the effects of forms of linked fate on black feminist ideology and feminist identity among black women. All of the right-hand side variables used in Table A2.1 are also used in this analysis. Each particular form of linked fate is separately added to the sets of structural and racial identity variables. Instead of presenting the results for each of the individual analyses, this table summarizes the effects of forms of linked fate for shaping black feminist ideology and feminist identity among black women. In all cells, numbers within parentheses are the ratio of the unstandardized coefficients to the standard error.
*Denotes statistically significant at the .05 level.
**Denotes statistically significant at the .10 level.

Table A2.15 Determinants of disillusioned liberalism and likelihood
of achieving racial equality

Variable	Disillusioned Liberalism (SE)	Likelihood of Achieving Racial Equality (SE)
Disillusioned Liberalism	◆	.70* (.16)
Likelihood of achieving racial equality (0 = have already achieved; 1 = will never achieve)	—	◆
Whites want blacks to get a better break? (0 = No, Whites want to keep blacks down)	−.11* (.03)	◆
Movement for black rights has affected you personally? (0 = No, not at all)	◆	—
Tied to black organizations (0 = no)	◆	.06* (.02)
Do you think blacks are economically worse off than whites? (0 = no)	.22* (.05)	◆
Do you think your fate is linked to that of black people? (0 = no)	.08* (.02)	—
Gender (0 = male)	—	—
Family income	—	.06* (.03)
Age	◆	.09* (.04)
Education	—	—
Census tract poverty	—	—
Interviewer perceived as white (0 = no)	−.06* (.02)	—

Table A2.15   (continued)

Variable	Disillusioned Liberalism (SE)	Likelihood of Achieving Racial Equality (SE)
Constant	.95*	—
	(.20)	
n	862	862
adjusted R^2	.	.
Root MSE	0.201	0.221

F-tests of Social Location Variables		
H_0 = Income = Education = Census tract poverty = 0		
	Disillusioned Liberalism (SE)	Likelihood of Achieving Racial Equality (SE)
F(d.f. denominator, d.f. numerator)	$F(3,852) = 0.10$	$F(3,851) = 1.85$
Prob > F	0.381	0.136

Source: 1993–94 National Black Politics Survey. Estimates were derived using *Stata Statistical Software.*

Notes: Each cell contains two-stage least-squares estimates. The figures in the parentheses represent the standard error.

H_0, the null hypothesis, is rejected at the 0.05 level of significance. A rejection of the null hypothesis infers that the slope coefficients of the social location variables are not all simultaneously zero.

*Denotes statistically significant at the .05 level.

♦Denotes variable not included in the model.

Dash denotes not statistically significant at the .05 or .10 levels.

Table A2.16   **Shifts in public opinion sample means induced by shifts in black conservatism**

	Selected Indicator of Black Public Opinion
Size of Shift	Opposition to formation of Black Party
−1 Standard Deviation	.41
No Shift	.47
+1 Standard Deviation	.52

Source: Compiled by author from 1993–1994 National Black Politics Survey.
Note: Each cell contains the estimated proportion of the population that adheres to the opinion listed at the top of each column. These proportions were obtained by first estimating probit equations using the variables that produced the estimates in Tables A2.5–2.8. Then the estimates (using the original probit coefficients) were recalculated after inducing a shift in black autonomy ranging from −1 to +1 standard deviations. The probabilities were then obtained using the cumulative distribution function. The program to implement this design was written by the author in Gauss-Markov.

Table A2.17   **Determinants of belief that one has been affected by the movement for black rights**

Variable	Movement for black rights has affected you personally (SE)
Do you think blacks are economically worse off than whites? (0 = no)	.23* (.06)
Do you think your fate is linked to that of black people? (0 = no)	.28* (.03)
Gender (0 = male)	—
Family income	—
Age	−.16* (.06)
Education	.01* (.00)
Tied to black information networks (0 = weak ties)	.20* (0.06)

Table A2.17   (continued)

Variable	Movement for black rights has affected you personally (SE)
Percentage of blacks in census tract	—
Census tract poverty	—
Is interviewer perceived as white? (0 = no)	—
Tied to black organizations (0 = no)	−.07* (.03)
Constant	—
n	932
adjusted R^2	0.196
Root MSE	0.376

Source: 1993–94 National Black Politics survey. Estimates were derived using *Stata Statistical Software.*
Note: Dash denotes not statistically significant at the .05 or .10 levels.
*Denotes statistically significant at the .05 level.
**Denotes statistically significant at the .10 level.

Table A2.18   Determinants of exposure to rap music

Variable	Exposure to Rap (0 = yes)
Do you think blacks are economically worse off than whites? (0 = no)	—
Do you think your fate is linked to that of black people? (0 = no)	.08* (2.11)
Gender (0 = male)	.08* (2.11)
Family income	—
Age	.76* (11.89)
Education	.01* (2.26)
Census tract poverty	—
Interviewer perceived as white (0 = no)	—
Constant	−1.38 (−4.62)
n	962
χ^2 (df)	187.82 (8)
Log likelihood	−572.77

Source: Compiled by M. Dawson from 1993–94 National Black Politics Survey. Estimates were derived using *Stata Statistical Software*.
Note: Dash denotes the coefficient was not statistically discernible from zero at the .10 level.
*Each unstarred cell contains an unstandardized probit estimate. Starred cells contain probabilities derived from probit estimates. These probabilities represent the percentage change in probability as one moves from the minimum value of the independent variable to the maximum value. In all cells, numbers within parentheses are the ratio of the unstandardized coefficient to the standard error.

Table A2.19 The effects of rap on issues of gender, black nationalism, and social orientation

Effects of rap on selected gender questions

	Pro-Choice? (0 = no)	Warmth for Gays?	Warmth for Lesbians?	Black Women Leaders Troublemakers? (0 = yes)	Black Feminists Divide Black Community? (0 = no)
Rap a Destructive Force? (0 = no)	-.10 (-2.57)	-.04 (-1.90)	-.04 (-1.82)	—	.12* (3.04)

Effects of rap on selected indicators of black nationalism

	Warmth for whites? (0 = yes)	Minister Farrakhan Positive Force? (0 = yes)	Blacks Form Own Political Party? (0 = yes)	Support Community Nationalism? (1 = yes)	Africa Is a Special Homeland? (0 = yes)	Black Children Should Study an African Language? (0 = yes)	Support Black Male Academies?

Rap a Destructive Force? (0 = no)	—	.16* (3.77)	.09 (2.44)	−.06 (−1.95)	—	.040 (1.93)	—

Effects of rap on selected indicators of orientations toward American society

	American Society Unfair? (0 = no)	Large Corporations Unfair to Blacks? (0 = no)	Problems of Racism, Poverty and Sexism are Linked? (0 = yes)	Police Contribute to Problem of Violence? (0 = no)
Rap a Destructive Force? (0 = no)	—	—	—	−.10* (−2.65)

Source: Compiled by author from 1993–94 National Black Politics Survey

Note: Dash denotes the coefficient was not statistically discernible from zero at the .10 level. A set of basic measures is used to model the effects of rap on components of black public opinion. All of the right-hand side variables used in table A2.1 are also used in this analysis. The "rap" variable is added to the sets of structural and racial identity variables used before. Instead of presenting the full results from each of the individual equations, these tables summarize the effects of rap on shaping various areas in black opinion.

*Each unstarred cell contains an unstandardized OLS coefficient. Starred cells contain probabilities derived from logic estimates. These probabilities represent the percentage change in probability as one moves from the view that rap is informative to the view that rap is a destructive force. In all cells, numbers within parentheses are the ratio of the unstandardized coefficient to the standard error.

Table A2.20 Determinants of belief that rap is destructive and support for black nationalism

Variable	Black Nationalism (SE)	Rap Destructive (SE)
Black Nationalism	◆	—
Exposed to rap music? (0 = Yes)	◆ −.08**	.36* (.04)
Belief that rap is destructive (0 = Rap informative)	(.04)	◆
Do you think blacks are economically worse off than whites? (0 = no)	.10* (.03)	◆
Do you think your fate is linked to that of black people? (no = no)	.08* (.02)	◆
Gender (0 = male)	—	—
Family income	—	.11** (.07)
Age	—	.36* (.08)
Education	—	—
Census tract poverty	—	.08** (.05)
Interviewer perceived as white (0 = no)	—	—
Constant	.60* (.04)	—
n	781	781
adjusted R^2	0.077	0.226
Root MSE	0.193	0.431

Source: 1993–94 National Black Politics Survey. Estimates were derived using *Stata Statistical Software*.
Note: Each cell contains two-stage least-squares estimates. The figures in the parentheses represent the standard error.
*Denotes statistically significant at the .05 level.
**Denotes statistically significant at the .10 level.
Dash denotes not statistically significant at the .05 or .10 levels.
◆ Denotes variable not included in the model.

Table A2.21 The effects of ideology on political participation

Variable	Member of an Organization Working to Improve Status of Blacks? (0 = yes)[a]	Contacted a Public Official or Agency? (0 = no)	Attended a Protest Meeting/ Demonstration? (0 = no)	Taken Part in a Neighborhood March? (0 = no)	Signed a Petition in Support of/ Against Something? (0 = no)	Talked to Family/Friends about Political Issues? (0 = no)
Black Autonomy[†]	.17* (2.25)	—	.17* (2.15)	—	—	—
Black Feminism[†]	—	—	—	—	—	—
Black Marxism[†]	—	.17* (1.96)	.15* (1.91)	—	.15* (1.74)	—
Disillusioned Liberalism[†]	—	—	.16* (1.79)	—	—	—
Radical Egalitarianism[†]	—	—	—	—	.24* (2.41)	—

(continued)

	Helped in a Voter Registration Drive? (0 = no)	Gave People Rides to Election Polls? (0 = no)	Gave Money to Political Candidates? (0 = no)	Attended a Fund Raiser for a Candidate? (0 = no)	Distributed Campaign Materials? (0 = no)	Signed a Petition Supporting a Candidate for Office? (0 = no)
Black Autonomy[†]	—	—	—	—	—	.18* (1.96)
Black Feminism[†]	-.11* (1.82)	—	—	-.15* (2.26)	-.11* (1.70)	—
Black Marxism[†]	—	—	—	—	—	—
Disillusioned Liberalism[†]	—	—	—	—	—	—
Radical Egalitarianism[†]	—	.19* (3.09)	—	—	—	—

Source: Compiled by M. Dawson from 1993–94 National Black Politics Survey. Estimates were derived using *Stata Statistical Software*.

Note: Dash denotes the coefficient was not statistically discernible from zero at the .10 level.

[†] A set of basic measures is used to model the effects of black ideologies on components of black political participation. All of the right hand side variables used in table A2.1 are also used in this analysis. Each ideology variable is separately added to the sets of structural and racial identity variables used before. Instead of presenting the results for each of the individual analyses, this table summarizes the effects of ideologies for shaping black political participation.

[a] In this particular analysis, the measure *member in an organization working to improve the status of blacks* is used a dependent variable of black political participation. With all other analyses in this table, it remains an independent variable as in table A2.1.

[b] In contrast to the first set of six dependent variables of black political participation, this second set of six was taken from a list of political activities that people sometimes do as part of their religious duties.

*Each cell contains probabilities derived from probit estimates. These probabilities represent the percentage change in probability as one moves from opposition to an ideology to strong support for that ideological predisposition. Numbers within parentheses are the ratio of the unstandardized coefficient to the standard error.

Table A3.1 Measurement coefficients for black ideologies

Construct	Item	Unstandardized λ (SE)	Θ_δ (SE)
Black Autonomy			
Support black male academies	X_1	0.45 (0.04)	0.80 (0.05)
Community control of government	X_2	0.80 (0.03)	0.61 (0.05)
Community control of economy	X_3	0.86 (0.03)	0.27 (0.06)
Shop in black stores	X_4	0.62 (0.04)	0.36 (0.06)

$n = 1072$; $\chi^2 = 1.28$, df = 2, p = 0.53; GFI = 1.00; AGFI = 0.99; CN ($\alpha = 0.05$) = 3611.08

Construct	Item	Unstandardized λ (SE)	Θ_δ (SE)
Black Feminism			
Problems linked	X_1	0.56 (0.10)	0.68 (0.12)
Black feminist groups help the black community	X_2	0.43 (0.09)	0.81 (0.08)
Black women should share leadership with black men	X_3	0.50 (0.10)	0.75 (0.10)
Black women have suffered from both sexism and racism	X_4	0.17 (0.08)	0.96 (0.04)

$n = 852$; $\chi^2 = 0.84$ df = 2, p = 0.66; GFI = 1.00; AGFI = 0.99; CN ($\alpha = 0.05$) = 2715.46

Construct	Item	Unstandardized λ (SE)	Θ_δ (SE)
Black Marxism			
Black middle class has abandoned the black poor	X_1	0.39 (0.06)	0.83 (0.06)
American economic system fair to poor people	X_2	0.73 (0.10)	0.46 (0.15)
Common interests despite economic differences	X_3	0.26 (0.06)	0.91 (0.04)
American corporations fair	X_4	0.44 (0.08)	0.79 (0.07)

$n = 1205$; $\chi2 = 5.43$ df = 2, p = 0.07; GFI = 0.99; AGFI = 0.97; CN ($\alpha = 0.05$) = 756.54

Construct	Item	Unstandardized λ (SE)	Θ_δ (SE)
Radical Egalitarianism-Black Conservatism			
So much racial progress that special programs for blacks are no longer needed	X_1	0.15 (0.11)	0.93 (0.06)
Poor people don't want to work	X_2	0.28 (0.10)	0.88 (0.07)
Blacks depend too much on government programs	X_3	0.81 (0.24)	0.34 (0.39)
Government should let individuals get ahead on their own	X_4	0.41 (0.13)	0.81 (0.11)

$n = 870$; $\chi^2 = 3.39$; df = 2, p = 0.18; GFI = 0.98;
AGFI = 0.92; CN ($\alpha = 0.05$) = 281.95

Construct	Item	Unstandardized λ (SE)	Θ_δ (SE)
America Fair			
American economic system fair to poor people	X_1	0.70 (0.04)	0.51 (0.07)
America's corporations fair	X_2	0.49 (0.05)	0.76 (0.05)
American society fair	X_3	0.87 (0.04)	0.24 (0.07)
American legal system fair	X_4	0.85 (0.04)	0.28 (0.07)

$n = 1205$; $\chi 2 = 0.71$; df = 2, p = 0.70; GFI = 1.00;
AGFI = 0.99; CN ($\alpha = 0.05$) = 2125.10

Source: 1993–94 National Black Politics Survey.
Note: The *PRELIS 2.20* and *LISREL 8.20* programs combine to estimate confirmatory factor analysis based on correlation matrices designed for ordinal-level variables. Asymptotic variances and covariances were used to calculate the measurement models using the weighted least-squares estimator.

Table A3.2   Scale reliability index of selected constructs

Construct	*Reliability Coefficient*
Black Autonomy	0.71
Support black male academies	
Community control of government	
Community control of economy	
Shop in black stores	
Black Feminism	0.26
Problems linked	
Black feminist groups help the black community	
Black women should share leadership with black men	
Black women have suffered from both sexism and racism	
Black Marxism	0.34
Black middle class has abandoned the black poor	
American economic system fair to poor people	
Common interests despite economic differences	
American corporations fair	
Disillusioned Liberalism	0.52
So much racial progress that special programs for blacks are no longer needed	
Poor people don't want to work	
Blacks depend too much on government programs	
Government should let individuals get ahead on their own	
American economic system fair to poor people	
America's corporations fair	
American society fair	
American legal system fair	
Radical Egalitarianism	0.28
So much racial progress that special programs for blacks are no longer needed	
Poor people don't want to work	
Blacks depend too much on government programs	
Government should let individuals get ahead on their own	
America Fair	0.62
American economic system fair to poor people	
America's corporation fair	
American society fair	
American legal system fair	

Construct	*Reliability Coefficient*
Economic Nationalism	0.62
Black people should shop in black stores whenever possible	
Blacks should have control over the economy in mostly black communities	

Black Information Networks	0.62
Read a novel by a black author	
Gone to a movie made by a black director	
Read a black newspaper	
Read a black magazine	
Listened to rap	
Listened to black news program on radio	
Watched a black TV program on cable	

Source: 1993–94 National Black Politics Survey. Estimates were derived using *Stata Statistical Software.*

Note: Reliability coefficient based on Cronbach's Alpha, which assesses the reliability of each summative rating scale composed of the specified set of items.

Table A4.1   Social and economic distributions among African Americans

Variable	1990 U.S. Census[a]	1993 NBPS[b]	1993 NBPS— Type 0[b]	1993 NBPS— Type 1[b]
Gender				
Male[†]	47.4%	35.2%	34.5%	36.0%
Female	52.6%	64.8%	65.5%	64.0%
N	33,141*	1,206	603	603
Age				
18–29	31.9%	22.7%	25.8%	19.6%
30–44	33.7%	33.5%	37.4%	29.6%
45–59	17.6%	21.5%	19.6%	23.3%
60–74	12.0%	13.3%	9.8%	16.8%
75 & over	4.8%	9.0%	7.3%	10.8%
N	20,653*	1,203	601	602
(Median Category)	(30–44)	(30–44)	(30–44)	(45–59)
Years of School Completed				
Elementary: 0–8 years	16.1%	6.9%	5.1%	8.6%
High School: 1–3 years	17.7%	10.4%	10.9%	9.8%
4 years	37.2%	28.7%	28.0%	29.4%
College: 1–3 years	17.6%	33.1%	36.2%	29.9%
4 years or more	11.3%	21.1%	19.7%	22.4%
N	16,751*	1,206	603	603
(Median Category)	(4 years high school)	(1–3 years college)	(1–3 years college)	(1–3 years college)
Income				
Less than $10,000	21.4%	13.7%	10.9%	16.4%
$10,000 to $14,999	11.5%	11.3%	12.0%	10.6%
$15,000 to $24,999	18.7%	23.5%	26.2%	20.9%
$25,000 to $49,999	28.2%	35.0%	35.5%	36.6%
$50,000 or more	20.1%	16.4%	17.4%	15.5%
N	7,740*	1,113	558	555
(Median Category)	($15,000– $24,999)	($25,000– $49,999)	($25,000– $49,999)	($25,000– $49,999)

Source: U.S. Bureau of the Census, Current Population Reports, P25-1095, (for column 2), and 1993 National Black Politics Study (for columns 3–5).
*In thousands.
[†]All subcategories represent a practical merging of the two dissimilar categorization methods used in the U.S. Census and the NBPS.

Table A4.2   Correlations between *Black Visions* Variables and Type

Variables	Type
Disillusioned Liberalism	−0.08
Age	0.12
Tied to black information networks (0 = weak ties)	−0.12
Support abortion (0 = no)	−0.30
Women linked fate (0 = no)	−0.08
Black women linked fate (0 = no)	−0.06
Non-white women linked fate (0 = no)	−0.09
Religion provides guidance in daily life (0 = no)	0.09
Signed a petition supporting candidate for office (0 = no)	−0.07
Attended a protest meeting demonstration (0 = no)	−0.10
Believe that rap is destructive (0 = no, rap informative)	0.07
Exposed to rap music (0 = yes)	0.12

Source: Compiled by M. Dawson from 1993–94 National Black Politics Survey. Estimates were derived using *Stata Statistical Software.*

Notes: 1. All noted correlation coefficients are significant at the .05 level.

2. Of the more than ninety five variables used in this study, only the thirteen presented in this table demonstrated a significant correlation with the variable TYPE. This result is expected. Although the correlation coefficients are statistically significant, substantively they are not. In a given sample, there typically tends to be a weak correlation between any two variables. This correlation is as likely to be positive as negative. Just as a coin would be unlikely to show exactly fifty heads in a series of one hundred flips, a correlation of exactly zero is highly unlikely.

REFERENCES

Aberbach, Joel D., and Jack L. Walker. 1970. The Meanings of Black Power: A Comparison of White and Black Political Interpretations of a Political Slogan. *American Political Science Review* 64: 367–88.

Achen, Christopher H. 1982. *Interpreting and Using Regression.* Paper Series: Quantitative Applications in the Social Sciences, no. 29. Beverly Hills: Sage.

African American Women. 1992. African Women in Defense of Ourselves. *Black Scholar* 22: 155.

Allen, Richard L.; Michael C. Dawson; and Ronald E. Brown. 1989. A Schema-Based Approach to Modeling African-American Racial Belief Systems. *American Political Science Review* 83: 421–41.

Anderson, Jervis. 1972. *A. Philip Randolph: A Biographical Portrait.* New York: Harcourt Brace Jovanovich.

Appiah, K. Anthony, and Amy Gutmann. 1996. *Color Conscious: The Political Morality of Race.* Princeton, NJ: Princeton University Press.

Aptheker, Herbert, ed., 1979. *A Documentary History of the Negro People in the United States.* Vol. 2. New York: Citadel Press.

Arendt, Hannah. 1958. *The Human Condition.* Chicago: University of Chicago Press.

———. 1966. *The Origins of Totalitarianism.* Rev. ed. New York: Harcourt, Brace & World.

Arnesen, Eric. 1994. "Like Banquo's Ghost, I Will Not Down": The Race Question and the American Railroad Brotherhoods, 1889–1920. *American Historical Review* 99: 1601–33.

Asante, Molefi Kete. 1988. *Afrocentricity.* Trenton, NJ: Africa World Press.

Bailyn, Bernard. 1967. *The Ideological Origins of the American Revolution.* Cambridge, MA: Harvard University Press.

Baker, Houston A., Jr. 1993. *Black Studies, Rap, and the Academy.* Chicago: University of Chicago Press.

Balibar, Etienne, and Immanuel Wallerstein. 1991. *Race, Nation, Class: Ambiguous Identities.* London: Verso.

Baraka, Amiri. 1974. Toward Ideological Clarity: Nationalism, Pan Africanism, Socialism. *Black World,* November 1974, 24–33, 84–95.

———. 1975. *Hard Facts.* Newark, NJ: Congress of Afrikan People.

———. 1981. Black Struggle in the '80s. *Black Nation* 1: 2–5.

———. 1982. Nationalism, Self-Determination, and Socialist Revolution. *Black Nation* 2: 4–10.

———. 1991a [1979]. The Autobiography of Leroi Jones/Amiri Baraka. In Harris 1991, 19.

———. 1991b [1984]. The Revolutionary Tradition in Afro-American Literature. In Harris 1991, 311–22.

———. 1991c [1989]. Black People and Jesse Jackson II. In Harris 1991, 457–80.

———. 1997 [1970]. Speech to the Congress of African Peoples. In Van Deburg 1997, 145–57.

Black Radical Congress. 1998. Principles of Unity. In *Black Radical Congress: Towards a Black Liberation Agenda for the Twenty-First Century* [Online]. 15 paragraphs. Available as of July 14, 2000, at <http://www.blackradicalcongress.com/BRC-POU.html>.

Bobo, Lawrence D. 1988. Group Conflict, Prejudice, and the Paradox of Contemporary Racial Attitudes. In Phyllis A. Katz and Dalmas A. Taylor, eds., *Eliminating Racism: Profiles in Controversy.* New York: Plenum, 85–114.

———. 2000. Racial Attitudes and Relations at the Close of the Twentieth Century. In Neil Smelser, William Julius Wilson, and Faith N. Mitchell, eds., *American Becoming: Racial Trends and Their Consequences,* vol. 1. Washington, DC: National Academy Press.

Bobo, Lawrence D., and Franklin D. Gilliam Jr. 1990. Race, Sociopolitical Participation, and Black Empowerment. *American Political Science Review* 84: 377–94.

Bobo, Lawrence D., and James R. Kluegel. 1997. Status, Ideology, and Dimensions of Whites' Racial Beliefs and Attitudes: Progress and Stagnation. In Steven A. Tuch and Jack K. Martin, eds., *Racial Attitudes in the 1990s: Continuity and Change.* Westport, CT: Praeger, 93–120.

Bobo, Lawrence D.; Camille L. Zubrinsky; James H. Johnson; and Melvin L. Oliver. 1995. Public Opinion before and after a Spring of Discontent. In Mark Baldassare, ed., *The Los Angeles Riots: Lessons for the Urban Future.* Boulder, CO: Westview Press, 103–33.

Boggs, James. 1970. *Racism and the Class Struggle: Further Pages from a Black Worker's Notebook.* New York: Monthly Review Press. (Articles cited by date and letter below.)

Boggs, James. 1970a. The American Revolution. In Boggs 1970, 161–90.

———. 1970b [1963]. Liberalism, Marxism, and Black Political Power. In Boggs 1970, 26–32.

————. 1970c [1967a]. Black Power: A Scientific Concept Whose Time Has Come. In Boggs 1970, 51–62.

————. 1970d [1967b]. Culture and Black Power. In Boggs 1970, 64–69.

————. 1970e [1968]. The Basic Issues of State and Nation. In Boggs 1970, 70–78.

Boggs, James, and Grace Lee Boggs. 1970 [1966]. The City Is the Black Man's Land. In Boggs 1970, 39–50.

Boxill, Bernard R. 1992. *Blacks and Social Justice.* Rev. ed. Lanham, MD: Rowman and Littlefield.

Boyd, Todd. 1994. Check Yo Self, before You Wrek Yo Self: Variations on a Political Theme in Rap Music and Popular Culture. *Public Culture* 7: 289–312.

Bracey, John H., Jr.; August Meir; and Elliot Rudwick. 1970. Introduction. In John H. Bracey Jr., August Meir, and Elliot Rudwick, eds., *Black Nationalism in America.* Indianapolis: Bobbs-Merrill, xxv–lx.

Breitman, George. 1967. *The Last Year of Malcolm X: The Evolution of a Revolutionary.* New York: Merit.

Briggs, Cyril V. 1973 [1918]. The Blood of Africa. In Vincent 1973, 126–27.

————. 1997 [1920]. The African Blood Brotherhood. In Van Deburg 1997, 35–37.

Brown, Elaine. 1992. *A Taste of Power: A Black Woman's Story.* New York: Pantheon Books.

Brown, Elsa Barkley. 1989. To Catch the Vision of Freedom: Reconstructing Southern Black Women's Political History, 1865–1885. The University of Michigan. Manuscript.

————. 1990a. Womanist Consciousness: Maggie Lena Walker and the Independent Order of Saint Luke. In Micheline R. Malson, Elisabeth Mudimbe-Boyi, Jean F. O'Barr, and Mary Wyer, eds., *Black Women in America: Social Science Perspectives.* Chicago: University of Chicago Press, 173–196.

————. 1990b. African-American Women's Quilting: A Framework for Conceptualizing and Teaching African-American Women's History. In Micheline R. Malson, Elisabeth Mudimbe-Boyi, Jean F. O'Barr, and Mary Wyer, eds., *Black Women in America: Social Science Perspectives.* Chicago: University of Chicago Press, 9–18.

————. 1995. Negotiating and Transforming the Public Sphere: African American Political Life in the Transition from Slavery to Freedom. In The Black Public Sphere Collective, eds., *The Black Public Sphere.* Chicago: University of Chicago Press, 111–150.

Bunche, Ralph J. 1995a. *Ralph J. Bunche: Selected Speeches and Writings.* Ed. Charles P. Henry. Ann Arbor: University of Michigan Press.

————. 1995b [1928]. Negro Political Philosophy. In Bunche 1995a, 27–34.

————. 1995c [1935]. A Critical Analysis of the Tactics and Programs of Minority Groups. In Bunche 1995a, 49–62.

————. 1995d [1936]. A Critique of New Deal Social Planning as It Affects Negroes. In Bunche 1995a, 63–70.

————. 1995e [1939]. Introduction to Confidential Report to the Republican Party. In Bunche 1995a, 85–92.

———. 1995f [1941]. The Negro in the Political Life of the U.S. In Bunche 1995a, 93–112.

———. 1995g [1951]. NAACP Convention Address. In Bunche 1995a, 238–48.

———. 1995h [1965]. March on Montgomery Speech. In Bunche 1995a, 259–62.

———. 1995i [1968]. The Black Revolution. In Bunche 1995a, 297–304.

———. 1995j [1969]. Race and Alienation. In Bunche 1995a, 305–16.

Butts, Calvin O., III. 1996. Rolling Out an Agenda for Rap. In Adam Sexton, ed., *Rap on Rap: Straight-Up Talk on Hip-Hop Culture*. New York: Delta Books, 75–77.

Calhoun, Craig. 1994. Nationalism and Civil Society: Democracy, Diversity, and Self-Determination. In Craig Calhoun, ed., *Social Theory and the Politics of Identity*. Oxford: Blackwell, 304–35.

———. 1995. *Critical Social Theory*. Oxford: Blackwell.

Campbell, Angus; Philip E. Converse; Warren E. Miller; and Donald E. Stokes. 1960. *The American Voter*. New York: John Wiley & Sons.

Carby, Hazel V. 1987. *Reconstructing Womanhood: The Emergence of the Afro-American Woman Novelist*. New York: Oxford University Press.

Carmichael, Stokely, and Charles V. Hamilton. 1967. *Black Power: The Politics of Liberation in America*. New York: Vintage Books.

Carmines, Edward G., and James A. Stimson. 1989. *Issue Evolution: Race and the Transformation of American Politics*. Princeton, NJ: Princeton University Press.

Carson, Clayborne. 1981. *In Struggle: SNCC and the Black Awakening of the 1960s*. Cambridge, MA: Harvard University Press.

———. 1991. *Malcolm X: The FBI File*. New York: Carroll & Graf.

Chatterjee, Partha. 1993. *The Nation and Its Fragments: Colonial and Postcolonial Histories*. Princeton, NJ: Princeton University Press.

Cohen, Cathy J. 1994. Contested Identities: Black Lesbian and Gay Identities and the Black Community's Response to AIDS. Yale University. Manuscript.

———. 1999. *The Boundaries of Blackness: AIDS and the Breakdown of Black Politics*. Chicago: University of Chicago Press.

Cohen, Cathy J., and Michael C. Dawson. 1993. Neighborhood Politics and African-American Politics. *The American Political Science Review* 87: 286–302.

———. 1994. Gender and Feminism in Black Communities: Modeling Black Feminist Thought. Manuscript.

Collins, Patricia Hill. 1991. *Black Feminist Thought: Knowledge, Consciousness, and the Politics of Empowerment*. Boston: Unwin-Hyman.

———. 1996. What's in a Name? Womanism, Black Feminism, and Beyond. *Black Scholar* 26: 9–17.

———. 1998. *Fighting Words: Black Women and the Search for Justice*. Minneapolis: University of Minnesota Press.

Combahee River Collective. 1981 [1977]. A Black Feminist Statement. In Moraga and Anzaldua 1981, 210–18.

COMINTERN. 1975. *The 1928 and 1930 COMINTERN Resolutions on the Black National Question in the United States*. Washington, DC: Revolutionary Review Press.

Cone, James H. 1991. *Martin and Malcolm and America: A Dream or a Nightmare?* Maryknoll, NY: Orbis Books.

Converse, Philip E. 1964. The Nature of Belief Systems in Mass Publics. In David Apter, ed., *Ideology and Discontent.* New York: Free Press, 206–261.

Cooper, Ana Julia. 1995 [1892]. The Status of Woman in America. In Guy-Sheftall 1995, 44–49.

Crenshaw, Kimberle. 1990. A Black Feminist Critique of Antidiscrimination Law and Politics. In David Kairys, ed., *The Politics of Law: A Progressive Critique.* New York: Pantheon Books, 195–218.

———. 1992. Whose Story Is It, Anyway? Feminist and Antiracist Appropriations of Anita Hill. In Toni Morrison, ed., *Race-ing Justice, En-gender-ing Power: Essays on Anita Hill, Clarence Thomas, and the Construction of Social Reality.* New York: Pantheon Books, 402–40.

Cruse, Harold. 1967. *The Crisis of the Negro Intellectual: From Its Origins to the Present.* New York: William Morrow.

Cube, Ice. 1995. Black Culture Still Getting a Bum Rap. In Adam Sexton, ed., *Rap on Rap: Straight-Up Talk on Hip-Hop Culture.* New York: Delta Books, 158–60.

Dahl, Robert. 1956. *Preface to Democratic Theory.* Chicago: University of Chicago Press.

Davis, Angela Y. 1981. *Women, Race, and Class.* New York: Vintage Books.

———. 1990a [1984]. Facing Our Common Foe: Women and the Struggle against Racism. In *Women, Culture, and Politics.* New York: Vintage Books, 16–34.

———. 1990b [1987]. Let Us All Rise Together: Radical Perspectives on Empowerment for Afro-American Women. In *Women, Culture, and Politics.* New York: Vintage Books, 3–15.

Dawson, Michael C. 1993a. Some Preliminary Thoughts on Poverty, Space, and Political Beliefs. University of Chicago. Manuscript.

———. 1993b. Demonization and Silence: Preliminary: Thoughts on the 1992 Presidential Election, the New Consensus on Race, and African-American Public Opinion. A paper presented at the Symposium on Race and American Political Culture, May 11, 1993 at the University of Chicago.

———. 1994a. *Behind the Mule: Race, Class, and African American Politics.* Princeton, NJ: Princeton University Press.

———. 1994b. A Black Counterpublic? Economic Earthquakes, Racial Agenda(s), and Black Politics. *Public Culture* 7: 195–223.

———. 1995. Desperation and Hope: Competing Visions of Race and American Citizenship. University of Chicago. Manuscript.

———. 1996. Black Discontent: The Report of the 1993–1994 National Black Politics Study. Report # 1 from the 1993–1994 National Black Politics Working Paper Series. University of Chicago.

———. 1997. Globalization, the Racial Divide, and a New Citizenship. In Theda Skocpol and Stan Greenberg, eds., *The New Majority.* New Haven, CT: Yale University Press, 264–78.

——. 1998. Twisting History: A Review of *America in Black and White* by Thernstrom, Stephan, and Abigail Thernstrom. *Common Quest* (winter 1998): 54–57.

——. 1999. Dis Beat Disrupts: Rap, Ideology, and Black Political Opinion. In Michèle Lamont, ed., *The Cultural Territories of Race: White and Black Boundaries.* Chicago: University of Chicago Press, 318–42.

——. n.d. The Black Prince? Speculations on Marcus Garvey and Machiavelli. Manuscript.

Dawson, Michael C., and Ernest J. Wilson III. 1991. Paradigms and Paradoxes: Political Science and the Study of African-American Politics. In William Crotty, ed., *Political Science: Looking to the Future,* vol. 1. Evanston, IL: Northwestern University Press, 189–234.

Delany, Martin R. 1993 [1852]. *The Condition, Elevation, Emigration, and Destiny of the Colored People of the United States.* Baltimore: Black Classic Press.

Dolan, Frederick M. 1994. *Allegories of America: Narratives, Metaphysics, Politics.* Ithaca, NY: Cornell University Press.

Douglass, Frederick. 1969a [1855]. *My Bondage and My Freedom.* New York: Dover Publications.

——. 1969b [1852]. What to the Slave Is the Fourth of July? In Douglass 1969a, 441–45.

Drake, St. Clair, and Horace R. Cayton. 1962. *Black Metropolis: A Study of Negro Life in a Northern City.* Vol. 2. New York: Harper & Row.

Du Bois, William Edward Burghardt. 1969 [1903]. *The Souls of Black Folk.* New York: Penguin Books.

——. 1971. [1935]. A Negro Nation within the Nation. In Andrew Paschal, ed. *W. E. B. Du Bois: A Reader.* New York: Collier Books, 69–79.

——. 1973 [1933]. Marxism and the Negro Problem. In Vincent 1973, 210–16.

——. 1979 [1935]. *Black Reconstruction in America, 1860–1880.* New York: Atheneum.

——. 1985a [1944]. A Program of Organization for Realizing Democracy in the United States by Securing to Americans of Negro Descent the Full Rights of Citizens. In Herbert Aptheker, ed., *Against Racism: Unpublished Essays, Papers, Addresses, 1887–1961, W. E. B. Du Bois.* Amherst: University of Massachusetts Press, 219–25.

——. 1985b [1949]. A Petition to the Human Rights Commission of the Social and Economic Council of the United Nations; and to the General Assembly of the United Nations; and to the Several Delegations of the Member States of the United Nations. In Herbert Aptheker, ed., *Against Racism: Unpublished Essays, Papers, Addresses, 1887–1961, W. E. B. Du Bois.* Amherst: University of Massachusetts Press, 261–65.

——. 1986 [1940]. *Dusk of Dawn.* In Nathan Huggins, ed., *Du Bois Writings.* New York: Library of America.

Dumm, Thomas L. 1994. *United States.* Ithaca, NY: Cornell University Press.

Dyson, Michael Eric. 1993. *Reflecting Black: African-American Cultural Criticism.* Minneapolis: University of Minnesota Press.

————. 1996. *Between God and Gangsta Rap: Bearing Witness to Black Culture.* New York: Oxford University Press.

Eagleton, Terry. 1991. *Ideology: An Introduction.* London: Verso Press.

Eley, Geoff. 1989. Nations, Publics, and Political Cultures: Placing Habermas in the Nineteenth Century. In Craig Calhoun, ed., *Habermas and the Public Sphere.* Cambridge: MIT Press, 289–339.

Epstein, Richard A. 1992. *Forbidden Grounds: The Case against Employment Discrimination Laws.* Cambridge, MA: Harvard University Press.

Farrakhan, Louis. 1989. *Back Where We Belong: Selected Speeches by Minister Louis Farrakhan.* Philadelphia: PC International Press.

————. 1996. *Let Us Make Man. Select Men Only and Women Only Speeches by Minister Louis Farrakhan.* New York: Uprising Communications.

Fields, Barbara J. 1982. Ideology and Race in American History. In J. Morgan Kousser and James M. McPherson, eds., *Region, Race, and Reconstruction: Essays in Honor of C. Vann Woodward.* New York: Oxford University Press, 143–77.

Floyd, Samuel A., Jr. 1995. *The Power of Black Music: Interpreting Its History from Africa to the United States.* New York: Oxford University Press.

Foner, Eric. 1980. *Politics and Ideology in the Age of the Civil War.* Oxford: Oxford University Press.

————. 1984. Reconstruction and the Black Political Tradition. In Richard S. McCormick, ed., *Political Parties and the Modern State.* New Brunswick: Rutgers University Press.

————. 1988. *Reconstruction: America's Unfinished Revolution, 1863–1877.* New York: Harper & Row.

Foner, Philip Sheldon, ed. 1995 [1970]. *The Black Panthers Speak.* New York: Da Capo Press.

Fortune, T. Thomas. 1973 [1926]. A Man without a Country. In Vincent 1973, 159–60.

Franklin, V. P. 1984. *Black Self-Determination: A Cultural History of the Faith of the Fathers.* Westport, CT: Lawrence Hill Books.

————. 1995. *Living Our Stories, Telling Our Truths: Autobiography and the Making of the African-American Intellectual Tradition.* New York: Scribner.

Fraser, Nancy. 1989. Rethinking the Public Sphere: A Contribution to the Critique of Actually Existing Democracy. In Craig Calhoun, ed., *Habermas and the Public Sphere.* Cambridge: MIT Press, 109–42.

Gailey, Christine Ward. 1987. *Kinship to Kingship: Gender Hierarchy and State Formation in the Tongan Islands.* Austin: University of Texas Press.

Gaines, Kevin K. 1996. *Uplifting the Race: Black Leadership, Politics, and Culture in the Twentieth Century.* Chapel Hill: University of North Carolina Press.

Garrow, David J. 1981. *The FBI and Martin Luther King, Jr.* New York: Penguin Books.

Garvey, Marcus. 1986. *Philosophy and Opinions of Marcus Garvey.* Ed. Amy Jacques-Garvey. New York: Atheneum.

Gates, Henry Louis, Jr.. 1996. W. E. B. DuBois and "The Talented Tenth." In Gates and West 1997, 115–32.

———. 1997. *Thirteen Ways of Looking at a Black Man*. New York: Random House.

Gates, Henry Louis, Jr., and Cornel West. 1997. Preface. In *The Future of the Race*. New York: Alfred A. Knopf, vii–xvii.

Georgakas, Dan, and Marvin Surkin. 1975. *Detroit, I Do Mind Dying : A Study in Urban Revolution*. New York: St. Martin's Press.

Geschwender, James A. 1977. *Class, Race, and Worker Insurgency: The League of Revolutionary Black Workers*. New York: Cambridge University Press.

Giddings, Paula. 1984. *When and Where I Enter: The Impact of Black Women on Race and Sex in America*. New York: William Morrow.

Gilliam, Franklin D., and Shanto Iyengar. 2000. Prime Suspects: The Influence of Local Television News on the Viewing Public. *American Journal of Political Science* 44 (3): 560–73.

Gilroy, Paul. 1991. *There Ain't No Black in the Union Jack: The Cultural Politics of Race and Nation*. Chicago: University of Chicago Press.

Gold, Jonathan. 1996. Why Rap Doesn't Cut It Live. In Adam Sexton, ed., *Rap on Rap: Straight-Up Talk on Hip-Hop Culture*. New York: Delta Books, 66–71.

Goodin, Robert E., and Philip Pettit eds. 1993. *A Companion to Contemporary Political Philosophy*. Oxford, U.K., and Cambridge, MA: Blackwell.

Goodin, Robert E., and Hans-Dieter Klingemann, eds. 1996. *A New Handbook of Political Science*. Oxford, U.K., and New York: Oxford University Press.

Greenstone, J. David. 1993. *The Lincoln Persuasion: Remaking American Liberalism*. Princeton, NJ: Princeton University Press.

Gurin, Patricia; Shirley Hatchett; and James S. Jackson. 1989. *Hope and Independence: Blacks' Response to Electoral and Party Politics*. New York: Russell Sage Foundation.

Guy-Sheftall, Beverly. 1992. Breaking the Silence: A Black Feminist Response to the Thomas/Hill Hearings (for Audre Lorde). *Black Scholar* 22: 35–37.

———. 1995. *Words of Fire: An Anthology of African-America Feminist Thought*. New York: New Press, 1–22.

Gwaltney, John L. 1980. *Drylongso: A Self-Portrait of Black America*. New York: Vintage Books.

Habermas, Jürgen. 1984. *The Theory of Communicative Action*. Vol. 1. Trans. Thomas McCarthy. Boston: Beacon Press.

———. 1989 [1962]. *The Structural Transformation of the Public Sphere: An Inquiry into a Category of Bourgeois Society*. Trans. Thomas Burger. Cambridge: MIT Press.

———. 1995. Citizenship and National Identity: Some Reflections on the Future of Europe. In Ronald Beiner, ed., *Theorizing Citizenship*. Albany: State University of New York Press, 255–81.

Hall, Stuart. 1992. What Is This "Black" in Black Popular Culture. In Gina Dent, ed. *Black Popular Culture: A Project by Michele Wallace*. Seattle: Bay Press, 21–33.

Hamilton, Charles V. 1982. Measuring Black Conservatism. In James Williams, ed., *The State of Black America*. New York: National Urban League, 113–40.

Hanchard, Michael G. 1991. Racial Consciousness and Afro-Diasporic Experiences: Antonio Gramsci Reconsidered. *Socialism and Democracy* 14: 83–106.

———. 1994. *Orpheus and Power: The Movimento Negro of Rio de Janeiro and São Paulo, Brazil, 1945–1988.* Princeton, NJ: Princeton University Press.

Hare, Nathan, and Julia Hare. 1992. The Clarence Thomas Hearings. *Black Scholar* 22: 37–40.

Harris, Angela P. 1994. Race and Essentialism in Feminist Legal Theory. In Susan Sage Heinzelman and Zipporah Batshaw Wiseman, eds., *Representing Women: Law, Literature, and Feminism.* Durham, NC: Duke University Press, 106–46.

Harris-Lacewell, Melissa. 1999. Barbershops, Bibles, and B. E. T.: Dialogue and the Development of Black Political Thought. Ph.D. diss. Duke University.

Harris, William J., ed. 1991. *The LeRoi Jones/Amiri Baraka Reader.* New York: Thunder's Mouth Press.

Hartz, Louis. 1955. *The Liberal Tradition in America: An Interpretation of American Political Thought Since the Revolution.* New York: Harcourt Brace Jovanovich.

Harvey, David. 1989. *The Condition of Postmodernity.* Cambridge, U.K.: Blackwell.

Haywood, Harry. 1977 [1957]. *For a Revolutionary Position on the Negro Question.* Chicago: Liberator Press.

———. 1978. *Black Bolshevik: Autobiography of an Afro-American Communist.* Chicago: Liberator Press.

Henry, Charles P. 1990. *Culture and African American Politics.* Bloomington: Indiana University Press.

———. 1992. Clarence Thomas and the National Black Identity. *Black Scholar* 22: 40–41.

Hess, Carla M. 1993. Introduction. In Greenstone 1993, xv–xxxiii.

Higginbotham, Evelyn Brooks. 1992. African-American Women's History and the Metalanguage of Race. *Signs* 17: 251–74.

———. 1993. *Righteous Discontent: The Women's Movement in the Black Baptist Church, 1880–1920.* Cambridge, MA: Harvard University Press.

Hill, Rickey. 1994. From a Culture of Struggle and Resistance to a Culture of Acquiescence and Displacement: Sketches on the Problematics of Contemporary Black Political Discourse. A paper presented at the Seventeenth Annual Black Studies Conference at Olive-Harvey College, Chicago, IL, April 20–23, 1994.

Hill, Robert A. 1987. Introduction. In Robert A. Hill, ed., *The Crusader: Volume 1, September 1918–August 1919.* New York: Garland, v–lxxiii.

Hilliard, David, and Lewis Cole. 1993. *This Side of Glory: The Autobiography of David Hilliard and the Story of the Black Panther Party.* Boston: Little, Brown.

Holmes, Stephen. 1995. *Passions and Constraint: On the Theory of Liberal Democracy.* Chicago: University of Chicago Press.

Holt, Thomas C. 1982a. An Empire over the Mind: Emancipation, Race, and Ideology in the British West Indies and the American South. In J. Morgan Kousser and James M. McPherson, eds., *Region, Race, and Reconstruction: Essays in Honor of C. Vann Woodward.* New York: Oxford University Press, 283–314.

————. 1982b. The Lonely Warrior: Ida B. Wells-Barnett and the Struggle for Black Leadership. In John Hope Franklin and August Meier, eds., *Black Leaders in the Twentieth Century*. Urbana: University of Illinois Press, 39–61.

————. 1990. *African-American History*. Washington, DC: American Historical Association.

Honig, Bonnie. 1993. *Political Theory and the Displacement of Politics*. Ithaca, NY: Cornell University Press.

hooks, bell. 1984. *Feminist Theory: From Margin to Center*. Boston: South End Press.

————. 1991. Theory as Liberatory Practice. *Yale Journal of Law and Feminism* 4: 1–11.

Hord, Fred Lee (Mzee Lasana Okpara), and Jonathan Scott Lee. 1995. "I Am Because We Are": An Introduction in Black Philosophy. In Fred Lee Hord (Mzee Lasana Okpara) and Jonathan Scott Lee, eds., *I Am Because We Are: Readings in Black Philosophy*. Amherst: University of Massachusetts Press, 1–16.

Horkheimer, Max. 1972. *Critical Theory: Selected Essays. Trans*. Matthew J. O'Connell. New York: Herder and Herder.

Horton, Carol. 1995. *Races, Liberalism, and American Political Culture*. Ph.D. diss. University of Chicago.

Howard-Pitney, David. 1990. *The Afro-American Jeremiad: Appeals for Justice in America*. Philadelphia: Temple University Press.

Huntington, Samuel P. 1981. *American Politics: The Promise of Disharmony*. Cambridge, MA: Belknap Press.

Hutchinson, Earl Ofari. 1995. *Blacks and Reds: Race and Class in Conflict, 1919–1990*. East Lansing: Michigan State University Press.

Innis, Roy. 1997 [1969]. From Separatist Economics: A New Social Contract. In Van Deburg 1997, 176–81.

Jackson, George. 1972. *Blood in My Eye*. New York: Bantam Books.

Jackson, Jesse. 1989. *Keep Hope Alive: Jesse Jackson's 1988 Presidential Campaign*. Ed. Frank Clemente. Boston: South End Press.

James, Winston. 1998. *Holding Aloft the Banner of Ethiopia: Caribbean Radicalism in Early Twentieth-Century America*. London: Verso.

Janofsky, Michael. 1993. Race and the American Workplace. *New York Times*. National edition, Sunday, June 20, 1993, section 3, p. 1.

Jaynes, Gerald D. 1986. *Branches without Roots: Genesis of the Black Working Class in the American South, 1862–1914*. New York: Oxford University Press.

Jencks, Christopher. 1990. Varieties of Altruism: Beyond Self-Interest. In Jane J. Mansbridge ed., *Beyond Self-Interest*. Chicago: University of Chicago Press.

————. 1992. *Rethinking Social Policy: Race, Poverty, and the Underclass*. New York: HarperCollins.

Jennings, James. 1992. *The Politics of Black Empowerment: The Transformation of Black Activism in Urban America*. Detroit: Wayne State University Press.

Johnson, James H., Jr., and Melvin L. Oliver. 1990. Economic Restructuring and Black Male Joblessness in U.S. Metropolitan Areas. *Urban Geography* 12 (6): 542–62.

Jones, Claudia. 1995 [1949]. An End to the Neglect of the Problems of Negro Women! In Guy-Sheftall 1995, 108–23.

Jones, LeRoi. 1967. *Black Music*. New York: William Morrow.

Karenga, Maulana. 1988. *The African American Holiday of Kwanza: A Celebration of Family, Community, and Culture*. Los Angeles: Sankore Press.

———. 1993. *Introduction to Black Studies*. 2d ed. Los Angeles: Sankore Press.

Katznelson, Ira. 1982. *City Trenches: Urban Politics and the Patterning of Class in the United States*. Chicago: University of Chicago Press.

Kelley, Robin. 1990. *Hammer and Hoe: Alabama Communists During the Great Depression*. Chapel Hill: University of North Carolina Press.

———. 1994. *Race Rebels: Culture, Politics, and the Black Working Class*. New York: Free Press.

Kerber, Linda K. 1990. The Revolutionary Generation: Ideology, Politics, and Culture in the Early Republic. In Eric Foner, ed., *The New American History*. Philadelphia: Temple University Press, 25–49.

Kilson, Martin. 1993. Anatomy of Black Conservatism. *Transition* 59: 4–19.

Kinder, Donald R. 1983. Diversity and Complexity in American Public Opinion. In Ada W. Finifter, ed., *Political Science: The State of the Discipline*. Washington, DC: American Political Science Association, 389–425.

Kinder, Donald, R.; Tali Mendelberg; Michael C. Dawson; Lynn M. Sanders; Steven J. Rosenstone; Jocelyn Sargent; and Cathy Cohen. 1989. Race and the 1988 American Presidential Election. Paper prepared for the Annual Meeting of the American Political Science Association, Atlanta, Georgia, August 30–September 3, 1989.

Kinder, Donald R, and Lynn M. Sanders. 1996. *Divided By Color: Racial Politics and Democratic Ideas*. Chicago: University of Chicago Press.

King, Gary. 1989. *Unifying Political Methodology: The Likelihood Theory of Statistical Inference*. New York: Cambridge University Press.

King, Gary; Robert O. Keohane; and Sidney Verba. 1994. *Designing Social Inquiry: Scientific Inference in Qualitative Research*. Princeton, NJ: Princeton University Press.

King, Martin Luther, Jr. 1967. *Where Do We Go from Here: Chaos or Community?* [book version]. Boston: Beacon Hill Press.

———. 1986a. *A Testament of Hope: The Essential Writings and Speeches of Martin Luther King, Jr*. Ed. James M. Washington. San Francisco: Harper & Row.

———. 1986b [1960]. The Rising Tide of Racial Consciousness. In King 1986a, 145–51.

———. 1986c [1961]. Equality Now: The President Has the Power. In King 1986a, 152–59.

———. 1986d [1961]. The American Dream. In King 1986a, 208–16.

———. 1986e [1967]. Where Do We Go from Here? [speech version]. In King 1986a, 245–52.

———. 1986f [1967]. The Trumpet of Conscience. In King 1986a, 634–53.

———. 1986g [1967]. Behind the Selma March. In King 1986a, 126–31.

————. 1986h [1968]. Conversation with Martin Luther King. In King 1986a, 657–79.

————. 1986i. [1963]. I Have a Dream. In King 1986a, 217–20.

————. 1986j. [1962a]. An Address Before the National Press Club. In King 1986a, 99–105.

————. 1986k. [1962b]. The Case Against 'Tokenism.' In King 1986a, 106–11.

————. 1986l. [1958]. Stride Toward Freedom. In King 1986a, 418–90.

Kirschenman, Joleen, and Kathryn M. Neckerman. 1991. "We'd Love to Hire Them, but . . .": The Meaning of Race for Employers. In Christopher Jencks and Paul E. Peterson, eds., *The Urban Underclass*. Washington, DC: The Brookings Institute, 203–32.

Kiss, Elizabeth. 1996. Five Theses on Nationalism. In Russell Hardin and Ian Shapiro, eds., *Political Order*. New York: New York University Press, 288–332.

Kitwana, Bakari. 1994. *The Rap on Gangsta Rap*. Chicago: Third World Press.

Kofsky, Frank. 1970. *Black Nationalism and the Revolution in Music*. New York: Pathfinder Press.

Kornweibel, Theodore, Jr. 1998. *Seeing Red: Federal Campaigns against Black Militancy, 1919–1925*. Bloomington: Indiana University Press.

Lane, Robert E. 1962. *Political Ideology: Why the American Common Man Believes What He Does*. New York: Free Press.

Larmore, Charles. 1996. *The Morals of Modernity*. Cambridge: Cambridge University Press.

Lee, Taeku. 1997a. Collective Agency and Frame Contestation: Black Insurgency and the Dynamics of Racial Attitudes During the Civil Rights Era, 1948–1965. Paper prepared for the annual meeting of the Midwest Political Science Association, April 10–12, 1997, Chicago, IL.

————. 1997b. Two Nations, Separate Grooves: Black Insurgency and the Dynamics of Mass Opinion—The United States from 1948 to 1972. Ph.D. diss. University of Chicago.

Lewis, Earl. 1991. *In Their Own Interests: Race, Class, and Power in Twentieth-Century Norfolk, Virginia*. Berkeley: University of California Press.

Lincoln, C. Eric, and Lawrence H. Mamiya. 1990. *The Black Church in the African American Experience*. Durham, NC: Duke University Press.

Lipsitz, George. 1988. *A Life in the Struggle: Ivory Perry and the Culture of Opposition*. Philadelphia: Temple University Press.

Locke, Mamie. 1987. Outsiders in Insider Politics: Black Women and the American Political System. In Franklin Jones et al., eds., *Readings in American Political Issues*. Dubuque, IA: Kendall/Hunt.

Lorde, Audre. 1984. *Sister/Outsider: Essays and Speeches*. Freedom, CA: The Crossing Press.

Loury, Glenn C. 1993. Self-Censorship in Public Discourse: A Theory of "Political Correctness" and Related Phenomena. Boston University. Manuscript.

———. 1995. *One by One from the Inside Out: Essays and Reviews on Race and Responsibility in America*. New York: Free Press.

———. 1998. *Selected Clips, January 1997–March 1998*. Boston: Institute on Race and Social Division, Boston University.

Lynn, Conrad. 1993 [1979]. *There Is a Fountain: The Autobiography of Conrad Lynn*. Brooklyn: Lawrence Hill Books.

Machiavelli, Niccolo. 1980. *The Prince*. Trans. Paul de Alvarez. Irving, TX: University of Dallas Press.

MacKinnon, Catherine A. 1991. From Practice to Theory, or What Is a White Woman Anyway? *Yale Journal of Law and Feminism* 4: 13–22.

Madhubuti, Haki R. 1994. *Claiming Earth: Race, Rage, Rape, Redemption: Blacks Seeking a Culture of Enlightened Empowerment*. Chicago: Third World Press.

Malcolm X. 1965. *Malcolm X Speaks*. New York: Grove Press.

———. 1970. *Malcolm X on Afro-American History*. New York: Pathfinder Press.

———. 1995 [1964]. The Black Revolution. In Fred Lee Hord (Mzee Lasana Okpara) and Jonathan Scott Lee, eds., *I Am Because We Are: Readings in Black Philosophy*. Amherst: University of Massachusetts Press, 272–84.

———. 1997 [1965]. From Basic Black Unity Program: Organization of Afro-American Unity. In Van Deburg 1997, 108–15.

Malveaux, Julianne. 1992. Popular Culture and the Economics of Alienation. In Gina Dent, ed., *Black Popular Culture: A Project by Michele Wallace*. Seattle: Bay Press, 200–208.

Mao Tse-Tung. 1968. *Statement by Comrade Mao Tse-Tung, Chairman of the Central Committee of the Communist Party of China, in Support of the Afro-American Struggle against Violent Repression*. Peking: Foreign Language Press.

Marable, Manning. 1983. *How Capitalism Underdeveloped Black America: Problems in Race, Political Economy, and Society*. Boston: South End Press.

———. 1995. *Beyond Black and White: Transforming African-American Politics*. London: Verso.

———. 1995a. History and Black Consciousness: The Political Culture of Black America. In Marable 1995, 216–29.

———. 1995b [1991]. Black America in Search of Itself. In Marable 1995, 13–25.

———. 1995c [1992]. At the End of the Rainbow. In Marable 1995, 55–61.

———. 1995d [1993]. Beyond Racial Identity Politics: Toward a Liberation Theory for Multicultural Democracy. In Marable 1995, 185–201.

———. 1995e. Affirmative Action and the Politics of Race. In Marable 1995, 81–90.

Marable, Manning, and Leith Mullings. 1995 [1994]. The Divided Mind of Black America: Race, Ideology and Politics in the Post–Civil Rights Era. In Marable 1995, 203–15.

Martin, Waldo E., Jr. 1990. Images of Frederick Douglass in the Afro-American Mind: The Recent Black Freedom Struggle. In Eric J. Sundquist, ed., *Frederick Douglass: New Literary and Historical Essays*. Cambridge: Cambridge University Press, 271–85.

Massey, Douglas S., and Nancy A. Denton. 1993. *American Apartheid: Segregation and the Making of the Underclass.* Cambridge, MA: Harvard University Press.

Mays, Andrea L. 1996. Women's Reaction Ran from Elation to Disdain. *USA Today,* online edition, February 16, 1996.

McAdam, Doug. 1982. *Political Process and the Development of Black Insurgency, 1930–1970.* Chicago: University of Chicago Press.

McDowell, Deborah E. 1995. *The Changing Same: Black Women's Literature, Criticism, and Theory.* Bloomington: Indiana University Press.

McKay, Nellie Y. 1992. Remembering Anita Hill and Clarence Thomas: What Really Happened When One Black Woman Spoke Out. In Toni Morrison, ed., *Race-ing Justice, En-gender-ing Power: Essays on Anita Hill, Clarence Thomas, and the Construction of Social Reality.* New York: Pantheon Books, 269–89.

Mills, Charles W. 1997. *The Racial Contract.* Ithaca, NY: Cornell University Press.

Moraga, Cherrie, and Gloria Anzaldua. 1981. *This Bridge Called My Back: Writings of Racial Women of Color.* Watertown, CT: Persephone Press.

Morgan, Joan. 1996. The Nigga Ya Hate to Love. In Adam Sexton, ed., *Rap on Rap: Straight-Up Talk on Hip-Hop Culture.* New York: Delta Books, 118–24.

Morrison, Toni. 1992a. Introduction: Friday on the Potomac. In Toni Morrison, ed., *Race-ing Justice, En-gender-ing Power: Essays on Anita Hill, Clarence Thomas, and the Construction of Social Reality.* New York: Pantheon Books, vii–xxx.

———. 1992b. *Playing in the Dark: Whiteness and the Literary Imagination.* Cambridge, MA: Harvard University Press.

Moses, Wilson Jeremiah. 1978. *The Golden Age of Black Nationalism, 1850–1925.* New York: Oxford University Press.

Mouledous, Joseph C. 1964. From Browderism to Peaceful Co-Existence: An Analysis of Developments in the Communist Position on the American Negro. *Phylon* 25: 79–90.

Muhammad, Elijah. 1997 [1965]. Know Thyself: Excerpts from *Message to the Blackman in America.* In Van Deburg 1997, 99–100.

Murray, Charles. 1984. *Losing Ground: American Social Policy, 1950–1980.* New York: Basic Books.

Murray, Hugh T., Jr. 1967. The NAACP versus the Communist Party: The Scottsboro Rape Cases, 1931–1932. *Phylon* 28: 276–87.

Naison, Mark. 1983. *Communists in Harlem During the Depression.* New York: Grove Press.

National Black Political Convention. 1997 [1972]. The Gary Declaration: Black Politics at the Crossroads. In Van Deburg 1997, 138–43.

Newton, Huey P. 1970a. Press Conference, August 21, 1970. From Black Panther Archives, Special Collections, Stanford University Libraries.

———. 1970b. Press Conference, September 5, 1970. From Black Panther Archives, Special Collections, Stanford University Libraries.

———. 1972. On Pan-Africanism or Communism. From Black Panther Archives, Special Collections, Stanford University Libraries.

Norton, Anne. 1993. *Republic of Signs: Liberal Theory and American Popular Culture.* Chicago: University of Chicago Press.

Nozick, Robert. 1974. *Anarchy, State, and Utopia.* New York: Basic Books.

Oakes, James. 1990. *Slavery and Freedom.* New York: Vintage Books.

———. 1992. The Liberal Dissensus. Northwestern University. Manuscript.

Ofari, Earl. 1970. *Black Liberation: Cultural and Revolutionary Nationalism.* Detroit: Radical Education Project.

Okin, Susan Moller. 1998. Feminism and Multiculturalism: Some Tensions. *Ethics* 108: 661–84.

———. 1991. John Rawls: Justice as Fairness—For Whom? in Mary Lyndon Shanley and Carole Pateman, eds., *Feminist Interpretations and Political Theory.* University Park: Pennsylvania State University Press, 181–98.

Oliver, Melvin L., and Thomas M. Shapiro. 1995. *Black Wealth/White Wealth: A New Perspective on Racial Inequality.* New York: Routledge.

Owen, Chandler. 1993 [1923]. White Supremacy in Organized Labor. In Vincent 1973, 145–50.

Page, Benjamin I., and Robert Y. Shapiro. 1992. *The Rational Public: Fifty Years of Trends in Americans' Policy Preferences.* Chicago: University of Chicago Press.

Painter, Nell Irvin. 1992. Hill, Thomas, and the Use of the Racial Stereotype. In Toni Morrison, ed., *Race-ing Justice, En-gender-ing Power: Essays on Anita Hill, Clarence Thomas, and the Construction of Social Reality.* New York: Pantheon Books, 200–214.

Paris. 1995. Yo! A Rapper's Domestic Policy Plan: How Clinton Can Bring Hope to Alienated Black America. In Adam Sexton, ed., *Rap on Rap: Straight-Up Talk on Hip-Hop Culture.* New York: Delta Books, 211–15.

Parker, Star. 1997. *Pimps, Whores, and Welfare Brats: The Stunning Conservative Transformation of a Former Welfare Queen.* New York: Pocket Books.

Payne, Charles. 1989. Ella Baker and Models of Social Change. *Signs* 14: 885–99.

Pearson, Hugh. 1994. *The Shadow of the Panther: Huey Newton and the Price of Black Power in America.* Reading, MA: Addison-Wesley.

Persons, Georgia. 1993. Introduction. *Dilemmas of Black Politics: Issues of Leadership and Strategy.* New York: HarperCollins College Publishers, 1–11.

Pinderhughes, Dianne. 1987. *Race and Ethnicity in Chicago Politics.* Urbana: University of Illinois Press.

Rabinowitz, Paula. 1987. Women and U.S. Literary Radicalism. In Charlotte Nekola and Paula Rabinowitz, eds., *Writing Red: An Anthology of American Women Writers, 1930–1940.* New York: Feminist Press, 1–16.

Randolph, A. Philip. 1965 [1919]. Lynching: Capitalism Its Cause; Socialism Its Cure. In Francis L. Broderick and August Meir, eds., *Negro Protest Thought in the Twentieth Century.* Indianapolis: Bobbs-Merrill, 71–77.

Randolph, A. Philip, and Chandler Owen. 1965 [1919]. Our Reason for Being. In Francis L. Broderick and August Meir, eds., *Negro Protest Thought in the Twentieth Century.* Indianapolis: Bobbs-Merrill, 67–71.

Ransby, Barbara. 1995. Black Popular Culture and the Transcendence of Patriarchal Illusions. In Guy-Sheftall 1995, 526–35.

———. 1996. Ella J. Baker and the Black Radical Tradition. Ph.D. diss. University of Michigan.

Ransby, Barbara, and Tracye Matthews. 1993. Black Popular Culture and the Transcendence of Patriarchal Illusions. *Race and Class* 35: 57–68.

Ransom, Roger L., and Richard Sutch. 1977. *One Kind of Freedom: The Economic Consequences of Emancipation.* Cambridge: Cambridge University Press.

Rawls, John. 1993. *Political Liberalism.* New York: Columbia University Press.

Raz, Joseph. 1986. *The Morality of Freedom.* New York: Oxford University Press.

Reed, Jr., Adolph. 1971. Marxism and Nationalism in Afroamerica. *Social Theory and Practice* (fall): 1–39.

———. 1986. *The Jesse Jackson Phenomenon: The Crisis of Purpose in Afro-American Politics.* New Haven, CT: Yale University Press.

———. 1992a. The Allure of Malcolm X. In Joe Wood, ed., *Malcolm X: In Our Own Image.* New York: St. Martin's Press, 201–32.

———. 1992b. Dubois's "Double Consciousness": Race and Gender in Progressive Era American Thought. *Studies in American Political Development* 6: 93–139.

———. 1997. *W. E. B. Du Bois and American Political Thought: Fabianism and the Color Line.* New York: Oxford University Press.

———. 1999a. The Black Urban Regime: Structural Origins and Constraints. In *Stirrings in the Jug: Black Politics in the Post-Segregation Era.* Minneapolis and London: University of Minnesota Press, 79–115.

———. 1999b. Sources of Demobilization in the New Black Political Regime: Incorporation, Ideological Capitulation, and Radical Failure in the Post-Segregation Era. In *Stirrings in the Jug: Black Politics in the Post-Segregation Era.* Minneapolis and London: University of Minnesota Press, 117–59.

Rivers, Eugene F., III. 1995. Beyond the Nationalism of Fools: Toward an Agenda for Black Intellectuals. *Boston Review* (October/November): online version. Supplementary url: <http://bostonreview.mit.edu/BR20.3/rivers.html>>.

Roberts, Dorothy. 1997. *Killing the Black Body: Race, Reproduction, and the Meaning of Liberty.* New York: Pantheon Books.

Robeson, Paul. 1973. *Equal Rights and an Equal Share.* Taped Message to Carnegie Hall Robeson Tribute on Seventy-fifth Birthday. Quoted on *Morning Edition.* National Public Radio, April 9, 1998 (transcript).

Robinson, Cedric J. 1983. *Black Marxism: The Making of the Black Radical Tradition.* London: Zed Books.

Robinson, Deborah M. 1987. The Effect of Multiple Group Identity among Black Women on Race Consciousness. Ph.D. diss. University of Michigan.

Roediger, David. 1994. *Toward the Abolition of Whiteness.* London: Verso.

Rokeach, Milton. 1976. *Beliefs, Attitudes, and Values: A Theory of Organization and Change.* San Francisco: Jossey-Bass.

————. 1979. Changes and Stability in American Value Systems, 1969–1971. In Milton Rokeach, ed., *Understanding Human Values*. New York: Free Press 129–47.

Rorty, Richard. 1989. *Contingency, Irony, and Solidarity*. Cambridge: Cambridge University Press.

————. 1991. On Ethnocentrism. In *Objectivity, Relativism, and Truth: Philosophical Papers*. Vol. 1. Cambridge: Cambridge University Press.

————. 1993. Human Rights, Rationality, and Sentimentality. *Yale Review* 81: 1.

————. 1994. Feminism, Ideology, and Deconstruction: A Pragmatist View. In Slavoj Žižek, ed., *Mapping Ideology*. London: Verso, 227–34.

Rose, Tricia. 1989. Orality and Technology: Rap Music and Afro-American Cultural Resistance. *Popular Music and Society* 13: 35–44.

————. 1991. Never Trust a Big Butt and a Smile. *Camera Obscura* 23: 104–31.

————. 1994. *Black Noise: Rap Music and Black Culture in Contemporary America*. Hanover: Wesleyan University Press.

————. 1995. Rhythmic Repetition, Industrial Forces, and Black Practice. In Adam Sexton, ed., *Rap on Rap: Straight-Up Talk on Hip-Hop Culture*. New York: Delta Books, 45–55.

Rosengarten, Theodore (Shaw, Nate). 1974. *All God's Dangers: The Life of Nate Shaw*. New York: Avon.

Rousseau, Jean-Jacques. 1978 [1762]. *The Social Contract*. Trans. Roger D. Masters. New York: St. Martin's Press

Ryan, Mary P. 1989. Gender and Public Access: Women's Politics in Nineteenth-Century America. In Craig Calhoun, ed., *Habermas and the Public Sphere*. Cambridge: MIT Press, 259–88.

Sandel, Michael J. 1996. *Democracy's Discontent: America in Search of a Public Philosophy*. Cambridge, MA: Harvard University Press.

Sanders, Lynn M. 1995a. The Racial Legacy of American Values. Ph.D. diss. University of Michigan.

————. 1995b. What Is Whiteness? Race of Interviewer Effects When All the Interviewers Are Black. University of Chicago. Manuscript.

————. 1997. Against Deliberation. *Political Theory* 22: 347–76.

————. Pornography: Pornography in Public. University of Chicago. Manuscript.

Satz, Debra. 1996. The World House Divided: The Claims of the Human Community in the Age of Nationalism. In Russell Hardin and Ian Shapiro, eds., *Political Order*. New York: New York University Press, 333–44.

Saville, Julie. 1994a. *The Work of Reconstruction: From Slave to Wage Laborer in South Carolina, 1860–1870*. Cambridge: Cambridge University Press.

————. 1994b. Civil Rites: Ex-Slaves and the Invention of Political Ritual in South Carolina, 1865–70. Paper prepared for delivery at the annual meeting of the Organization of American Historians, Atlanta, GA, April 14–17, 1994.

Schank, Roger, and Robert Abelson. 1977. *Scripts, Plans, Goals, and Understanding: An Inquiry into Human Knowledge Structures*. Hillsdale, NJ: Lawrence Erlbaum Associates.

Scott, James C. 1990. *Domination and the Arts of Resistance: Hidden Transcripts*. New Haven, CT: Yale University Press.

Sewell, William H., Jr. 1992. A Theory of Structure: Duality, Agency, and Transformation. *American Journal of Sociology* 98: 1–29.

———. 1994. *A Rhetoric of Bourgeois Revolution: The Abbè Sieyes and "What Is the Third Estate?"* Durham, NC: Duke University Press.

Sexton, Adam. 1995. Don't Believe the Hype: Why Isn't Hip-Hop Criticism Better? In Adam Sexton, ed., *Rap on Rap: Straight-Up Talk on Hip-Hop Culture*. New York: Delta Books, 1–13.

Shakur, Assata. 1987. *Assata: An Autobiography*. London: Zed Books.

Sheftall, Beverly. 1995. Introduction: The Evolution of Feminist Consciousness among African-American Women. In Beverly Guy-Sheftall, ed., *Words of Fire: An Anthology of African-American Feminist Thought*, 1–22.

Shklar, Judith N. 1995. *American Citizenship: The Quest for Inclusion*. Cambridge, MA: Harvard University Press.

———. 1998. *Redeeming American Political Thought*. Ed. Dennis F. Thompson. Chicago: University of Chicago Press.

Skinner, Quentin. 1988. Meaning and Understanding in the History of Ideas. In James Tully, ed., *Meaning and Context: Quentin Skinner and His Critics*. Princeton, NJ: Princeton University Press, 29–67.

Smith, Barbara, and Beverly Smith. 1981. Across the Kitchen Table: A Sister-to-Sister Dialogue. In Moraga and Anzaldua 1981, 114–27.

Smith, Robert C. 1993. Ideology as the Enduring Dilemma of Black Politics. In Georgia Persons, ed., *Dilemmas of Black Politics: Issues of Leadership and Strategy*. New York: HarperCollins College Publishers, 211–24.

Smith, Robert C., and Richard Seltzer. 1992. *Race, Class, and Culture: A Study in Afro-American Mass Opinion*. Albany: State University of New York Press.

Smith, Rogers M. 1997. *Civic Ideals: Conflicting Visions of Citizenship in U.S. History*. New Haven, CT: Yale University Press.

Souljah, Sister. 1994. *No Disrespect*. New York: Times Books.

Sowell, Thomas. 1992. *Inside American Education: The Decline, the Deception, the Dogmas*. New York: Free Press.

———. 1994. *Race and Culture: A World View*. New York: Basic Books.

Spillers, Hortense J. 1987 Mama's Baby, Papa's Maybe: An American Grammar Book. *Diacritics* (summer): 65–81.

———. 1996. "All The Things You Could Be by Now If Sigmund Freud's Wife Was Your Mother": Psychoanalysis and Race. *Critical Inquiry* 22: 710–34.

Sposito, Frank Andreas. 1998. Liberalism and the Emaciated Conception. University of Chicago. Manuscript.

Starks, Robert. 1995. *Million Man March Manifesto*. Northeastern Illinois University. Manuscript.

Stepto, Robert. B. 1991. *From Behind the Veil: A Study of Afro-American Narrative*. 2d ed. Urbana: University of Illinois Press.

Stimson, James A. 1991. *Public Opinion in America: Moods, Cycles, and Swings.* Boulder, CO: Westview Press.

Storing, Herbert J. 1995. The Case against Civil Disobedience. In Joseph M. Bessette, ed., *Toward a More Perfect Union: Writings of Herbert J. Storing.* Washington, DC: AEI Press, 236–58.

Stuckey, Sterling. 1987. *Slave Culture: Nationalist Theory and the Foundations of Black America.* New York: Oxford University Press.

Sunstein, Cass R. 1998. Beyond the Republican Revival. *The Yale Law Journal* 97: 539–90.

T., Ice. 1995. The Controversy. In Adam Sexton, ed., *Rap on Rap: Straight-Up Talk on Hip-Hop Culture.* New York: Delta Books, 177–88.

Tate, Katherine. 1993. *From Protest to Politics: The New Black Voters in American Politics.* Cambridge, MA: Harvard University Press.

Taylor, Charles. 1992. *Multiculturalism and "the Politics of Recognition."* Princeton, NJ: Princeton University Press.

Thernstrom, Stephan, and Abigail Thernstrom. 1997. *America in Black and White: One Nation, Indivisible.* New York: Simon and Schuster.

Thompson, John B. 1984. *Studies in the Theory of Ideology.* Berkeley: University of California Press.

Truth, Sojourner. 1995a [1851]. Woman's Rights. In Guy-Sheftall 1995, 36.

———. 1995b [1867]. When Woman Gets Her Rights Man Will Be Right. In Guy-Sheftall 1995, 37–38.

Unger, Roberto Mangabeira, and Cornel West. 1998. *The Future of American Progressivism: An Initiative for Political and Economic Reform.* Boston: Beacon Press.

Van Deburg, William. ed., 1997. *Modern Black Nationalism: From Marcus Garvey to Louis Farrakhan.* New York: New York University Press.

Van Woodward, C. 1966. *The Strange Career of Jim Crow.* 2d rev. ed. New York: Oxford Press.

Van Zanten, John W. 1967. Communist Theory and the American Negro Question. *Review of Politics* 29: 435–56.

Venkatesh, Sudhir A. 1993. The Killing of Rail: Black Gangs and the Reconstitution of "Community" in an Urban Ghetto. Paper prepared for the Politics of Race and the Reproduction of Racial Ideologies Workshop, November 12. University of Chicago.

Vincent, Theodore G., ed. 1973. *Voices of a Black Nation: Political Journalism in the Harlem Renaissance.* Trenton, NJ: Africa World Press, 55.

Waldron, Jeremy. 1993. *Liberal Rights: Collected Papers, 1981–1993.* Cambridge: Cambridge University Press.

Walker, Alice. 1993 [1974]. In Search of Our Mothers' Gardens: Womanist Prose. In Deirdre Mullane, ed., *Crossing the Danger Water: Three Hundred Years of African-American Writing.* New York: Anchor Books, 722–31.

Walzer Michael. 1990. The Communitarian Critique of Liberalism. *Political Theory* 18: 6–23.

———. 1992. *What It Means to Be an American: Essays on the American Experience*. New York: Marsilio.

Washington, Booker T. 1995 [1895]. The Atlanta Exposition Address. In Fred Lee Hord (Mzee Lasana Okpara) and Jonathan Scott Lee, eds., *I Am Because We Are: Readings in Black Philosophy*. Amherst: University of Massachusetts Press, 243–46.

Wells, Ida B. 1970. *Crusade for Justice: The Autobiography of Ida B. Wells*. Ed. Alfreda Duster. Chicago: University of Chicago Press.

West, Cornel. 1982. *Prophesy Deliverance! An Afro-American Revolutionary Christianity*. Philadelphia: Westminster Press.

———. 1988. Marxist Theory and the Specificity of Afro-American Oppression. In Gary Nelson and Lawrence Grossberg, eds., *Marxism and the Interpretation of Culture*. Urbana: University of Illinois Press, 17–33.

———. 1989. *The American Evasion of Philosophy: A Genealogy of Pragmatism*. Madison: University of Wisconsin Press.

———. 1993a. Nihilism in Black America. In *Race Matters*. Boston: Beacon Press, 9–20.

———. 1993b. Race, Class, and Power in Contemporary America. In *Prophetic Reflections: Notes on Race and Power in America*. Monroe, ME: Common Courage Press, 145–62.

———. 1993c [1987]. Rethinking Marxism. In *Prophetic Reflections: Notes on Race and Power in America*. Monroe, ME: Common Courage Press, 177–82.

———. 1993d [1988]. Black Radicalism and the Marxist Tradition. In *Prophetic Reflections: Notes on Race and Power in America*. Monroe, ME: Common Courage Press, 169–75.

———. 1993e [1991]. We Socialists. In *Prophetic Reflections: Notes on Race and Power in America*. Monroe, ME: Common Courage Press, 239–44.

Whatley, Warren, and Gavin Wright. 1994. Race, Human Capital, and Labour Markets in American History. Working Paper no. 7. Center for Afroamerican and African Studies, University of Michigan.

White, E. Frances. 1990. Africa on My Mind: Gender, Counter Discourse, and African-American Nationalism. *Journal of Women's History* 2: 73–97.

Williams, Armstrong. 1995. *Letters to a Young Victim: Hope and Healing in America's Inner Cities*. New York: Free Press.

Williams, Walter E. 1982. *The State against Blacks*. New York: McGraw-Hill.

Wilson, William J. 1987. *The Truly Disadvantaged: The Inner City, the Underclass, and Public Policy*. Chicago: University of Chicago Press.

Wittgenstein, Ludwig. 1958 [1953]. *Philosophical Investigations*. 3d ed. Trans. G. E. M. Anscombe. New York: Macmillan.

Wright, Richard. 1966 [1937]. *Black Boy*. New York: Harper & Row.

———. 1977 [1944]. *American Hunger*. New York: Harper & Row.

Yeshitela, Omali. 1988. This Time Till It's Won: Power in Our Own Hands. Oakland, CA: African People's Socialist Party.

Young, Iris Marion. 1990. Socialist Feminism and the Limits of Dual Systems Theory. In Iris Marion Young, ed., *Throwing Like a Girl and other Essays in Feminist Philosophy and Social Theory*. Bloomington: Indiana University Press, 21–35.

———. 1997. *Intersecting Voices: Dilemmas of Gender, Political Philosophy, and Politics*. Princeton, NJ: Princeton University Press.

Zaller, John R. 1992. *The Nature and Origins of Mass Opinion*. New York: Cambridge University Press.

Žižek, Slavoj. 1994. Introduction. In Slavoj Žižek, ed., *Mapping Ideology*. London: Verso, 1–33.

107; in black middle class, 48; Boggs on, 202; of Farrakhan, 105–11; war with revolutionary nationalism, 93, 117–18; on women's role, 110–11

culture: black Marxism on, 229; outcomes seen as determined by, 290–91. *See also* cultural nationalism

Dahl, Robert, 68, 242, 250

Daley, Richard J., 259, 269

Daly, Mary, 148

Davis, Angela, 7, 18, 197

Dawson, Michael C., 46n.4, 66n, 69, 69n, 128n.14, 300n

Declaration of Independence, 55

Delaney, Martin: on black Americans as nation within a nation, 6; black Americans compared with oppressed peoples of Europe by, 98; as black nationalist, 21, 85; scholars missing significance of, 30; on a state for black Americans, 94–95

Dellums, Ron, 248

Democratic Leadership Council (DLC), 220, 225

Democratic Party: black Marxism on, 234, 235; blacks' blind loyalty to, 225, 281; radical egalitarians supporting, 316; social democrats as critical of, 316; softening of black support for, 321

Democratic Socialists of America, 176, 217

Detroit: influx of blacks into, 202–3; League of Revolutionary Black Workers, 200–211; Marxism in, 200, 210; riots in, 198, 203; Young, 38, 207

Dewey, John, 223

Dirksen, Everett, 261, 266

discrimination: antidiscrimination efforts, 236, 262, 277, 292; rational, 250, 265, 266, 292. *See also* segregation

disillusioned liberalism, 273–80; and the American Creed, 14, 255; antecedents of support for, 307–8; and a black homeland, 95; and black Marxism, 174; and black nationalism, 100–102; and community nationalism, 316; core components of, 17–18; distributions of, 304–6; *305, 306*; measures of, 303; ties with

other ideologies, *317*; true believers and true haters in, *83*; as unstable, 312, 320

DLC (Democratic Leadership Council), 220, 225

Dodge Revolutionary Union Movement (DRUM), 36–37, 200, 203, 205

Dolan, Frederick M., 8, 13

Dole, Robert, 9

"Double V" campaign, 195

Douglass, Frederick: on activism and egalitarianism, 259; on autonomy, 254, 272–73; and black nationalism, 85; on blacks fighting in Civil War, 178; and competing visions of freedom, 2; contacts with whites, 34; debate with Shields, 1, 30; and liberalism, 29; *North Star*, 51; on private property, 31; and radical egalitarianism, 15, 16; on struggle as condition of progress, 258; on violence, 17n; Washington contrasted with, 286

Douglass, Lewis, 284

Drake, St. Clair, 172

DRUM (Dodge Revolutionary Union Movement), 36–37, 200, 203, 205

Du Bois, W. E. B.: and activism, 53, 263; agenda as radical, 268; in anti-Garvey crusade, 182; and a black homeland, 95; and black Marxism, 18, 19, 229; on black middle class, 270; black nationalism in conflict with, 23; on Black Reconstruction, 51, 173; on black revolutionaries, 172; on blacks fighting in World War I, 178; and Bunche, 248; categorization of thought of, 275, 275n.6; contacts with whites, 34; and Council of African Affairs, 196; on differences between blacks and whites, xi, 4; and disillusioned liberalism, 17–18, 274–79; *Dusk of Dawn*, 17–18, 26n.13, 32, 136, 248, 278; on equality, 23, 268; on federal action to stop terrorism against blacks, 264; forums provided by, 51; on Freedman's Bureau, 263–64; as independent radical, 176; internationalizing plight of blacks, 100, 264; on liberalism, 31–32, 243, 244, 248; "A Negro Nation within the Nation," 312; and radical egalitarianism,